Ultimate Visual Studio for Developers

A Practical Guide to Modern Visual Studio Development

Kapil Thakur

www.orangeava.com

First Published: February 2026

Published By: Orange Education Pvt Ltd, AVA®

Address: 9, Daryaganj, Delhi, 110002, India

275 New North Road Islington Suite 1314 London,
N1 7AA, United Kingdom

ISBN (PBK): 978-93-49887-51-0

ISBN (E-BOOK): 978-93-49887-44-2

Scan the QR code to explore our entire catalogue

www.orangeava.com

Get a Free eBook

We hope you're enjoying your recent book purchase! Your feedback is incredibly valuable to us and helps other readers discover books that truly make a difference.

If you found this book useful or enjoyable, we'd greatly appreciate it if you could leave a short review with a 5-star rating on Amazon. Your review supports our work and allows us to reach more learners worldwide.

As a thank-you, we're happy to offer you a **free digital copy of this book** plus a **30% discount code** for your next purchase on our official websites:

www.orangeava.com

www.orangeava.in (For the Indian Subcontinent).

☑ **How it works:**

Leave your review on Amazon, take a screenshot of the confirmation or use the following link to submit the claim and email it to **info@orangeava.com.** Once received the required detail, we will send your rewards within 24 hours, **along with one month free subcription to the book on AVA SkillShelf!**

Claim Form
https://rebrand.ly/4d2477

Thank you for your support–it truly means a lot to us.

Enjoy 1 Month of Free Access to AVA SkillShelf!

The future belongs to lifelong learners. With AVA SkillShelf, you go beyond reading books and start building real, job-ready skills curated by industry experts.

Your membership unlocks **200+ learning products** covering AI, Cloud, Python, Cybersecurity, Data Science, DevOps, and more—all in one platform. Our bestselling technical books are transformed into structured courses designed for practical, real-world application.

Learn directly from experienced professionals and published authors, with no filler—just actionable insights. Earn **verified digital certifications** to strengthen your CV, LinkedIn profile, and professional credibility.

Learn anytime, anywhere, on any device, at your own pace. Ideal for students, professionals, career switchers, and tech leaders.

For full access to all current and future courses, choose our **Annual Membership**. Simply scan the QR to get started!

For 1 month Free access, simply refer to the steps on the previous page titled: Get a Free ebook!

https://www.avaskillshelf.com/

Downloading the code bundles and colored images

Please follow the links or scan the QR codes to download the
Code Bundles and Images of the book:

https://github.com/ava-orange-education/Ultimate-Visual-Studio-for-Developers

The code bundles and images of the book are also hosted on
https://rebrand.ly/ae017c

In case there's an update to the code, it will be updated on the existing GitHub repository.

Errata

We take immense pride in our work at **Orange Education Pvt Ltd,** and follow the best practices to ensure the accuracy of our content to provide an indulging reading experience to our subscribers. Our readers are our mirrors, and we use their inputs to reflect and improve upon human errors, if any, that may have occurred during the publishing processes involved. To let us maintain the quality and help us reach out to any readers who might be having difficulties due to any unforeseen errors, please write to us at:

errata@orangeava.com

Your support, suggestions, and feedback are highly appreciated.

Dedicated To

My Beloved Wife, Teena, Whose Unwavering Support, Patience, and Encouragement Have Been the Foundation of Every Endeavor.

And to My Cherished Daughters, Mishika and Nyra, Whose Curiosity, Laughter, and Love Inspire Me to Create, Learn, and Share – Today and Always.

With All My Heart,

About the Author

Kapil Thakur is a distinguished software enthusiast and Microsoft .NET expert with over two decades of experience building enterprise-grade applications across the globe. His journey began with a Bachelor's degree from the University of Delhi followed by Masters of Computer Applications (MCA) from Graphic Era University, establishing a strong academic foundation. As a Microsoft Certified Professional and Microsoft Certified Solutions Associate, he has consistently stayed at the forefront of Microsoft technologies, from the early .NET Framework 1.0 to modern .NET Core and cloud-native Azure solutions.

Beginning his career at leading firms such as Cognizant and AON Services, he developed deep expertise in full-stack .NET development before bringing his skills to the United States in 2017. His impressive portfolio spans IT Consulting, Pharmaceuticals, Analytics, Automobiles, Finance, Insurance, and Real Estate, demonstrating a remarkable ability to adapt and deliver value across diverse industry domains. He specializes in architecting scalable solutions using technologies such as ASP.NET Core, C#, React Angular, SQL Server, MongoDB, and Azure, and is proficient in the entire DevOps lifecycle with tools such as Azure DevOps, Jenkins, and Octopus.

Beyond his professional achievements, he is passionate about knowledge sharing and continuous learning, believing that robust, well-architected software can transform businesses and user experiences. When not designing systems or writing codes, he enjoys exploring new programming paradigms, contributing to tech communities, and staying updated with the latest in cloud computing and application security. He teaches .Net, React and Python to students and upcoming developers.

About the Technical Reviewer

Jeevanram Kasiviswanathan has 14 years of experience designing and delivering scalable, robust enterprise applications. With a strong .NET background, he specializes in API-first architecture, building APIs as products, and enabling data access through modern API platforms. He is also an expert in exposing real estate data, and developing in-house solutions such as an advanced address search system built on MongoDB. Jeevanram has expertise in building intelligent AI agents using OpenAI's agent frameworks, enabling models to reason across workflows, integrate external tools, and perform complex tasks beyond standard conversational interfaces.

Currently, Jeevanram serves as Assistant Vice President of Systems Architecture at Xome, part of Rocket Mortgage, where he focuses on modernizing applications, enterprise APIs, and data platforms. He is actively involved in initiatives integrating Microsoft Fabric and other advanced data technologies, driving data-driven transformation, enhancing system scalability and reliability, and mentoring teams to deliver high-impact solutions.

Acknowledgments

There are a few people I want to thank for their ongoing support and encouragement during the writing of this book. First and foremost, I would like to thank my wife and kids for their unwavering belief in me, and for constantly motivating me throughout this journey–I could not have completed this without their love and support.

I am deeply grateful to the many companies and professional environments I have been a part of over my two-decade career in .NET development. Each experience contributed to the depth and practicality of the insights shared in this book.

Special thanks to my colleagues and mentors who have shared their knowledge and challenged me to grow– particularly in mastering Visual Studio, .NET architecture, and modern DevOps practices. I also extend my sincere appreciation to **Mr. Jeevanram Kasiviswanathan** for providing valuable feedback, ensuring that the content remains accurate, relevant, and truly useful for developers at all levels.

My gratitude also goes to the editorial and production team at Orange Education Pvt. Ltd. for their flexibility, patience, and support in bringing this project to life. Writing a comprehensive guide on a tool as vast and evolving as Visual Studio is no small task, and their understanding allowed me to structure this book in a way that balances depth with accessibility, ensuring that it serves both the newcomers and seasoned professionals, alike.

Preface

This book is your definitive guide to **mastering Visual Studio, the world's leading Integrated Development Environment (IDE)** for building modern applications. It goes far beyond simply teaching the interface, focusing instead on how to use Visual Studio's powerful, deep feature set to maximize developer productivity, ensure code quality, and confidently tackle complex enterprise projects.

In today's fast-paced tech world, efficiency is paramount. This book solves the challenge of transitioning from being a basic IDE user to a professional powerhouse by systematically unlocking the advanced tools–from robust debugging and comprehensive unit testing to seamless database and cloud integration–that are essential for success in the .NET ecosystem. It emphasizes a practical, hands-on approach, ensuring learners can immediately apply techniques to their real-world applications, regardless of the technology stack (Web, API, Mobile, or Desktop).

This book is meticulously organized into various chapters, guiding you from the initial setup to advanced cloud-based development and optimization.

Chapter 1 is your foundation or your launch pad, and your orientation to the environment where you will spend countless hours bringing ideas to life. Think of Visual Studio not just as software, but as your development cockpit. Here, we will learn how to set it up, adjust it to fit your personal workflow, and understand its core controls. From choosing the right edition to customizing panels and themes, we are building a workspace that is both powerful and personal–one that will support you from your first "Hello, World" to your most complex enterprise project.

Chapter 2 sets the stage before you write your first line of code. This chapter explores the foundation of every new project: Templates. Think of them as architectural blueprints–pre-configured, technology-specific starting points that eliminate redundant setup, and establish best practices from day one. You will learn how to choose the right template for your project's needs, align it with your team's expertise, and avoid the technical debt that comes from starting with the wrong foundation.

Chapter 3 is about transforming intention into execution, and ideas into reliable software. Visual Studio is your workshop–a place of both creation and refinement. Here, we move beyond simply writing lines of text to understanding how to engineer solutions efficiently and collaboratively. We will also explore how the editor accelerates your flow, how IntelliSense anticipates your needs, and how integrated tools help to keep your code clean and under control.

More than a set of features, this is a guide to building a sustainable coding practice within Visual Studio.

Chapter 4 talks about how Debugging and Diagnostics are the keystones of professional software development–transforming good code into reliable, high-performing applications. This chapter unlocks the full power of Visual Studio's debugging toolkit, guiding you from vital breakpoints and diagnostics to advanced performance profiling. Through practical examples, you will learn to systematically trace errors, analyze bottlenecks, and refine your problem-solving approach.

Chapter 5 is your guide to building that necessary safety net such as unit testing. We will move beyond theory into practice, using Visual Studio's integrated tools to create, manage, and automate tests that catch bugs early, and give you the confidence to refactor and extend your applications.

You will also learn how to select the right framework, write meaningful tests, and integrate testing seamlessly into your daily workflow. By the end, you will not only be writing tests but leveraging them to build more reliable, maintainable, and robust software–turning testing from a chore into a cornerstone of professional development.

Chapter 6 deep dives into how an application is only as strong as its ability to handle information securely and efficiently. This chapter demystifies database integration in Visual Studio, moving beyond basic connections to explore the modern toolset that makes data persistence seamless and scalable. From hands-on examples with Entity Framework Core to cloud-ready Azure SQL, you will learn how to turn raw data into your application's greatest asset–ensuring that it is not just stored, but truly empowered.

Chapter 7 introduces you to the core components of the .NET platform–starting with the foundational Common Language Runtime (CLR)–and explores the frameworks that empower you to create everything from robust server-side applications to modern, interactive client-side experiences. We will walk through ASP.NET Core, the open-source, cross-platform heart of .NET web development, and examine how it enables patterns such as MVC, integrates seamlessly with databases through Entity Framework Core, and supports real-time features via SignalR. You will also discover Blazor, an innovative framework that lets you build dynamic client-side UIs entirely with C#, unifying your full-stack development under one language and toolset. Thus, by the end of this chapter, you will understand how the .NET ecosystem fits together, and how to choose the right tools—whether you are crafting a high-traffic API, a real-time dashboard, or a rich single-page application—ensuring that your projects are secure, maintainable, and ready to scale.

Chapter 8 delves into Visual Studio Extensions, the modular add-ons that transform the IDE from a powerful tool into your personal development cockpit. We will explore how these add-ons, ranging from Microsoft's own utilities to community-driven innovations, can automate mundane tasks, integrate cutting-edge tools, and fundamentally enhance your productivity. By the end of this chapter, you will know how to discover, install, and leverage extensions to create a development environment that is perfectly tailored to ensure that you spend less time configuring, and more time creating exceptional software.

Chapter 9 talks about Performance and Memory Management which is the heartbeat of software—often overlooked until a system slows, crashes, or scales. This chapter is not just about tools; it is about developing a disciplined approach to optimization. You will move from guessing why an app is slow to knowing exactly where inefficiencies live, using Visual Studio's diagnostic suite like a professional. Thus, whether you are hunting memory leaks, tuning CPU-intensive tasks, or architecting for scalability, the practices here will transform how you build, debug, and deliver.

Chapter 10 discusses how Cloud development and Containerization are not merely trends; they are the foundational pillars of modern application architecture. This chapter explores how these two forces combine to redefine how we build, deploy, and scale software. You will learn to leverage cloud platforms and container tools directly within Visual Studio, turning complexity into capability, and transforming your development workflow into a seamless, future-ready engine of innovation.

Finally, **Chapter 11** talks about how a thoughtfully configured development environment is not a luxury today, but a necessity. This chapter is your blueprint for transforming Visual Studio from a standard integrated development environment into a personalized productivity powerhouse. We will walk you through essential configurations, hidden settings, and powerful extensions that streamline workflows, eliminate distractions, and align your workspace with modern development rhythms. Hence, whether you work solo or as part of a distributed team, the steps outlined here will help you build faster, debug smarter, and collaborate seamlessly—turning your IDE into a true partner in innovation!

DID YOU KNOW

Did you know that Orange Education Pvt Ltd offers eBook versions of every book published, with PDF and ePub files available? You can upgrade to the eBook version at **www.orangeava.com** and as a print book customer, you are entitled to a discount on the eBook copy. Get in touch with us at: **info@orangeava.com** for more details.

At **www.orangeava.com**, you can also read a collection of free technical articles, sign up for a range of free newsletters, and receive exclusive discounts and offers on Print Books and eBooks.

PIRACY

If you come across any illegal copies of our works in any form on the internet, we would be grateful if you would provide us with the location address or website name. Please contact us at **info@orangeava.com** with a link to the material.

ARE YOU INTERESTED IN AUTHORING WITH US?

If there is a topic that you have expertise in, and you are interested in either writing or contributing to a book, please write to us at **business@orangeava.com**. We are on a journey to help developers and tech professionals to gain insights on the present technological advancements and innovations happening across the globe and build a community that believes Knowledge is best acquired by sharing and learning with others. Please reach out to us to learn what our audience demands and how you can be part of this educational reform. We also welcome ideas from tech experts and help them build learning and development content for their domains.

REVIEWS

Please leave a review. Once you have read and used this book, why not leave a review on the site that you purchased it from? Potential readers can then see and use your unbiased opinion to make purchase decisions. We at Orange Education would love to know what you think about our products, and our authors can learn from your feedback. Thank you!

For more information about Orange Education, please visit **www.orangeava.com**.

Table of Contents

CHAPTER 1

Getting Started with Visual Studio

Introduction

We will begin by exploring the significance of Visual Studio in the realm of software development, while discussing why it stands out as the go-to choice for millions of developers worldwide. From its intuitive interface to its extensive array of functionalities, Visual Studio provides a versatile platform to tackle projects of all sizes and complexities.

As we progress through the chapter, we will navigate through the landscape of Visual Studio versions, and shed light on the different editions available, while helping you choose the one that best suits your needs. Additionally, we will walk you through the step-by-step installation process for a seamless setup experience for both newcomers and experienced users alike.

Once Visual Studio is up and running on your system, we will embark on an exploration of its core components. You will be introduced to the IDE and gain familiarity with its layout, navigation tools, and essential features. From creating and opening projects to customizing your development environment, this chapter lays the groundwork for your journey with Visual Studio.

Furthermore, we will dive into the intricacies of the menu bar and its sub-menu items, which will act as a treasure trove of tools and options at your disposal. Hence, whether you are looking to configure project settings, access debugging tools, or explore advanced features, the menu bar will be the gateway to a wealth of functionalities within Visual Studio.

At the end of this chapter, you will be well-equipped with the knowledge and skills necessary to harness the full potential of Visual Studio 2022. Thus, whether you are aiming to build simple applications or tackle complex software projects, this chapter provides the foundation upon which you can build your expertise, and embark on a rewarding journey in software development with Visual Studio.

Structure

In this chapter we will cover the following topics:

- Introduction to Visual Studio
- Choosing Your Visual Studio Edition
- Visual Studio 2022 System Requirements for Installation
- Visual Studio 2022 Installation Guide
- Customizing Panels
- Working with Documents
- Synchronizing Accounts and Settings
- Customizing the Menu bar and Toolbars
- Understanding the VS Menu bar

Introduction to Visual Studio

Visual Studio is a cornerstone of software development and offers a comprehensive **Integrated Development Environment (IDE)** that covers the entire development cycle in one cohesive platform. It serves as a complete application development tool with features for designing, developing, debugging, deploying and finally maintaining and enhancing any .Net application. It supports several technologies apart from .Net.

Visual Studio is designed to streamline software development across various platforms and languages. Unlike other IDEs, Visual Studio offers incredible versatility and supports many programming languages such as C#, C++, Python, and JavaScript, along with robust tools and features tailored to each language's ecosystem.

With its rich array of tools and features, Visual Studio provides an unparalleled environment for writing, editing, debugging, building, and deploying code across several languages and platforms, which makes it a preferred choice for developers worldwide. It is the most comprehensive IDE for .NET and C++ developers on Windows for building web, cloud, desktop, mobile apps, services and games.

Let us take a closer look at the key components, features, and benefits that make Visual Studio the preferred choice for developers worldwide.

One of the key advantages of Visual Studio lies in its seamless integration with Microsoft Azure and other cloud platforms. This ability facilitates cloud development and direct deployment from the IDE. Additionally, Visual Studio stands out for its rich ecosystem of extensions and plug-ins, which allows developers to customize their development environment according to their specific needs and preferences.

As a developer, understanding the significance of Visual Studio is important to navigate the vast landscape of software development tools. What sets Visual Studio apart is its unwavering commitment to providing developers with a holistic experience. Through an intuitive user interface and a plethora of productivity-enhancing features, Visual Studio streamlines the entire software development lifecycle, from coding and debugging, to testing and deployment. Its extensibility is another hallmark, as it allows developers to augment its capabilities with several extensions and plug-ins tailored to meet their specific needs.

The advantages of Visual Studio over other IDEs are manifold. Firstly, its unparalleled integration with Microsoft's ecosystem, including Azure cloud services, enables seamless development and deployment of cloud-native applications. Additionally, Visual Studio's support for many programming languages, frameworks, and platforms ensures that developers can work with their preferred tools and technologies without constraints. Moreover, its robust debugging tools like IntelliTrace and Live Share facilitate collaborative debugging and troubleshooting, which makes the development process more efficient.

At the heart of Visual Studio lie its main features that empower developers to streamline their workflows. These include:

- **Code Editor:** A powerful and feature-rich code editor with syntax highlighting, code completion, and refactoring capabilities
- **Debugger:** Advanced debugging tools for identifying and resolving software issues quickly and efficiently
- **Integrated Git Support:** Refers to the built-in Git integration for version control, which enables seamless collaboration and code management
- **Testing Tools:** Comprehensive testing tools like unit testing and code coverage analysis ensure the quality and reliability of applications
- **Extensibility:** A vibrant ecosystem of extensions and plug-ins that extend Visual Studio's capabilities and cater to diverse development needs
- **Cloud Integration:** Provides seamless integration with Microsoft Azure for cloud development, deployment, and management
- **Cross-Platform Development:** Grants support for cross-platform development across Windows, macOS, and Linux, while ensuring that applications can reach a wider audience

In essence, Visual Studio transcends the boundaries of a conventional IDE and is a comprehensive platform that empowers developers to bring their ideas to life. Its unparalleled versatility, robust feature set, and seamless integration with various services have set the standard for modern software development environments.

Reasons to Use Visual Studio

Visual Studio is not just another IDE; it is a complete ecosystem designed to enhance developer productivity and efficiency. Here is why developers choose Visual Studio:

- **Workload-Based Installer**: Install only what you need as per your specific development requirements to ensure a streamlined and efficient setup process.
- **Powerful Coding Tools and Features**: From code completion tools and compilers, to source control integration and AI-assisted development, Visual Studio provides everything developers need to build high-quality applications efficiently.
- **Multiple Language Support**: With support for languages such as C++, C#, JavaScript, TypeScript, Python, and more, Visual Studio accommodates the requirements of developers working across diverse tech stacks and projects.
- **Cross-Platform Development**: Whether building for Windows, web, mobile, or the cloud, Visual Studio offers tools and frameworks targeting a wide range of platforms, which enables developers to reach a broader audience with their applications.
- **Version Control Integration**: Collaborate seamlessly with team members using integrated version control systems like Git, which allows for efficient code management and collaboration.
- **AI-Assisted Development**: Leverage AI-powered tools like GitHub Copilot and IntelliCode to write code faster with greater accuracy and gain deeper insights into your codebase.

Choosing Your Visual Studio Edition

There are 3 versions of Visual Studio as provided by Microsoft:

- Community Edition
- Professional Edition
- Enterprise Edition

Let us understand the features and differences between these versions.

Community Edition

The VS Community edition is a free complimentary offering from Microsoft which encompasses the essential functionalities for .NET application development such as creation, building, debugging, and deployment, alongside the collaborative features of Visual Studio. Designed for non-enterprise entities, it can only accommodate a maximum of five users and caters primarily to students, freelancers, independent developers, and small businesses. It can only be used for open source, academic research, and classroom learning environments. It cannot be used for creating enterprise level applications.

Here are the key features of VS Community:

- **Complete Debugging Tools**: Facilitate code inspection during debugging processes
- **Performance and Diagnostics Hub**: Assesses application performance and memory utilization
- **Refactoring Tools**: Streamline code maintenance and adherence to coding best practices
- **Unit Testing Capabilities**: Navigate, execute, and aggregate results from unit tests
- **Peek Definition Functionality**: Provides expedited navigation to method or function definitions
- **VS Live Share**: Facilitates real-time collaborative development

While VS Community encompasses essential tools for daily use, certain scenarios like unit testing, memory management, or code inspection may necessitate additional functionalities. For instance, Live Unit Testing, which provides real-time feedback from continuously running unit tests, is not available in the VS Community edition.

Professional Edition

Visual Studio Professional is a licensed edition of Visual Studio that is available through a subscription model. This version is typically recommended for enterprise-level applications and development teams with more than five members.

The Visual Studio Professional edition includes all the core tools and features found in the Community edition, but also comes with some additional capabilities. For instance, it integrates CodeLens, a feature that helps developers quickly identify references, changes, and unit test information directly within the code.

In terms of pricing, the current subscription cost for an individual user of Visual Studio Professional is $45 per month. This subscription provides several additional benefits, including:

- Access to training resources
- Technical support services
- Integration with the basic Azure DevOps plan

The higher cost of the Professional edition is justified by the expanded feature set and the enterprise-grade tools it provides. Organizations with more complex development requirements and larger team sizes are likely to find the Professional edition better suited to their needs.

While the Community edition covers the essential needs of many individual developers and small teams, the Professional subscription unlocks a more robust set of capabilities for larger and more sophisticated software projects.

Enterprise Edition

Visual Studio Enterprise is the highest-tier subscription offering within the Visual Studio product lineup. Building upon the capabilities of the Professional edition, the Enterprise subscription includes all the features available in the Community version, along with additional advanced tools and capabilities.

One of the exclusive features of the Enterprise edition is IntelliTrace, which is a powerful debugging tool that records the state of the application. It allows developers to inspect the system in detail before an exception occurs. This provides valuable information about events, exceptions, and function calls, which can be helpful during the debugging process.

Other notable features of the Visual Studio Enterprise edition include:

- **Live Unit Testing:** Automatically re-runs unit tests after code changes and provides immediate feedback
- **Snapshot Debugger:** Saves snapshots of the application during debugging, thereby enabling in-depth analysis of errors and issues
- **Performance Analysis Tools:** Advanced tools for profiling and optimizing the performance of mobile applications
- **Architectural Layer Diagrams:** Visualize the logical architecture of your application for designing and planning

The Visual Studio Enterprise subscription comes with a monthly fee of $250 per user. However, this subscription includes several additional benefits, such as:

- $150 in monthly Azure credits
- Access to Power BI Pro
- Enhanced Azure DevOps features, including test plans
- All the features and capabilities that are available in the lower-tier Visual Studio editions

To compare the pricing and features of the different Visual Studio offerings, you can visit the official Visual Studio pricing page at https://visualstudio.microsoft.com/vs/pricing/

Here is the official link to download Visual Studio: https://visualstudio.microsoft.com/downloads/

**This book uses the Visual Studio 2022 Professional version as base edition for all its examples.*

Visual Studio 2022 is a 64-bit application. Please check system requirements before installing it for your development machine.

Visual Studio Code

It is a lighter standalone source code editor that runs on Windows, macOS, and Linux. It is the top pick for JavaScript and Java and web developers as it provides several extensions to support just about any programming language.

Features of Visual Code:

- **Cross-Platform Compatibility**: Visual Studio Code is a lightweight, open-source code editor that runs on Windows, macOS, and Linux. This makes it a versatile choice for developers operating different platforms.
- **Extensive Language Support**: VS Code supports a wide range of programming languages, including C++, C#, Java, JavaScript, TypeScript, Python, and many more, with excellent syntax highlighting and code completion.
- **Integrated Terminal**: VS Code includes a built-in terminal that allows developers to run and interact with command-line tools and shells directly within the editor.
- **Intelligent Code Editing**: VS Code provides advanced code editing features like IntelliSense, code folding, bracket matching, and code formatting to enhance productivity.
- **Debugging Tools**: VS Code includes robust debugging tools that allow developers to set breakpoints, step through code, and inspect variables, making it easier to identify and fix issues.
- **Extensions and Customization**: VS Code has a vast ecosystem of extensions and plugins that can be installed to add support for additional languages, frameworks, and development tools, as well as customize the editor's appearance and behavior.
- **Git and Source Control Integration**: VS Code integrates seamlessly with Git and other version control systems, which allow developers to manage their code repositories, view diffs, and perform common Git operations directly within the editor.
- **Live Share**: This feature enables real-time collaboration, allowing developers to share their workspace, code, and debugging sessions with others, thereby fostering remote collaboration.

- **Lightweight and Fast**: Compared to the full-featured Visual Studio IDE, VS Code is a lightweight, fast, and efficient code editor that can run on lower-powered machines.
- **Open-Source and Community-Driven**: Visual Studio Code is an open-source project, which allows developers to make contributions and improvements.

In conclusion, Visual Studio empowers developers with the tools and resources they need to succeed. With its robust features, comprehensive support, and seamless integration, Visual Studio remains the IDE of choice for developers worldwide, as it enables them to build with confidence and innovate without being hindered by limits.

Visual Studio 2022 System Requirements for Installation

Visual Studio 2022 is supported on the following 64-bit operating systems (as it is not supported on 32 bit operating systems):

Windows 11

- Home, Pro, Pro Education, Pro for Workstations, Enterprise, and Education
- Minimum supported OS version or higher

Windows 10

- Home, Professional, Education, and Enterprise
- Minimum supported OS version or higher

Windows Server

- Windows Server 2022: Standard and Datacenter
- Windows Server 2019: Standard and Datacenter
- Windows Server 2016: Standard and Datacenter

Hardware Requirements

- ARM64 or x64 processor
- Minimum 4GB RAM
- Minimum 20-50GB of available space
- Administrator rights are required for installing or updating Visual Studio.

Visual Studio 2022: Harnessing the Power of 64-Bit Architecture

Visual Studio 2022 brings a significant yet subtle enhancement under the hood: a transition to a 64-bit architecture. While this change may not be immediately visible to users, its impact on performance is profound. By leveraging the capabilities of modern 64-bit CPUs found in today's laptops and PCs, Visual Studio 2022 enhances efficiency and reduces latency, particularly while you are executing multiple tasks concurrently.

One of the most notable advantages of moving to a 64-bit architecture is the removal of the previous 4 GB memory access limitation which is inherent in 32-bit systems. With this upgrade, Visual Studio can tap into a significantly larger pool of memory, which is limited only by the physical hardware's capabilities. This expansion in memory access translates to smoother operation, while mitigating time constraints and preventing frustrating IDE freezes or crashes.

To illustrate the difference, one needs to compare the performance of Visual Studio 2022 when it is running on a 64-bit platform alongside its predecessor, Visual Studio 2019, which operates on a 32-bit architecture. Task Manager in Windows provides a tangible demonstration of the enhanced efficiency, which highlights the distinct advantages of the 64-bit environment.

Moreover, this shift to a 64-bit architecture represents a forward-looking investment in performance optimization. The Visual Studio development team has diligently fine-tuned the software to deliver improved performance across various scenarios, which is particularly noticeable when working on large-scale projects. As Visual Studio evolves in future iterations, users can expect continued enhancements in performance, which provides for a more seamless and efficient development experience.

In essence, the adoption of a 64-bit architecture in Visual Studio 2022 marks a significant milestone in optimizing performance, as it lays a robust foundation for the software's evolution and ensures a smoother, more productive development workflow for users.

Introducing .NET 8: A Powerful Upgrade for Developers

.NET, the popular open-source software framework, has just released its latest version, which is called .NET 8. This new release brings a host of exciting improvements and features that benefit developers operating across various domains like web, desktop, mobile, and more.

New Features in .NET 8

- **Native AOT for Apps**: .NET 8 introduces a new feature called Native AOT (Ahead-of-Time) compilation, which allows developers to create native, standalone applications. This advancement offers improved performance and smaller application sizes, thereby making it especially beneficial for resource-constrained environments.
- **C# 12 Compatibility**: The .NET 8 framework is fully compatible with the latest version of the C# programming language, C# 12. This means that developers can leverage the latest language features and enhancements to write more efficient and expressive code.
- **Continuous Improvements**: As with each annual release of .NET, .NET 8 builds upon the foundation of its predecessors and introduces various refinements and optimizations to improve overall performance, stability, and developer productivity.

Seamless Integration with Visual Studio 2022

The release of .NET 8 is well-timed, as it coincides with the availability of Visual Studio 2022. Developers can now seamlessly create, compile, and publish their projects using the latest version of the .NET framework directly within the Visual Studio 2022 IDE.

Staying Up-to-Date

To learn more about the specific improvements and features in .NET 8, we encourage you to visit the official Microsoft documentation at https://docs.microsoft.com/en-us/dotnet/core/whats-new/dotnet-8.

Whether you are a seasoned .NET developer or just starting out, the release of .NET 8 presents an exciting opportunity to leverage the latest advancements in the framework and take your applications to new heights.

Visual Studio 2022 Installation Guide

Improving the Visual Studio Installation Experience:

With each iteration, the installation process for Visual Studio (VS) has seen enhancements, which offer users greater convenience and flexibility. Notably, the latest versions allow for seamless upgrades and customization of workloads to cater to various project requirements.

- **Obtaining the Installer**: Acquiring the VS installer is a straightforward process, which is devoid of complexities or the need for an account. Users can easily access the installer by visiting the official Visual Studio website at visualstudio.microsoft.com/downloads. From there, navigate to the Visual Studio section and select the desired option such as the Community edition to initiate the download process.

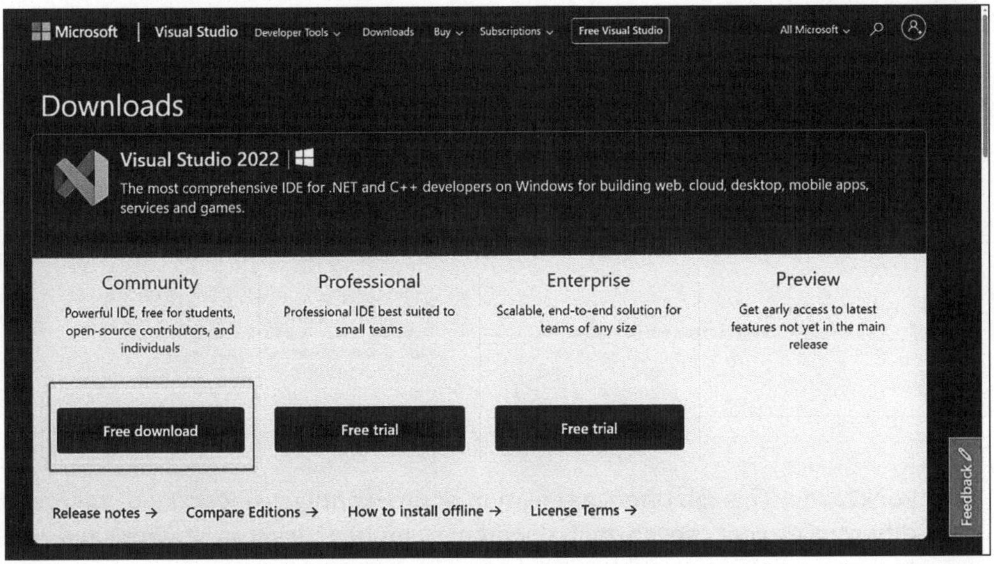

Figure 1.1: *Visual Studio Versions*

Should users prefer older versions, links to download VS 2022 and previous iterations are available at https://visualstudio.microsoft.com/vs/older-downloads.

- **Installation Procedure**: Upon downloading the VS installer, running it triggers an update process for the installer itself, which ensures that it is up-to-date with the latest improvements. The installer is designed to seek out and incorporate the latest updates from the development team seamlessly.

Updating the VS Installer

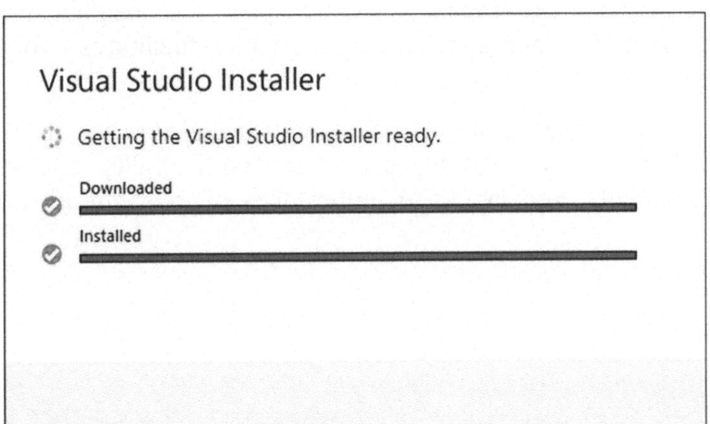

Figure 1.2: VS *Installer*

Upon completion of the update, users are presented with the initial screen of the installer, which features four primary configuration options that are accessible from the top menu.

The VS Workloads Tab

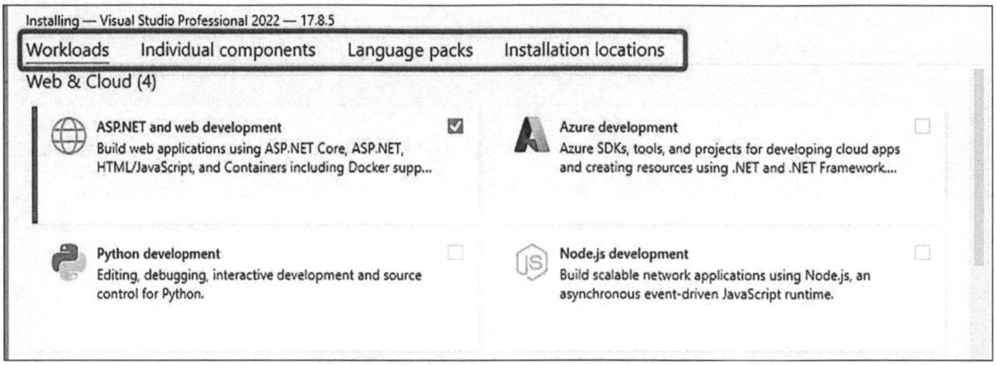

Figure 1.3: *VS Workloads Tab*

- `Workloads`: This tab offers a selection of pre-configured workloads tailored to different project types which encompass mobile, desktop, Python, and other technologies. Each workload includes a curated set of tools and components specific to the chosen technology stack.
- `Individual Components`: Here, users can peruse and select individual components to install, even if they are not part of the selected workloads, which allows for a more granular customization of the installation.
- `Language Packs`: Users can choose from a list of 14 languages for the VS interface for seamless development in their preferred language(s). This flexibility extends to the ability to switch between languages during the development process.
- `Installation Locations`: This tab provides insights into the space requirements for each installation path, which facilitates informed decision-making.

Once satisfied with the configurations, users can proceed with the installation process by clicking the Install button. Notably, users have the flexibility to modify workloads, individual components, and language preferences by re-running the downloaded installer.

VS Installation in Progress

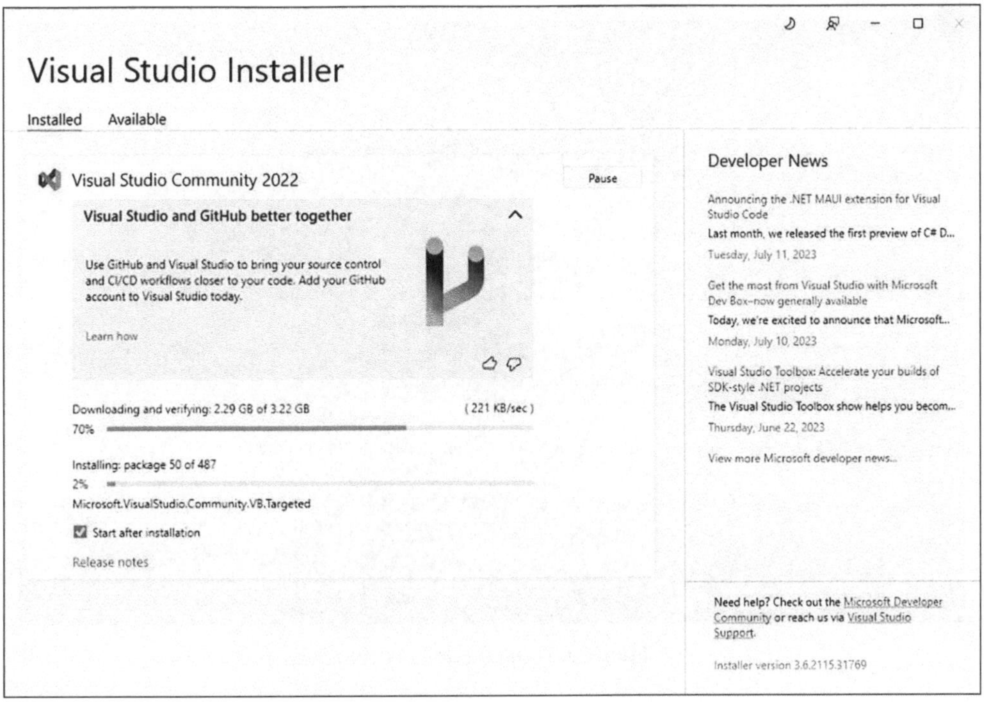

***Figure 1.4**: Visual Studio Installer Progress Page*

Upon initiating the installation, users are presented with a detailed overview of the download and installation progress, while ensuring transparency throughout the process.

With the installation complete, users are now ready to explore the Visual Studio interface, and embark on their development journey.

Introduction to Visual Studio IDE

Now that Visual Studio 2022 is successfully installed, you will encounter the startup screen presenting options for creating, cloning, or opening projects.

Tip: *Always run the Visual Studio in "**`run-as Administrator`**" mode.*

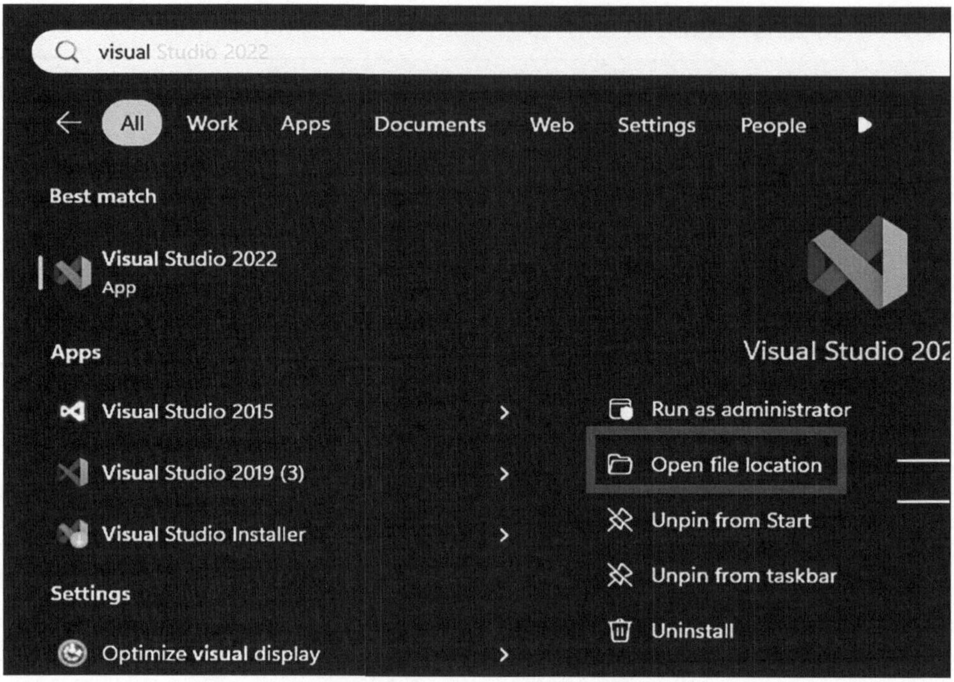

Figure 1.5: *Open File Location*

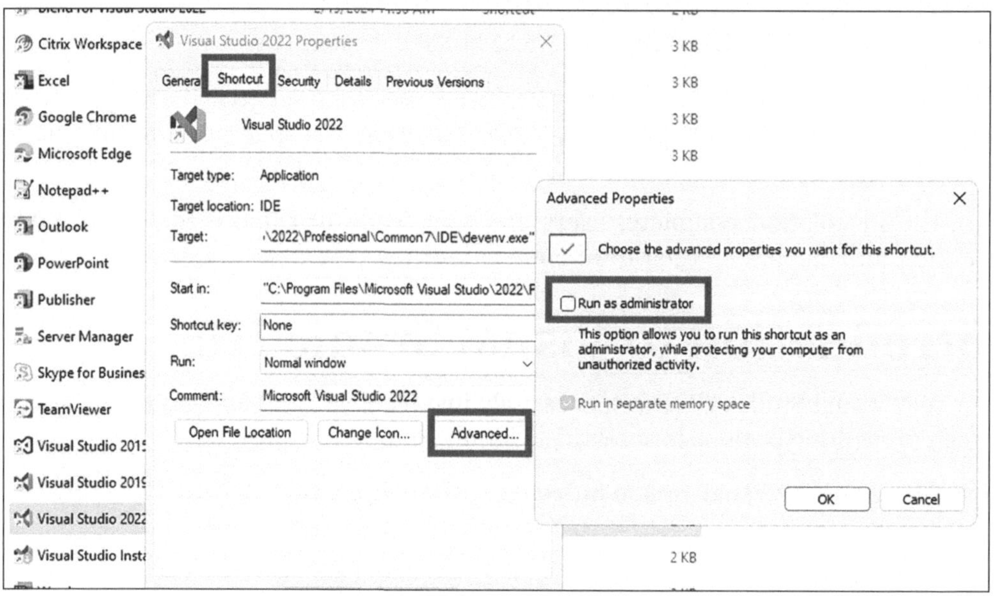

Figure 1.6: *Run as administrator*

Check "**`Run as administrator`**" and click on **`Ok`**. Now every time you open the visual studio it will always run in Admin mode by default. So, you will not encounter any hassle of remembering to manually run VS in admin mode.

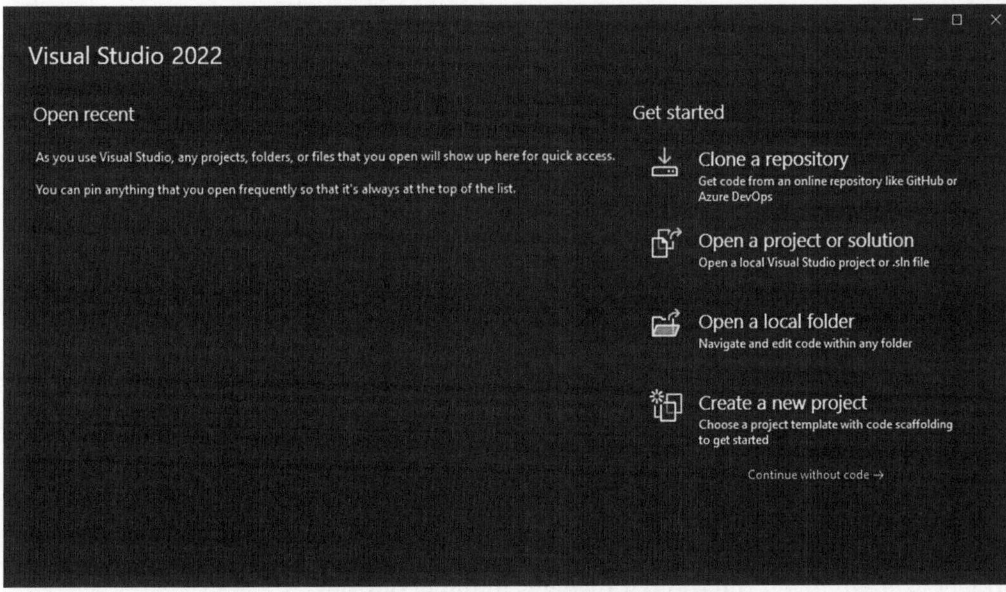

Figure 1.7: *VS Getting Started Screen*

It is noteworthy that multiple versions of Visual Studio can coexist on the same machine. This flexibility is particularly useful for maintaining compatibility with older technologies like Visual Studio 2010 for Silverlight development.

Let us delve into the interface without creating a project yet by selecting the "**`Continue without code`**" option. Upon entering the main interface, you will notice the "**`Options`**" menu at the top, which offers a plethora of tools for various purposes, alongside buttons for common actions like starting application execution and debugging.

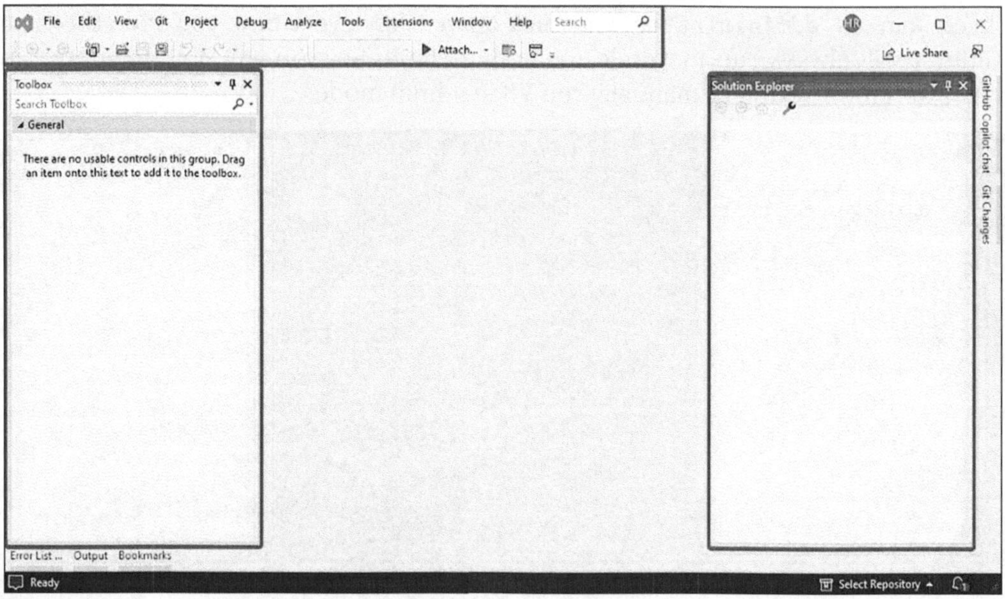

Figure 1.8: *VS General Interface*

The available tools may vary depending on the open project. For instance, since no project is created yet, the toolbar displays minimal options.

In the left and right sections, you will find panels containing tools specific to the type of project you are working on. These panels typically include commonly used tools like Solution Explorer, Toolbox, Properties, and Code Editor.

Customizing Panels

Visual Studio panels provide access to project-specific tools. These panels consist of tools and document editors that are essential for development tasks.

Visual Studio 2022 offers a wide array of tools that you can show or hide according to your requirements. Access these tools from the "**`View`**" menu, where commonly used ones are listed upfront, with additional options available under "**`Other Windows`**."

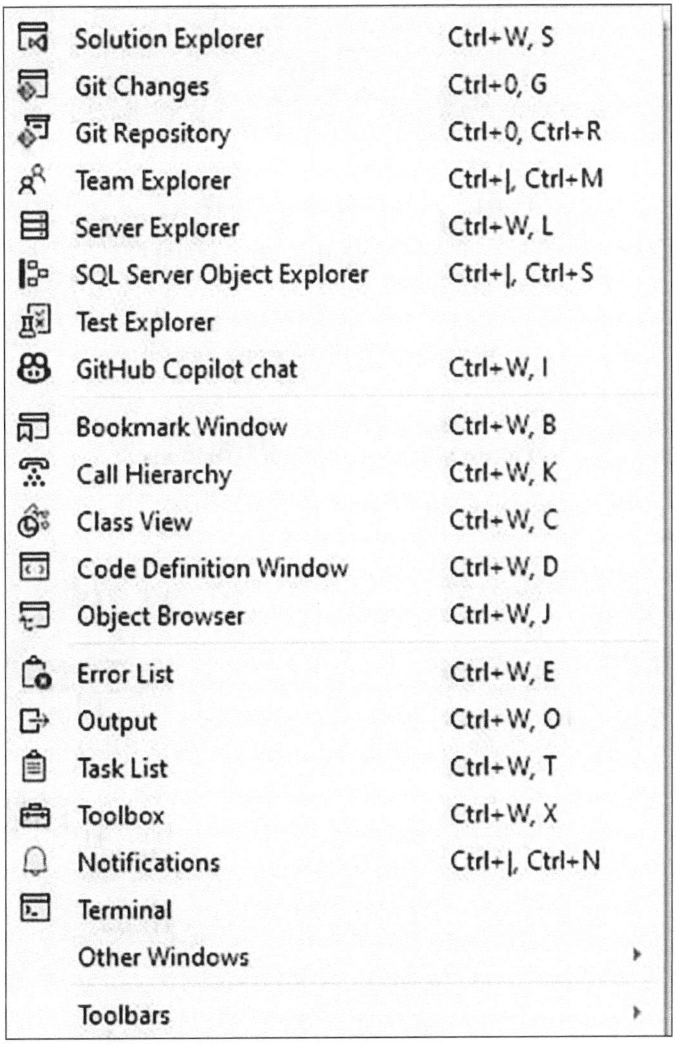

Figure 1.9: *View Menu Options*

To add a tool to a panel, simply select it. For instance, adding the Server Explorer tool places it in the left panel, while adding the Output tool places it at the bottom pane.

One of the advantages of Visual Studio is the ability to arrange tool panels according to your preferences. Each panel comprises five sections where tools can be placed. The IDE simplifies this process by indicating possible locations for tool placement. Additionally, you can detach panels from the main window for standalone use.

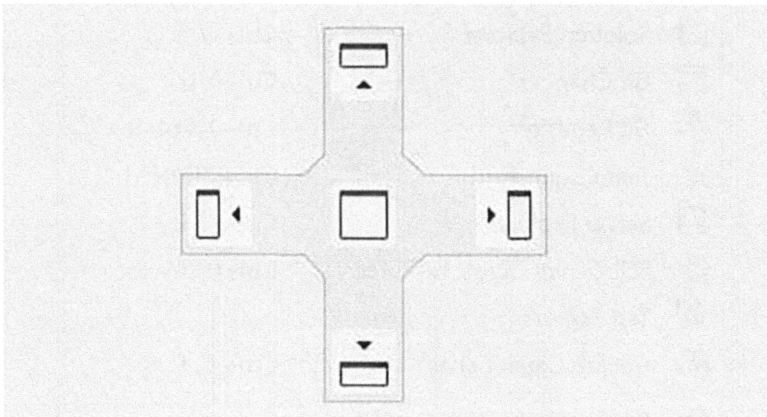

Figure 1.10: *Showing Panel Locations*

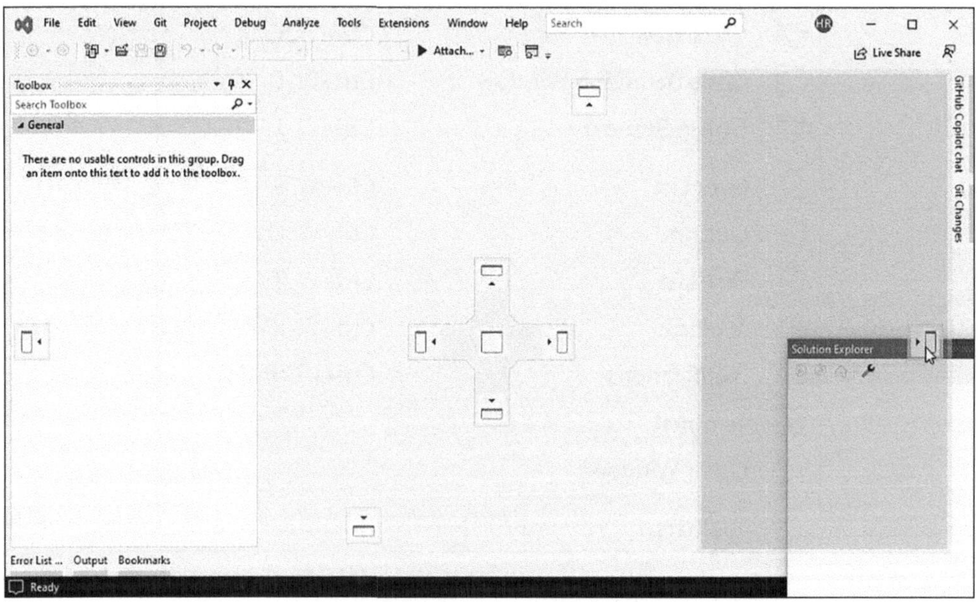

Figure 1.11: *Available Panel Locations*

Working with Documents

Document editors, like Code Editor, offer special options to enhance productivity. Right-clicking on an open document tab reveals options like floating the editor into a separate window, pinning the tab, or adjusting the tab layout to suit your workflow.

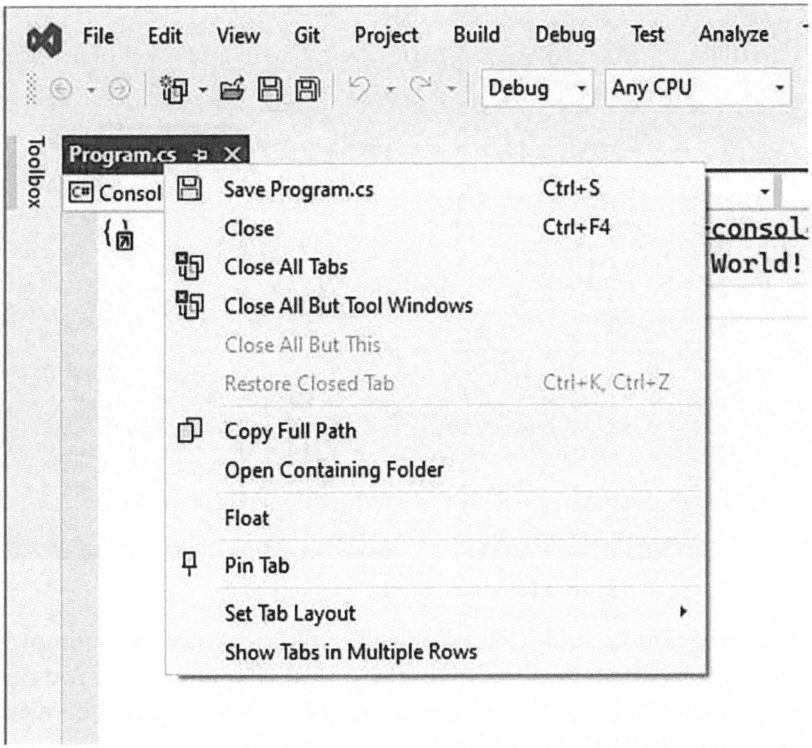

Figure 1.12: *Context Menu for Code Editor*

Utilize the *Ctrl* + F1 shortcut to access Visual Studio documentation for guidance and updates.

- **Customizing the IDE:** Software developers often have different preferences when it comes to coding environments. Visual Studio 2022 offers various customization options, including theme selection and font customization.
- **Selecting a VS Theme:** Upon startup, Visual Studio defaults to a dark theme, though several pre-installed themes are available. These themes cater to different preferences and environmental conditions, with the dark theme offering reduced eye strain in low-light conditions.

To change the theme, navigate to the "`Tools`" menu, select "`Themes`", and choose from the available options. Additional themes can be obtained from the Visual Studio Marketplace.

Figure 1.13: *Visual Studio Marketplace*

- **Customizing Fonts and Colors:** Visual Studio allows for comprehensive customization of fonts and colors to suit individual preferences. You can access these settings from the "`Tools`" menu, where you can adjust the environment font and the font settings for the code editor.

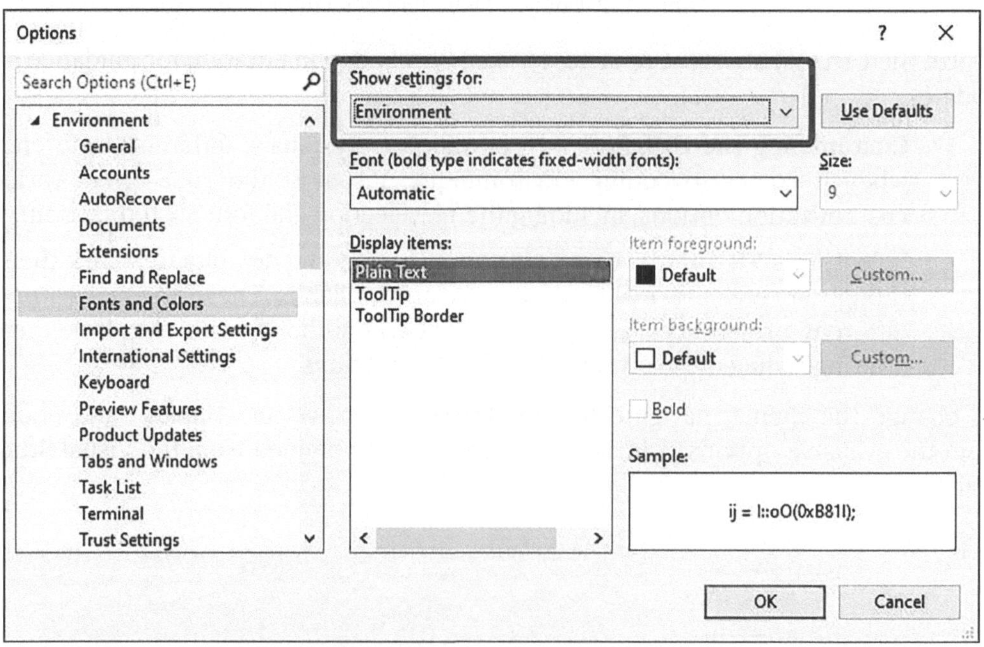

Figure 1.14: *Changing the Environment Font Settings*

Moreover, Visual Studio introduces the Cascadia font as the default font, which is known for its improved code readability.

Synchronizing Accounts and Settings

Visual Studio facilitates synchronization of configurations across different devices through a Microsoft account. Key settings such as user-defined window layouts, themes, fonts, keyboard shortcuts, and text editor settings can be synchronized seamlessly.

To enable or disable synchronization, access the "**`Tools`**" menu, navigate to "**`Options`**," and select the "**`Environment`**" and "**`Accounts`**" sections.

[VS – Sign in (at the top right of the main screen)](link-to-image)

Figure 1.15: *VS Account Sign In*

Customizing the Menu Bar and Toolbars

Menus and toolbars provide quick access to frequently used commands. Visual Studio allows users to customize these elements to streamline their development workflow.

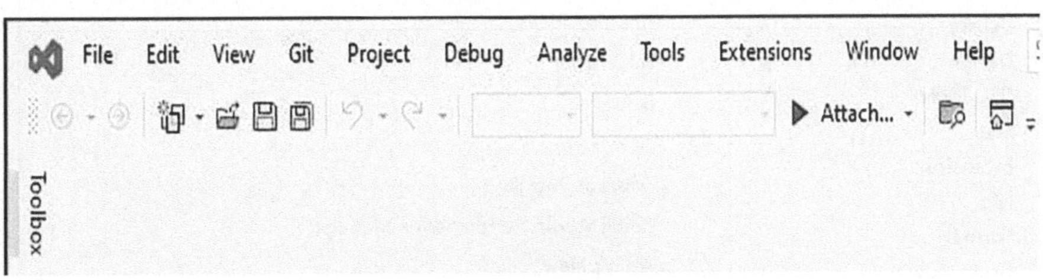

Figure 1.16: *VS Menu Bar*

Customizing the Menu Bar

The menu bar, located at the top of the IDE, offers dropdown menus for executing tasks and accessing tools. Customize the menu bar by selecting the "**`Tools`**" menu, followed by "**`Customize`**." From here, you can modify the main and secondary menu bars by adding, deleting, or rearranging menu items.

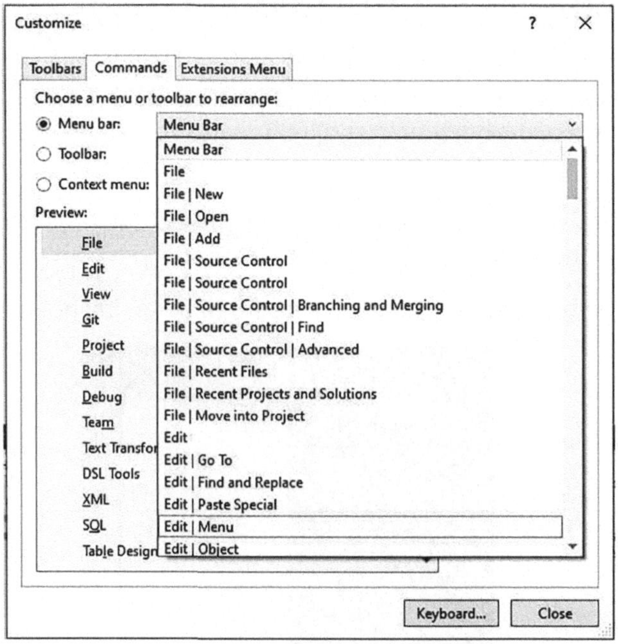

Figure 1.17: *Customizing Menu Bar*

Select the command you want to add in menu bar and click **`OK`** (as shown in image).

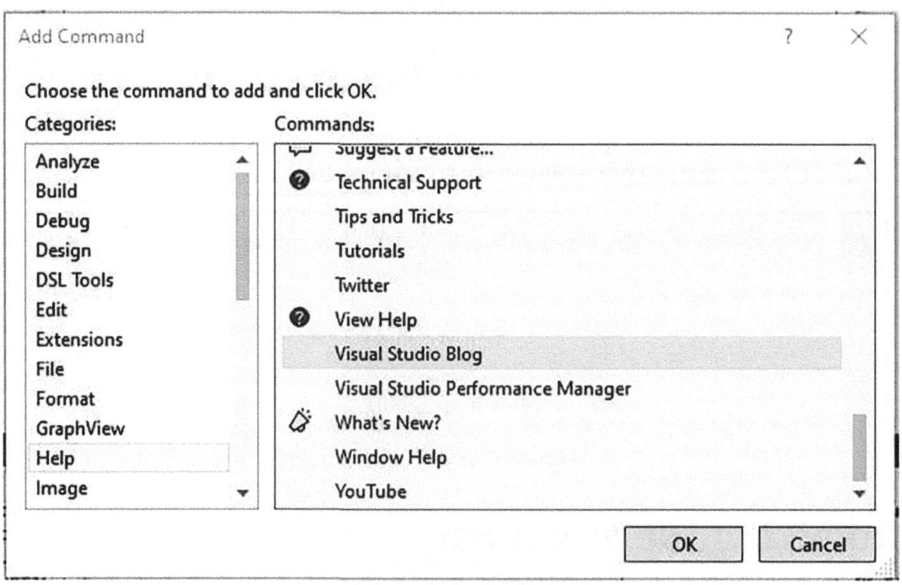

Figure 1.18: *Add Command*

You can delete the menu item if you think you will not be using it often during development.

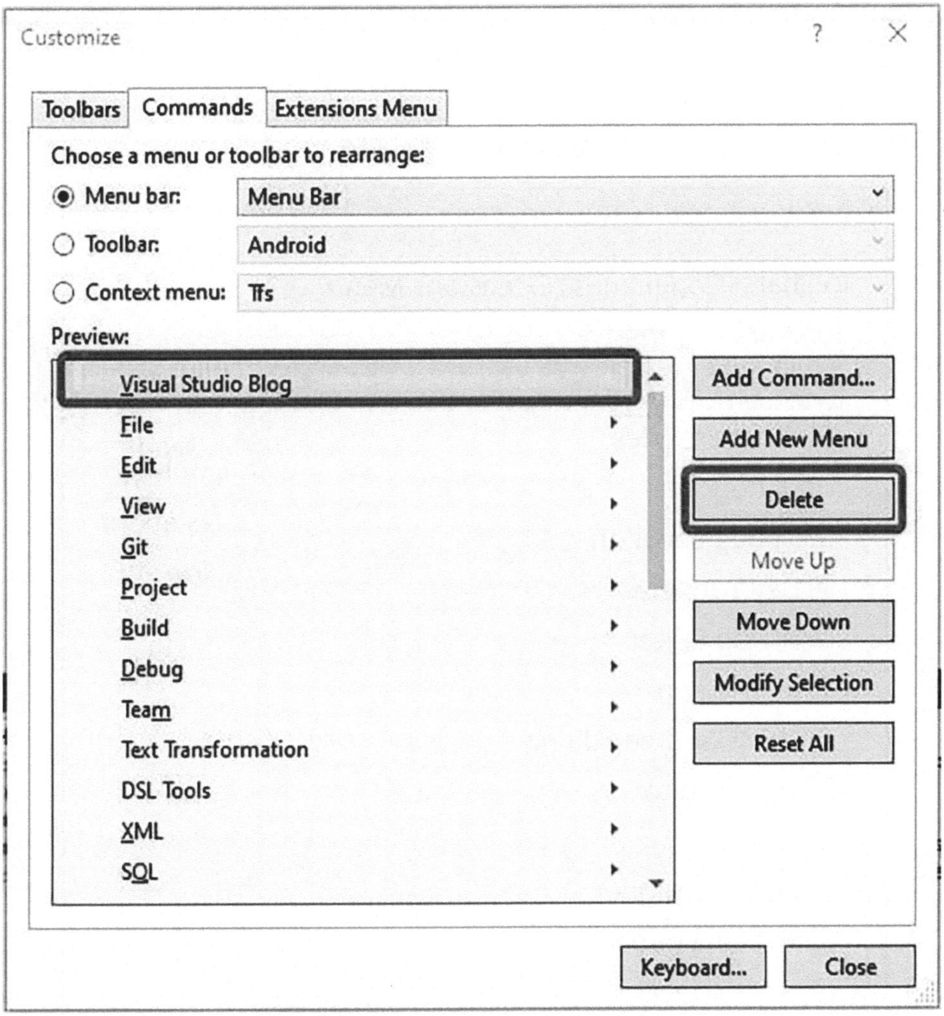

Figure 1.19: *Customizing Menu Bar Items*

Customizing Toolbars

Toolbars offer direct access to commands without the need for dropdown menus. You can customize toolbars by selecting the desired options from the "**`Tools`**" menu and "**`Customize`**" submenu. You can add or remove toolbars and commands to tailor the IDE to your preferences.

Toolbar can also be modified to add or remove which options to be displayed in IDE.

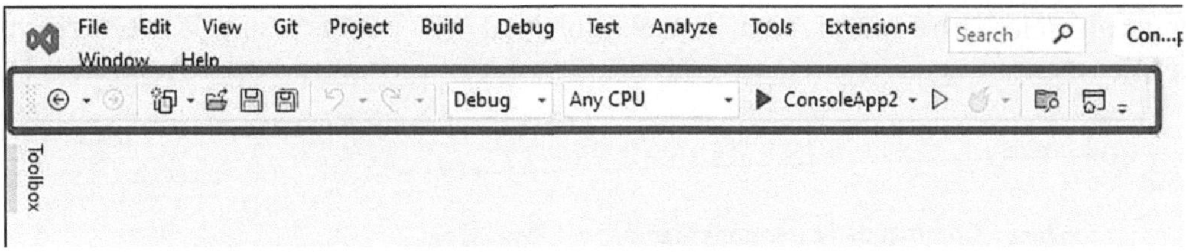

Figure 1.20: *Toolbar Icons*

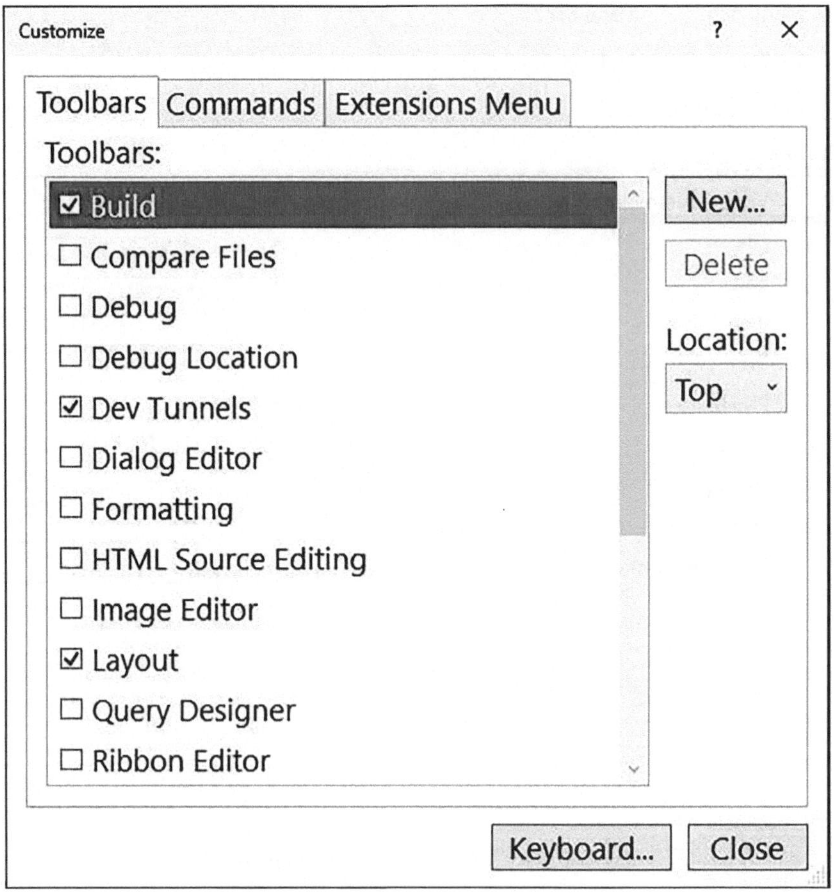

Figure 1.21: *Customizing ToolBar Items*

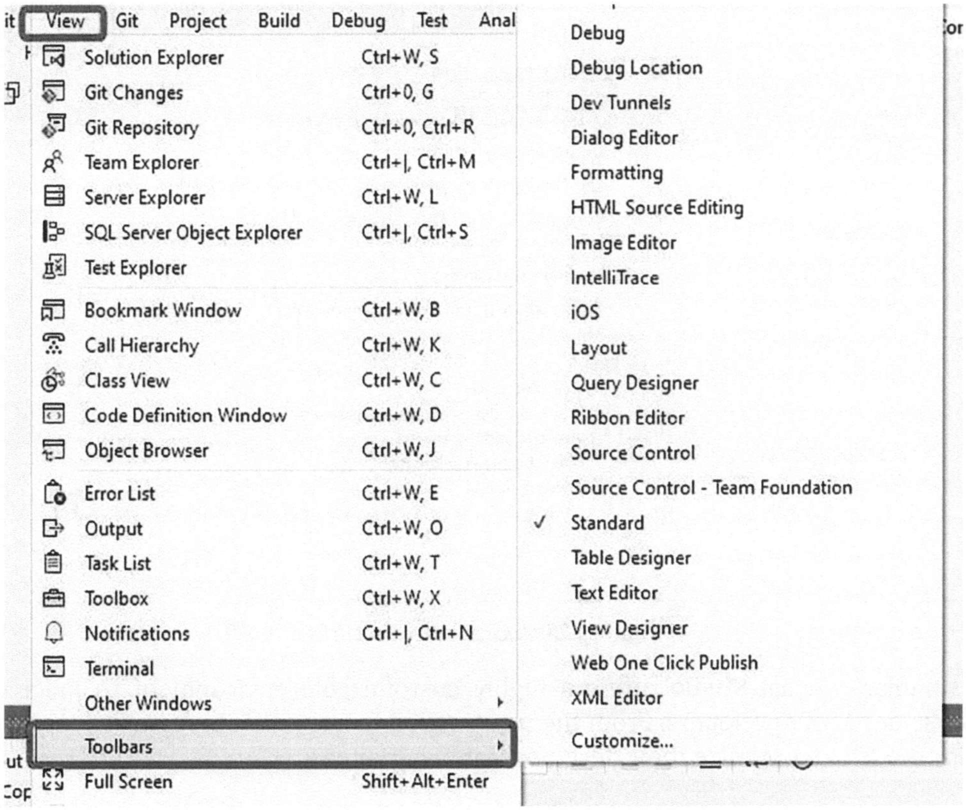

Figure 1.22: *Additional Menu Items under View→Toolbars*

Accessibility Features

Visual Studio includes accessibility features to accommodate users with visual impairments. These features include a high-contrast blue theme and the ability to add sounds for various IDE events. Users can also utilize keyboard shortcuts for common tasks, which enhances accessibility and productivity.

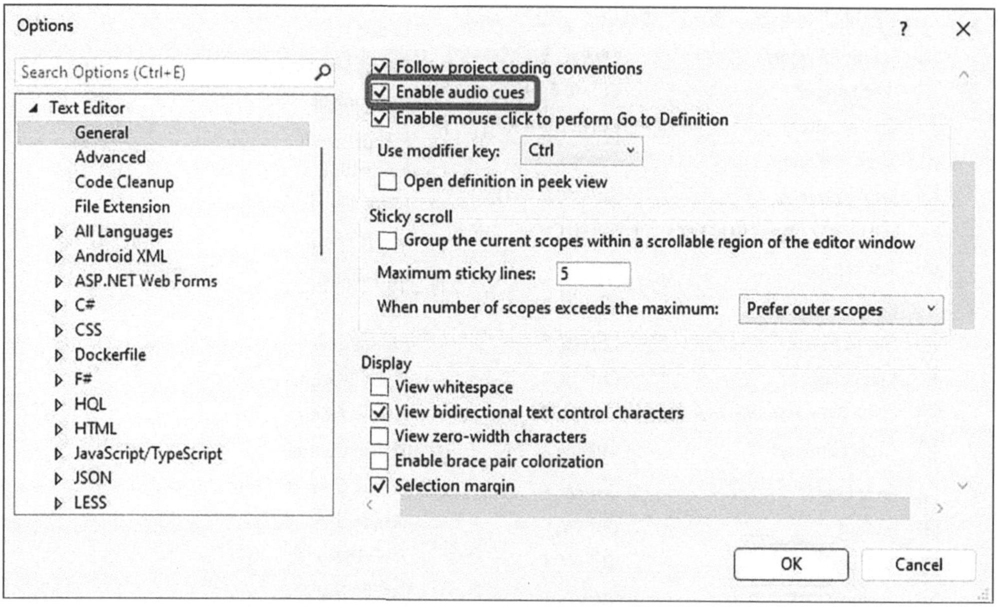

Figure 1.23: *Accessibility Features*

In summary, Visual Studio offers a highly customizable environment to meet the diverse needs of developers. From theme selection to accessibility features, users can tailor the IDE to optimize their development experience.

Understanding the VS Menu Bar

The Visual Studio menu bar is the primary navigation tool in the IDE, and it provides access to a wide range of features and options that are essential for the software development process. Let us go through each menu and explain its purpose and the options it offers to a new software engineer:

Figure 1.24: *VS Menu Bar*

These options may vary slightly depending on the specific version of Visual Studio 2022 you are using and any installed extensions or customizations.

File Menu

The "**`File`**" menu typically contains various options and features related to file operations, project management, and other general functionalities. Here is a comprehensive list of options you might find under the "**`File`**" menu along with their typical uses:

`New`

- Create a new project, file, or item within your project.
- Select from various project templates and file types depending on your development needs.

`Open`

- Open an existing project, solution, file, or folder in Visual Studio.
- Navigate to the location of the desired file or project and open it directly from the file system.

`Close`

- Close the currently active document or project without closing the entire Visual Studio instance.
- Useful for managing multiple open files or projects.

`Save`

- Save any changes made to the active document or project.
- If the document or project has not been saved previously, this option will prompt you to specify a location and filename.

`Save As`

- Save a copy of the active document or project with a different filename or in a different location.
- This option is helpful for creating new versions of a file without overwriting the original.

`Save All`

- Save all open documents and projects in Visual Studio.
- It is convenient when you have multiple unsaved changes across several files and want to save them all at once.

`Print`

- Print the contents of the active document or active page.
- Configure print settings such as printer selection, page layout, and number of copies.

`Recent Files`

- Display a list of recently opened files
- Quickly access documents you have been working on without navigating through your file system.

`Recent Projects and Solutions`

- Display a list of recently opened projects and solutions.
- Quickly resume work on previous projects.

`Exit`

- Close Visual Studio and exit the application.
- Used when you are done with your work and want to close Visual Studio entirely.

`New Repository`

- Create a new Git repository directly within Visual Studio.
- Start version controlling a new project from the beginning using Git.

Create a Git repository (**`File □ New □ Repository`**) :

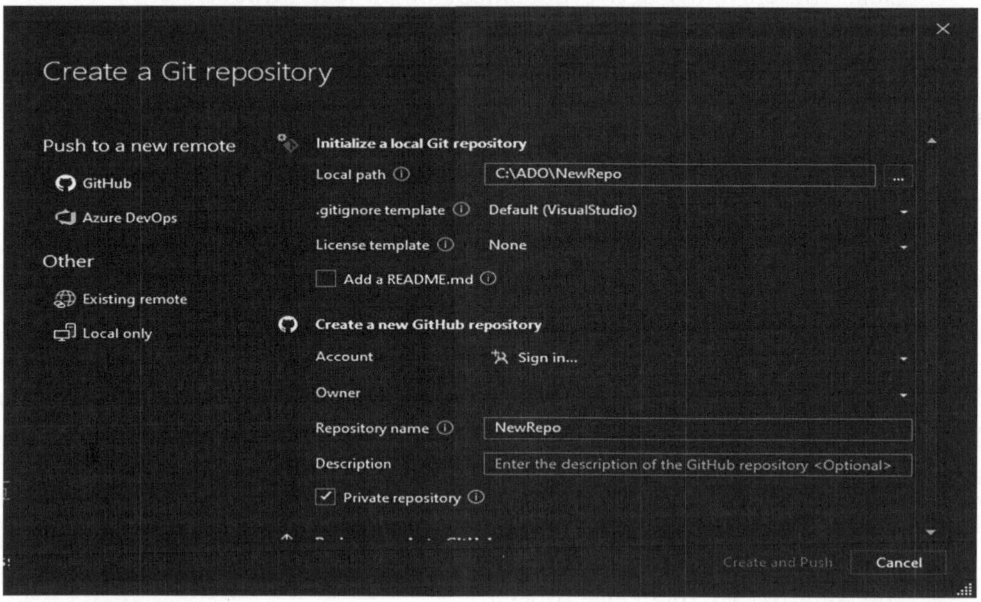

***Figure 1.25:** Create Git Repository*

In Visual Studio 2022, you can create a new repository by navigating to "**`File`** > **`New`** > **`New Repository`**" option under the "**`File`**" menu allows you to create a new Git repository directly within Visual Studio. This feature is particularly useful when you want to start a new project and version control it from the beginning using Git.

When you select the "**`New Repository`**" option, Visual Studio will guide you through the process of creating a new Git repository. This typically involves specifying a location for the repository on your local filesystem, providing a name for the repository, and optionally choosing a **`.gitignore`** file template to exclude certain files from version control.

Once the repository is created, Visual Studio will initialize it with an initial commit containing any files you have added to the project. From there, you can continue to work on your project, staging and committing changes as needed using the built-in Git integration in Visual Studio.

Creating a new repository directly within Visual Studio streamlines the process of setting up version control for your projects, making it easier to manage changes and collaborate with others on your code.

`File > Clone a Repository`

Figure 1.26: *Clone Repository*

In Visual Studio 2022, the "**`Clone Repository`**" option under the "**`File`**" menu allows you to clone an existing Git repository from a remote location, such as GitHub, Azure DevOps, or a self-hosted Git server, directly within Visual Studio.

When you select the "**`Clone Repository`**" option, Visual Studio will prompt you to provide the URL of the Git repository you want to clone and specify a local directory where the repository will be cloned to. Additionally, you can choose the branch to clone or leave it to the default branch.

Once you provide the necessary information and confirm, Visual Studio will initiate the cloning process. It will download all the files and commit history from the remote repository to your local machine, while creating a new local Git repository in the specified directory.

After the cloning process is complete, you can start working with the cloned repository in Visual Studio. You will have access to all the files and commit history, and you can use Visual Studio's built-in Git tools to manage changes, commit new code, and push/pull changes to and from the remote repository.

The "`Clone Repository`" option in Visual Studio simplifies the process of getting started with an existing project hosted on a remote Git repository, which will enable you to quickly bring the codebase onto your local development environment and start contributing.

Edit Menu

This menu provides options for editing and modifying the code in your project.

Its constituent options include:

- **`Undo`:** Reverts the most recent action performed in the active document
- **`Redo`:** Reapplies the most recently undone action in the active document
- **`Cut`:** Removes the selected text or content from the active document and places it in the clipboard
- **`Copy`:** Copies the selected text or content from the active document to the clipboard
- **`Paste`:** Inserts the content from the clipboard into the active document at the current cursor position
- **`Duplicate`:** If no selection is made, it typically duplicates the entire line where the cursor is positioned. If a selection is active, it duplicates the selected text.
- **`Delete`:** Deletes the selected text or content from the active document
- **`Find and Replace`:** Opens the Find and Replace dialog, allowing you to search for specific text within the active document and optionally replace it with different text
- **`Go To`:** Opens the Go To dialog, which allows you to navigate to a specific line number or declaration within the active document
- **`Advanced`:** This submenu often contains additional editing options such as toggling word wrap, indenting or unindenting text, and formatting selections.
- **`Select All`:** Selects all text or content within the active document
- **`Format`:** This submenu usually contains options for formatting code, such as applying code styling rules, organizing using directives, and removing and sorting using directives.
- **`Comment/Uncomment`:** These options allow you to comment or uncomment selected lines of code, depending on the language you are working with.
- **`IntelliSense`:** This submenu provides options related to IntelliSense such as refreshing IntelliSense suggestions or displaying parameter info.

- **`Bookmarks`:** Allows you to set, navigate to, and manage bookmarks within the active document
- **`Snippets`:** Provides access to code snippets that can be inserted into the active document to speed up coding tasks
- **`Outlining`:** This submenu offers options for collapsing and expanding code blocks, which makes it easier to navigate and focus on specific sections of code.
- **`Spelling`:** Contains options for spell checking the active document

View Menu

In Visual Studio 2022, the "**`View`**" menu contains various options and features to customize the layout, appearance, and functionality of the IDE. Here is a detailed list of the options along with their usage and specific examples of how they can be helpful during software development:

`Solution Explorer`: This option toggles the visibility of the Solution Explorer window, which displays the structure of your solution and its projects, folders, and files. You can use it to navigate through your project hierarchy, add or remove files, and manage project settings.

In Visual Studio 2022, the "**`View`**" menu provides options related to various aspects of the development environment, including **`Git Changes`** and **`Git Repository`**. Here is a breakdown of these options and their purposes:

`Git Changes`: This option opens the Git Changes tool window, which displays changes made to files in your Git repository.

- **Purpose**: It allows you to review and manage changes to your code, including additions, modifications, and deletions, before committing them to the repository.
- **Example**: You can use Git Changes to review the modifications you've made to your codebase, stage specific changes for commit, and discard changes if needed.

`Git Repository`: This option opens the Git Repository tool window, which provides a summary of the current Git repository and its status.

- **Purpose**: It allows you to view information about the repository, such as the current branch, recent commits, untracked files, and branch history.
- **Example**: You can use the Git Repository tool window to switch between branches, view the commit history, perform Git operations like branching, merging, and pushing changes, and manage repository settings.

These options are particularly useful for developers working with Git version control within Visual Studio. They provide easy access to Git-related features and help streamline the process of managing changes and collaborating on code with a team.

Properties Window: The Properties window displays properties for the currently selected item in the IDE, such as a control on a form or a file in Solution Explorer. You can use it to view and modify properties, which can be particularly useful when designing user interfaces or configuring project settings.

Output: This window displays diagnostic messages, build output, debugging information, and other output generated by Visual Studio and your projects. It is helpful for troubleshooting errors, monitoring build progress, and viewing runtime messages during debugging sessions.

Error List: The Error List window displays compiler errors, warnings, and other issues detected in your code. You can use it to quickly navigate to errors, fix syntax issues, and address other problems that may prevent your code from building or running correctly.

Task List: The Task List window displays tasks, comments, and other annotations within your code. You can use it to keep track of TODO comments, code review feedback, and other items that require attention during development.

Code Definition Window: This window displays the definition of the symbol at the current cursor position in your code. You can use it to quickly view the definition of a class, method, variable, or other code element without navigating away from your current location.

Document Outline: The Document Outline window provides a hierarchical view of the elements within the currently active document, such as classes, methods, and controls. You can use it to navigate through the structure of your code and quickly locate specific elements.

Toolbox: The Toolbox window contains controls and components that you can drag and drop onto your forms or design surfaces when building user interfaces. You can use it to quickly access and add common UI elements like buttons, text boxes, and labels to your projects.

Code Snippet Manager: This option opens the Code Snippet Manager, where you can manage and customize code snippets for common programming tasks. You can use it to create, edit, import, and export snippets to streamline your coding workflow and promote code reuse.

Server Explorer: Server Explorer provides access to data connections, servers, and services within your development environment. You can use it to browse databases, interact with Azure resources, and manage connected services during application development.

`SQL Server Object Explorer`: This window allows you to interact with SQL Server databases directly within Visual Studio. You can use it to browse database objects, execute queries, manage table data, and perform other database-related tasks without leaving the IDE.

`Command Window`: The Command Window in Visual Studio provides a command-line interface for executing commands, especially those related to debugging, editing, and navigation.

- It allows developers to execute commands directly without navigating through menus or toolbars.
- Developers can use the **`Command Window`** to perform various tasks such as executing debugging commands, setting breakpoints, navigating to specific files or lines, and interacting with the Visual Studio IDE programmatically through commands.
- Example usage of some common scenarios:
    - Executing a debugging command to set a breakpoint at a specific line of code
    - Navigating to a specific file by entering its path in the Command Window

`Immediate Window`: The **`Immediate Window`** is primarily used during debugging sessions in Visual Studio.

- It provides a way to interactively execute code statements and evaluate expressions while debugging.
- Developers can use the **`Immediate Window`** to inspect variables, evaluate expressions, call methods, and perform calculations during debugging sessions.
- It can help in debugging by allowing developers to quickly test and evaluate code snippets without modifying the source code.
- Example usage of some common scenarios:
    - Inspecting the value of a variable by typing its name and pressing Enter in the Immediate Window
    - Evaluating an expression to understand its result during debugging
    - Calling a method with specific arguments to observe its behavior at runtime

***Tip**: Both the `Command Window` and `Immediate Window` are powerful tools in Visual Studio that aid developers in debugging and interacting with their code efficiently during development sessions. They provide a command-line interface and an interactive environment for executing commands and evaluating expressions during debugging sessions, respectively.*

Project Menu

This menu is focused on managing and configuring your project settings and build options.

The options in this menu are:

`Add New Item`: Add a new file or item to your project.

`Add Existing Item`: Add an existing file to your project.

`Properties`: Access the project properties, where you can configure build settings, target frameworks, and other project-specific options.

Build Menu

This menu is used to control the build process for your project.

In Visual Studio, both "**`Build Solution`**" and "**`Rebuild Solution`**" are options used to compile the code and produce the output, but they differ in their approach and behavior.

`Build Solution:`

- When you select "**`Build Solution`**," Visual Studio compiles only those project files that have changed since the last build, along with their dependencies.
- It is a faster operation compared to "**`Rebuild Solution`**" because it only rebuilds what is necessary.
- If the project has already been built and there are no changes, selecting "**`Build Solution`**" will not rebuild anything, which results in no changes to the output files.

`Rebuild` Solution:

- When you select "**`Rebuild Solution`**," Visual Studio performs a clean build by first cleaning all output files (that is, removing all previously built files) and then compiling all project files from scratch, regardless of whether they have changed or not.
- It ensures that the entire solution is built from a clean state, which can be useful in situations where the build might be corrupted or inconsistent due to various reasons.
- "**`Rebuild Solution`**" takes more time compared to "**`Build Solution`**" because it compiles all files, regardless of whether they have changed or not.

In summary, "**`Build Solution`**" is generally faster and is used for incremental builds, compiling only what has changed since the last build. "**`Rebuild Solution`**" is slower but ensures a clean and consistent build by compiling all project files from scratch, regardless of changes. The choice between them depends on the specific needs and circumstances of your project.

`Clean Solution`: This option is used to remove all intermediate and output files generated during the build process. When you clean a solution, Visual Studio deletes all the compiled binaries, temporary files, and other artifacts associated with the projects in the solution. Here is what the "`Clean Solution`" option does:

Remove Output Files:

- Deletes all compiled output files, such as executable files, DLLs, and object files, generated by the build process for each project in the solution.
- Clears the output directories where the build artifacts are stored, ensuring a clean slate for the next build.

Clears Temporary Files:

- Removes any temporary files generated during the build process, including intermediate files and compiler-generated files.
- Clears the temporary directories used by the compiler and build tools, freeing up disk space and reducing clutter.

Cleans Project Dependencies:

- Cleans any build outputs for projects within the solution.
- Removes any dll(s) and other files ensuring a clean and consistent build environment.

Resets Build State:

- Resets the build state of the solution, so the next build operation starts from scratch.
- Ensures that the next build operation recompiles all source files and regenerates all output files, regardless of whether they have changed or not.

Using the "`Clean Solution`" option can be helpful in various scenarios, such as:

- Resolving build errors or inconsistencies that may arise due to outdated or corrupted build artifacts
- Ensuring a clean and consistent build environment before performing a fresh build or rebuilding the solution
- Cleaning up unnecessary files and freeing up disk space by removing temporary and intermediate build artifacts

It is important to note that "`Clean Solution`" does not remove source code files or project settings. It only removes the output files and temporary build artifacts generated during the build process.

`Cancel`: Cancel the current build process (Keyboard shortcut: *Ctrl + Break*).

Debug Menu

The "`Debug`" menu provides various options and features to assist developers in debugging their applications effectively. Below is a detailed list of the options, features, and sub-menu items available in the "`Debug`" menu, along with specific examples of how to use them during software development:

`Start Debugging`: Launches the application in debug mode, allowing breakpoints and other debugging features to be utilized. **Example**: Launching a .NET application to debug and step through code execution

`Start Without Debugging`: Launches the application without enabling debugging features. **Example**: Launching a .NET application to run it normally without any debugging intervention

`Attach to Process`: Allows you to attach the debugger to a running process for debugging. **Example**: Attaching the debugger to an already running web server process to debug an issue

`Step Over`: It steps over the current line of code during debugging, without stepping into any function calls. **Example**: Stepping over a method call to quickly move to the next line of code in the current method.

`Step Into`: It steps into and inside the currently selected function or method during debugging. **Example**: Stepping into a method call to debug the code within that method

`Step Out`: It steps out of the current function or method during debugging, returning to the calling function. **Example**: Stepping out of a method to return to the caller and continue debugging from there

`Continue`: It resumes execution of the application until the next breakpoint is reached. **Example**: Continuing execution after fixing an issue to see if it is resolved

`Stop Debugging`: It stops the debugging session and terminates the application. **Example**: Stopping debugging after identifying and fixing all the issues

`Restart`: It terminates the current debugging session and immediately starts a new one with the debugger attached. It does not preserve the state of the previous session. **Example**: Restarting the application to test changes made during debugging and automatically reattaching the debugging session

`Break All`: It Pauses the execution of the application, allowing you to inspect the current state. **Example**: Using "`Break All`" to pause the application and investigate unexpected behavior

`Windows`: It provides various debugging-related windows such as "**`Breakpoints`**," "**`Call Stack`**," "**`Locals`**," and so on, to inspect the state of the application during debugging

These options and features in the "**`Debug`**" menu facilitate efficient debugging workflows, which allows developers to diagnose and fix issues in their applications effectively during software development.

Git Menu

This menu is focused on source control and collaboration features.

The options under this menu include:

`Clone Repository`: Connect your project to a team collaboration platform, such as Azure DevOps or GitHub.

`Commit`: Commit your changes to the source control repository

`Pull`: Pull the latest changes from the source control repository

`Push`: Push your local changes to the source control repository.

Tools Menu

This menu provides access to various tools and utilities within Visual Studio.

The options under this menu include:

`NuGet Package Manager`: Manage NuGet packages for your project.

`Extensions and Updates`: Explore and install additional extensions and tools for Visual Studio.

`Options`: Access the Visual Studio options and settings.

Help Menu

This menu offers access to the documentation, resources, and support for Visual Studio.

The options under this menu include:

`Visual Studio Help`: Access the Visual Studio documentation and user guide.

`Send Feedback`: Submit feedback or report issues with Visual Studio.

`Check for Updates`: It will check for any latest versions or updates available for currently installed VS.

`About Microsoft Visual Studio`: View information about the current version of Visual Studio.

Search Menu

The **`Search`** option in the Visual Studio menu bar is a powerful tool that can greatly improve your productivity and workflow. Let us dive into the details of this feature:

The **`Search`** option is located in the top-right corner of the Visual Studio IDE, next to the Help menu. This search bar provides a centralized way to quickly find and access various elements within your codebase, the Visual Studio interface, and the development tools.

Here are the key features and use cases of the Visual Studio Search option:

`Code` Search:

- You can use the search bar to quickly find and navigate to specific classes, methods, variables, or other code elements within your project.
- As you type in the search bar, Visual Studio will provide live suggestions and preview the matching code elements.
- This helps you quickly jump to the desired code location, which will save you time and improve your overall productivity.

`Command` Search:

- The search bar can also be used to find and execute Visual Studio commands like build, debug, or project management actions.
- By typing in a command or its description, Visual Studio will suggest you the matching commands, which will allow you to quickly access and execute them.
- This is particularly useful when you are trying to find a specific command or feature within the Visual Studio interface, but you are unsure of its exact location.

`Settings` Search:

- The search bar can be used to search for and modify Visual Studio settings and options.
- You can type in keywords related to the setting you are looking for, and Visual Studio will provide suggestions and direct you to the relevant settings page.
- This can be helpful when you need to customize the IDE's behavior or appearance to suit your preferences or project requirements.

Extension Manager:

- It can be found in **`Extensions`** menu.

- The search pr browse option can also be used to find and install Visual Studio extensions and tools from the Visual Studio Marketplace.
- By typing in keywords related to the extension you are looking for, Visual Studio will display relevant search results, which allows you to quickly discover and install the desired extensions.

Documentation Search:

- The search bar can be used to search the Visual Studio documentation and online resources.
- This can be particularly useful when you are trying to find information about a specific feature, an API, or a development best practice.

Thus, by mastering the Visual Studio Search option, you can significantly improve your development workflow, quickly navigate your codebase, access important features and commands, and stay informed about the various tools and resources available within the Visual Studio ecosystem.

Also, by familiarizing yourself with the Visual Studio menu bar and the options available in each menu, you will be able to efficiently navigate the IDE, access the necessary tools and features, and streamline your software development process.

Conclusion

In this inaugural chapter, we explored a powerful development environment called Visual Studio 2022.

We began by delving into the rationale behind utilizing Visual Studio, while emphasizing on its significance as a comprehensive integrated development environment (IDE) that caters to a wide array of programming languages and platforms. We examined the various iterations of Visual Studio, while highlighting the evolution of this indispensable toolset over the years.

Our journey continued with a step-by-step guide to the installation process, which ensured a seamless setup experience for readers who are eager to harness the capabilities of Visual Studio 2022. Through clear instructions and visual aids, we navigated the installation procedure and empowered users to embark on their development journey with confidence.

Upon successful installation, we then ventured into the heart of Visual Studio—the IDE itself. After introducing the readers to the interface, we provided insights into the myriad options available within the menu bar and its submenus. From essential tools for project management, to customizable settings for personalization, we explored the diverse functionalities available.

As readers acquaint themselves with the intuitive layout and extensive feature set of Visual Studio 2022, they will be able to embark on a journey of exploration and innovation in the realm of software development. Armed with a foundational understanding of Visual Studio's capabilities and customization options, readers will be poised to delve deeper into the intricacies of this indispensable toolset in the chapters that follow.

With the groundwork laid in this chapter, readers will be equipped to harness the full potential of Visual Studio 2022 and embark on a transformative journey of creativity, productivity, and innovation in software development. As we bid adieu to this introductory chapter, we look forward to accompanying readers on their journey through the Ultimate Guide to Visual Studio 2022.

The upcoming chapter will delve into project creation within VS, and will cover popular templates and project types.

CHAPTER 2
Understanding Projects and Solutions

Introduction

This chapter undertakes a thorough examination of the primary templates in Visual Studio. These templates serve as excellent starting points for new projects and include pre-configured files, references, project properties, and compilation options that are tailored for specific technologies and frameworks. By using templates, developers can quickly set up a project structure and access boilerplate code to build it, rather than starting from scratch.

The available templates depend on the workloads that are selected during VS installation. Some templates, such as class libraries, are installed by default. Developers can choose from different template options based on the project requirements and technologies that they plan to use. Selecting an appropriate template that aligns with the project's scope, requirements, and the team's expertise can help avoid technical debt and future architectural issues.

Structure

In this chapter, we will cover the following topics:

- Benefits of Using Templates in Visual Studio
- Choosing the Right Templates
- Understanding Projects and Solutions
- Web Application-Based Templates
- Web API Templates
- Swagger
- Desktop Templates
- MAUI Templates

- Blazor Hybrid App
- Class Library
- SPA Templates
- Blazor Templates

Benefits of Using Templates in Visual Studio

Using templates in Visual Studio offers several benefits such as:

- **Saves Time and Boosts Productivity:** Templates provide a pre-configured starting point for new projects, which saves developers from the tedious task of setting up project structures, references, and configurations from scratch. This allows them to focus on writing code, and implementing business logic, while increasing productivity.
- **Promotes Consistency and Standardization:** By adopting custom project templates within an organization, development teams can ensure a consistent project structure, coding conventions, and best practices across all projects. This consistency facilitates collaboration, code maintainability, and knowledge sharing among team members.
- **Reduces Technical Debt and Architectural Issues:** Templates often encapsulate industry best practices and proven architectural patterns. By selecting the appropriate template that aligns with project requirements and the team's expertise, developers can avoid technical debt and potential architectural pitfalls from the outset.
- **Facilitates Onboarding and Knowledge Transfer:** Well-designed templates can serve as a learning resource for new team members, as they provide a clear understanding of the project structure, coding standards, and development workflows. This can accelerate the onboarding process and knowledge transfer within the team.
- **Supports Rapid Prototyping and Experimentation:** Visual Studio provides a wide range of templates for various project types such as web development, desktop applications, and cross-platform development. These templates enable developers to quickly set up and experiment with different technologies, frameworks, and architectures, fostering innovation and exploration.
- **Extensibility and Customization:** Visual Studio allows developers to create custom project and item templates tailored to their specific needs. These custom templates can encapsulate company-specific coding standards, third-party libraries, and reusable components, thereby enhancing productivity and consistency across projects.

By leveraging the power of templates in Visual Studio, development teams can streamline their workflows, maintain consistency, reduce technical debt, facilitate knowledge sharing, and deliver high-quality software more efficiently.

The following section will explore the main templates provided by Visual Studio, and discuss how to choose the most suitable template for your projects.

Choosing the Right Templates

Visual Studio offers a wide range of templates. You can find the right one through its built-in search functionality. Developers can search for templates based on keywords, technologies, or project types to quickly locate the most relevant options. *Figure 2.1* shows the "**`Create a new project`**" window (**`File`** → **`New`** → **`Project`**).

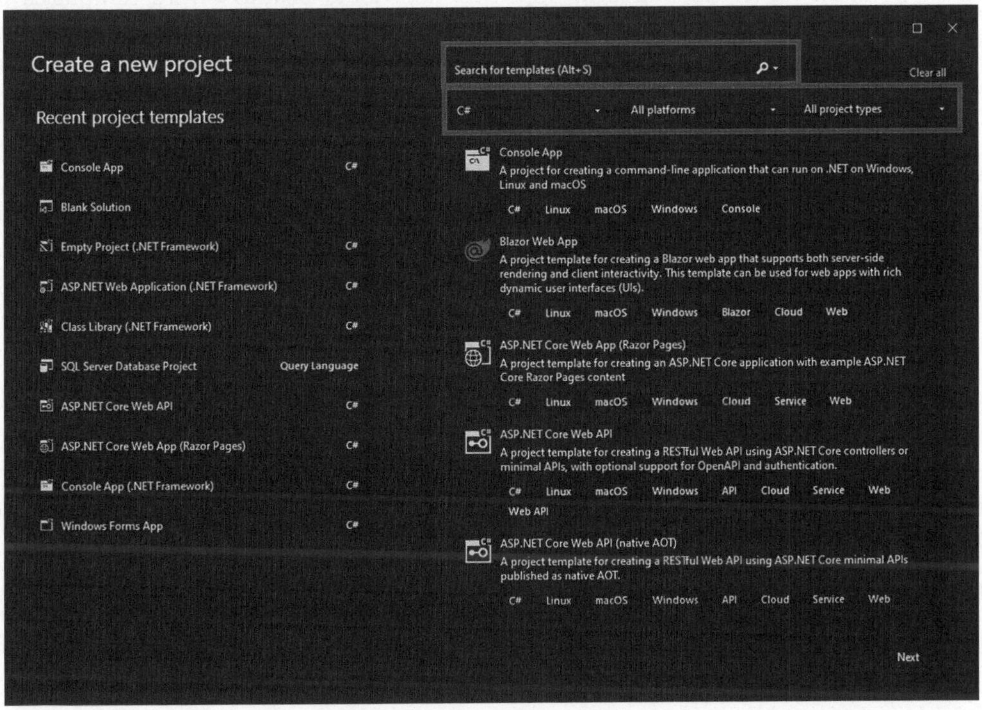

Figure 2.1: *Create New Project*

The illustrated window has a search option which you can use to search for specific templates by keywords like web, desktop, API, mobile, and so on.

It also has options to target specific languages like C#, Visual Basic, Python, JavaScript, and so on.

It also has options to target final platforms such as Web, Windows, Android, Azure, Linux, and so on, for platform specific development.

Finally, "`All project types`" dropdown allows you to target projects for Web API, Console, Desktop, NUnit, MAUI, and others.

Here are some of the differences between available templates:

- **Web Applications Development Templates:** Visual Studio provides several templates that are specifically designed for web development projects. These templates include pre-configured settings and boilerplate code for popular web frameworks and technologies such as ASP.NET, Angular, React, and Vue.js. After selecting a web development template, developers can jumpstart their projects with a solid foundation and focus on implementing their unique business logic.
- **Multiplatform Applications Development Templates:** With the increasing demand for cross-platform applications, Visual Studio offers templates for developing apps that can run on multiple devices like smartphones and desktop environments. These templates support technologies like Xamarin, Flutter, and .NET MAUI, which enable developers to create native-like experiences across various operating systems.
- **Desktop Applications Development Templates:** Visual Studio also provides templates for building desktop applications that cater to different user interface frameworks and technologies. Developers can choose from templates for Windows Forms, Windows Presentation Foundation (WPF), or Universal Windows Platform (UWP) projects, depending on their specific requirements and the target audience.

By understanding the available templates, and selecting the most appropriate one for their projects, developers can save time, reduce the risk of architectural pitfalls, and ensure a consistent starting point for their applications. Visual Studio's template system empowers developers to focus on delivering value by acting as a solid foundation for their projects.

Also, "`Search`" bar provides the option to search for specific project templates.

Figure 2.1 shows all projects related to creating `Console` apps, as follows:

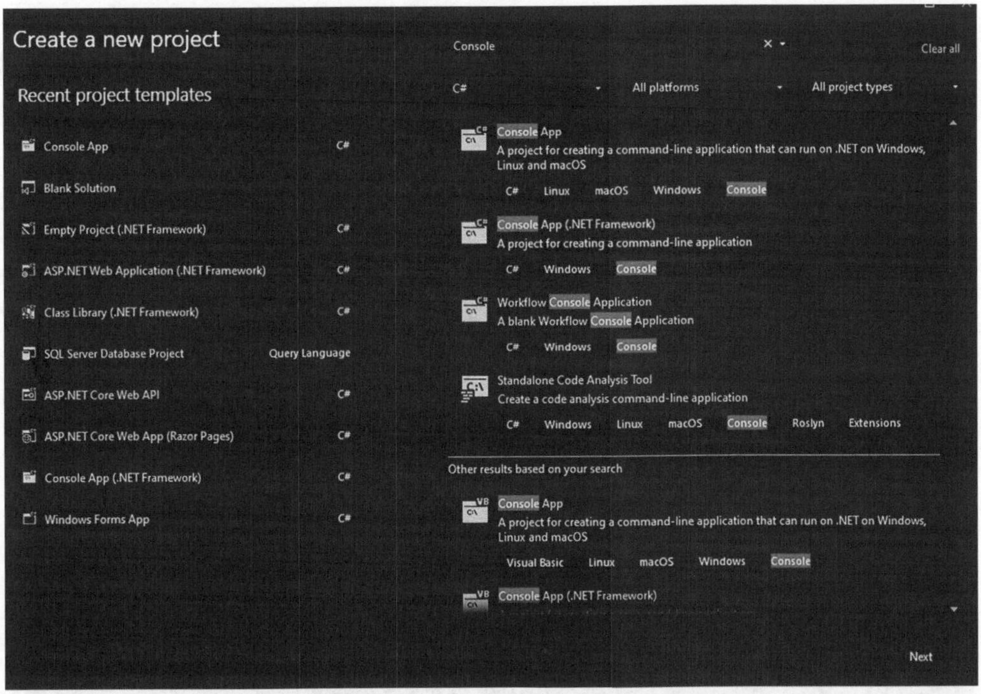

Figure 2.2: Console App Templates

Figure 2.3: All Projects Targeting .Net Core Apps

In case, you could not find the right template for your selected language or platform type, then you will find an option to "**`install more tools and features`**" right at the bottom of the search results, as shown in *Figure 2.4*:

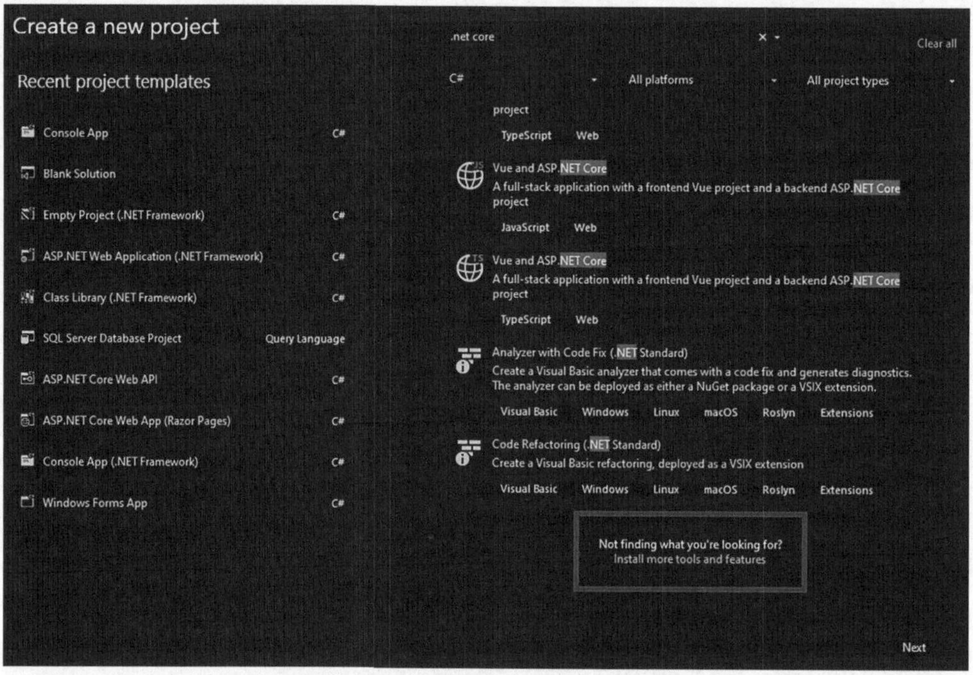

Figure 2.4: *.Net Core Templates*

Clicking the link will provide the option to install more features to the visual studio through the installer window, as is indicated in *Figure 2.5*:

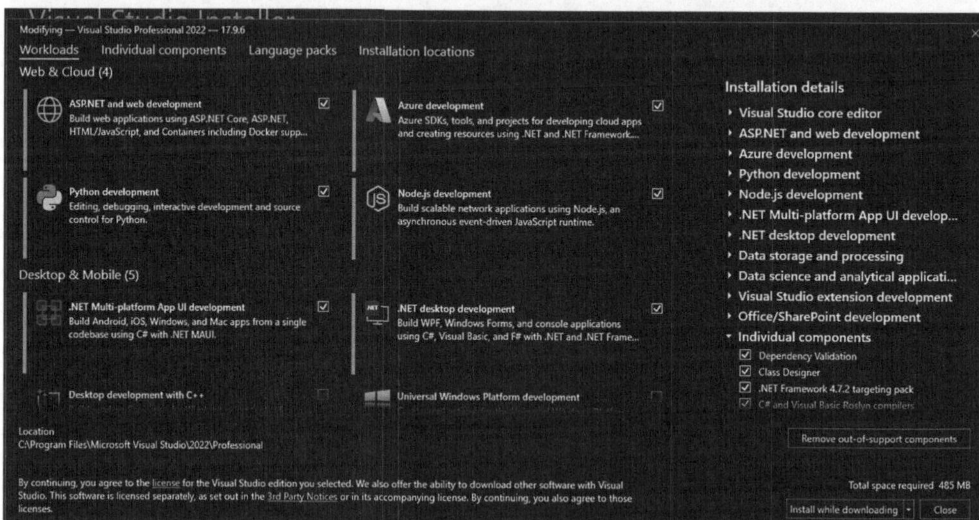

Figure 2.5: *Adding Features to Install Visual Studio*

Empty Templates/Projects

In Visual Studio, the "**`Empty Template`**" concept is a starting point to create new projects. Essentially, selecting the Empty Template means to initiate a project with no predefined code or structure. Instead, it provides developers with a clean slate, which offers them complete freedom and flexibility to build their application from scratch according to their preferences.

The purpose of the **`Empty Template`** is to cater to developers who have a clear vision of their project architecture and prefer to construct their codebase without any predefined conventions or constraints. This template is particularly helpful for experienced developers or those working on highly customized or unique projects where pre-existing templates might not align with their needs.

By starting with the **`Empty Template`**, developers can exercise maximum control over their project including directory structure, file naming conventions, and code organization. This allows for a tailored approach to development, which allows developers to implement the features and components that are necessary for their application without confronting any unnecessary bloat or overhead.

Furthermore, the **`Empty Template`** encourages developers to gain a deeper understanding of the underlying technologies and frameworks they are working with, as they are responsible for building out the entire project structure themselves. This can result in creating a more comprehensive understanding of the project's architecture and fostering better decision-making throughout the development process.

In summary, the **`Empty Template`** in Visual Studio serves as a blank canvas for developers, which empowers them to create projects precisely tailored to their needs and preferences and promote deeper understanding and control of the project's architecture and implementation.

Understanding Projects and Solutions

When creating a new project in Visual Studio, it is essential to understand the distinctions between a project and a solution, as well as between project files and solution files. *Figure* 2.6 shows how to set the Project name, Solution name and Project location, while creating new projects.

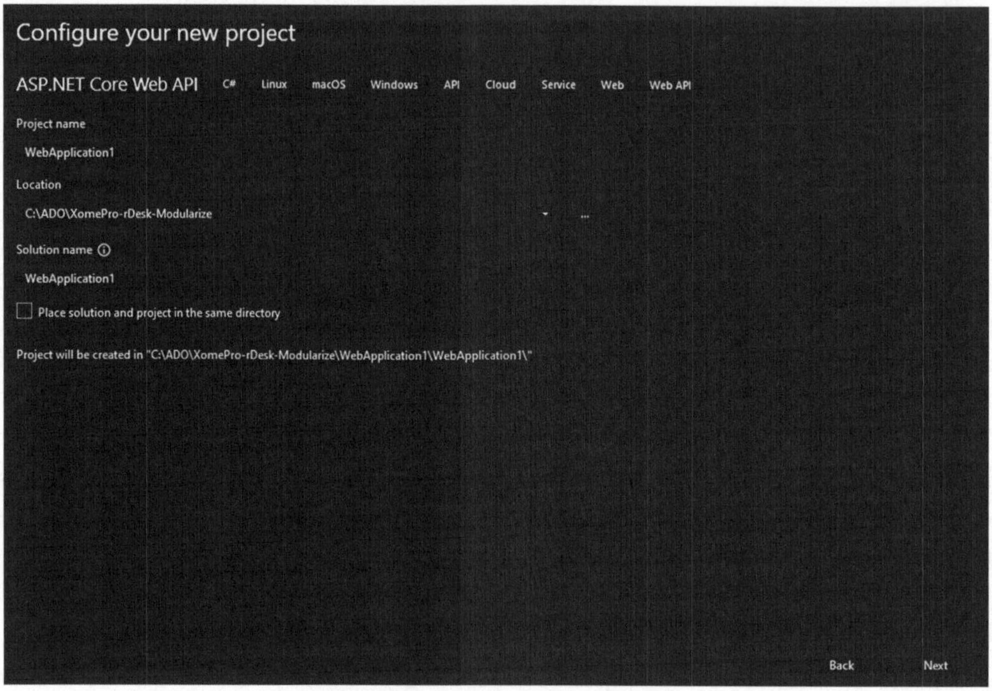

Figure 2.6: *Configuring New Project*

Project vs. Solution:

- **Project:** A project in Visual Studio is a collection of files and resources that are compiled into a single output. It represents a specific software application, component, or library that you are developing. A project contains source code files, configuration files, assets (such as images or resource files), and references to external libraries or frameworks. Each project has its own settings, dependencies, and build configurations.
- **Solution:** A solution is a container that can hold one or more projects. It provides a way to organize and manage multiple related projects within a single workspace. Solutions are useful for managing complex applications that consist of multiple components or modules. They allow developers to work on different parts of an application independently while still maintaining dependencies and relationships between projects.

Project File vs. Solution File:

- **Project File:** A project file is a configuration file specific to each project within a solution. It contains metadata about the project, such as its name, type, dependencies, build settings, and other project-specific configurations. The project file typically has an extension like '`.csproj`' for C# projects, '`.vbproj`' for VB.NET projects, or '`.vcxproj`' for C++ projects. This file is used by Visual Studio and the build system to compile the project into the desired output.
- **Solution File:** A solution file is a file with a '`.sln`' extension that defines the structure and contents of a Visual Studio solution. It serves as a top-level container for one or more projects within the solution. The solution file contains references to the individual project files, as well as solution-wide settings and configurations. It provides a centralized entry point for opening and managing all the projects within the solution.

In summary, a project represents a specific software component or application, while a solution is a container for organizing and managing multiple related projects. Project files contain project-specific configurations, while solution files define the structure and contents of the entire solution. Understanding these distinctions is crucial for effectively managing and developing projects in Visual Studio.

Now, we will explore the types of templates provided by Visual Studio.

Web Application-Based Templates

Figure 2.7 shows the various web based templates available in VS:

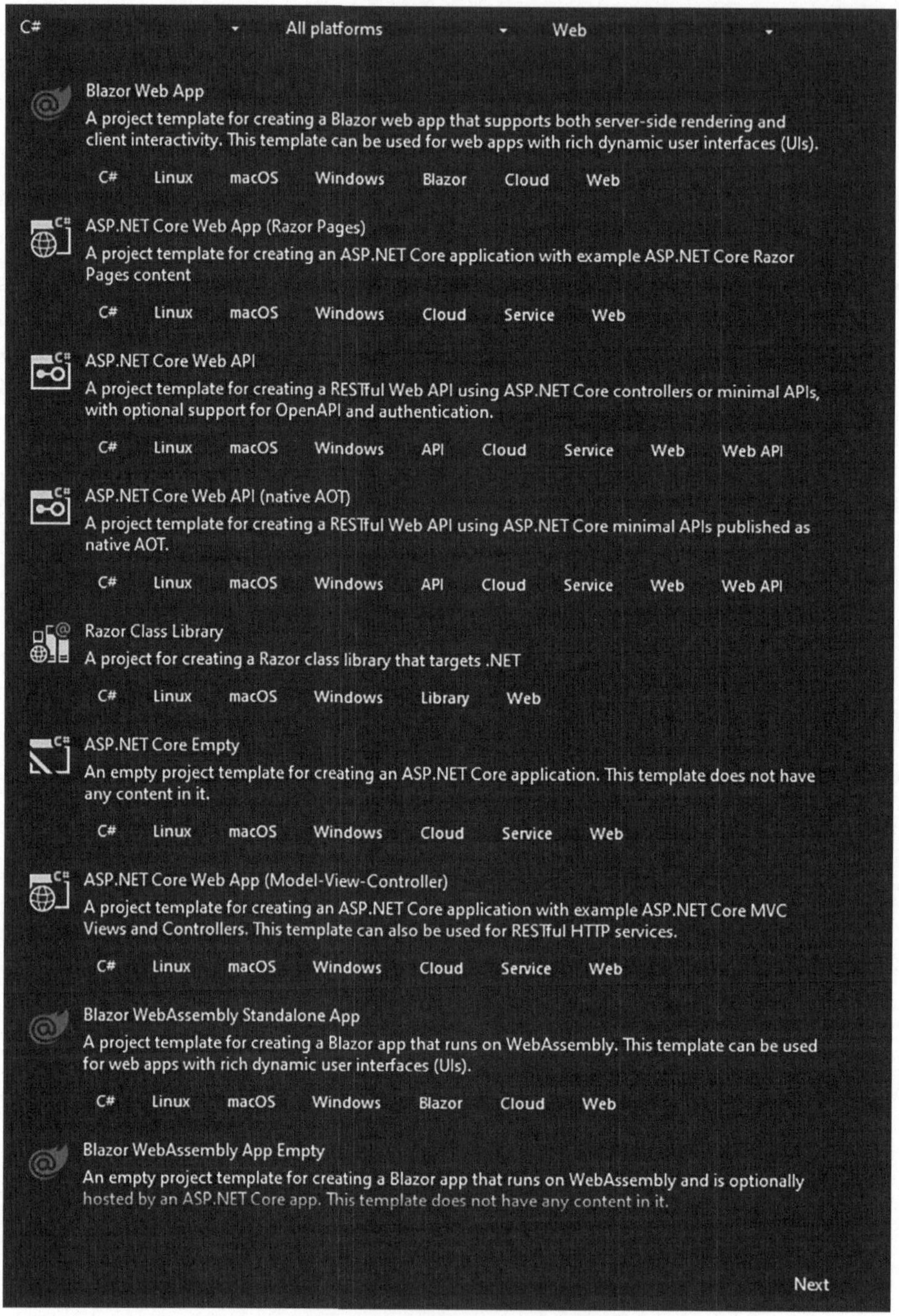

Figure 2.7: *Web-Based Templates*

In Visual Studio, web-based templates are pre-configured project structures designed to kickstart web development projects. These templates provide a starting point for developers by including essential files, folders, and configurations tailored to various types of web applications. The different types of web templates cater to specific use cases and frameworks, where each serves a distinct purpose. Here are some common types of web templates and their purposes:

ASP.NET Core Web Applications

This template is used for creating modern web applications using ASP.NET Core, a cross-platform framework for building web apps. The types of web applications available in VS are as follows:

- **Web Application:** A template for building general-purpose web applications
- **Web API:** Designed specifically for building RESTful APIs
- **Empty:** Provides a bare-bones project structure with minimal files and configurations, while offering maximum flexibility for customization
- **Razor Pages:** Introduces the Razor Pages programming model for creating page-focused web applications with minimal ceremony

Features and Advantages:

- **Cross-Platform Development:** ASP.NET Core supports development on Windows, macOS, and Linux environments.
- **High Performance:** Optimized for speed and scalability, thereby making it suitable for high-traffic applications
- **Modular Architecture:** Allows developers to include only the necessary components, reducing overhead
- **Integrated Dependency Injection:** Built-in support for dependency injection simplifies application design and testing
- **Built-in Middleware:** Middleware components handle requests and responses, while providing features like routing, authentication, and logging.

ASP.NET MVC Web Applications

This template is used for creating web applications following the Model-View-Controller (MVC) architectural pattern.

- **Web Application:** Standard MVC template for building full-fledged web applications
- **Web API:** Similar to the ASP.NET Core Web API template; used for building RESTful APIs using MVC
- **Empty:** Offers an empty MVC project structure and allows developers to start from scratch

Features and Advantages:

- **Separation of Concerns:** MVC architecture separates the application into model, view, and controller components, while promoting maintainability and testability.
- **Extensible Routing:** Flexible routing mechanism allows developers to define custom URL patterns.
- **Powerful Templating Engine:** Razor syntax enables dynamic content rendering and code reuse.
- **Testability:** Components can be unit tested independently, which enhances the overall code quality.
- **Rich Ecosystem:** This provides access to a vast ecosystem of libraries, extensions, and community resources.

Angular/React/Vue.js Web Applications

These templates are tailored for building single-page applications (SPAs) using popular front-end JavaScript frameworks. These templates facilitate the development of dynamic, interactive web applications with rich user interfaces. Most Commonly used javascript based framework templates are mentioned as follows:

- **Angular:** A template for creating Angular applications
- **React.js:** A template for creating React.js applications
- **Vue.js:** A template for creating Vue.js applications

Features and Advantages

- **Component-Based Architecture:** Frameworks like Angular, React.js, and Vue.js promote component-based development, enhancing modularity and reusability.
- **Virtual DOM (React.js):** Efficient rendering and updates for improved performance
- **Reactive Data Binding (Angular, Vue.js):** Automatic data synchronization between components and UI elements
- **Rich Ecosystem:** Access to a plethora of third-party libraries, plug-ins, and tools for rapid development
- **Community Support:** Active communities that provide resources, tutorials, and support forums for developers

Static Web Application

- This template is used for creating static websites or simple web projects without server-side logic.

- **HTML/JavaScript:** Provides a basic project structure with HTML, CSS, and JavaScript files
- **SPA:** Enables building interactive web UIs through C# and .NET running on WebAssembly

Features and Advantages

- **Lightweight:** There is no server-side processing, which results in faster load times and less hosting requirements.
- **Simplicity:** Ideal for small projects or static content websites that do not require dynamic server-side functionality.
- **Cost-Effective:** Hosting static websites is often more affordable compared to dynamic websites.
- **Secure:** There is a reduced attack surface as there is no server-side processing or database interaction.

In summary, each web template in Visual Studio is designed to streamline the development process by offering a predefined project structure, configurations, and often integrated tooling tailored to the specific technology stack or framework. Developers can choose the most suitable template based on their project requirements, technology preferences, and familiarity with the chosen framework.

Web API Templates

In Visual Studio, Web API templates are project templates designed to facilitate the creation of RESTful APIs through ASP.NET Core. These templates provide a structured foundation for building web services that can be consumed by client applications, such as web, mobile, or desktop applications. Here are the different types of Web API templates in Visual Studio, along with their purposes, features, and advantages:

ASP.NET Core Web API

The ASP.NET Core Web API template is a general-purpose template for building RESTful APIs using ASP.NET Core. It provides a basic project structure with controllers, models, and configuration files to get started with API development.

Features and Advantages

- **MVC Architecture:** Follows the Model-View-Controller (MVC) architectural pattern, where controllers handle incoming HTTP requests, models represent data entities, and views (in this case, not present) format the response data
- **Attribute Routing:** Supports attribute-based routing, thereby allowing developers to define API endpoints and routes using attributes on controller actions

- **Dependency Injection:** Built-in support for dependency injection, which enables the injection of services and dependencies into controllers and other components
- **Middleware Pipeline:** Utilizes the ASP.NET Core middleware pipeline for processing HTTP requests and responses, which enables custom middleware to be added for additional functionality
- **Content Negotiation:** Supports content negotiation to determine the appropriate response format (for example, JSON, XML) based on client preferences

ASP.NET Core Empty

The ASP.NET Core Empty template provides a minimalistic starting point for building custom web APIs from scratch. It includes only the essential project files and folders, which allows developers to add components and features as needed.

Features and Advantages

- **Flexibility:** Offers maximum flexibility for customizing the project structure and adding specific components tailored to the requirements of the API
- **Lightweight:** Provides a lightweight starting point with minimal boilerplate code, thereby reducing unnecessary overhead and complexity
- **Customization:** Allows developers to choose and integrate specific libraries, frameworks, and tools based on project requirements without any predefined conventions

ASP.NET Core with Docker Support

The ASP.NET Core with Docker Support template extends the ASP.NET Core Web API template by adding Docker support for containerization and deployment.

Features and Advantages

- **Containerization:** Includes Dockerfiles and Docker Compose configuration for packaging the ASP.NET Core application into containers, which enables consistent deployment across different environments
- **DevOps Integration:** Facilitates integration with continuous integration and continuous deployment (CI/CD) pipelines, which enables automated testing, building, and deployment of containerized applications
- **Scalability:** Enables horizontal scaling of the application by deploying multiple container instances across container orchestration platforms like Kubernetes

In summary, Web API templates in Visual Studio provide developers with a structured starting point for building RESTful APIs using ASP.NET Core. These templates offer features such as MVC controller pattern, attribute routing, dependency injection, and Docker support that empower developers to create scalable, maintainable, and interoperable APIs efficiently. Depending on project requirements and preferences, developers can choose the appropriate template that best suits their needs and customize it as per their goals.

Web API Project Structure:

Controllers: This folder contains C# classes that define the API endpoints, and handle the incoming HTTP requests. Each controller class typically corresponds to a logical grouping of related API endpoints. They contain action methods that execute business logic and return responses to clients.

Controllers contain action methods that represent individual API endpoints, each corresponding to a specific HTTP verb (**`GET`**, **`POST`**, **`PUT`**, **`DELETE`**, and so on.) and route. These action methods perform operations such as retrieving data, creating resources, updating resources, or deleting resources.

Here are some of the commonly used action methods that are supported by controllers in Web APIs:

- **`GET`:** Retrieves data from the server; typically used for fetching resources or querying data
- **`POST`:** Creates a new resource on the server; used for submitting data or creating new records
- **`PUT`:** Updates an existing resource on the server; used for modifying existing data
- **`DELETE`:** Deletes a resource from the server; used for removing records or resources
- **`PATCH`:** Partially updates an existing resource; used for making partial modifications to resource properties
- **`OPTIONS`:** Returns the supported HTTP methods and other information about the server or resource
- **`HEAD`:** Similar to a GET request but returns only the headers of the response, without the body; used for retrieving metadata about a resource

Controllers also handle various HTTP status codes in the responses they generate. Here are some of the commonly used response codes and their meanings:

- **`200 (OK)`:** Indicates that the request was successful and the server has returned the requested resource
- **`201 (Created)`:** Indicates that the request has been fulfilled and resulted in the creation of a new resource

- `204 (No Content)`: Indicates that the server successfully processed the request, but does not need to return any content in the response body
- `400 (Bad Request)`: Indicates that the server cannot process the request due to client error, such as invalid input or missing parameters
- `401 (Unauthorized)`: Indicates that the request requires authentication and the client needs to provide valid credentials
- `404 (Not Found)`: Indicates that the server cannot find the requested resource
- `500 (Internal Server Error)`: Indicates that the server encountered an unexpected condition that prevented it from fulfilling the request

These are just a few examples of the action methods and response codes supported by controllers in Web APIs. Controllers play a crucial role in defining the behavior and functionality of the API endpoints, handling incoming requests, and generating appropriate responses based on the request context and business logic.

- `Models`: This folder contains C# classes that represent data entities or models used within the API. These classes define the structure of the data exchanged between the client and the server.
- `Services`: This folder (optional) may contain C# classes that encapsulate business logic or application services used by the API controllers.
- `wwwroot`: This folder contains static files (for example, HTML, CSS, JavaScript) that are served by the web server middleware. It is commonly used for hosting client-side assets in conjunction with server-side APIs.
- `appsettings.json`: This JSON file contains configuration settings for the API, such as database connection strings, logging configuration, or other application-specific settings.
- `package.json`: This file is typically used in Node.js-based projects to manage dependencies and scripts. It may not be present in a standard ASP.NET Core Web API project unless frontend assets are included.
- `Program.cs`: This C# file contains the entry point for the application. It is responsible for creating the web host and configuring the startup process. It also contains the configuration logic for the ASP.NET Core application. It defines middleware, services, and other components that are needed to bootstrap the application at runtime.

Swagger

Swagger is an open-source tool for documenting and testing APIs. It generates interactive API documentation from API specifications, which makes it easier for developers to understand and interact with the API. Swagger will automatically generate documentation based on the API controllers and models, while providing a visual representation of the API endpoints, request/response models, and allowing developers to test the API directly from the Swagger UI.

To Use Swagger in a .NET Core Web API Project:

1. Install the **`Swashbuckle.AspNore`** NuGet package.
2. Configure Swagger in the **`Program.cs`** file by adding **`services.AddSwaggerGen()`** during service registration and **`app.UseSwagger()`** in the middleware pipeline through **`ConfigureServices`** and **`Configure`** methods, respectively.
3. Customize Swagger settings such as API versioning and document generation options in the **`ConfigureServices`** method.
4. Access the Swagger UI by navigating to **`/swagger/index.html`** in your web browser. Here, you can explore and interact with the API documentation.

Here is a sample image of how Swagger index should look:

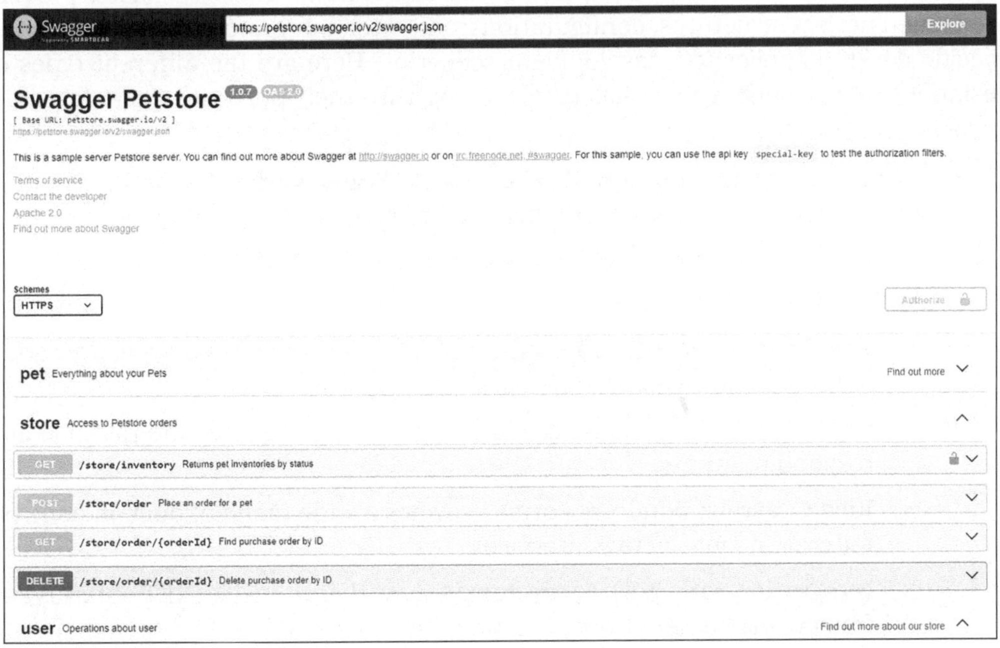

Figure 2.8: *Swagger*

Importance of Web APIs in Industry:

- **Scalability:** Web APIs allow for horizontal scaling by distributing load across multiple instances or servers. This enables applications to handle increasing traffic and user demand effectively.

- **Robustness:** Web APIs promote loose coupling between client and server, while allowing for independent development, deployment, and scaling of components. This enhances system robustness and fault tolerance.
- **Microservices Architecture:** Web APIs are a fundamental building block of microservices architectures, as they enable the decomposition of monolithic applications into smaller, independently deployable services. This promotes agility, scalability, and maintainability.

Overall, Web APIs play a crucial role in modern software development as they bring about interoperability, scalability, and flexibility in building distributed systems. They are the backbone of microservices architectures, and facilitate seamless integration between disparate systems and applications.

Desktop Templates

In Visual Studio, desktop-based templates are the starting points for developing applications that run on desktop platforms such as Windows. These templates provide predefined project structures, configurations, and often integrated tooling tailored to specific desktop application development scenarios. Here are the different types of desktop-based templates in Visual Studio, along with their purposes, main features, and advantages:

- **Windows Forms App (.NET Core/.NET Framework):** Used for creating traditional Windows desktop applications with graphical user interfaces (GUIs) using Windows Forms technology

  Features and Advantages

  - **Rapid Development:** Drag-and-drop UI designer allows for quick creation of user interfaces.
  - **Event-Driven Programming Model:** Easily handle user interactions and respond to events.
  - **Rich Controls:** Windows Forms provides a wide range of built-in controls for creating interactive interfaces.
  - **Integration with .NET Ecosystem:** Access the extensive .NET libraries and frameworks for additional functionality.
  - **Compatibility:** It can target both .NET Core and .NET Framework runtime environments.
- **WPF App (.NET Core/.NET Framework):** Designed for building modern, rich-client desktop applications using Windows Presentation Foundation (WPF)

Features and Advantages

- **Powerful UI Composition:** Allows for the creation of visually stunning interfaces using XAML markup language
- **Data Binding:** Support for two-way data binding simplifies interaction between the UI and underlying data models
- **Customization:** Extensible styling and templating capabilities that enable highly customizable UI designs
- **Vector Graphics:** Utilizes hardware-accelerated graphics rendering for smooth animations and effects
- **MVVM Pattern:** Encourages separation of concerns and testability through the Model-View-ViewModel architectural pattern

- **Console App (.NET Core/.NET Framework):** Used for creating command-line applications that run in a console window

  Features and Advantages

  - **Lightweight:** Minimal overhead, which makes it suitable for simple utility or automation scripts
  - **Text-Based Interface:** Interacts with users through text input and output, suitable for certain types of applications like batch processing or system administration tools
  - **Platform Independence:** Console applications that can be run on any platform that supports the .NET runtime
  - **Scripting Support:** Can be used for scripting tasks or automating repetitive tasks

- **Windows Service (.NET Core/.NET Framework):** Designed for creating long-running background services and daemons that run without a user interface

  Features and Advantages

  - **Background Processing:** Executes tasks asynchronously in the background without user intervention
  - **System-Level Interaction:** Can interact with system resources and perform tasks such as monitoring folders, processing data, or managing services
  - **Scalability:** Can be scaled to handle large workloads and can run continuously without user intervention
  - **Configuration Flexibility:** Can be configured to start automatically with the system or on-demand based on specific triggers

In summary, desktop-based templates in Visual Studio facilitate the development of applications for desktop platforms such as Windows. They offer a range of features and advantages tailored to specific desktop application development scenarios, including rapid development, powerful UI composition, extensibility, and platform compatibility. These templates empower developers to create robust and feature-rich desktop applications efficiently.

MAUI Templates

In Visual Studio, MAUI (Multi-platform App UI) templates are specifically designed for building cross-platform applications that target multiple devices and platforms, including Windows, macOS, iOS, and Android. MAUI leverages .NET MAUI, a framework built on top of `Xamarin.Forms`, to enable developers to create native user interfaces and share code across different platforms. Here are the different types of MAUI templates in Visual Studio, along with their purposes, main features, and advantages:

Blank MAUI App

It provides a clean slate for starting a new MAUI application.

Features and Advantages

- **Cross-Platform Development:** Allows developers to write code once and deploy it across multiple platforms, including Windows, macOS, iOS, and Android
- **Native UI Components:** Utilizes native controls and UI elements to ensure a consistent and familiar user experience on each platform
- **XAML-Based UI Development:** Supports XAML markup language for defining user interfaces, while enabling rapid UI development with familiar tools and workflows
- **Shared Codebase:** Enables sharing of application logic, data models, and business logic across platforms, which reduces development time and effort
- **Integration with .NET Ecosystem:** Seamlessly integrates with the broader .NET ecosystem, including libraries, frameworks, and tools

Blank MAUI App (Preview)

It offers an early preview of new features and enhancements in MAUI development.

Features and Advantages

- **Early Access:** Provides developers with access to upcoming features and improvements in MAUI development

- **Feedback Opportunity:** Allows developers to test new functionality and provide feedback to shape the future direction of the MAUI framework
- **Experimentation:** Enables experimentation with new features and capabilities before they are officially released, while helping developers stay ahead of the curve

Blazor Hybrid App

It combines Blazor, a framework for building interactive web UIs with .NET, with MAUI to create hybrid desktop and mobile native apps.

Features and Advantages

- **Single Codebase:** Enables sharing of code between web and desktop applications, while maximizing code reuse and reducing duplication
- **Modern Web Technologies:** Utilizes web standards and technologies such as HTML, CSS, and JavaScript to build rich user interfaces
- **Hybrid Deployment:** Allows developers to deploy applications as both desktop and web applications, thereby reaching a broader audience and enhancing accessibility
- **Progressive Enhancement:** Supports progressive enhancement, while allowing applications to deliver a consistent experience across devices and leveraging platform-specific features whenever they are available

In summary, MAUI templates in Visual Studio empower developers to create cross-platform applications targeting multiple devices and platforms. These templates offer features such as native UI components, shared codebases, and integration with the .NET ecosystem, which enable developers to build robust and feature-rich applications efficiently. Additionally, preview templates provide early access to upcoming features and enhancements that allow developers to experiment and provide feedback to shape the future of MAUI development.

Class Library

In Visual Studio, class library templates are used for creating reusable libraries of code that can be referenced and utilized by other projects or applications. These libraries typically contain classes, interfaces, and other types that provide specific functionality or services. Here are the different types of class library templates in Visual Studio, along with their purposes, main features, and advantages:

Class Library (.NET Standard/.NET Core/.NET Framework): Provides a basic template for creating class libraries targeting the .NET Standard, .NET Core, or .NET Framework runtime environments

Features and Advantages

- **Reusability:** Enables the creation of reusable components that can be shared across multiple projects and applications
- **Encapsulation:** Facilitates encapsulation of functionality into cohesive units, promoting modularity and code organization
- **Versioning:** Supports versioning and dependency management, thereby allowing consumers to reference specific versions of the library
- **Cross-Platform Compatibility:** Class libraries targeting .NET Standard and .NET Core support cross-platform compatibility, which allows them to run on multiple runtime environments such as Windows, Linux, and macOS. In contrast, class libraries targeting .NET Framework are limited to Windows and do not offer cross-platform support.
- **Integration with .NET Ecosystem:** Seamlessly integrates with the broader .NET ecosystem, including tools, libraries, and frameworks

Class Library (.NET Standard/.NET Core/.NET Framework) with Unit Tests: Extends the basic class library template by including a project for unit testing using a testing framework such as NUnit or MSTest

Features and Advantages

- **Test-Driven Development (TDD):** Supports test-driven development practices by providing a framework for writing and executing unit tests
- **Automated Testing:** Facilitates automated testing of library functionality, thereby ensuring code correctness and reliability
- **Test Coverage:** Helps measure test coverage to identify areas of the codebase that require additional testing
- **Continuous Integration (CI) Support:** Integrates with CI/CD pipelines to automate the execution of tests and ensure code quality throughout the development process
- **Improved Code Quality:** Promotes the development of high-quality, robust code by encouraging the creation of comprehensive unit tests

Class Library (Windows Runtime): Designed for creating class libraries targeting the Windows Runtime (WinRT) platform; primarily used for developing Windows Store and Universal Windows Platform (UWP) applications

Features and Advantages

- **Native Windows Integration:** Provides access to WinRT APIs and platform-specific features for building native Windows applications

- **Modern App Development:** Supports the development of modern Windows applications with rich user interfaces and seamless integration with Windows features
- **Cross-Platform Compatibility:** Allows targeting of multiple Windows platforms, including desktop, mobile, and IoT devices
- **Deployment Flexibility:** Enables distribution of libraries through the Microsoft Store or sideloading, depending on the application's deployment requirements
- **Integration with Visual Studio Tools:** Integrates with Visual Studio development tools and workflows for efficient Windows app development

In summary, class library templates in Visual Studio facilitate the creation of reusable code libraries for use in various projects and applications. These templates offer features such as reusability, encapsulation, versioning, and integration with testing frameworks, which enables developers to build high-quality, maintainable codebases efficiently. Additionally, class libraries targeting specific platforms like .NET Standard, .NET Core, .NET Framework, and the Windows Runtime provide flexibility and compatibility with different runtime environments and development scenarios.

SPA Templates

SPA (Single Page Application) templates in Visual Studio 2022 are designed to facilitate the development of modern web applications that provide a seamless and responsive user experience by dynamically updating the content on a *single web page*, without requiring full page reloads. These templates typically leverage popular front-end frameworks like Angular, React.js, or Vue.js to achieve this behavior. Here are the main features of SPA templates in Visual Studio 2022, along with their advantages and steps to create a test SPA application:

Main Features of SPA Templates

- **Framework Integration:** SPA templates integrate with popular front-end frameworks like Angular, React.js, or Vue.js, which provide a foundation for building dynamic user interfaces.
- **Component-Based Architecture:** SPA applications are built using a component-based architecture, where UI elements are encapsulated into reusable components to promote code reusability and maintainability.
- **Routing:** SPA templates include routing mechanisms that allow navigation between different views or components within the application without page reloads to provide a smoother user experience.
- **State Management:** Many SPA templates include state management libraries or patterns (such as Redux for React.js or Vuex for Vue.js) to manage application state and data flow, thereby ensuring consistency and predictability.

- **API Integration:** SPA applications can interact with backend APIs to fetch and update data asynchronously, which enables real-time updates and interaction with server-side resources.
- **Responsive Design:** SPA templates often include responsive design principles and tools to ensure that applications are optimized for various devices and screen sizes.

Advantages of Using SPA Templates

- **Improved User Experience:** SPA applications provide a more fluid and interactive user experience compared to traditional multi-page web applications, thanks to dynamic content updates and smoother transitions.
- **Faster Load Times:** Since SPA applications only load the required resources and content once and subsequent interactions typically result in faster load times and improved performance.
- **Code Reusability:** SPA templates encourage code reusability through component-based architecture, thereby reducing duplication and promoting maintainability.
- **Enhanced Development Productivity:** SPA templates often come with pre-configured build tools, development servers, and other utilities that streamline the development process and improve developer productivity.
- **Scalability:** SPA architectures can easily scale to accommodate growing user bases and evolving application requirements, which makes them suitable for large-scale applications.

Steps to Create a Test SPA Application

1. Open Visual Studio 2022.
2. Click on "`Create a new project`" or go to "`File`" > "`New`" > "`Project`".
3. In the "`Create a new project`" window, search for "`SPA`" or the specific framework you want to use (for example, "`Angular`", "`React.js`", "`Vue.js`"). (*Figure* 2.7)
4. Select the desired SPA template (for example, "`ASP.NET Core with Angular`", "`ASP.NET Core with React.js`", "`ASP.NET Core with Vue.js`") from the available options.
5. Choose a location and provide a name for your project.
6. Click "`Create`" to create the project.
7. Follow the instructions to configure the project settings and dependencies as needed.

8. Once the project is created, you can start developing your SPA application by adding components, defining routes, integrating with APIs, and implementing desired functionality.

By following these steps, you can quickly create a test SPA application using Visual Studio 2022, while leveraging the features and advantages offered by SPA templates for modern web development.

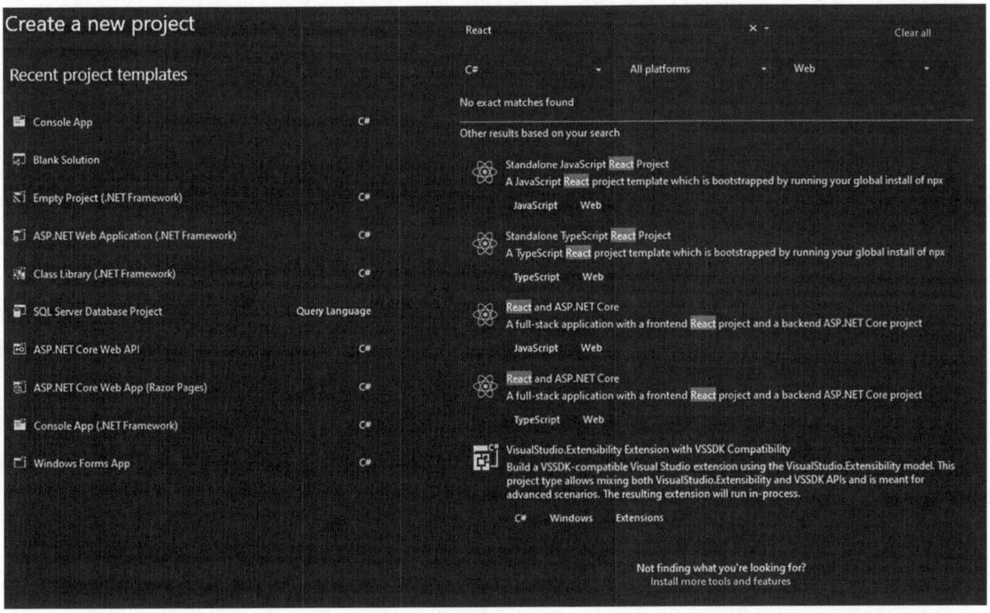

Figure 2.9: *Showing the Options Available for Creating React Based Projects in VS*

Single Page Applications (SPAs) are beneficial in Visual Studio for several reasons that are mentioned as follows:

- **Streamlined Development:** SPAs allow developers to build applications with a single HTML page that dynamically updates content based on user interactions, which reduces the complexity associated with managing multiple pages and server-side rendering.
- **Enhanced User Experience:** SPAs provide a seamless and responsive user experience by minimizing page reloads and delivering fast, fluid interactions. This improves user engagement and satisfaction.
- **Framework Integration:** Visual Studio provides templates and tooling support for popular front-end frameworks like Angular, React.js, and Vue.js, which makes it easy for developers to create SPAs using their preferred technologies.
- **Code Reusability:** SPAs encourage a modular and component-based approach to development, thereby promoting code reusability and maintainability.

Components can be reused across different parts of the application, reducing duplication and improving consistency.

- **API Integration:** SPAs can interact with backend APIs to fand so on and update data asynchronously, which enables real-time updates and seamless integration with server-side resources. Visual Studio facilitates API integration through tools like HttpClient and Axios.
- **Debugging and Testing:** Visual Studio provides robust debugging and testing tools for SPAs, which allows developers to diagnose and fix issues efficiently. Features like browser debugging tools, unit testing frameworks, and integration testing support enhance the development and testing experience.
- **Cross-Platform Compatibility:** SPAs can target multiple platforms and devices, including desktops, mobile devices, and tablets. Visual Studio supports cross-platform development, which allows developers to create SPAs that run on Windows, macOS, iOS, and Android.
- **Performance Optimization:** Visual Studio offers performance profiling tools and optimization techniques for SPAs to help developers identify and address performance bottlenecks and ensure optimal application performance.

Overall, SPAs are helpful in Visual Studio for building modern web applications that deliver a rich, interactive user experience while benefiting from streamlined development processes, code reusability, and cross-platform compatibility.

Blazor Templates

Blazor is a web framework for building interactive web UIs using C# and .NET. It enables developers to create rich, single-page applications (SPAs) with the same tools and languages they use for server-side development. Blazor allows for the creation of web applications that run entirely in the browser, thereby eliminating the need for JavaScript and enabling full-stack development using C#.

Key Features of Blazor

Component-Based Architecture: Blazor applications are built using a component-based architecture, where UI elements are encapsulated into reusable components. These components can be composed and nested to create complex UI structures.

Example:

```
<Counter />
   <UserProfile />
   <ProductList />
```

Razor Syntax: Blazor uses Razor syntax, which is a mix of HTML and C#, for defining UI components. This allows developers to write UI markup and logic in a familiar and expressive syntax.

Example:

```
<h1>Welcome, @userName!</h1>
```

Two-Way Data Binding: Blazor supports two-way data binding, allowing changes to UI elements to automatically update the associated data model and vice versa.

Example:

```
<input @bind="userName" />
```

Routing: Blazor applications can define client-side routes for navigation between different views within the application, which is similar to traditional SPAs.

Example:

```
@page "/profile"
```

Dependency Injection: Blazor provides built-in support for dependency injection, which allows services to be registered and injected into components.

Example:

```
@inject IHttpClientFactory HttpClientFactory
```

Code Sharing: With Blazor, developers can share code between client and server for full-stack development using C# and .NET. This reduces code duplication and promotes code reuse.

Advantages of Using Blazor Templates for Development

- **Familiar Development Experience:** Developers can leverage their existing knowledge of C# and .NET to build web applications, thereby eliminating the need to learn new languages or frameworks like JavaScript.
- **Full-Stack Development:** Blazor enables full-stack development using C# and .NET, which allows developers to use the same language and tools for both client-side and server-side development.
- **Rich Ecosystem:** Blazor benefits from the extensive .NET ecosystem, including libraries, frameworks, and tools to provide access to a wide range of resources and capabilities for building web applications.
- **Performance:** Blazor applications are compiled to WebAssembly (client-side) or run on the server, which results in fast load times for apps running on server and responsive user interfaces.
- **Security:** Blazor applications benefit from the security features provided by the .NET runtime, including built-in protections against common web vulnerabilities.

When to Develop Blazor Applications

Blazor applications are suitable for a variety of use cases, including:

- Building modern web applications with rich, interactive user interfaces
- Developing line-of-business applications, internal tools, or enterprise applications
- Creating applications that require tight integration with .NET backend services or the existing .NET codebases

Steps to Create a Test Blazor Application

1. Open Visual Studio 2022.
2. Click on "**`Create a new project`**" or go to "**`File`**" > "**`New`**" > "**`Project`**".
3. In the "**`Create a new project`**" window, search for "**`Blazor`**" or select "**`Blazor App`**" from the list of project templates (*Figure* 2.8).
4. Choose the desired Blazor template (for example, "**`Blazor Server App`**" or "**`Blazor WebAssembly App`**").
5. Provide a name and location for your project, then click "**`Create`**" to create the project.
6. Follow the instructions to configure the project settings and dependencies as needed.
7. Once the project is created, you can start developing your Blazor application by adding components, defining routes, integrating with backend services, and implementing desired functionality.

Thus, by following these steps, you can quickly create a test Blazor application using Visual Studio 2022, while leveraging the features and advantages of Blazor for modern web development.

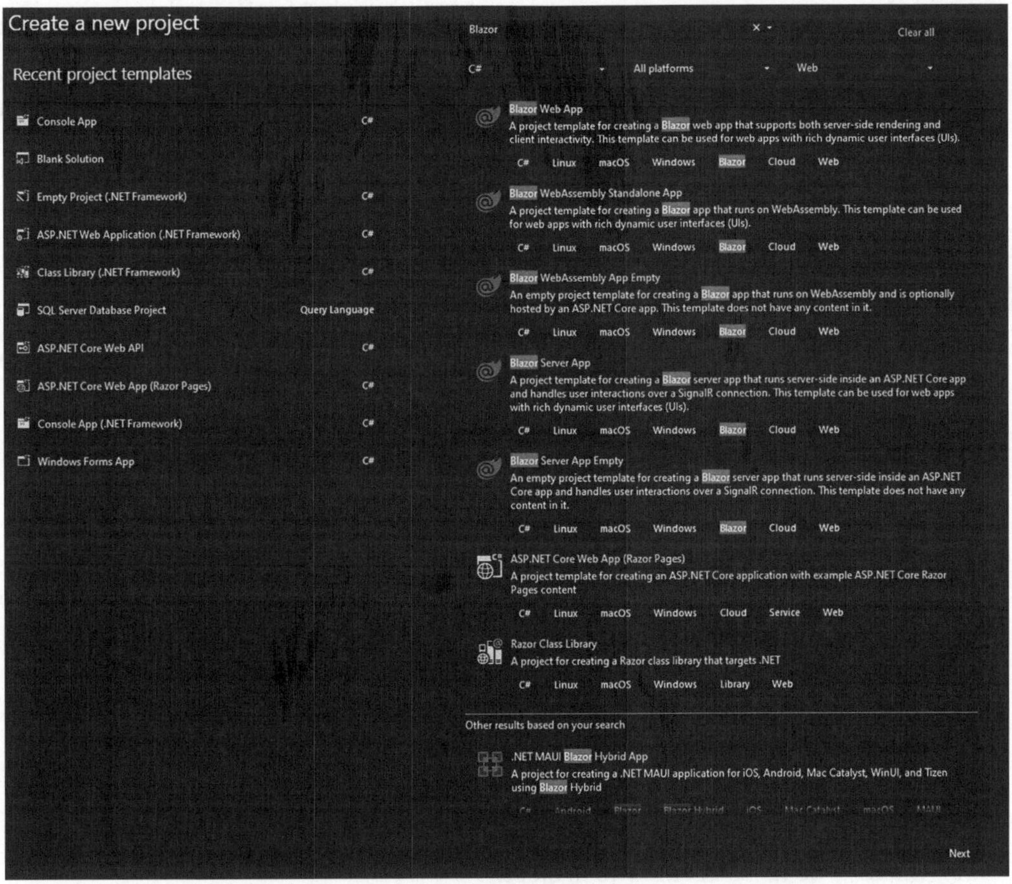

Figure 2.10: *The New Project Templates Available for Blazor*

In Visual Studio 2022, there are several JavaScript framework-based templates available for creating web applications. Here are some of the commonly used ones:

- **Angular:** Angular is a popular front-end framework for building single-page applications (SPAs). Visual Studio provides templates for creating Angular applications with .NET backend support.
- **React.js:** React.js is a JavaScript library for building user interfaces. Visual Studio offers templates for creating React.js applications with .NET backend support.
- **Vue.js:** Vue.js is a progressive JavaScript framework for building interactive web interfaces. Visual Studio provides templates for creating Vue.js applications with .NET backend support.
- **Node.js Express Application:** Node.js is a JavaScript runtime for building server-side applications. Visual Studio offers templates for creating Node.js

Express applications, which can be used to build APIs or server-rendered web applications.

- **React Native:** React Native is a framework for building native mobile applications using JavaScript and React.js. Visual Studio provides templates for creating React applications targeting iOS and Android platforms.

Steps to Create a Project Using a JavaScript Framework-Based Template

Here, let us outline the steps to create a project using the React.js template in Visual Studio 2022:

1. Open Visual Studio 2022.
2. Click on "**`Create a new project`**" or go to "**`File`**" > "**`New`**" > "**`Project`**".
3. In the "**`Create a new project`**" window, search for "**`React.js`**" or "**`ASP.NET Core with React.js`**". **`ASP.NET Core with React.js`**
4. Select the "**`ASP.NET Core with React.js`**" template from the list of project templates.
5. Provide a name and location for your project.
6. Choose additional options such as target framework and authentication if needed.
7. Click "**`Create`**" to create the project.
8. Visual Studio will scaffold the project structure for you, including the necessary files and folders for a React.js application.

   Visual Studio will create a new solution with two projects: an ASP.NET Core Web API project for the backend, and a separate React.js project for the frontend. The React.js project will be pre-configured with the latest version of React and other dependencies.
9. Once the project is created, you can start developing your React.js application by adding components, defining routes, integrating with backend services, and implementing desired functionality.

You can run the application by pressing **`F5`** or clicking the **`"Start"`** button in the toolbar. This will launch both the backend and frontend projects simultaneously, with the React.js application running in your default web browser

The steps are similar for creating projects with Angular or Vue.js templates, with the main difference being the selected template in Step 4.

Therefore, by following these steps, you can create a new project using a JavaScript framework-based template in Visual Studio 2022 and begin developing your web application using the chosen framework.

Conclusion

In this section, we have explored the primary workloads and prevalent templates offered in VS for developing diverse project types. We have delved into specific templates tailored for web development, encompassing ASP.NET Core applications, Single Page Applications (SPAs), and web APIs. The abundance of templates dedicated to ASP.NET and web development underscores VS's commitment not only to .NET developers but also to the broader web development community.

Moreover, we have examined templates facilitating cross-platform development through .NET MAUI to enable deployment across Android, iOS, and Windows platforms primarily. Lastly, we have outlined the available templates for desktop development.

In the forthcoming chapter, we will delve into the array of tools available in VS, while empowering developers to debug applications for error detection, alongside performance analysis tools to optimize application performance.

Chapter 3
Writing Code in Visual Studio

Introduction

In the realm of software development, the ability to craft clean, efficient, and maintainable code is an important skill to master. As developers, our tools play a crucial role in enabling us to translate our ideas into functional software solutions. Among these tools, Visual Studio offers a robust and feature-rich integrated development environment (IDE) that is trusted by millions of developers worldwide.

In this chapter, we will delve into the art and science of writing code in Visual Studio. Whether you are a seasoned developer or just beginning your coding journey, mastering the tools and techniques available in Visual Studio can significantly enhance your productivity and proficiency. From its powerful code editing capabilities to its seamless integration with debugging and testing tools, Visual Studio empowers developers to bring their code to life with precision and confidence.

Throughout this chapter, we will explore the various features and functionalities that make Visual Studio a preferred choice for software development across a wide range of platforms and languages. We will learn how to navigate the IDE, customize our development environment, write and refactor code efficiently. We will explore the code editor, which offers features such as IntelliSense, code formatting, and code snippets, which are designed to enhance productivity and ensure code consistency.

Furthermore, we will cover the integration of Visual Studio with source control systems like Git and Team Foundation Version Control (TFVC). Source control is essential for collaborative development, as it enables multiple developers to work on the same codebase while tracking changes and managing conflicts.

Hence, whether you are writing a simple script or developing a complex enterprise application, Visual Studio provides the tools and support you need to turn your vision into reality. So, let us embark on this journey together, as we uncover the secrets of writing code in Visual Studio, and unlock the full potential of our development endeavors.

Now, let us explore how to create a console application in Visual Studio 2022 using C# and SQL Server. Follow the mentioned steps to create and run an application. Then we will understand the behind-the-scenes implementation of each step.

Structure

- Creating a New Console Application
- Setting up SQL Server
- Adding Entity Framework Core
- Configuring & using the Database Context
- Class, Methods, Encapsulation, Inheritance, Polymorphism, Abstraction, Interfaces
- Adding Code Snippets
- Intellisense
- Task List and Code Navigation
- Refactoring
- Version Control using Git
- Live Share

Prerequisites:

- Visual Studio 2022 installed
- SQL Server installed and running
- Basic knowledge of C and SQL

Step 1: Creating a New Console Application

a. Open Visual Studio 2022.

b. Create a new project:

   i. Click on '`Create a new project`' from the start window.

   ii. Select '`Console App (.NET Core)`' or '`Console App (.NET Framework)`' (depending on your requirement) and click on 'Next'.

c. Configure your new project:

   - `Name`: '`MyConsoleApp`'
   - `Location`: Choose your desired location.
   - `Solution Name`: '`MyConsoleAppSolution`'
   - Click on '`Create`'.

Step 2: Setting Up SQL Server

- Open SQL Server Management Studio (SSMS).
- Create a new database in the mentioned way:
  i. Right-click on '**`Databases`**' and select '**`New Database...`**'
  ii. Name your database '**`MyDatabase`**' and click '**`OK`**'.
- Create a new table as mentioned here:
  i. Expand the '**`MyDatabase`**' node.
  ii. Right-click on '**`Tables`**' and select '**`New Table...`**'
  iii. Add columns (for example, '**`Id`**' as '**`int`**', '**`Name`**' as '**`nvarchar(50)`**', '**`Age`**' as '**`int`**').
  iv. Set '**`Id`**' as the primary key.
  v. Save the table as '**`Persons`**'.

4. Insert sample data into the table in the following way:

```
INSERT INTO Persons (Name, Age) VALUES (John Doe, 30);
INSERT INTO Persons (Name, Age) VALUES (Jane Smith, 25);
```

Step 3: Adding Entity Framework Core to your Project

a. Install the Entity Framework Core packages.
   i. Open the **`Package Manager Console`** from **`Tools`** -> **`NuGet Package Manager`** -> **`Package Manager Console`**.
   ii. Run the following PowerShell commands to install EF Core and SQL Server provider:

```
Install-Package Microsoft.EntityFrameworkCore.SqlServer
Install-Package Microsoft.EntityFrameworkCore.Tools
```

b. Create a new folder for models.
   i. Right-click on the project in **`Solution Explorer`**, select **`Add`** -> **`New Folder`**, and name it '**`Models`**'.

c. Create a Person model.
   i. Right-click on the '**`Models`**' folder, select **`Add`** -> **`Class`**, and name it '**`Person.cs`**'.
   ii. Define the '**`Person`**' class in C# as indicated here:

```
namespace MyConsoleApp.Models
{
    public class Person
```

```
        {
            public int Id { get; set; }
            public string Name { get; set; }
            public int Age { get; set; }
        }
    }
```

Step 4: Configuring the Database Context

a. Create a new folder for data context, as shown here:

   i. Right-click on the project in **Solution Explorer**, select **Add** -> **New Folder**, and name it '**Data**'.

b. Create the database context class, as indicated here:

   i. Right-click on the Data folder, select **Add** -> **Class**, and name it '**MyDatabaseContext.cs**'.

   ii. Define the '**MyDatabaseContext**' class, as shown here:

```
using Microsoft.EntityFrameworkCore;
using MyConsoleApp.Models;

     namespace MyConsoleApp.Data
     {
         public class MyDatabaseContext : DbContext
         {
             public DbSet<Person> Persons { get; set; }

             protected override void OnConfiguring
(DbContextOptionsBuilder optionsBuilder)
             {
                 optionsBuilder.UseSqlServer("Server=YOUR_
SERVER_NAME;Database=MyDatabase;Trusted_Connection=True;");
             }
         }
     }
```

   iii. Replace **YOUR_SERVER_NAME** with your actual SQL Server name.

Step 5: Using the Database Context in the Program

a. Open **Program.cs** and update the code to interact with the database, as shown:

```
using System;
 using MyConsoleApp.Data;
 using MyConsoleApp.Models;
 using System.Linq;

 namespace MyConsoleApp
```

```
    {
        class Program
        {
            static void Main(string[] args)
            {
                using (var context = new MyDatabaseContext())
                {
                    // Read data from database
                    var persons = context.Persons.ToList();
                    foreach (var person in persons)
                    {
                        Console.WriteLine($"Id: {person.Id}, Name: 
{person.Name}, Age: {person.Age}");
                    }
                }
            }
        }
    }
```

Step 6: Running Your Application

Build and run your application in the following manner:

a. Press *Ctrl* + F5 to build and run the console application.

b. You should see the data from the Persons table displayed in the console.

Congratulations! You have successfully created a console application in Visual Studio 2022 using C# and SQL Server.

Now, let us consider each step in detail:

Step 1: Creating a Console Application

A console application in C is a program that runs in a command-line or terminal window, rather than in a graphical user interface (GUI). It is designed to interact with users via text-based commands and outputs, which makes it a straightforward and efficient way to develop applications for tasks that do not require graphical elements. Console applications are often used for:

- **Automation scripts**: Automating repetitive tasks
- **Batch processing**: Handling multiple tasks in bulk
- **Simple utilities**: Creating tools for specific functions
- **Learning and testing**: Gaining familiarity with C and .NET without dealing with complex GUI elements

Key Characteristics of a Console Application

- **Text-based Interface**: Input and output are handled through text, using the console window
- **Simplicity**: Often simpler and faster to develop compared to GUI applications
- **Use of Standard Input/Output**: Utilizes '**`Console.ReadLine()`**' for input and '**`Console.WriteLine()`**' for output
- **Runs in a Terminal**: Executed in a command-line interface (CLI) like Command Prompt, PowerShell, or Terminal

Basic Structure of a Console Application in C#

A typical console application in C# includes the `Main` method, which acts as the entry point of the application. Here is an example of a simple C# console application:

```
using System;
namespace MyConsoleApp
{
    class Program
    {
        static void Main(string[] args)
        {
            Console.WriteLine("Hello, World!");

            Console.Write("Enter your name: ");
            string name = Console.ReadLine();

            Console.WriteLine($"Hello, {name}!");
        }
    }
}
```

Explanation:

Namespace: Organizes the code and avoids name conflicts

In C#, a namespace is a way to organize and group related classes, interfaces, structs, enums, and delegates. Namespaces provide a hierarchical means of organizing code and helps in avoiding naming conflicts in larger projects by providing a scope for the identifiers (names of types, functions, variables, and so on).

Key Points about Namespaces

- **Organization:** Namespaces help organize your code logically, which makes it easier to manage and navigate, especially in large projects.

- **Avoiding Naming Conflicts:** By encapsulating classes within namespaces, you can prevent naming conflicts that might arise when different classes in a project have the same name.
- **Hierarchy:** Namespaces can be nested, which creates a hierarchical structure that further organizes your code.

Declaring a Namespace: Namespaces are declared using the '**namespace**' keyword followed by the namespace name. Here is an example:

```
namespace MyApplication
{
    class Program
    {
        static void Main(string[] args)
        {
            Console.WriteLine("Hello, World!");
        }
    }
}
```

Using Namespaces: To use types defined in a namespace, you can either do it via the fully qualified name or through the '**using**' directive. The `**using**` directive makes it easier to access the members of a namespace without having to specify the full name.

Fully Qualified Name: You can reference a class by its fully qualified name, which includes the following namespace:

```
System.Console.WriteLine("Hello, World!");
```

Using Directive: The '**using**' directive allows you to import a namespace, so that you do not have to use the fully qualified name, as indicated here:

```
using System;

namespace MyApplication
{
    class Program
    {
        static void Main(string[] args)
        {
            Console.WriteLine("Hello, World!"); // No need to use
System.Console
        }
    }
}
```

Nested Namespaces: Namespaces can be nested to create a more structured organization, which is shown as follows:

```
namespace Company
{
    namespace Project
    {
        class Example
        {
            public void PrintMessage()
            {
                Console.WriteLine("Hello from Company.Project!");
            }
        }
    }
}
```

You can also use a shorthand syntax for declaring nested namespaces, as shown here:

```
namespace Company.Project
{
    class Example
    {
        public void PrintMessage()
        {
            Console.WriteLine("Hello from Company.Project!");
        }
    }
}
```

Summary

- **Definition:** A namespace acts as a mechanism to organize and group related code elements such as classes, interfaces, structs, enums, and delegates, into logical units. They are crucial for managing code in larger projects and preventing naming conflicts.
- **Purpose:** It helps in organizing code and preventing naming conflicts.
- **Usage:** You can access members of a namespace using fully qualified names or by importing the namespace with the '**`using`**' directive.
- **Hierarchy:** Namespaces can be nested to create a hierarchical structure for better organization.

Namespaces are an essential feature of C# that contribute to clean, maintainable, and organized code, especially in larger applications.

Thus, before we move further, let us look at the important components that forms the base for any C# working code file.

Class Program: Contains the code for the application

In C#, a class is a fundamental building block of Object-Oriented Programming (OOP). It serves as a blueprint for creating objects, which are instances of that class. A class encapsulates data for the object and methods to manipulate that data. The '`Program`' class is a common convention in C# console applications that defines the entry point of the application where the execution begins.

The '`Program`' class typically contains the '`Main`' method, which is the starting point of a C# application. Here is a simple example of a '`Program`' class in a console application:

```
using System;

namespace MyConsoleApp
{
    class Program
    {
        static void Main(string[] args)
        {
            Console.WriteLine("Hello, World!");
        }
    }
}
```

Here, we have broken down the preceding code to understand each component better:

1. **Namespace:** `namespace MyConsoleApp`
    - A namespace is a logical container used to organize code and control the scope of class and method names in larger programming projects.
2. **Class Definition: `class Program`**
    - A class is defined using the `` `class` `` keyword followed by the class name. In this case, '`Program`' is the name of the class.
3. **Main Method: `static void Main(string[] args)`**
    - The '`Main`' method is the entry point of the application. It is the method that is called when the program starts.
    - **`static`**: Indicates that the method belongs to the class itself, rather than an instance of the class
    - **`void`**: Specifies that the method does not return a value
    - **`Main`**: The name of the method.
    - **`string[] args`**: An array of strings which represents the command-line arguments passed to the application.

Functionality: In the previous example, the 'Main' method performs a simple task: it outputs "**`Hello, World!`**" to the console using the '**`Console.WriteLine`**' method.

Key Points

- **Static Methods:** The '**`Main`**' method is static, which means it can be called without creating an instance of the 'Program' class. This is necessary because the method needs to be accessible when the program starts, before any objects are instantiated.
- **Entry Point:** The '**`Main`**' method is always the entry point of a C# application. There can be multiple classes in a project, but the '**`Main`**' method defines where the execution begins.
- **Encapsulation:** A class in C# can contain fields, properties, methods, and events. It includes the data (fields) and the behavior (methods) that operate on the data.

Example with More Details

Here is a more detailed example of a '**`Program`**' class with additional methods and properties:

```
using System;

namespace MyConsoleApp
{
    class Program
    {
        static void Main(string[] args)
        {
            // Create an instance of the Greeting class
            Greeting greeting = new Greeting();
            greeting.Message = "Hello, World!";
            greeting.DisplayMessage();
        }
    }

    class Greeting
    {
        public string Message { get; set; }

        public void DisplayMessage()
        {
            Console.WriteLine(Message);
        }
    }
}
```

In this example:

- The '**`Program`**' class contains the 'Main' method that creates an instance of the 'Greeting' class.
- The '**`Program`**' class has a property '**`Message`**' and a method '**`DisplayMessage`**' to display the message on the console.

This example illustrates how classes can interact with each other and demonstrates object-oriented principles in a simple C console application.

Main Method: The entry point where the program starts execution.

`Console.WriteLine`: Outputs text to the console

`Console.ReadLine`: Reads input from the user

Running the Application

1. **Compile and Run:** Through an IDE like Visual Studio, you can compile and run the application and it will execute in the terminal/console window.
2. **Interaction:** Users can interact with the application through text-based input and output.

In summary, console applications in C# are ideal for scenarios where a graphical interface is unnecessary. They provide a quick and efficient way to develop applications that perform various tasks using a simple, text-based interface.

Step 2: Setting Up SQL Server

This is a pretty straight-forward step of creating a new database and then creating a new table and populating it with sample data to display in the console application.

Step 3: Adding Entity Framework Core to your Project

We will introduce Entity Framework (EF) in this step. EF helps in interacting with databases using .Net objects.

Entity Framework (EF)

Entity Framework (EF) is an open-source Object-Relational Mapping (ORM) framework for .NET. It enables developers to work with relational data using domain-specific objects, which eliminates the need for most of the data-access code that developers usually need to write. EF provides an abstraction over the database layer, allowing developers to interact with databases using .NET objects and LINQ (Language Integrated Query).

Key Features of Entity Framework:

- **Modeling**: EF allows you to create a conceptual model of your data using .NET classes.
- **Querying**: You can use LINQ to query your data, which provides compile-time syntax checking and IntelliSense support.
- **Change Tracking**: EF automatically tracks changes made to the objects so that the correct updates can be sent to the database.
- **Saving**: EF can generate SQL commands to insert, update, or delete data based on the changes made to the objects.
- **Concurrency**: EF provides built-in support to handle concurrency conflicts.
- **Caching**: EF includes a first-level cache, which reduces the number of database queries by caching query results.

Types of Entity Framework:

- **EF Core**: A lightweight, extensible, and cross-platform version of Entity Framework. EF Core is recommended for new projects.
- **EF6**: This is the traditional version of Entity Framework, which is still maintained but is not recommended for new projects in favor of EF Core.

How Entity Framework Works:

- **Model Creation**: Create a model that defines the shape of your data and relationships between your data.
- **DbContext**: This is the central class in EF that manages the database connection and is used to query and save data.
- **Migration**: EF allows you to create and apply database schema changes through migrations.

Example of Entity Framework in Action

1. Install the Entity Framework.

```
Tools → Nuget Package Manager → Package Manager Console
 Install-Package Microsoft.EntityFrameworkCore
 Install-Package Microsoft.EntityFrameworkCore.SqlServer
 Install-Package Microsoft.EntityFrameworkCore.Tools
 ```
```

2. Define a Model (example shown as follows).

```
public class Person
{
    public int Id { get; set; }
    public string Name { get; set; }
```
```

```
        public int Age { get; set; }
    }
```

3. Create a DbContext.

```
    public class MyDatabaseContext : DbContext
    {
        public DbSet<Person> Persons { get; set; }

        protected override void OnConfiguring(DbContextOptions-
Builder optionsBuilder)
        {
            optionsBuilder.UseSqlServer("Server=YOUR_SERVER_NAME;-
Database=MyDatabase;Trusted_Connection=True;");
        }
    }
```

4. **Perform CRUD Operations:**

```
    using (var context = new MyDatabaseContext())
    {
        // Create
        var person = new Person { Name = "John Doe", Age = 30 };
        context.Persons.Add(person);
        context.SaveChanges();

        // Read
        var persons = context.Persons.ToList();

        // Update
        person.Age = 31;
        context.SaveChanges();

        // Delete
        context.Persons.Remove(person);
        context.SaveChanges();
    }
```

Importance of Entity Framework for .NET

- **Productivity**: EF reduces the amount of boilerplate code required for data access, which allows developers to focus on the business logic.
- **Maintainability**: Through EF, data access logic is abstracted from the business logic, which makes the codebase cleaner and easier to maintain.
- **Scalability**: EF supports multiple database providers, which makes it easier to switch databases if needed.
- **Performance**: While EF might introduce some overhead compared to raw ADO. NET, its caching and lazy loading features can optimize performance in many

scenarios. Lazy loading, if not managed carefully, it can cause performance issues (N+1 query problem).

- **Testability**: EF allows you to create mock contexts and repositories, which makes it easier to write unit tests for your data access code.
- **Cross-Platform**: With EF Core, you can build applications that run on multiple platforms, including Windows, Linux, and macOS.

In summary, Entity Framework is a powerful ORM tool that simplifies data access in .NET applications, boosts productivity, and enhances code maintainability, which makes it an essential component for modern .NET development.

Step 4: Configuring the Database Context

This is a pretty straight-forward step of defining and configuring the DbContext, which represents the session with the database.

Step 5: Using the Database Context in the Program

This is a pretty straight-forward step of creating a new database, then creating a new table, and populating it with sample data to display in the console application.

Step-by-Step Guide to Creating a Namespace

1. **Understanding Namespace Syntax**:
   - Namespaces in C# are declared using the '`namespace`' keyword followed by the namespace name and curly braces `{}` to enclose the code within the namespace.
   - Typically, namespaces are used at the beginning of a file, before any other code elements.
2. **Creating a New Namespace**: To create your own namespace, you simply use the '`namespace`' keyword followed by the desired name. Here is an example:

```
namespace MyNamespace {
    // Code goes here
}
```

   Replace `MyNamespace` with your preferred namespace name.

3. **Placing Code inside the Namespace**: Once you have declared the namespace, you can place any valid C# code inside it. Consider this example:

```
namespace MyNamespace {
    public class MyClass {
        public void MyMethod() {
            Console.WriteLine("Inside MyMethod");
        }
    }
}
```

Here, **`MyClass`** and **`MyMethod`** are contained within the **`MyNamespace`**.

4. **Using the Namespace**: To use types (classes, structs, interfaces, and so on) defined within your namespace in other parts of your code or in other namespaces, you need to either fully qualify the type name or import the namespace via a '**`using`**' directive, as shown here:

```
// Fully qualified name
MyNamespace.MyClass instance = new MyNamespace.MyClass();

// Using directive
using MyNamespace;
// Now you can directly use MyClass
MyClass instance = new MyClass();
```

Example Explained

Let us create a practical example to illustrate namespaces in action, which is illustrated here:

```
// Define a namespace called MyNamespace
namespace MyNamespace {
    // Define a class inside the namespace
    public class MyClass {
        public void MyMethod() {
            Console.WriteLine("Inside MyMethod");
        }
    }
}

// Usage outside the namespace
class Program {
    static void Main() {
        // Create an instance of MyClass from MyNamespace
        MyNamespace.MyClass instance = new MyNamespace.MyClass();

        // Call MyMethod
        instance.MyMethod();
    }
}
```

Best Practices

- **Naming Conventions**: Use meaningful names for namespaces that reflect the purpose or domain of the contained code.
- **Avoid Overly Deep Nesting**: Keep namespaces concise and avoid nesting too deeply, as it can make code harder to navigate.
- **Organize Code**: Use namespaces to logically group related classes, interfaces, and other types.

Thus, by following these steps and best practices, you can effectively organize your C# code using namespaces, which improves the readability and maintainability of your projects.

In C#, **Object-Oriented Programming (OOP)** concepts form the foundation for creating modular, reusable, and maintainable code. Here is an overview of some key OOP concepts in C#:

Class

A class is a blueprint or template for creating objects. It defines the data and behavior (methods) that objects of the class will have. Classes in C are declared using the '`class`' keyword.

Example:

```
public class Person {
    // Fields (data members)
    public string Name;
    public int Age;

    // Constructor
    public Person(string name, int age) {
        Name = name;
        Age = age;
    }

    // Method
    public void DisplayInfo() {
        Console.WriteLine($"Name: {Name}, Age: {Age}");
    }
}
```

Properties

Properties provide a way to encapsulate fields and expose them through getter and setter methods. They provide controlled access to class fields and help maintain encapsulation.

Example:

```
public class Person {
    // Auto-implemented properties
    public string Name { get; set; }
    public int Age { get; set; }

    // Constructor
    public Person(string name, int age) {
        Name = name;
        Age = age;
    }

    // Method
    public void DisplayInfo() {
        Console.WriteLine($"Name: {Name}, Age: {Age}");
    }
}
```

Methods (Functions)

Methods in C# are functions defined within a class that perform actions or compute values. They encapsulate behavior and are called using an instance of the class.

Example:

```
public class Calculator {
    public int Add(int a, int b) {
        return a + b;
    }

    public int Subtract(int a, int b) {
        return a - b;
    }

    public int Multiply(int a, int b) {
        return a * b;
    }

    public double Divide(int a, int b) {
        if (b != 0)
            return (double)a / b;
        else
```

```
                throw new DivideByZeroException("Cannot divide by
zero.");
        }
    }
```

Encapsulation

Encapsulation is the principle of bundling data (fields) and methods that operate on the data within a single unit (class). It also restricts access to some of the object's components. This helps in achieving data hiding and abstraction.

Example:

```
public class BankAccount {
    private decimal balance;

    // Property to access balance (encapsulated field)
    public decimal Balance {
        get { return balance; }
        private set {
            if (value >= 0)
                balance = value;
            else
                throw new ArgumentException("Balance cannot be
negative.");
        }
    }

    // Method to deposit money
    public void Deposit(decimal amount) {
        Balance += amount;
    }

    // Method to withdraw money
    public void Withdraw(decimal amount) {
        if (amount <= Balance)
            Balance -= amount;
        else
            throw new InvalidOperationException("Insufficient
funds.");
    }
}
```

Inheritance

Inheritance allows one class (derived class or subclass) to inherit properties and behavior from another class (base class or superclass). It promotes code reusability and enables hierarchical relationships between classes.

Example:

```
public class Animal {
    public void Eat() {
        Console.WriteLine("Animal is eating.");
    }
}

public class Dog : Animal {
    public void Bark() {
        Console.WriteLine("Dog is barking.");
    }
}
```

Polymorphism

Polymorphism allows objects of different types to be treated as objects of a common base type. It infuses flexibility and extensibility in code by allowing methods to be overridden in derived classes.

Example:

```
public class Shape {
    public virtual void Draw() {
        Console.WriteLine("Drawing a shape.");
    }
}

public class Circle : Shape {
    public override void Draw() {
        Console.WriteLine("Drawing a circle.");
    }
}

public class Rectangle : Shape {
    public override void Draw() {
        Console.WriteLine("Drawing a rectangle.");
    }
}
```

Abstraction

Abstraction focuses on the essential features of an object, while hiding its complex implementation details. Abstract classes and interfaces are used to achieve abstraction in C#.

Example:

```
public abstract class Shape {
    public abstract void Draw();
}

public class Circle : Shape {
    public override void Draw() {
        Console.WriteLine("Drawing a circle.");
    }
}

public class Rectangle : Shape {
    public override void Draw() {
        Console.WriteLine("Drawing a rectangle.");
    }
}
```

Interface

An interface defines a contract that classes can implement. It specifies a set of methods, properties, events, or indexers that implementing classes must define. Interfaces promote loose coupling and support multiple inheritances in C#.

Example:

```
public interface IShape {
    void Draw();
}

public class Circle : IShape {
    public void Draw() {
        Console.WriteLine("Drawing a circle.");
    }
}

public class Rectangle : IShape {
    public void Draw() {
        Console.WriteLine("Drawing a rectangle.");
    }
}
```

These concepts are fundamental to understanding and effectively using Object-Oriented Programming in C. They provide a structured approach to software development, while promoting modularity, reusability, and maintainability of code.

Adding Code Snippets

Code snippets in C# are predefined blocks of code that you can quickly insert into your program to speed up coding and ensure consistency. These snippets can be simple, like inserting a property or a method, or complex, including larger structures like classes and entire algorithms. Code snippets help developers by reducing the amount of repetitive coding tasks and minimizing errors.

To add code snippets in C#, you can use Visual Studio, which provides a variety of built-in code snippets to speed up your development process. You can also create your own custom code snippets. Here is how you can use both built-in and custom code snippets in Visual Studio:

Using Built-In Code Snippets

- **Invoking the Snippet Manager**: You can open the Snippet Manager by pressing `*Ctrl* + K, *Ctrl* + B` or by right-clicking in the code editor, selecting `**Insert Snippet**`, and then choosing from the available snippets.
- **Using Shortcut Keywords**: You can type shortcut keywords followed by pressing the *Tab* key twice to insert a snippet. For example, typing '**prop**' and pressing *Tab* twice will insert a property snippet.
- Common Built-In Snippets:
  - **prop**: Inserts a property
  - **cw**: Inserts a **Console.WriteLine** statement
  - **for**: Inserts a for loop
  - **foreach**: Inserts a foreach loop

Creating Custom Code Snippets

1. **Creating a Snippet File**: Create a new XML file with a **.snippet** extension. Here is an example of a custom snippet for a '**Hello World**' program:

```
    <CodeSnippets xmlns="http://schemas.microsoft.com/Visual
Studio/2005/CodeSnippet">
      <CodeSnippet Format="1.0.0">
        <Header>
          <Title>Hello World</Title>
          <Shortcut>hw</Shortcut>
          <Description>A simple Hello World snippet</Description>
          <Author>Your Name</Author>
          <SnippetTypes>
            <SnippetType>Expansion</SnippetType>
          </SnippetTypes>
        </Header>
        <Snippet>
```

```
        <Declarations>
          <Literal>
            <ID>name</ID>
            <ToolTip>Type your name here</ToolTip>
            <Default>World</Default>
          </Literal>
        </Declarations>
        <Code Language="csharp">
          <![CDATA[
          using System;

          namespace $rootnamespace$
          {
              class Program
              {
                  static void Main(string[] args)
                  {
                      Console.WriteLine("Hello, $name$!");
                  }
              }
          }
          ]]>
        </Code>
      </Snippet>
    </CodeSnippet>
  </CodeSnippets>
```

2. **Importing the Snippet into Visual Studio:**
   a. Open Visual Studio.
   b. Go to **`Tools`** > **`Code Snippets Manager`**, or press *Ctrl* + K, *Ctrl* + B.
   c. Select the language (for example, Visual C#).
   d. Click on **`Import`** and navigate to the **`.snippet`** file you have created.
   e. Click on Open to add the snippet to your available code snippets.

Using the Custom Snippet

Once the custom snippet is imported, you can use it just like a built-in snippet. Type the shortcut keyword (for example, **`'hw'`**) in the code editor and press '**`Tab`**' twice to insert the snippet.

Example of Using a Code Snippet

Here is a demonstration of using the **`'prop'`** snippet to create a property in a class:

1. Type '**prop**' in the code editor and press *Tab* twice:

```
public class MyClass
{
    public int MyProperty { get; set; }
}
```

2. **Customize the snippet as needed:**

```csharp
public class MyClass
{
    private int myField;

    public int MyProperty
    {
        get { return myField; }
        set { myField = value; }
    }
}
```

Using snippets can significantly speed up your coding by reducing the amount of repetitive code you otherwise would have to write manually.

Using IntelliSense in C#

IntelliSense is a powerful code-completion tool in Visual Studio that helps developers write code more efficiently and accurately. It offers several key features that assist in the coding process by providing real-time suggestions, completions, and documentation. It includes a number of features: List Members, Parameter Info, Quick Info, and Complete Word. These features help you to write code faster and with fewer errors.

Step-by-Step Guide to Using IntelliSense

1. **Enabling IntelliSense**: IntelliSense is enabled by default in Visual Studio. If it's not working, you can enable it from **`Tools`** -> **`Options`** -> **`Text Editor`** -> **`C#`** -> **`IntelliSense`**.

2. **Listing Members**:

    - Start typing a variable name, method name, or class name. IntelliSense will automatically show a list of possible completions.
    - Use the arrow keys to navigate the list and press *Tab* or *Enter* to select an item.

Example:

```
string exampleString = "Hello, World!";
   exampleString. // IntelliSense will show methods like
'Length', 'Substring', etc.
```

3. **Parameter Info**: When you type the opening parenthesis after a method name, IntelliSense will show the method's parameters.

Example:

```
Console.WriteLine( // IntelliSense shows parameter info for
'WriteLine' method
```

4. **Quick Info**: Hover the mouse pointer over a variable, method, or class name to see a tooltip with information about the element.

Example:

```
int number = 5;
   // Hover over 'number' to see its type and value
```

5. **Completing the Word**: Type part of a word and press *Ctrl + Space* to complete the word.

Example:

```
str // Press 'Ctrl + Space' to complete to 'string'
```

Advantages of IntelliSense

- **Increased Productivity:**
    - Reduces the amount of typing needed
    - Provides quick access to documentation and information about APIs
- **Error Reduction:**
    - Helps avoid typos and syntactical errors by suggesting correct options
    - Highlights errors in real-time, thereby allowing for immediate correction
- **Ease of Learning:**
    - Provides insights into unfamiliar APIs and methods
    - Displays parameter information, making it easier to use methods correctly
- **Improved Code Quality**: Encourages the use of best practices by suggesting proper method names and properties

Ways to Implement and Use IntelliSense

1. **Using IntelliSense in Visual Studio**:

- **Automatic Suggestions**: IntelliSense provides suggestions automatically as you type.

- **Manual Trigger**: Press *Ctrl* + J or *Ctrl* + *Space* to manually invoke IntelliSense.
- **Method Parameters**: While typing method parameters, use *Ctrl* + *Shift* + *Space* to view the parameter info.

2. **Configuring IntelliSense**:
   - Customize IntelliSense settings from **`Tools`** -> **`Options`** -> **`Text Editor`** -> **`C`** -> IntelliSense.
   - **Options include**:
     - Show completion list after a character is typed
     - Highlight matching portions of completion list items
3. **Using IntelliSense in Other Environments**:
   - **Visual Studio Code:**
     - IntelliSense is also available in VS Code with similar features.
     - Use extensions like C for Visual Studio Code to enhance IntelliSense.
   - JetBrains Rider: Another IDE with robust IntelliSense support for C#
4. **Customizing IntelliSense**:
   a. Create custom code snippets to use with IntelliSense.
   b. Go to **`Tools`** -> **`Code Snippets Manager`** to create and manage snippets.
5. **Using IntelliSense with Third-Party Libraries**:
   a. IntelliSense works with third-party libraries by providing information about their methods and properties.
   b. Install the library via NuGet and IntelliSense will integrate it into its suggestions.

Example of Using IntelliSense

Consider writing a small program that uses IntelliSense:

```
using System;
using System.Collections.Generic;

namespace IntelliSenseDemo
{
    class Program
    {
        static void Main(string[] args)
        {
            List<string> names = new List<string>();
            names.Add("Alice");
            names.Add("Bob");
```

```
                foreach (var name in names)
                {
                    Console.WriteLine(name);
                }

                // Hover over 'names' to see its type and informa-
tion.
                // Type 'names.' to see a list of available methods
and properties.
                // Type 'Console.WriteLine' and open parenthesis to
see parameter info.
            }
        }
    }
```

In this example, IntelliSense helps you by showing available methods for 'names', while providing parameter info for '`Console.WriteLine`' and offering quick information about variables and methods.

Using Task List and Code Navigation in Visual Studio 2022

Task List and Code Navigation features play an important role in improving productivity and maintaining code quality in Visual Studio 2022.

Task List

The Task List in Visual Studio helps you keep track of tasks, comments, and other important notes in your code. It can be used to manage TODOs, HACKs, and custom tokens.

Step-by-Step Guide to Using the Task List

1. **Opening the Task List**: Go to `View` -> `Task List` or press *Ctrl* + \ and then T.

2. **Adding Tasks to Your Code**: Use predefined tokens such as **TODO**, **HACK**, or **UNDONE** in your comments to create tasks.

Example:

```
// TODO: Refactor this method
// HACK: This is a temporary fix
// UNDONE: This feature is not complete
```
```
```

3. **Create Custom Tokens:**

   a. Go to **`Tools`** -> **`Options`**.

   b. Navigate to **`Environment`** -> **`Task List`**.

   c. Add new tokens (for example, **`NOTE`**, **`FIXME`**) and assign priority levels.

Example:

```
// NOTE: Check this logic later
    // FIXME: Correct this calculation
    ```
```

4. **View and Manage Tasks:**

   a. Tasks will appear in the **`Task List`** window.

   b. Click on a task to navigate to its location in the code.

   c. Filter tasks by type, priority, or custom tokens using the drop-down menu in the Task List window.

**Advantages of the Task List**

- **Organized Workflow**: Keeps track of tasks and code-related notes, while improving organization
- **Prioritization**: Allows you to prioritize tasks and focus on important issues
- **Navigation**: Quick navigation to specific tasks or comments within your code

# Code Navigation

Code Navigation in Visual Studio helps you quickly find and navigate to different parts of your codebase, which enhances productivity and efficiency.

# Step-by-Step Guide to Using Code Navigation

1. **Navigate to Definition**: Right-click on a symbol (class, method, variable) and select '**`Go To Definition`**' or press F12.

**Example**:

```
    MyClass myObject = new MyClass();
    myObject.MyMethod(); // Right-click 'MyMethod' and select
'Go To Definition'
```

2. **Peek Definition**:

   a. Right-click on a symbol and select '**`Peek Definition`**' or press Alt + F12.
```

b. A small window will appear and show the definition without navigating away from your current location.

Example:

```
myObject.MyMethod(); // Right-click 'MyMethod' and select
'Peek Definition'
```

3. **Find All References**:

   a. Right-click on a symbol and select '**`Find All References`**' or press *Shift* + F12.

   b. A window will display all the instances where the symbol is used.

Example:

```
myObject.MyMethod(); // Right-click 'MyMethod' and select
'Find All References'
```

4. **Navigate Backwards and Forwards**:

   a. Use *Ctrl* + - to navigate back to the previous location.

   b. Use *Ctrl* + *Shift* + - to navigate forward to the next location.

5. **CodeLens**:

   a. CodeLens provides information about code references, changes, and tests directly above your code.

   b. It is enabled by default in Visual Studio Enterprise and Professional editions.

Advantages of Code Navigation

- **Efficiency**: Quickly navigate to definitions, references, and other code locations.
- **Context**: Peek at definitions without losing your place in the code.
- **Insight**: Find all references and understand where and how symbols are used.
- **History**: Navigate back and forth through code locations.

Ways to Implement and Use Task List and Code Navigation

- **Integrating with Team Workflows:**
  - Use Task List tokens to assign tasks to team members.
  - Track code reviews and pending changes through comments and custom tokens.
- **Code Reviews and Refactoring:**
  - Utilize Code Navigation to review code changes, refactor methods, and ensure code quality.

    - Use '**`Find All References`**' to understand the impact of changes across the codebase.
- **Debugging and Testing**:
    - Navigate to method definitions and references while debugging to understand call stacks and logic flows.
    - Use CodeLens to see test results and code changes directly in the editor.
- **Documentation and Learning**:
    - Annotate code with TODOs, HACKs, and notes to provide context and documentation for future reference.
    - New team members can use Code Navigation to explore and understand the codebase.

Summary

The Task List and Code Navigation features in Visual Studio 2022 are essential tools for managing tasks, organizing code, and navigating large codebases efficiently. Through predefined and custom tokens, you can keep track of important notes and tasks. Code Navigation allows you to quickly find definitions, references, and navigate through your code, which enhances productivity and code quality. Integrating these tools into your development workflow can significantly improve organization, collaboration, and efficiency.

Using Refactoring Tools in Visual Studio 2022

Refactoring tools in Visual Studio 2022 help developers improve the structure of their code without changing its external behavior. These tools provide automated ways to perform common refactoring tasks, thereby making the code easier to read, maintain, and extend.

Step-by-Step Guide to Using Refactoring Tools

1. **Renaming Identifiers**:

Steps:

   a. Right-click on the identifier (variable, method, class) you want to rename.

   b. Select '**`Rename`**' from the context menu, or press F2.

   c. Type the new name and press *Enter*.

   d. Review the changes in the preview window and click on '**`Apply`**'.

Example:

```
int myVariable = 5;
   // Rename 'myVariable' to 'newVariableName'
```

2. **Extract Method**:

Steps:

a. Select the block of code you want to extract into a new method.

b. Right-click and choose **`Refactor`** -> **`Extract Method`**, or press *Ctrl* + R, *Ctrl* + M.

c. Enter the new method name and press *Enter*.

d. The selected code is replaced with a call to the new method.

Example:

```
void MyMethod()
{
    // Select the following code block to extract
    int result = Calculate(5, 10);
    Console.WriteLine(result);
}
```

3. **Extract Interface**:

Steps:

a. Right-click on the class name.

b. Select **`Quick Actions`** and **`Refactorings`** -> **`Extract Interface`**, or press *Ctrl* + . and choose '**`Extract Interface`**'.

c. Select the members to include in the interface and click on OK.

Example:

```
public class MyClass
   {
       public void Method1() { }
       public void Method2() { }
   }
   // Extract an interface 'IMyClass' from 'MyClass'
```

4. **Encapsulate Field:**

Steps:

a. Place the cursor on the field you want to encapsulate.

b. Right-click and select Refactor -> Encapsulate Field, or press Ctrl + R, Ctrl + E.

c. The field is converted to a property with a private field.

Example:

```
public int myField;
// Encapsulate 'myField' to create a property 'MyField'
```

5. **Inline Temporary Variable**:

Steps:

a. Place the cursor on the variable you want to inline.

b. Right-click and choose Refactor` **->** `Inline, or press *Ctrl* + R, *Ctrl* + I.

c. Confirm the inline operation in the preview window.

Example:

```
int temp = GetValue();
Console.WriteLine(temp);
// Inline 'temp' to directly use 'GetValue()'
```

Advantages of Refactoring Tools

- **Improved Code Quality:**
  - Enhances code readability and maintainability
  - Simplifies complex code structures
- **Increased Productivity:**
  - Automates repetitive refactoring tasks
  - Reduces the time needed to perform manual code improvements
- **Reduced Errors:**
  - Minimizes the risk of introducing bugs during manual refactoring
  - Ensures consistent and accurate code changes
- **Enhanced Collaboration:**
  - Standardizes code refactoring practices across the team
  - Facilitates better code reviews and knowledge sharing

Ways to Implement and Use Refactoring Tools

1. **Regular Code Maintenance**:

a. Schedule regular intervals to refactor code and improve its structure.

b. Use tools like Code Cleanup to apply code style preferences and fix common issues.

2. **During Code Reviews**:
   a. Identify refactoring opportunities during code reviews.
   b. Use refactoring tools to address issues such as long methods, duplicated code, or improper naming conventions.
3. **When Adding New Features**:
   a. Refactor related parts of the codebase before adding new features to ensure a solid foundation.
   b. Use Extract Method and Extract Interface to create reusable and testable code components.
4. **Improving Legacy Code**:
   a. Gradually refactor legacy code to modernize and improve its structure.
   b. Use tools like Code Metrics to identify areas that need refactoring.
5. **Automated Refactoring**:
   a. Integrate static analysis and code-fixing tools within continuous integration/continuous deployment (CI/CD) pipelines.
   b. Use tools like Roslyn Analyzers to enforce coding standards and apply automatic code fixes where possible.

Example of Refactoring in Action:

Consider the following code snippet that can benefit from refactoring:

```
public class OrderProcessor
{
    public void ProcessOrder(Order order)
    {
        // Validate order
        if (order == null)
        {
            throw new ArgumentNullException(nameof(order));
        }
        if (string.IsNullOrEmpty(order.CustomerName))
        {
            throw new ArgumentException("Customer name is
required.");
        }
```

```
            // Calculate total
            decimal total = 0;
            foreach (var item in order.Items)
            {
                total += item.Price * item.Quantity;
            }

            // Process payment
            PaymentService paymentService = new PaymentService();
            paymentService.ProcessPayment(order.PaymentDetails, total);
        }
    }
```

Using refactoring tools, you can improve this code as follows:

1. **Extract Method**: Extract validation, total calculation, and payment processing into separate methods.
2. **Rename Identifier**: Rename '**total**' to '**orderTotal**' for clarity.
3. **Encapsulate Field**: If '**OrderProcessor**' had a public field, encapsulate it as a property.

Refactored Code:

```
public class OrderProcessor
{
    public void ProcessOrder(Order order)
    {
        ValidateOrder(order);
        decimal orderTotal = CalculateOrderTotal(order);
        ProcessPayment(order.PaymentDetails, orderTotal);
    }

    private void ValidateOrder(Order order)
    {
        if (order == null)
        {
            throw new ArgumentNullException(nameof(order));
        }
        if (string.IsNullOrEmpty(order.CustomerName))
        {
            throw new ArgumentException("Customer name is
required.");
        }
    }

    private decimal CalculateOrderTotal(Order order)
    {
```

```
            decimal total = 0;
            foreach (var item in order.Items)
            {
                total += item.Price * item.Quantity;
            }
            return total;
        }

        private void ProcessPayment(PaymentDetails paymentDetails,
    decimal amount)
        {
            PaymentService paymentService = new PaymentService();
            paymentService.ProcessPayment(paymentDetails, amount);
        }
    }
```

Summary

Refactoring tools in Visual Studio 2022 is essential for maintaining high-quality, clean, and maintainable code. By leveraging these tools, developers can efficiently rename identifiers, extract methods and interfaces, encapsulate fields, and inline variables, among other tasks. These automated refactoring features help improve code readability, reduce errors, and enhance overall productivity. Implementing regular refactoring practices can significantly improve the structure and maintainability of your codebase.

Version Control using GIT

Version control is a system that records changes to files over time, which allows you to recall specific versions later. In Visual Studio, version control is integrated to help developers manage changes to their code, collaborate with others, and maintain a history of their work. The most commonly used version control systems in Visual Studio are Git, Azure DevOps (ADO) and Team Foundation Version Control (TFVC).

Key Features of Version Control in Visual Studio

- **Source Control Integration:** Visual Studio provides built-in support for Git and TFVC, which allows you to manage version control directly within the IDE.
- **Version History:** Keeps a detailed history of changes, which enables you to view and revert to previous versions of your code
- **Branching and Merging:** Facilitates working on different features or fixes in isolated branches and merging them when ready
- **Commit and Sync:** Allows you to commit changes to the local repository and sync with remote repositories

- **Collaboration:** Supports collaborative development by enabling multiple developers to work on the same project simultaneously
- **Conflict Resolution:** Provides tools to identify and resolve conflicts when merging changes from different branches

Advantages of Version Control in Visual Studio

a. **Improved Collaboration:**
    - Multiple team members can work on the same project without overwriting each other's changes.
    - Facilitates code reviews and collaborative development through pull requests and code sharing

b. **Change Tracking:**
    - Records every change made to the codebase by providing a detailed history that can be reviewed at any time
    - Enables tracking of who made specific changes and why, thus enhancing accountability and traceability

c. **Backup and Restore:**
    - Maintains a backup of the entire codebase, which allows you to revert to previous versions in case of errors or issues
    - Protects against data loss by keeping a history of all changes

d. **Branching and Merging:**
    - Isolates work on new features or bug fixes in separate branches, while minimizing the risk of introducing bugs into the main codebase
    - Merges branches when changes are ready to be integrated, which ensures a smooth workflow

e. **Continuous Integration and Deployment (CI/CD):**
    - Integrates with CI/CD pipelines to automate testing, building, and deployment processes, while ensuring high code quality and faster releases

f. **Conflict Resolution:**
    - Provides tools to identify, manage, and resolve conflicts, which ensures smooth integration of changes from different sources

Version control is essential for tracking changes, collaborating with others, and managing different versions of your codebase. Git is a popular version control system that integrates seamlessly with Visual Studio 2022.

Step-by-Step Guide to Implementing Git in Visual Studio 2022

1. **Setting Up Git in Visual Studio**

    a. **Install Git**: Download and install Git from git-scm.com (https://git-scm.com/).

    b. **Open Visual Studio**: Launch Visual Studio 2022.

    c. **Enable Git Integration**: Git integration is enabled by default in Visual Studio 2022. If not, go to **`Tools`** -> **`Options`** -> **`Source Control`** -> **`Plug-in Selection`** and select **`Git`**.

2. **Creating a New Repository**

    a. **Create a New Project**:

        i. Go to **`File`** -> **`New`** -> **`Project`**.

        ii. Create a new project or open an existing one.

    b. **Initialize a Git Repository**:

        i. Go to **`Git`** -> **`Create Git Repository`**.

        ii. Choose a local path for your repository and provide a name for it.

        iii. Click on **`Create`**.

    c. **Add Solution to Source Control**:

        i. Right-click on your solution in the **`Solution Explorer`**.

        ii. Select **`Add Solution to Source Control`**.

        iii. This will initialize the repository and add your project files to it.

3. **Committing Changes**

    a. **Make Changes**: Make changes to your code as needed.

    b. **Stage Changes**:

        i. Go to **`Git`** -> **`Changes`**.

        ii. Review the changes listed under **`Unstaged Changes`**.

        iii. Select the changes you want to commit and click the **`+`** button to stage them.

c. **Commit Changes**:

   i. Enter a commit message in the **`Message`** field.

   ii. Click on **`Commit Staged`** to commit the changes to the local repository.

4. **Pushing and Pulling Changes**

   a. **Push Changes to Remote Repository**:

      i. Go to **`Git`** -> **`Push`**.

      ii. If you don't have a remote repository, you can create one on GitHub, GitLab, or any other Git hosting service.

      iii. Follow the prompts to link your local repository to the remote repository.

   b. **Pull Changes from Remote Repository**:

      i. Go to **`Git`** -> **`Pull`**.

      ii. This will fetch and merge changes from the remote repository into your local repository.

5. **Branching and Merging**

   a. **Create a New Branch**:

      i. Go to **`Git`** -> **`Manage Branches`**.

      ii. Click on **`New Branch`**.

      iii. Enter a name for your branch and click on **`Create`**.

   b. Switch Between Branches: In the Branches pane, right-click on the branch you want to switch to and select Checkout.

   c. **Merge Branches:**

      i. Go to **`Git`** -> **`Manage Branches`**.

      ii. Right-click on the branch you want to merge into and select '**`Merge From...`**'.

      iii. Choose the branch you want to merge from and complete the merge.

6. **Resolving Conflicts**

   a. **Identify Conflicts**:

      i. Conflicts occur when changes in different branches affect the same lines of code.

      ii. Conflicts will be highlighted in the Git Changes window.

b. **Resolve Conflicts**:

   i. Open the conflicting files.

   ii. Manually resolve the conflicts by choosing the changes you wish to retain.

   iii. Stage the resolved files and commit the changes.

Advantages of Using Git in Visual Studio

- **Improved Collaboration**:
  - Multiple developers can work on the same project simultaneously.
  - Changes can be merged and conflicts resolved efficiently.
- **Change Tracking**:
  - Track all changes made to the codebase over time.
  - Revert to previous versions if needed.
- **Branching and Merging**:
  - Work on new features or bug fixes in isolated branches.
  - Merge branches when changes are ready to be integrated.
- **Backup and Restore:**
  - Maintain a complete history of the codebase.
  - Restore previous versions in case of issues.

Ways to Implement and Use Git

- **Local Repositories**: You can use Git locally for individual projects without needing a remote repository.
- **Remote Repositories:**
  - Use services like GitHub, GitLab, Bitbucket, or Azure Repos to host remote repositories.
  - Collaborate with others by pushing and pulling changes.
- **Continuous Integration/Continuous Deployment (CI/CD)**: Integrate Git with CI/CD pipelines to automate testing, building, and deployment.
- **Code Reviews**: Use pull requests and code reviews to ensure code quality and consistency.
- **Issue Tracking**: Link commits and branches to issues or tasks in project management tools for better traceability.

Example Workflow (All Code is in PowerShell)

1. **Create a Repository**:

```
git init
```

2. **Add Remote Repository**:
```
git remote add origin https://github.com/username/repository.git
```
3. **Commit Changes**:
```
git add .
git commit -m "Initial commit"
```
4. **Push Changes**:
```
git push -u origin master
```
5. **Create and Switch to a New Branch:**
```
git checkout -b new-feature
```
6. **Merge Branches**:
```
git checkout master
git merge new-feature
```
7. **Pull Changes**:
```
git pull origin master
```

Summary

Using Git in Visual Studio 2022 provides powerful version control capabilities, which enhance collaboration, track changes, and manage different versions of your codebase. By following the detailed steps for setting up, committing, pushing, pulling, branching, merging, and resolving conflicts, developers can maintain a well-organized and efficient workflow. Integrating Git with remote repositories, CI/CD pipelines, and issue tracking systems further enhances project management and code quality.

Collaborative Coding with Visual Studio Live Share in Visual Studio 2022

Visual Studio Live Share allows multiple developers to collaborate in real-time within Visual Studio 2022. It allows you to share your codebase, debugging sessions, and more with others without having to clone repositories or set up environments.

Step-by-Step Guide to Using Visual Studio Live Share

1. **Setting Up Live Share:**

    a. **Install Visual Studio Live Share**:

        i. Live Share is integrated into Visual Studio 2022 by default. If you have not installed it yet, go to **`Extensions`** -> **`Manage Extensions`**.

   ii. Search for "`Live` Share" and install it. Restart Visual Studio if needed.

   b. **Sign In**: Open Visual Studio and sign in with your Microsoft account or GitHub account.

2. **Starting a Live Share Session:**

   a. **Open Your Project**: Open the project or solution you want to share.

   b. **Start Live Share**:

      i. Click the `Live Share` button in the top-right corner of the Visual Studio window or go to `File` -> `Live Share` -> `Start Collaboration Session`.

      ii. A link will be generated for you to share with collaborators.

   c. **Share the Link**: Copy the link and share it with the collaborators you want to invite to your session.

3. **Joining a Live Share Session:**

   a. **Receive the Link**:

      i. Open the link provided by the host in a web browser.

      ii. The link will prompt you to open Visual Studio if it's installed.

   b. **Join the Session**: Visual Studio will open and join the session automatically.

4. **Collaborating in a Live Share Session:**

   a. **Shared Editing**: All participants can edit the code simultaneously. Changes are reflected in real-time.

   b. **Follow Mode**: Participants can follow each other to see what others are working on. Right-click on a participant's name and select Follow.

   c. **Shared Debugging**:

      i. Share debugging sessions, including breakpoints and call stacks.

      ii. Participants can step through code together and view the same debugging data.

   d. **Shared Terminals**:

      i. Share terminal instances to run commands and see output.

      ii. Start a shared terminal from the `Live Share` toolbar.

   e. **Shared Servers**:

      i. Share local servers (for example, web servers) with participants.

ii. Use the Share Server option in the Live Share toolbar.

5. **Ending a Live Share Session:**

   a. **End Session:**

      i. The host can end the session by clicking `End Collaboration Session` in the `Live Share` toolbar.

      ii. All participants will be disconnected from the session.

Advantages of Visual Studio Live Share

- **Real-Time Collaboration**: Collaborate with team members in real-time, enhancing productivity and communication.
- **No Environment Setup**: Participants do not need to clone repositories or set up environments. Everything is shared directly from the host's setup.
- **Shared Debugging**: Debug together in real-time to easily identify and fix issues collaboratively.
- **Remote Pair Programming**: Facilitate pair programming sessions regardless of physical location.
- **Efficient Code Reviews**: Conduct code reviews interactively, discussing changes and improvements in real-time.
- **Educational Use**: Ideal for teaching and mentoring, allowing instructors to guide students through code examples and exercises.

Ways to Implement and Use Live Share

- **Pair Programming**: Two developers work together on the same codebase, while taking turns writing and reviewing code.
- **Code Reviews**: Conduct interactive code reviews with multiple reviewers, while providing immediate feedback and suggestions.
- Debugging Sessions: Collaboratively debug complex issues and leverage the expertise of multiple team members.
- **Workshops and Training**: Host coding workshops or training sessions where participants can follow along and interact with the instructor's code.
- **Mentoring**: Mentors can guide mentees through coding challenges and projects, while providing real-time assistance and feedback.
- **Remote Collaboration**: Enable remote teams to work together seamlessly, regardless of geographical location.

Example Workflow

1. **Start a Live Share Session**: Host starts the session and shares the link with a team member.

2. **Join the Session**: The team member clicks the link and joins the session in Visual Studio.
3. **Collaborate on Code**: Both developers edit and debug the code in real-time, while discussing changes via integrated chat or a separate communication tool.
4. **Share Terminals and Servers**: Host shares a terminal for running commands and a local server for testing.
5. **End the Session**: After completing the collaboration, the host ends the session and both developers can continue their work independently.

Summary

Visual Studio Live Share in Visual Studio 2022 enables seamless real-time collaboration for developers. It simplifies the process of working together on code by eliminating the need for environment setup and providing powerful tools for shared editing, debugging, and more. By following the step-by-step guide to setting up and using Live Share, developers can enhance productivity, improve code quality, and facilitate better teamwork. Whether for pair programming, code reviews, debugging, or training, Live Share is a valuable tool for modern software development.

Conclusion

This chapter has provided a hands-on exploration of the core workflows for writing, organizing, and managing code within Visual Studio. We've moved from creating a basic console application to integrating databases with Entity Framework, applying object-oriented principles, and leveraging powerful IDE features like IntelliSense, refactoring, code snippets, collaboration tools such as Git for version control and Live Share for real-time co-development.

The true skill of a developer is often measured not just by their ability to write code, but by their proficiency in efficiently identifying, understanding, and resolving problems within it. The next chapter, "*Debugging and Diagnostics*," delves into the powerful suite of tools Visual Studio provides for this critical task.

CHAPTER 4
Debugging and Diagnostics

Introduction

Debugging and diagnostics lie at the heart of successful software development. They are the processes through which we ensure that our applications not only run but run well. This chapter explores the essential tools and techniques for effectively debugging and diagnosing issues within the applications in Visual Studio.

Visual Studio 2022 provides a robust and sophisticated debugging environment which is designed to help you pinpoint the root cause of errors, unexpected behavior, and performance bottlenecks. Hence, whether you are dealing with a simple bug or a complex issue, the tools in Visual Studio can make the process of identifying and resolving problems much more manageable.

In this chapter, you will learn how to set up and configure unit tests, write effective test cases, and integrate testing into your development workflow. We will also explore advanced testing features in Visual Studio, such as code coverage analysis and Test-Driven Development (TDD). These can further enhance the robustness and reliability of your applications. Thus, by the end of this chapter, you will be well-equipped to leverage unit testing to improve the quality and maintainability of your C# code. You will also be well-equipped to confidently navigate the debugging process in Visual Studio. You can easily resolve application issues efficiently, and ensure that your code functions as intended. Debugging is not just about fixing bugs; it is about understanding your code better and making it more robust, reliable, and performant.

Structure

In this chapter, we will cover:

- Setting Breakpoints and Step Debugging
- Managing Breakpoints

- Conditional Breakpoints
- Function Breakpoints
- Data Breakpoints
- Temporary Breakpoints
- Using Watch Windows and QuickWatch
- Autos and Local Windows
- Analyzing Call Stacks and Threads
- Intellitrace

Setting Breakpoints and Step Debugging

Let us get started on this critical aspect of software development and unlock the full potential of Visual Studio 2022 for debugging and diagnostics.

Debugging in Visual Studio is the process of identifying, analyzing, and resolving bugs or defects within an application using the integrated tools and features provided by the Visual Studio IDE. Debugging is an essential part of the software development lifecycle, which enables developers to ensure that their code behaves as expected, performs efficiently, and is free of errors that could lead to crashes, incorrect results, or other unintended behavior.

Key Features of Debugging in Visual Studio

- **Breakpoints:** Breakpoints allow you to pause the execution of your program at specific lines of code. This enables you to inspect the current state of your application, including variable values, memory usage, and execution flow.
- **Step Execution:** Step through your code one line at a time (`Step Over`), dive into method calls (`Step Into`), or skip over methods (`Step Out`) to understand how your code executes and interacts with different components.
- **Watch Windows and QuickWatch:** These tools allow you to monitor the values of variables and expressions in real-time. You can add variables to the Watch Window to keep track of their values throughout the debugging session or use QuickWatch for a quick, temporary inspection.
- **Call Stack:** The Call Stack window shows the sequence of method calls that led to the current point of execution. This is useful for understanding the context of the current code and tracing the flow of execution.
- **Locals and Autos Windows:** These windows display the values of variables that are in the current scope (Locals) and those that are automatically determined to be relevant to the current line of execution (Autos).

- **Exception Handling:** Visual Studio can be configured to break execution when an exception is thrown, which allows you to inspect the state of the application and determine the cause of the exception.
- **Diagnostic Tools:** These include performance profilers, memory analyzers, and other tools that help you identify performance bottlenecks, memory leaks, and other issues that may not be immediately apparent through code inspection alone.
- **Intellitrace:** Intellitrace captures a historical record of your application's execution, which allows you to navigate back in time to see how the state of the application has changed over time. This is especially useful for debugging complex issues that are difficult to reproduce.
- **Live Debugging:** Visual Studio supports live debugging of running applications, including those hosted on remote servers or in the cloud. This allows you to debug issues in real-time without needing to reproduce them in a local development environment.
- **Debugging Managed and Unmanaged Code:** Visual Studio supports debugging both managed code (for example, C#, VB.NET) and unmanaged code (for example, C++), which makes it a versatile tool for developers working with different programming languages.

The Debugging Process

- **Identify the Issue:** Start by identifying the symptoms of the problem you are trying to solve. This could be a crash, incorrect output, performance issues, or any other unexpected behavior.
- **Set Breakpoints:** Place breakpoints at strategic locations in your code where you suspect the issue might be occurring. This allows you to pause execution and inspect the state of your application.
- **Run the Application:** Start your application in Debug mode. Visual Studio will run the application and pause at the breakpoints you have set.
- **Inspect State:** Use the debugging windows (Locals, Watch, Call Stack, and so on) to inspect the current state of your application. Look for any discrepancies or unexpected values that might indicate the cause of the issue.
- **Step Through Code:** Step through your code line by line to see how it executes and how the state changes. This can help you identify the exact location and cause of the problem.
- **Analyze and Fix:** Once you have identified the cause of the issue, modify your code to fix it. Then, rerun the application to verify that the fix resolves the problem.

- **Repeat as Necessary:** Debugging is often an iterative process. You may need to repeat these steps multiple times to fully resolve complex issues.

By utilizing the robust debugging tools in Visual Studio, developers can effectively diagnose and fix issues in their applications, leading to the development of reliable and high-quality software.

Therefore, before diving into debugging techniques we will take a quick look between **`Clean` Solution**, **`Build` Solution**, **`Rebuild` Solution**. Understanding the difference between "`Clean`", "`Build`", and "`Rebuild`" in Visual Studio is crucial for developers for several reasons:

Efficiency in Development Workflow

- **Build Time Optimization**: Knowing when to use "`Build`" versus "`Rebuild`" can significantly save time. "`Build`" compiles only the changes made since the last build, which is faster than recompiling the entire project. This efficiency is especially important in large projects where a full rebuild can take considerable time.
- **Avoiding Redundant Compilations**: Using "`Build`" after every minor change ensures that only modified files are recompiled, which avoids unnecessary recompilation of unchanged files.

Ensuring Clean Builds

- **Preventing Build Artifacts Issues**: Sometimes, leftover build artifacts (like object files or binaries) from previous builds can cause issues, such as linking errors or outdated dependencies. Using "`Clean`" helps remove these artifacts to prevent such issues.
- **Consistency**: A "`Rebuild`" ensures that all code is compiled from scratch, which can be essential when changing project-wide settings or dependencies. This helps ensure that all components are in sync and built against the latest code.

Troubleshooting and Debugging

- **Isolating Issues**: If a build is producing unexpected results or errors, starting with a "`Clean`" followed by a "`Build`" or "`Rebuild`" can help isolate the problem by ensuring that no stale artifacts are causing the issue.
- **Verification**: Sometimes, subtle bugs or issues can arise from incremental builds. A "`Rebuild`" can help verify that the problem is not due to any leftover state from previous builds.

Resource Management

- **Disk Space**: Regularly using "`Clean`" can help manage disk space by removing unnecessary intermediate and output files that accumulate over time.

- **Project Size Management**: For large projects, frequent "`Clean`" operations can keep the project directory from becoming cluttered with obsolete files, thereby making it easier to manage and navigate.

Understanding Build Processes and Dependencies

- **Learning Build Mechanics**: Understanding these commands helps developers gain insights into how the build process works, how dependencies are managed, and how different files and components interact during compilation and linking.
- **Configuration Management**: Different configurations (for example, Debug, Release) might require different build strategies. Knowing when to "`Clean`", "`Build`", or "`Rebuild`" helps in effectively managing and switching between these configurations.

Understanding the difference between "`Clean`", "`Build`", and "`Rebuild`" allows developers to optimize their development workflow, ensure clean and consistent builds, troubleshoot and debug effectively, manage resources, and understand the build process better. This knowledge is fundamental for maintaining high productivity and quality in software development.

In Visual Studio, the "`Clean`", "`Build`", and "`Rebuild`" commands are essential operations for managing your project's build process.

Clean

The "`Clean`" operation removes all compiled files (binaries) and intermediate files generated during the build process. This includes object files, executable files, libraries, and any other files that were produced by the compiler and linker.

- **Purpose**: To clear out all previously compiled files and start with a fresh slate.
- **When to Use**: Use "`Clean`" when you want to ensure that no old binaries or intermediate files are left over, which might cause issues with your build.

How to Clean a Project:

1. Right-click on the project in Solution Explorer.
2. Select "`Clean`" from the context menu.

Build

The "`Build`" operation compiles and links only those source files that have changed since the last build, along with any files that depend on them. It aims to produce an up-to-date executable, library, or other output files without recompiling everything.

- **Purpose**: To compile the latest changes in your code efficiently
- **When to Use**: Use "`Build`" when you have made incremental changes to your project and want to compile and link only those changes.

How to Build a Project:

1. Right-click on the project in Solution Explorer.
2. Select "`Build`" from the context menu.
3. Alternatively, you can use the "`Build`" option from the main menu or press *Ctrl* + *Shift* + B.

Rebuild

The "`Rebuild`" operation is a combination of the "`Clean`" and "`Build`" commands. It first performs a "`Clean`" operation to remove all the existing compiled and intermediate files, and then performs a "`Build`" operation to compile and link all the source files from scratch.

- **Purpose**: To ensure a completely fresh build of your project.
- **When to Use**: Use "`Rebuild`" when you suspect that the build output might be corrupted, when you have changed project-wide settings, or when you want to ensure that all code is recompiled from scratch.

How to Rebuild a Project:

1. Right-click on the project in Solution Explorer.
2. Select "`Rebuild`" from the context menu.
3. Alternatively, you can use the "`Rebuild`" option from the main menu.

Summary

- `Clean`: Removes all previously compiled binaries and intermediate files
- `Build`: Compiles and links only the files that have changed since the last build
- `Rebuild`: Performs a "`Clean`" operation followed by a "`Build`" operation, while recompiling everything from scratch

Using these commands appropriately helps maintain an efficient and effective development workflow and ensures that your project builds correctly and consistently.

Breakpoints

Breakpoints are crucial tools for debugging in Visual Studio, which allow you to pause the execution of your code at specific points. This enables you to inspect variables, check the call stack, and troubleshoot issues.

Setting Breakpoints in Source Code

You can place a breakpoint on any executable line of code. For instance, in the following C# snippet, breakpoint is set on line number 14 (*Figure* 4.1). Breakpoints cannot be placed on method signatures, namespace or class declarations, or variable declarations without assignments or getters/setters.

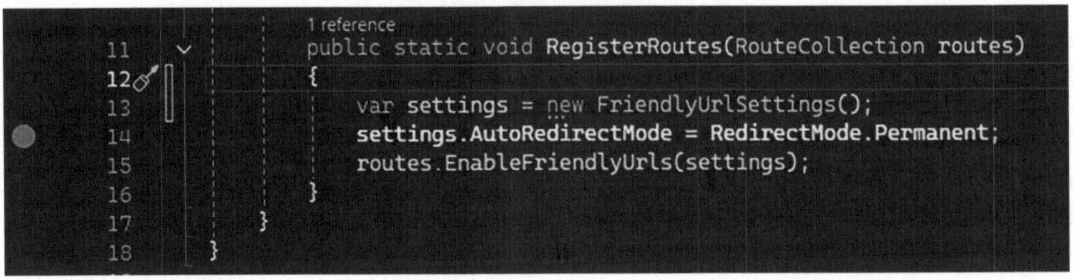

***Figure 4.1**: Breakpoint Set at Line Number 14 in Code Snippet*

How to Set a Breakpoint:

1. Click in the left margin next to a line of code.
2. Select the line and press **F9**.
3. Go to **Debug > Toggle Breakpoint**.
4. Right-click the line and select **Breakpoint > Insert breakpoint**.

Note : *Make sure Visual Studio has Debug mode selected (Figure 4.2)*

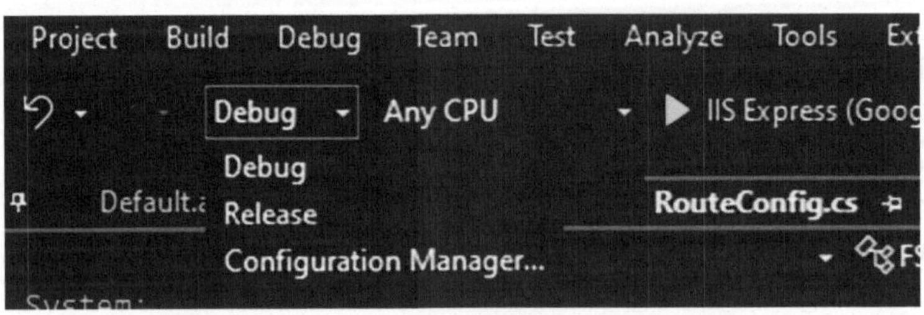

***Figure 4.2**: Showing "Debug" Mode Selected in VS*

In most languages like C#, breakpoints and current execution lines are highlighted. For C++, enable this by selecting **Tools** (or **Debug**) > **Options** > **Debugging** > **Highlight** entire source line for breakpoints and current statement (C++ only).

Breakpoint Execution

When you start debugging, execution halts at the breakpoint before executing the code on that line, indicated by a yellow arrow (*Figure* 4.3). You can then inspect variable values and the call stack.

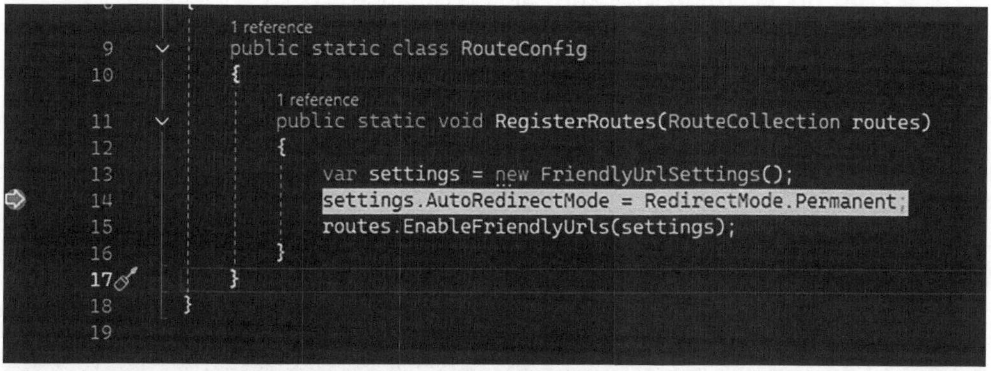

Figure 4.3: *Breakpoint Activated When Execution Reaches the Code*

General Instructions for Managing Breakpoints:

- Toggle breakpoints by clicking them, pressing F9, or using **`Debug > Toggle Breakpoint`**.
- To disable a breakpoint, right-click and select **`Disable breakpoint`**. Re-enable it by selecting **`Enable breakpoint`**.
- Right-click on a breakpoint to set conditions, add actions, labels, or export it (*Figure* 4.4).

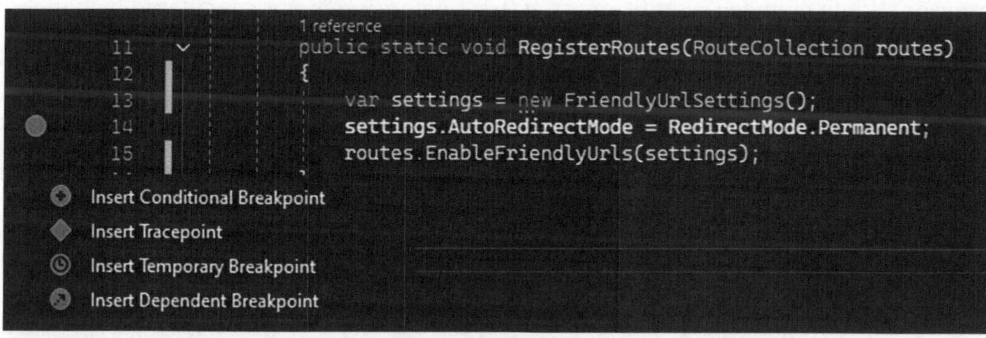

Figure 4.4: *Right Click Breakpoint to Display the Available Options*

Advanced Breakpoint Features (*Figure* 4.5**):**

- **Tracepoints:** A tracepoint logs a message to the Output window, without pausing code execution. Set a tracepoint via the Breakpoint Settings window.

- **Breakpoint Conditions:** Conditions control when and where a breakpoint activates. Right-click on a breakpoint and select **`Conditions`** to set a conditional expression, hit count, or filter.
- **Conditional Expressions:**

  Is true: Breaks when the expression is satisfied.
  When changed: Breaks when the value changes.

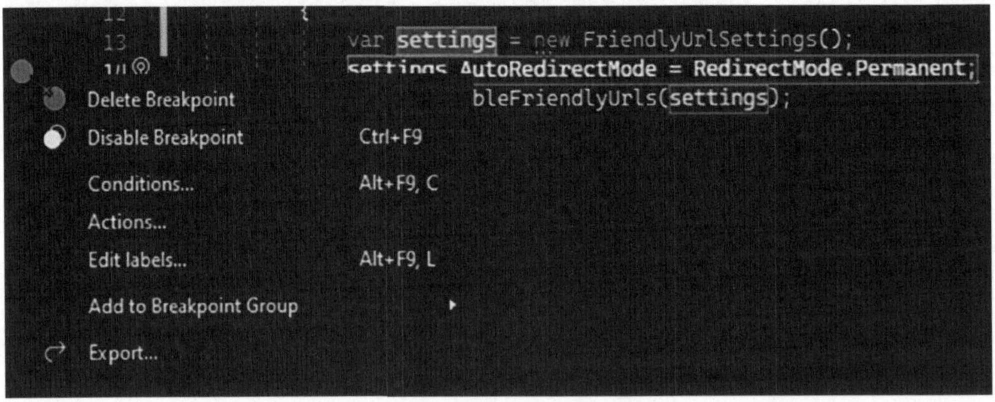

***Figure 4.5**: Right Click to View the Advanced Breakpoint Features*

Example: For a breakpoint to hit only when '**`testInt`**' is 4:

```
int testInt = 4;
```

If the syntax is invalid, a warning appears. If semantics are invalid, a warning shows when the breakpoint was first hit.

Note: *For "When changed" conditions, the first evaluation is not considered a change.*

- **Object IDs (C# and F#):** To track a specific object instance, create an Object ID in the Locals window. Use this ID in breakpoint conditions to observe specific object behavior.
- **Hit Count:** Set a breakpoint to activate after a specific number of iterations, useful for debugging loops (*Figure* 4.6).
- **Filters:** Limit breakpoints to specific devices, processes, or threads by setting filters (*Figure* 4.6).

***Figure 4.6**: Showing the Various Available Breakpoint Settings*

Specialized Breakpoints

- **Function Breakpoints**: Break execution when a specific function is called; useful for unknown locations or overloaded functions.

How to Set a Function Breakpoint:

a. Select **`Debug`** > **`New Breakpoint`** > **`Function Breakpoint`** (*Figure* 4.7).

b. Enter the function name and use fully qualified names or parameters to specify the function.

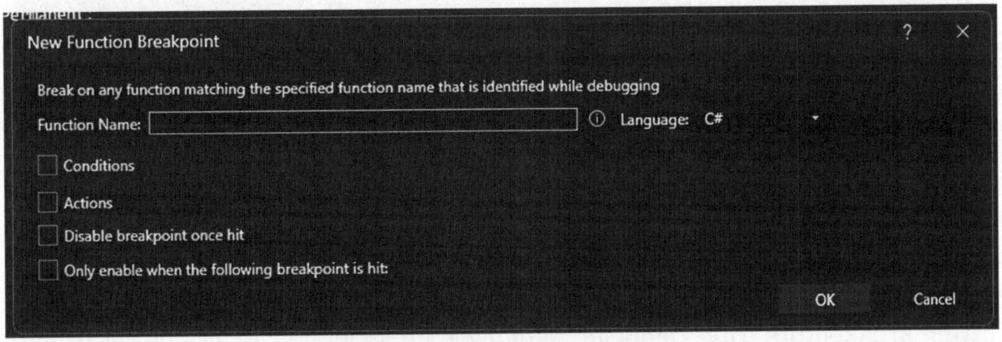

***Figure* 4.7**: *New Function Breakpoint*

- **Memory Address Breakpoints (C++ only):** Set a function breakpoint using an object's memory address.
- **Data Breakpoints:** For .NET Core 3.x or .NET 5+, break when a specific property changes. For C++, break when a value at a specific memory address changes.

  Note: *Data breakpoints depend on memory addresses, which change between debugging sessions. They also have hardware limits.*
- **Dependent Breakpoints:** Activate only if another breakpoint is hit first; useful for complex scenarios like multi-threaded applications.
- **Temporary Breakpoints:** These breakpoints pause execution once, and then remove themselves.

Managing Breakpoints: Use the Breakpoints window (*Figure* 4.8) to manage all breakpoints in your solution. This window allows you to search, sort, filter, enable/ disable, or delete breakpoints, and set conditions and actions. It can be accessed via Tool bar: **`Debug`** → **`Windows`** → **`Breakpoints`**.

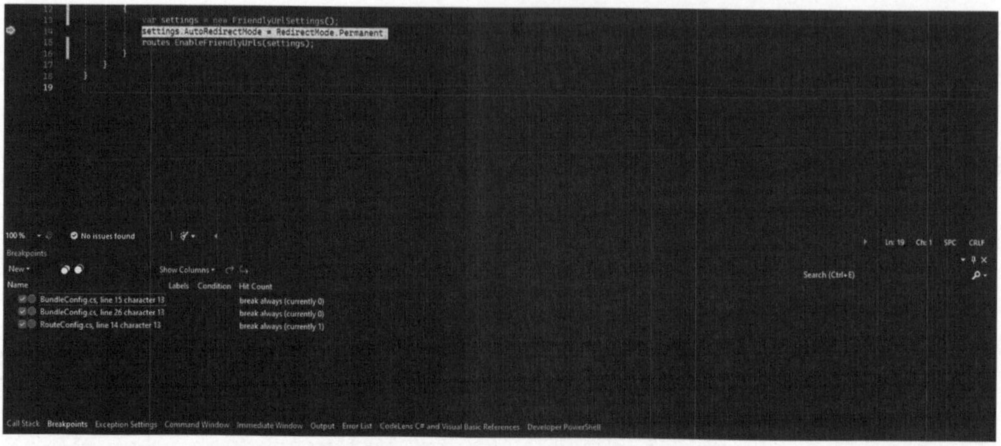

Figure 4.8: *Displaying the Breakpoints Window with All Breakpoints within the Project*

Exporting and Importing Breakpoints:

- Export single or multiple breakpoints to an XML file.
- Import breakpoints from an XML file to save or share your debugging setup.

Setting Breakpoints from Debugger Windows: Breakpoints can also be set from the Call Stack and Disassembly windows.

In the Call Stack Window: Right-click on the calling function and select **`Breakpoint`** > **`Insert Breakpoint`**.

In the Disassembly Window: Click in the left margin of an instruction or press F9.

Using these features effectively will enhance your debugging process, which makes it easier to find and fix issues in your code.

Step Execution or Navigation through Breakpoints

When a breakpoint is hit, you can then step through your code using various commands to understand its behavior, and identify any issues. The three primary stepping commands are **`Step Into`**, **`Step Over`**, and **`Step Out`**. Here is what each of these commands does (*Figure* 4.9):

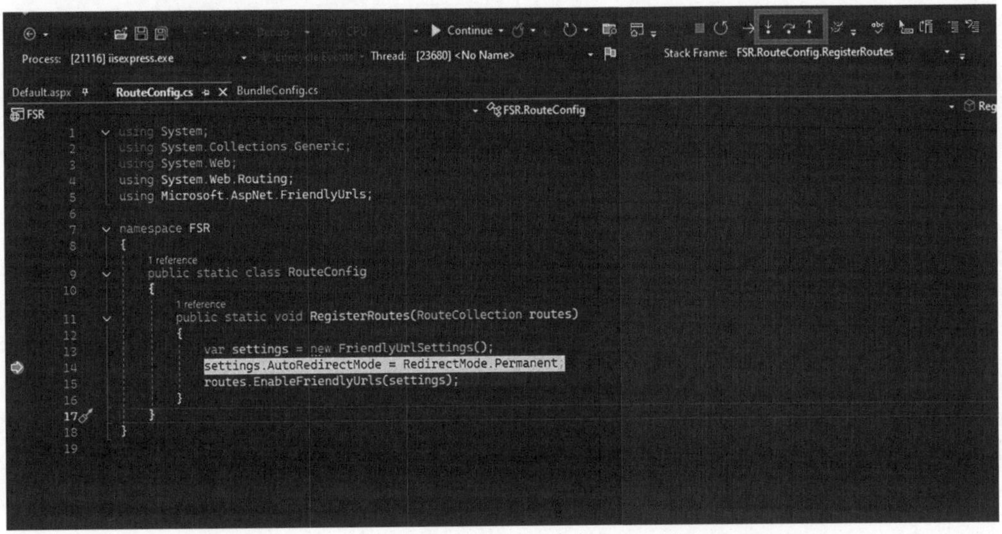

***Figure 4.9**: The Steeping Commands When a Breakpoint is Hit*

Step Into (F11): When you use the "**Step Into**" command, the debugger will move into the method or function that the current line of code is calling. If the line of code is a method call, the debugger will pause the execution at the first line inside that method. This is indicated via the code example here:

```
public void Main()
{
    int result = Add(5, 3); // If you Step Into here, it will go
into the Add method.
}

public int Add(int a, int b)
{
    return a + b; // The debugger will stop here.
}
```

Step Into is particularly useful when you want to debug the internal workings of a method or function call. It allows you to delve deeper into the code.

Step Over (F10): This command executes the current line of code and pauses at the next line in the same scope. If the current line contains a method call, the entire method will be executed, but the debugger will not enter into that method.

```
public void Main()
{
    int result = Add(5, 3); // If you Step Over here, the Add
method executes, but you stay in Main.
    Console.WriteLine(result); // The debugger will stop here
next.
```

```
}

public int Add(int a, int b)
{
    return a + b; // The debugger does not stop here if Step Over
is used.
}
```

Step Over is useful when you want to quickly move through your code without getting into the details of every method call. It maintains a higher-level view of the execution flow.

Step Out (*Shift* + F11): The **`Step Out`** command continues execution until the current method or function has finished running, and then pauses execution at the line where the method was called. It is indicated in the following example:

```
public void Main()
{
    int result = Add(5, 3); // If you Step Into this method and
then Step Out, the debugger will return here.
    Console.WriteLine(result); // The debugger will stop here
after Step Out.
}

public int Add(int a, int b)
{
    return a + b; // If you Step Out here, the debugger will jump
back to where Add was called.
}
```

`Step Out` is useful when you have stepped into a method and realize that you do not need to examine the rest of it. It allows you to return to the calling method without finishing the step-by-step execution of the current method.

Here are the differences between these commands:

1. **`Step Into`**: Enter into the method being called to inspect it line by line.
2. **`Step Over`**: Execute the entire line of code, including any method calls, and move to the next line in the current scope.
3. **`Step Out`**: Complete execution of the current method and return to the line where the method was originally called.

Therefore, by understanding and using these commands effectively, you can navigate through your code more efficiently, and focus on the areas that matter most during debugging.

Conditional Breakpoints

Conditional breakpoints are a powerful debugging feature in Visual Studio 2022 that allows developers to pause program execution only when certain conditions are met. Unlike standard breakpoints which halt the program every time the line of code is executed, conditional breakpoints give you the flexibility to specify conditions, such as variable values, expressions, or even hit counts, under which the breakpoint should trigger. This makes them particularly useful in complex debugging scenarios where you only want to investigate specific cases or data states.

Advantages of Conditional Breakpoints:

- **Focused Debugging:** Conditional breakpoints help in narrowing down issues by allowing the code to run normally until a specific condition is met, while reducing the noise and making it easier to pinpoint the problem.
- **Time Efficiency:** By avoiding unnecessary breaks in execution, you save time, particularly in large codebases or loops where the same line of code may be executed multiple times.
- **Simplified Troubleshooting:** They simplify the process of reproducing and isolating bugs that occur under specific conditions, which makes it easier to track down elusive issues.
- **Customizable Conditions:** You can set a wide range of conditions, from simple variable checks to complex expressions, which offers flexibility in how and when the breakpoint is triggered.

When to Use Conditional Breakpoints:

Conditional breakpoints are particularly useful in the following scenarios:

- **Debugging Loops:** When you want to inspect the state of the application only after a loop has iterated a certain number of times or when a specific condition within the loop is true.
- **Investigating Complex Conditions:** When you are dealing with bugs that manifest only under certain conditions, such as specific input values, states, or configurations.
- **Large Codebases:** In larger projects where stepping through every instance of a breakpoint would be time-consuming, conditional breakpoints help focus on the relevant instances.
- **Intermittent Issues:** When a bug does not occur consistently, using a conditional breakpoint to trigger only under specific circumstances can make it easier to identify the root cause.

How to Create and Use Conditional Breakpoints: A Step-by-Step Guide

1. **Set a Standard Breakpoint:** Click in the margin to the left of the code line where you want to place the breakpoint, or press F9 while the cursor is on the desired line (*Figure* 4.10).
2. **Open the Breakpoint Settings:** Right-click on the red breakpoint icon in the margin and select Conditions from the context menu. This will open the Breakpoint Settings window.
3. **Define the Condition:** In the Condition section, you can enter an expression that will be evaluated each time the breakpoint is reached. For example, '`x > 10`' or '`myList.Count == 5`'. The breakpoint will only be triggered when this condition is true.

   You can also choose whether the condition is based on an expression or a hit count (that is, the number of times the breakpoint has been hit before it triggers).

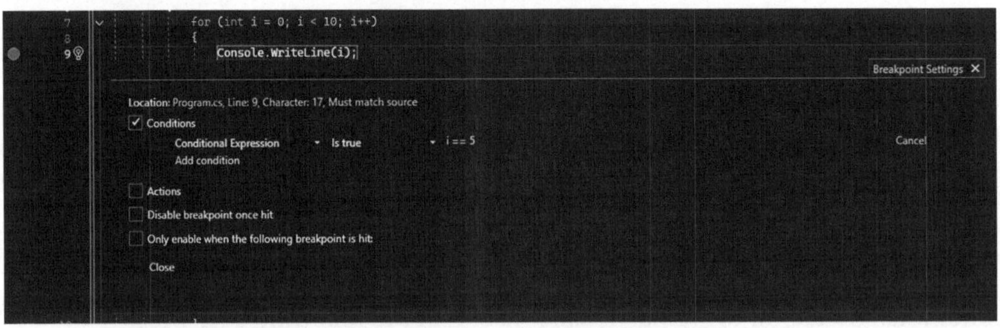

***Figure 4.10**: Setting a Conditional Breakpoint*

4. **Configure Additional Settings (Optional):** You can also set actions such as logging a message to the output window when the condition is met, or even continue execution automatically after the action is performed.
5. **Resume Execution:** Start or resume debugging by pressing F5. The code will execute normally until the specified condition is met, at which point the debugger will pause execution.
6. **Modify or Remove Conditions:** You can revisit the Breakpoint Settings at any time to modify or remove the condition, which gives you full control over your debugging session.
7. **Importance of Conditional Breakpoints in Debugging:** From a debugging perspective, conditional breakpoints are invaluable for reducing the complexity of debugging sessions. They allow you to bypass irrelevant iterations or cases and allow you to focus on the exact scenarios where things go wrong. This

precision in debugging not only speeds up the process but also improves the accuracy with which you can diagnose and fix issues.

8. **How Developers Can Benefit from Using Conditional Breakpoints:** For developers, the use of conditional breakpoints translates into more efficient and effective debugging. They can avoid the tedium of stepping through code that is not relevant to the issue at hand, which allows them to concentrate on the specific conditions under which a problem occurs. This focused approach reduces frustration, speeds up the debugging process, and ultimately leads to quicker resolutions and more robust software. By leveraging conditional breakpoints, developers can gain deeper insights into their code's behavior, which makes them more adept at identifying and solving complex issues.

Function Breakpoints

Function breakpoints are a debugging feature in Visual Studio 2022 that allow developers to pause the execution of their application whenever a specific function is called, regardless of where it is invoked in the code. Unlike traditional line breakpoints, which are set at a specific line in the code, function breakpoints are set on a function itself. This makes them particularly useful when you need to monitor function calls that occur across various parts of your application or when the function's implementation is spread across multiple files.

Advantages of Function Breakpoints:

- **Global Monitoring:** Function breakpoints enable you to monitor all invocations of a function, irrespective of where it is called in the codebase. This is particularly useful in large projects where the same function might be called from multiple locations.
- **No Need to Navigate Code:** You do not need to locate the exact line of code where the function is called. Simply setting a breakpoint on the function allows you to catch every instance of its invocation.
- **Focus on Specific Functionality:** When debugging, you can concentrate on a particular function without worrying about the surrounding code, which makes it easier to isolate and troubleshoot issues.
- **Cross-File Debugging:** For functions that are used in multiple files or modules, a function breakpoint saves time and effort by allowing you to set the breakpoint once and apply it across all relevant code files.

When to Use Function Breakpoints?

Function breakpoints are particularly beneficial in the following scenarios:

- **Tracking Function Invocations:** When you need to track every instance of a function being called, particularly in large or complex projects where the function might be invoked from various locations.

- **Debugging Library or API Functions:** When working with libraries or APIs, function breakpoints allow you to monitor when certain library or API functions are executed and help you understand how they interact with your code.
- **Investigating Unintended Behavior:** If a function is behaving unexpectedly, setting a function breakpoint can help you identify when and how it is being called, providing clues about the source of the problem.
- **Refactoring Code:** During refactoring, when functions are moved, renamed, or have their logic altered, function breakpoints ensure that their usage across the codebase continues to function as expected.

How to Create and Use Function Breakpoints: A Step-by-Step Guide

1. **Open the Breakpoints Window:** Go to **`Debug`** > **`Windows`** > **`Breakpoints`** or press *Ctrl* + *Alt* + B to open the Breakpoints window.
2. **Add a New Function Breakpoint:** Click on the New button (or right-click within the Breakpoints window and select **`New Breakpoint`** > **`Function Breakpoint`**), as shown in *Figure* 4.11.

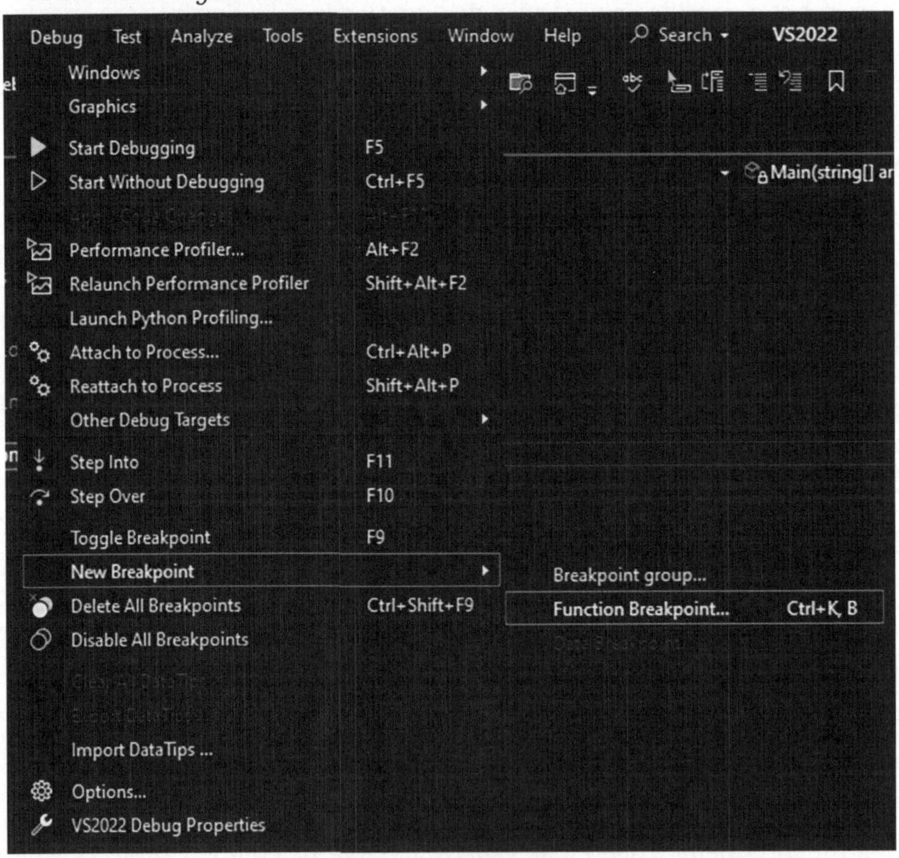

Figure 4.11: *Showing Function Breakpoint Option in Menu Bar*

A dialog box (*Figure* 4.12) will appear where you can enter the name of the function. You can enter the function name directly (for example, **`MyFunction`**), or specify the full namespace (for example, **`MyNamespace.MyClass.MyFunction`**).

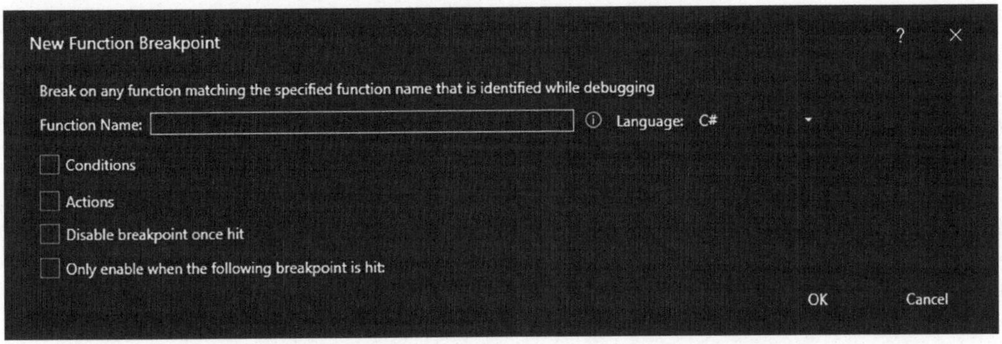

***Figure 4.12**: Displaying New Function Breakpoint Dialog Box*

3. **Set Additional Conditions (Optional):**
    - Just like with conditional breakpoints, you can add conditions to your function breakpoint. For example, you can specify that the breakpoint should only be triggered if a certain argument to the function is a particular value.
    - You can also specify hit counts or log messages, which can be particularly useful if the function is called frequently.
4. **Start Debugging:** Start or resume debugging by pressing F5. The debugger will pause execution whenever the specified function is called, which will allow you to inspect the current state of the application.
5. **Modify or Remove the Breakpoint:** You can manage your function breakpoints from the Breakpoints window. Right-click on the breakpoint to edit, enable/disable, or remove it as needed.

Importance of Function Breakpoints in Debugging

Function breakpoints play a critical role in debugging by allowing developers to monitor the execution of specific functions across an entire application. This is especially important in scenarios where a function's behavior is inconsistent or where it is invoked from multiple parts of the code. By providing a centralized way to capture all calls to a function, function breakpoints simplify the process of identifying the root cause of bugs, which makes debugging more efficient and focused.

How Developers Can Benefit from Using Function Breakpoints

Function breakpoints offer developers a streamlined and effective way to track the behavior of specific functions, which is especially useful in complex or large-scale projects. By enabling a breakpoint on a function, developers can quickly identify when and how a function is being called, which can significantly reduce the time spent on debugging. This level of control over function execution not only aids in identifying bugs but also in ensuring that changes to code, such as during refactoring, do not introduce new issues. Overall, function breakpoints are a powerful tool that can enhance the debugging process, which leads to faster development cycles and more reliable software.

Data Breakpoints

Data breakpoints are a powerful debugging feature in Visual Studio 2022 that allow developers to pause the execution of an application when the value of a specific variable or memory location changes. Unlike traditional line breakpoints, which halt execution at a particular line of code, data breakpoints monitor changes to data regardless of where those changes occur in the codebase. This makes them incredibly useful for tracking down hard-to-find bugs that result from unexpected or unintended modifications to critical variables.

Data breakpoints are particularly effective when debugging complex applications where the source of a data change is not immediately apparent. They work by monitoring the memory address of a variable and triggering a breakpoint whenever the content at that address is altered. This enables developers to pinpoint exactly where and when a variable's value changes, while facilitating a more efficient and targeted debugging process.

Advantages of Data Breakpoints

- **Precise Tracking of Data Changes:** Data breakpoints provide exact information about when and where a variable's value changes, while eliminating the need to manually search through code to find modifications.
- **Efficient Debugging:** They reduce debugging time by automatically halting execution upon data change, which allows developers to inspect the program state immediately and identify issues quickly.
- **Monitoring Across the Entire Codebase:** Data breakpoints monitor changes to specific memory locations, regardless of the scope or module, which makes them ideal for large and complex projects.
- **Minimal Intrusion:** Unlike traditional breakpoints that may require multiple

placements throughout the code, a single data breakpoint can monitor all changes, which results in a less cluttered and more manageable debugging session.

- **Dynamic Analysis:** They are particularly useful for observing how variables interact and change during runtime, which provides insights that static code analysis cannot offer.
- **Support for Multithreaded Applications:** Data breakpoints are effective in multithreaded environments, which helps developers to identify race conditions and synchronization issues by tracking unintended data modifications across threads.

When to Use Data Breakpoints

- **Tracking Unexpected Value Changes:** When a variable is changing value unexpectedly and the location of the change is unknown, data breakpoints help identify the exact point of modification.
- **Debugging Complex or Legacy Code:** In large, unfamiliar, or legacy codebases where tracing through all possible code paths is impractical, data breakpoints simplify the process of locating where data alterations occur.
- **Identifying Side Effects:** To detect unintended side effects caused by function calls or operations that modify data they should not, data breakpoints can be employed to monitor and catch these changes.
- **Multithreaded Debugging:** When dealing with concurrency issues where multiple threads may be altering the same data, data breakpoints assist in identifying and resolving synchronization problems.
- **Monitoring External Library Interactions:** When using external libraries or APIs that modify your application's data, data breakpoints help ensure that these interactions are occurring as expected.
- **Validating Assumptions During Refactoring:** While refactoring code, data breakpoints can be used to verify that data modifications occur only where intended, while ensuring the integrity of the application logic.

How to Create and Use Data Breakpoints: A Step-by-Step Guide

Note: *Data breakpoints are only available for native code debugging (for example, C/C++). They are not supported for managed code (for example, C#, VB.NET). However, starting from Visual Studio 2019, there is limited support for managed data breakpoints when debugging .NET Core applications.*

Step 1: Start Debugging the Application.

a. Open your project in Visual Studio 2022.

b. Start debugging by pressing F5 or selecting **`Debug`** > **`Start Debugging`** from the menu.

c. Ensure that you are debugging in a mode that supports data breakpoints (native code).

Step 2: Run to a Point Where the Variable is in Scope.

a. Navigate your application to a point where the variable you want to monitor is in scope and has been initialized.

b. You can use traditional breakpoints (F9) to pause execution at a specific line where the variable is accessible.

Step 3: Set the Data Breakpoint.

a. Once execution is paused and the variable is in scope, locate the variable in the Watch, Autos, Locals, or QuickWatch window.

b. Right-click on the variable and select Break When Value Changes from the context menu.

Alternatively:

In the Command Window (accessible via `**View** > **Other Windows** > **Command Window**`), you can use the **`DataBreak`** command by typing:

- DataBreak **`<expression>`**
- Replace **`<expression>`** with the variable you want to monitor.

Step 4: Configure Data Breakpoint Settings (Optional)

a. Visual Studio allows you to specify conditions under which the data breakpoint should trigger.

b. You can configure these settings in the Breakpoints window (*Ctrl*+*Alt*+B).

c. Right-click on your data breakpoint and select **`Conditions`** to add expressions that control when the breakpoint activates.

Step 5: Resume Execution

a. Continue running your application by pressing F5.

b. The debugger will automatically pause execution when the value of the monitored variable changes.

Step 6: Inspect and Analyze

a. Once execution is halted, inspect the call stack, variables, and program state to understand the context of the change.

b. Use this information to identify and fix any issues related to the unexpected data modification.

Step 7: Manage Data Breakpoints

a. Data breakpoints can be enabled, disabled, or deleted from the Breakpoints window.

b. Keep in mind that most systems limit the number of active data breakpoints (often to 4), so manage them accordingly.

c. To remove a data breakpoint, right-click on it in the **`Breakpoints`** window and select **`Delete`**.

Additional Considerations

- **Limitations:**
  - Data breakpoints are only valid while the application is running. If you stop debugging, you will need to recreate them in the next session.
  - They cannot be set on variables that change location in memory, such as those that are moved by the garbage collector in managed environments.
- **Performance Impact:** Monitoring data changes can have a performance overhead. Use data breakpoints judiciously to minimize impact on debugging performance.

Importance of Data Breakpoints in Debugging

From a debugging perspective, data breakpoints are essential tools for diagnosing and resolving issues related to unintended data modifications. They provide a proactive approach to error detection by automatically monitoring critical variables and halting the execution precisely during moments when anomalies occur.

This capability is particularly valuable in scenarios where traditional debugging techniques fall short, such as:

- **Elusive Bugs**: Catching sporadic or non-deterministic bugs that are difficult to reproduce and trace
- **Security**: Detecting unauthorized or unexpected changes to sensitive data, which could indicate security vulnerabilities or breaches
- **Integrity Assurance**: Ensuring data consistency throughout application

execution, which is crucial for applications that rely heavily on accurate and stable data states

Thus, by offering real-time insights into how and when data changes, data breakpoints enable developers to maintain high code quality and reliability, which ultimately leads to more robust and secure software applications.

How Developers Can Benefit from Using Data Breakpoints

- **Accelerated Debugging Process:** Developers can quickly locate and address issues without manually sifting through extensive code, while significantly reducing the time spent on debugging.
- **Enhanced Code Understanding:** Observing when and how data changes provide deeper insights into code behavior and execution flow, which improves overall understanding and facilitates better code maintenance.
- **Improved Code Quality:** Early detection and resolution of data-related bugs contribute to more stable and reliable software, which enhances user experience and reduces post-deployment issues.
- **Effective Troubleshooting of Legacy Systems:** Inherited or poorly documented codebases become easier to manage and debug, as data breakpoints help uncover hidden dependencies and unintended data manipulations.
- **Resource Optimization:** By efficiently identifying and fixing bugs, developers can allocate more time and resources to feature development and optimization rather than prolonged debugging sessions.
- **Facilitation of Concurrent and Parallel Programming:** In multi-threaded and parallel processing environments, data breakpoints aid in identifying and resolving complex synchronization and data access issues.

Data breakpoints in Visual Studio 2022 are indispensable tools that empower developers to monitor and control data flow within their applications effectively. By providing precise and automated tracking of variable changes, they streamline the debugging process, enhance code reliability, and contribute significantly to the development of high-quality software solutions. Mastery of data breakpoints equips developers with advanced capabilities to tackle some of the most challenging debugging scenarios with confidence and efficiency.

Temporary Breakpoints

Visual Studio 2022 supports temporary breakpoints, also known as "*one-time*" breakpoints, are a special type of breakpoint in Visual Studio 2022 that automatically remove themselves once they are hit. These breakpoints are designed for scenarios where you only need to pause the execution of your application at a specific line of code just once, while allowing you to inspect the current state without leaving a lingering breakpoint that needs to be manually cleared afterward. This feature is particularly useful for quick, ad-hoc debugging tasks where you want to check something in the code without affecting subsequent runs.

Advantages of Temporary Breakpoints

- **Simplified Debugging**: Temporary breakpoints reduce the clutter of lingering breakpoints in your code, while keeping the debugging environment clean and focused.
- **Time Efficiency**: They save time by automatically removing themselves after being hit, which eliminates the need for manual breakpoint management and cleanup.
- **Ad-Hoc Inspection**: Ideal for quick checks and verifications during debugging, temporary breakpoints allow you to pause the execution, inspect the state, and then continue without leaving any unnecessary breakpoints.
- **Minimal Disruption**: They ensure that your debugging session is minimally invasive, as they do not interrupt the flow of code execution more than necessary.
- **Reduced Risk of Forgetting**: Since temporary breakpoints remove themselves after execution, there is no risk of accidentally leaving breakpoints in the code, which can cause unexpected pauses in future debugging sessions.

When to Use Temporary Breakpoints:

Temporary breakpoints are particularly useful in the following scenarios:

- **Quick Inspections**: When you want to check the state of the application at a specific point in the code, without needing to stop at that point repeatedly.
- **One-Time Debugging Needs**: When you are debugging a specific issue, and know that you only need to break at a certain line of code once to understand the problem.
- **Code Exploration**: When exploring new or unfamiliar code, and you want to pause execution at a particular point to understand what is happening without cluttering the code with multiple breakpoints.
- **Avoiding Manual Cleanup**: When you want to ensure that breakpoints do not remain in the code after a debugging session and cause confusion or issues during subsequent runs.

How to Create and Use Temporary Breakpoints: A Step-by-Step Guide

Step 1: Start Debugging the Application.

a. Open your project in Visual Studio 2022.

b. Begin debugging by pressing F5 or by selecting **`Debug`** > **`Start Debugging`**.

Step 2: Set a Temporary Breakpoint.

a. Navigate to the line of code where you want to set the temporary breakpoint.

b. Hold down the Ctrl key and then click in the margin next to the line of code where you want the breakpoint.

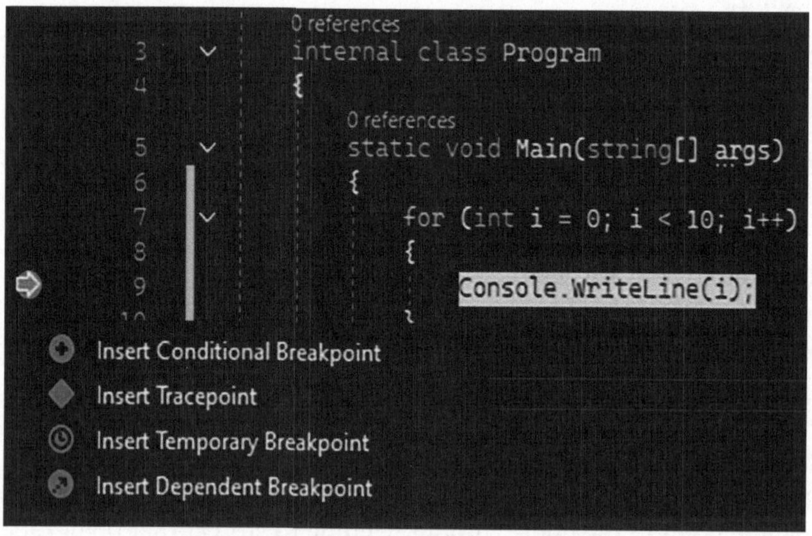

***Figure 4.13**: Setting Temporary Breakpoint*

Alternatively: Right-click on the line of code, select **`Breakpoint`** > **`Insert Temporary Breakpoint`** from the context menu.

Step 3: Run to the Temporary Breakpoint

Continue running the application. When the code execution reaches the temporary breakpoint, the debugger will pause, which allows you to inspect the state of the application at that moment.

Step 4: Inspect and Resume Execution

a. After the temporary breakpoint is hit, examine the values of variables, the call stack, and any other relevant information to understand the state of the application.

b. Resume execution by pressing F5. The temporary breakpoint will automatically be removed, and the application will continue running without further interruption.

Step 5: Verify Breakpoint Removal

After the application resumes, the temporary breakpoint should no longer exist in the code. You can verify this by checking the line where it was set; there should be no breakpoint indicator.

Importance of Temporary Breakpoints in Debugging

From a debugging perspective, temporary breakpoints are invaluable for maintaining a streamlined and efficient debugging process. They allow developers to pause execution at a critical point just once, enabling quick inspections without the risk of cluttering the code with multiple, forgotten breakpoints. This capability is especially useful in scenarios where you need to validate a hypothesis or inspect the state of an application at a specific point without leaving any trace after the inspection.

Temporary breakpoints also help in keeping the debugging environment clean, ensuring that the focus remains on the code itself rather than on managing breakpoints. By reducing the need for manual cleanup, they minimize the risk of disrupting subsequent debugging sessions, thus leading to a smoother and more productive workflow.

Breakpoint Groups

Breakpoint Groups in Visual Studio 2022 allow developers to organize multiple breakpoints into logical collections or groups for more effective management during debugging sessions. By grouping related breakpoints together, you can easily enable, disable, or configure them as a set rather than individually. This feature is particularly useful in complex debugging scenarios where multiple breakpoints are needed across different files or modules, thereby allowing you to manage them collectively based on specific debugging needs or phases.

Advantages of Breakpoint Groups

- Organized Debugging: Breakpoint groups help in organizing your breakpoints into meaningful collections, thereby making it easier to manage large numbers of breakpoints in complex projects.
- **Efficient Management**: Instead of toggling individual breakpoints on or off, you can control an entire group, which saves time and reduces the risk of missing a breakpoint that should be active.

- **Improved Focus**: By grouping breakpoints relevant to specific debugging tasks or scenarios, you can focus on a particular aspect of the code, which makes debugging more efficient and targeted.
- **Scalability**: In larger projects with many breakpoints, grouping them helps scale the debugging process by allowing you to handle breakpoints in bulk, rather than dealing with each one individually.
- **Customization**: Breakpoint groups allow for customization of debugging sessions, where different groups can be tailored to different testing scenarios or stages of development.

When to Use Breakpoint Groups

- **Debugging Complex Applications**: When working on complex applications with multiple modules, functions, or classes, breakpoint groups help in managing the breakpoints related to specific areas of the codebase.
- **Testing Different Scenarios**: If you need to test different scenarios or cases that require different sets of breakpoints, grouping them allows you to easily switch between these scenarios.
- **Phased Debugging**: When debugging in phases, such as initial testing, bug fixing, and final verification, you can group breakpoints by phase and enable or disable them as needed.
- **Collaborative Debugging**: In team environments, breakpoint groups allow different team members to organize their debugging tasks without interfering with each other's breakpoints.

How to Create and Use Breakpoint Groups: A Step-by-Step Guide

Step 1: Open the Breakpoints Window.

a. Open your project in Visual Studio 2022.

b. Go to `Debug` > `Windows` > `Breakpoints` or press *Ctrl* + *Alt* + B to open the Breakpoints window where all breakpoints are listed.

Step 2: Create a New Breakpoint Group.

a. In the `Breakpoints` window, right-click on any existing breakpoint, and select `Add to Group`.

b. If no groups exist, you can create a new group by selecting `New Group`, then providing a name for this group.

c. You can also create a group directly from the Breakpoints Window by clicking the `New` button and selecting `Breakpoint Group`.

Step 3: Assign Breakpoints to the Group.

a. After creating a group, you can add breakpoints to it by right-clicking on each breakpoint and selecting Add to Group followed by the name of the group.

b. You can add multiple breakpoints to the same group and organize them based on your debugging needs.

Step 4: Manage Breakpoint Groups.

a. In the Breakpoints window, you will see your groups listed with their associated breakpoints.

b. You can enable or disable an entire group by right-clicking on the group name and selecting Enable Group or Disable Group.

c. To remove a breakpoint from a group, right-click on the breakpoint and choose Remove from Group.

Step 5: Switch Between Groups.

If you have multiple groups, you can easily switch between them by enabling one group while disabling others. This allows you to focus on specific sets of breakpoints depending on the current debugging task.

Step 6: Delete a Breakpoint Group.

To delete a group, right-click on the group name in the Breakpoints window and select Delete Group. Deleting a group will not delete the breakpoints themselves, but it will remove the group organization.

Importance of Breakpoint Groups in Debugging

From a debugging perspective, breakpoint groups are crucial for managing complex projects with numerous breakpoints. They provide a structured way to organize breakpoints, allowing developers to focus on specific debugging tasks without the distraction of unrelated breakpoints. By enabling or disabling groups of breakpoints with a single action, developers can streamline their debugging process, making it more efficient and less prone to errors.

Breakpoint groups also enhance collaboration in team settings by enabling different developers to manage their own sets of breakpoints without affecting others. This organization is particularly beneficial in larger projects or when working on different aspects of the codebase concurrently.

How Developers Can Benefit from Using Breakpoint Groups

- **Increased Productivity**: By reducing the time spent managing individual breakpoints, developers can focus more on debugging and less on setup, which will boost productivity.
- **Enhanced Debugging Workflow**: Grouping breakpoints based on tasks or phases allows developers to follow a more structured and systematic debugging workflow, which reduces the likelihood of missing critical breakpoints.
- **Better Code Analysis**: With organized breakpoints, developers can analyze the code more effectively, as they can easily switch between different sets of breakpoints to investigate specific issues.
- **Simplified Debugging Management**: Managing large numbers of breakpoints becomes simpler with groups, as developers can quickly enable, disable, or modify sets of breakpoints in bulk.
- **Improved Team Collaboration**: In a team environment, breakpoint groups allow for better collaboration by ensuring that each developer can organize their debugging process without interfering with others, which makes it easier to work on different parts of the code simultaneously.

Breakpoint groups in Visual Studio 2022 are an essential feature for developers working on complex or large-scale projects. By allowing breakpoints to be organized into logical collections, developers can manage their debugging sessions more effectively, which will improve both productivity and code quality. Whether you are working individually or as part of a team, mastering the use of breakpoint groups can significantly enhance your ability to debug complex applications efficiently.

Watch Window in Visual Studio 2022

Watch Window in Visual Studio 2022 is a powerful debugging tool that allows developers to monitor and evaluate the values of variables and expressions during a debugging session. This feature provides an interactive way to inspect the state of your application, which will allow you to track specific variables, expressions, or even complex data structures over time as the program executes. The Watch Window is particularly useful for debugging, as it allows you to observe how values change in real-time and to identify unexpected behavior in your code.

Advantages of the Watch Window

- **Real-Time Monitoring**: The Watch Window provides real-time updates to the values of variables and expressions, which allows developers to observe changes as they step through their code.

- **Enhanced Debugging Insight**: By allowing you to inspect and evaluate expressions, the Watch Window helps you gain deeper insights into how your code is behaving during execution, while facilitating more effective troubleshooting.
- **Customization and Flexibility**: You can add, remove, and modify the expressions in the Watch Window at any time during the debugging session, which provides a flexible and customizable debugging experience.
- **Support for Complex Data Structures**: The Watch Window supports complex data types, including objects, arrays, and collections, which allows you to drill down into nested structures and inspect individual elements.
- **Multiple Watch Windows**: Visual Studio allows you to use multiple Watch Windows simultaneously (Watch 1, Watch 2, and so on), which will enable you to organize and group variables or expressions based on different debugging tasks or scenarios.

When to Use the Watch Window

- **Tracking Variable Changes**: When you need to monitor the value of specific variables as your code executes to identify when and why they change
- **Evaluating Expressions**: When you want to evaluate the result of expressions or functions in real-time, especially if you suspect that a particular calculation or operation is not producing the expected result.
- **Inspecting Data Structures**: When dealing with complex data structures such as objects, arrays, or collections, and you need to inspect individual elements or properties.
- **Debugging Logical Errors**: When you suspect that logical errors in your code are causing incorrect behavior, the Watch Window can help you verify the logic by observing how variables and expressions behave during execution.
- **Testing Hypotheses**: When you want to test different scenarios by manually changing variable values or by evaluating different expressions to see how they affect the program's behavior.

How to Create and Use the Watch Window: A Step-by-Step Guide

Step 1: Start Debugging the Application.

a. Open your project in Visual Studio 2022.

b. Begin a debugging session by pressing F5 or selecting `Debug` > `Start Debugging`.

Step 2: Open the Watch Window.

The Watch Window can be accessed by selecting `Debug` > `Windows` > `Watch` > `Watch 1` from the menu, or by pressing *Ctrl* + *Alt* + W, then press W to open

`Watch 1`. Additional Watch Windows (`Watch 2`, `Watch 3`, `Watch 4`) can be accessed similarly by pressing **2**, **3**, or **4** after *Ctrl* + *Alt* + W.

Step 3: Add Variables or Expressions to the Watch Window.

To add a variable or expression to the Watch Window:

a. Type the name of the variable or the expression directly into a new row in the Watch Window and press *Enter*.

b. Alternatively, highlight a variable or expression in your code, right-click, and select Add Watch from the context menu.

Step 4: Monitor Values During Debugging.

a. As you step through your code using F10 (`Step Over`) or F11 (`Step Into`), the `Watch Window` will update the values of the variables and expressions you have added in real-time.

b. You can expand complex data types like objects or arrays to inspect individual members or elements.

Step 5: Modify Values and Expressions.

a. You can modify the values of variables directly in the `Watch Window` by clicking on the value field and typing a new value. This is useful for testing how changes to variables affect program execution.

b. You can also edit the expressions in the Watch Window to evaluate different scenarios or hypotheses.

Step 6: Remove or Organize Watch Items.

a. To remove an item from the `Watch Window`, right-click on it, and select `Delete`.

b. You can reorder items by dragging them up or down in the list, which will help you organize the Watch Window according to your needs.

Step 7: Continue or Restart Debugging.

a. Continue stepping through your code or resume execution by pressing F5. The Watch Window will remain active and continue updating values as the program runs.

b. If you restart the debugging session, the items in the Watch Window will persist, which will allow you to pick up where you left off.

Importance of the Watch Window in Debugging

From a debugging perspective, the Watch Window is an essential tool for gaining visibility into the internal state of your application. It allows you to monitor variables and expressions dynamically, providing immediate feedback on how changes in the code impact the program's execution. This real-time monitoring is crucial for identifying bugs, understanding the flow of data, and verifying the correctness of algorithms and logic within the code.

The ability to evaluate expressions and modify variable values on the fly also empowers developers to experiment with different scenarios, test assumptions, and quickly isolate the root cause of issues. This makes the Watch Window an indispensable component of a developer's debugging toolkit, especially when working with complex or unfamiliar codebases.

How Developers Can Benefit from Using the Watch Window

- **Improved Debugging Accuracy:** By monitoring variable values and expressions in real-time, developers can catch errors as they occur, leading to more accurate and efficient debugging sessions.
- **Enhanced Understanding of Code:** The Watch Window provides insights into how the code operates at a detailed level, which helps developers understand the flow of data and the behavior of functions and expressions.
- **Quick Problem Isolation:** Developers can quickly isolate and identify problematic areas in the code by observing where and when values change unexpectedly, thus facilitating faster bug resolution.
- **Increased Productivity:** The ability to track multiple variables and expressions simultaneously in multiple Watch Windows allows developers to manage complex debugging scenarios more effectively, while improving overall productivity.
- **Flexible Debugging:** The Watch Window's flexibility in adding, modifying, and evaluating expressions makes it a versatile tool that can adapt to various debugging needs, from simple checks to complex investigations.

Summary

The Watch Window in Visual Studio 2022 is a critical feature for any developer aiming to perform thorough and efficient debugging. By offering real-time monitoring of variables and expressions, it provides the insights necessary to understand and resolve issues in your code quickly. Mastering the use of the Watch Window can significantly enhance your debugging capabilities and lead to faster development cycles, higher code quality, and more reliable software.

Autos and Locals Windows in Visual Studio 2022

In Visual Studio 2022, the Autos and Locals windows are essential debugging tools that automatically display variables and their values within the current scope of execution. These windows provide a quick and convenient way to inspect the state of your application as it runs, while showing the variables that are relevant to the current line of execution (Autos) or all variables that are local to the current method (Locals). These windows are especially useful in C# development, where understanding the flow of data and variable states is crucial for debugging and optimizing code.

- **Autos Window:** Displays variables that are used on the current line of code and the preceding line. It is particularly useful for seeing the variables that are most likely to be affected by the current operation.
- **Locals Window:** Displays all local variables that are within the current method's scope. This includes parameters passed to the method, variables declared within the method, and any objects or data structures currently in scope.

Advantages of the Autos and Locals Windows

- **Automatic Contextual Display**: Both the Autos and Locals windows automatically populate with relevant variables, which save your time and effort by providing immediate access to the data that is most pertinent to the current execution context.
- **Real-Time Updates**: These windows update in real-time as you step through your code, while providing instant feedback on how variable values change during execution.
- **Enhanced Debugging Focus**: The Autos window helps you focus on variables directly related to the code you are currently debugging, while the Locals window provides a broader view of all variables in the current scope, which allows for a comprehensive understanding of the current state.
- **Ease of Use**: Both windows are user-friendly, requiring no configuration or setup. They are designed to present information in a clear and organized manner, which makes them accessible even to developers new to debugging in Visual Studio.
- **Support for Complex Data Types**: The Autos and Locals windows support complex data structures, which allow you to drill down into objects, arrays, and collections to inspect their individual members or elements.

When to Use the Autos and Locals Windows

- **Stepping Through Code**: When you are stepping through your code line by line (F10 for Step Over, F11 for Step Into), the Autos and Locals windows provide immediate visibility into how variables are affected by each line of code.

- **Tracking Variable Changes**: Use the Autos window to monitor variables directly involved in the current operation and the Locals window to observe all variables in the method. These options track changes and identify potential issues.
- **Debugging Methods**: When debugging a specific method, the Locals window allows you to see all local variables at a glance, which is crucial for understanding the method's logic and behavior.
- **Inspecting Function Parameters**: The Locals window is particularly useful for inspecting the values of parameters passed into a function, which helps you verify that the inputs are as expected.
- **Analyzing Data Structures**: Both windows are invaluable when you need to inspect the contents of complex data structures such as objects or collections to ensure that they are being manipulated correctly.

How to Create and Use the Autos and Locals Windows: A Step-by-Step Guide

Step 1: Start Debugging the Application.

a. Open your C# project in Visual Studio 2022.

b. Start a debugging session by pressing F5 or by selecting `Debug` > `Start Debugging` from the menu.

Step 2: Access the Autos and Locals Windows.

- **Autos Window:** The Autos window will automatically appear when you begin stepping through your code. If it does not, you can manually open it by selecting `Debug` > `Windows` > `Autos` from the menu.
- **Locals Window:** Similarly, the Locals window can be accessed automatically when debugging or manually by selecting `Debug` > `Windows` > `Locals`.

Step 3: Step Through the Code.

Use the F10 (`Step Over`) or F11 (`Step Into`) keys to step through your code. As you do so, the Autos and Locals windows will update to reflect the current state of variables relevant to the line of code being executed.

Step 4: Inspect Variables.

- **Autos Window:** Inspect the variables that are shown in the Autos window to see how they are affected by the current and previous lines of code. This window will show the most immediate variables in use, which is useful for understanding the current operation.

- **Locals Window:** In the Locals window, review all the local variables in the current method. Expand complex data structures like objects or arrays to inspect their individual properties or elements.

Step 5: Modify Variables (Optional).

If you want to test how changes to variable values affect the program's execution, you can modify the values directly in the Autos or Locals windows by clicking on the value and typing a new one.

Step 6: Continue Debugging.

Continue stepping through your code or resume normal execution by pressing F5. The Autos and Locals windows will continue to update in real-time, which provides ongoing insights into the state of your application.

Importance of Autos and Locals Windows in Debugging

From a debugging perspective, the Autos and Locals windows are invaluable tools that provide immediate visibility into the state of your application. They enable you to see how variables are manipulated in real-time, which is crucial for identifying and fixing bugs. The Autos window is particularly important for tracking variables directly involved in the current operation, while the Locals window gives a broader view of the method's entire context.

These windows reduce the need for manual inspection and configuration, while allowing you to understand how your code behaves and identify the root cause of issues quickly. Their ability to display complex data structures also makes them essential for debugging more sophisticated applications.

How Developers Can Benefit from Using the Autos and Locals Windows

- **Faster Debugging Sessions:** By automatically displaying relevant variables, the Autos and Locals windows help you identify issues more quickly, which leads to faster resolution of bugs.
- **Increased Insight into Code Behavior:** These windows provide real-time updates on variable values, giving you deeper insights into how your code operates, which is essential for troubleshooting and optimization.

- **Streamlined Code Analysis:** The ability to see all local variables at a glance allows for more effective analysis of methods and functions, which helps you understand the flow of data and logic.
- **Enhanced Productivity:** With the Autos and Locals windows handling much of the variable tracking automatically, you can focus more on problem-solving and less on setup, which improves your overall productivity.
- **Support for Complex Debugging:** The ability to inspect and manipulate complex data structures within these windows makes them powerful tools for tackling more challenging debugging scenarios.

The Autos and Locals windows in Visual Studio 2022 are essential components of the debugging toolkit for C# developers. By providing automatic and real-time visibility into the state of your application's variables, these windows help streamline the debugging process, making it faster and more efficient. Whether you are stepping through code, analyzing data structures, or tracking down bugs, mastering the use of the Autos and Locals windows will significantly enhance your ability to debug effectively and maintain high-quality code.

Intellitrace in Visual Studio 2022

Intellitrace is an advanced debugging feature in Visual Studio 2022 that extends the capabilities of traditional debugging by recording and replaying the history of an application's execution. This feature allows developers to "go back in time" and examine the state of the application at previous points in the execution, even after the application has continued running. Intellitrace captures events such as method calls, exceptions, and variable values, providing a rich and detailed history of what has occurred in your application. This makes it easier to diagnose complex issues that might be difficult to reproduce or understand using standard debugging techniques.

Advantages of using Intellitrace:

- **Historical Debugging:** Intellitrace enables developers to navigate back to a previous point in the application's execution, which allows them to inspect variables, objects, and execution paths as they were at that moment. This historical perspective is invaluable for understanding how and why a problem occurred.
- **Efficient Issue Diagnosis:** By recording a detailed history of application events, Intellitrace reduces the need to reproduce issues multiple times, which is particularly useful for diagnosing intermittent bugs or problems that are hard to replicate.
- **Enhanced Context Awareness:** Intellitrace provides context by showing how the application reached its current state, which helps developers to better

understand the flow of execution and the sequence of events leading to a bug.

- **Time-Saving:** Intellitrace can significantly reduce the time spent on debugging by eliminating the need to restart the application and reproduce the issue. Developers can simply review the recorded execution history to identify and fix the problem.
- **Integrated with Visual Studio:** As part of Visual Studio, Intellitrace is seamlessly integrated into the IDE, which makes it easy to use alongside other debugging tools. This integration ensures a smooth and efficient debugging experience.

When to Use Intellitrace

- **Debugging Complex Issues**: Intellitrace is particularly useful when dealing with complex bugs that involve multiple steps or interactions between different parts of the code. It helps track down the root cause of issues by providing a detailed history of execution.
- **Investigating Intermittent Bugs**: For bugs that occur sporadically or under specific conditions that are hard to reproduce, Intellitrace's recording capabilities allow you to capture the bug when it happens and analyze it later.
- **Understanding Legacy Code**: When working with unfamiliar or legacy code, Intellitrace helps developers understand how the code operates by showing the sequence of method calls and events that lead to a particular state.
- **Analyzing Performance Issues**: Intellitrace can also be used to analyze performance-related issues by reviewing the execution history to identify bottlenecks or inefficient code paths.
- **Collaborative Debugging**: In a team environment, Intellitrace recordings can be shared among team members, which allows others to analyze the same debugging session and contribute to problem resolution.

How to Create and Use Intellitrace: A Step-by-Step Guide

Step 1: Ensure that `Intellitrace` is Enabled.

a. Intellitrace is available in the Enterprise edition of Visual Studio 2022. To check if Intellitrace is enabled:

b. Go to **`Tools`** > **`Options`** > **`Intellitrace`**.

   - Ensure that the option Enable Intellitrace is selected. You can also configure specific events and calls that Intellitrace should capture.

Step 2: Start Debugging with Intellitrace.

Begin a debugging session by pressing F5 or by selecting `Debug` > `Start Debugging`. Intellitrace will automatically start recording the execution history as the application runs.

Step 3: Use Intellitrace Events and Calls.

During debugging, Intellitrace captures two types of data:

- `Events`: These include exceptions, breakpoints, and other significant events.
- `Calls`: These include method calls, their parameters, and return values.

You can view these in the Intellitrace Events window, accessible via `Debug` > `Windows` > Intellitrace Events.

Step 4: Navigate Through Execution History.

a. While debugging, you can pause the application (*Ctrl+Alt+Break*) and open the Intellitrace Events window.

b. This window shows a list of captured events and method calls. You can click on any entry to "`go back`" to that point in time.

c. When you select an event or call, the Code window will update to show the relevant code at that time and the Locals and Watch windows will display the state of variables and objects as they were.

Step 5: Analyze and Debug.

a. Use the information provided by Intellitrace to analyze the flow of your application. You can inspect variables, review the sequence of method calls, and understand the context leading up to an issue.

b. If needed, you can modify your code and re-run the application to see how changes affect the execution.

Step 6: Save and Share Intellitrace Sessions (Optional).

You can save an Intellitrace session by selecting `File` > `Save Intellitrace Session As`. This allows you to revisit the session later or share it with other team members for collaborative debugging.

Step 7: Disable or Adjust Intellitrace Settings.

If you find that Intellitrace is capturing too much information or impacting performance, you can adjust its settings under `Tools` > `Options` > `Intellitrace`. You can choose to capture fewer events or limit the recording to specific areas of your application.

Importance of Intellitrace in Debugging

Intellitrace is an essential tool for debugging complex or hard-to-reproduce issues in C#. By providing a detailed execution history, Intellitrace allows developers to understand the exact sequence of events leading to a bug, which makes it easier to identify and fix the root cause. This ability to "`rewind`" and inspect previous states of the application is particularly valuable when dealing with issues that are difficult to replicate or when debugging unfamiliar code.

Intellitrace also enhances the overall debugging experience by reducing the need for repeated trial-and-error cycles, saving time, and increasing efficiency. For teams, Intellitrace sessions can be shared and reviewed collaboratively, which improves communication and accelerates the debugging process.

How Developers Can Benefit from Using Intellitrace

- **Faster Issue Resolution:** Intellitrace helps developers quickly identify and fix issues by providing a clear and detailed history of the application's execution, which reduces the time spent on debugging.
- **Improved Code Understanding:** By showing the exact flow of execution, Intellitrace aids developers in understanding how different parts of the code interact, especially in large or complex projects.
- **Increased Productivity:** The ability to review and analyze past execution states without rerunning the application increases productivity by allowing developers to focus on solving the problem rather than reproducing it.
- **Collaborative Debugging:** Intellitrace sessions can be saved and shared with team members, which enables collaborative debugging and allows multiple developers to contribute to resolving complex issues.
- **Better Insight into Application Behavior:** Intellitrace provides deeper insights into the behavior of your application, which helps you optimize performance and ensure that your code is functioning as intended.

Intellitrace in Visual Studio 2022 is a powerful tool for C# developers, which offers a unique and advanced approach to debugging by recording the history of application execution. By enabling developers to go back in time and examine the state of their application at various points, Intellitrace greatly enhances the ability to diagnose and resolve complex issues. Whether you are dealing with difficult-to-reproduce bugs, unfamiliar code, or performance problems, Intellitrace provides the tools and insights needed to debug effectively and efficiently.

Conclusion

In this chapter, we delved into the essential tools and techniques for debugging and diagnostics in C# using Visual Studio 2022. We began by exploring breakpoints, including conditional, function, data, and temporary breakpoints, each of which allows developers to control and manage the flow of their applications during execution. We also discussed the use of breakpoint groups, which facilitate the organization and management of multiple breakpoints in complex projects.

The chapter continued with an examination of the Watch, Autos, and Locals windows, which provide real-time visibility into the state of variables and expressions during debugging sessions. These tools are invaluable for tracking down bugs and understanding the behavior of your code as it runs. We also covered IntelliTrace, a powerful feature that allows developers to record and replay the execution history of an application, thereby providing a unique capability to diagnose hard-to-reproduce issues by "**`rewinding`**" the program's execution.

Through these tools and techniques, this chapter provided a comprehensive guide to mastering the debugging and diagnostics capabilities in Visual Studio, which will equip developers with the knowledge needed to identify, isolate, and resolve issues efficiently, thereby improving code quality and application stability.

As we conclude our exploration of debugging and diagnostics in C#, we turn our attention to another critical aspect of software development: unit testing.

The next chapter will guide you through the fundamentals of writing, executing, and managing unit tests within the Visual Studio environment. Unit testing is an essential practice that helps ensure the correctness of individual components in your application, while making it easier to identify and fix bugs early in the development process.

CHAPTER 5
Unit Testing with Visual Studio

Introduction

In the world of software development, ensuring that your code works as expected is not just a best practice, but an essential requirement. Unit testing, which is a critical component of any robust development process, allows developers to verify that individual units of code are functioning correctly in isolation. By catching bugs early and providing a safety net for code changes, unit tests maintain the reliability and stability of your applications over time.

Visual Studio offers a powerful and integrated environment for creating, running, and managing unit tests. Whether you are working on a small project or a large enterprise application, Visual Studio provides you the essential tools to ensure that your code is solid, maintainable, and ready for production. This chapter will guide you through the fundamentals of unit testing within Visual Studio, right from setting up your first test to running comprehensive test suites as part of your continuous integration pipeline.

We will explore the various testing frameworks supported by Visual Studio, including **MSTest**, **NUnit**, and **xUnit**, and demonstrate how to write effective unit tests that cover different scenarios. Additionally, you will learn how to leverage Visual Studio's testing tools to debug failing tests, measure code coverage, and even run tests in parallel to speed up your development workflow.

By the end of this chapter, you will be equipped with the knowledge and skills to confidently use Visual Studio's unit testing features, which will your development process more efficient and your codebase more resilient. Whether you are new to unit testing or looking to deepen your understanding, this chapter will provide the comprehensive overview you need to harness the full potential of Visual Studio in your testing endeavors.

Structure

In this chapter, we will cover the following topics:

- Introduction to Unit Testing
- Getting Started with Unit Testing in Visual Studio
- Understanding the Visual Studio Testing Environment
- Writing Effective Unit Tests
- Running and Managing Tests
- Debugging Unit Tests
- Advanced Unit Testing Techniques
- Integrating Unit Tests with Continuous Integration (CI)
- Best Practices for Unit Testing in Visual Studio

Introduction to Unit Testing

Unit testing is an essential practice in modern software development, which provides a safety net that ensures individual components of your application work as intended. Visual Studio, as a comprehensive integrated development environment (IDE), offers a robust set of tools to create, manage, and run unit tests, thereby making it easier for developers to maintain high-quality code throughout the development lifecycle.

Visual Studio supports multiple testing frameworks like **MSTest**, **NUnit**, and **xUnit**, which give developers the flexibility to choose the framework that best fits their project's needs. The seamless integration of these frameworks within Visual Studio allows for an intuitive testing experience, where you can write, execute, and debug tests without leaving the IDE.

This introduction will guide you through the fundamentals of unit testing within Visual Studio, from setting up your testing environment to understanding the tools and features that make unit testing effective. By the end of this section, you will be equipped with the foundational knowledge to start implementing unit tests in your Visual Studio projects, which will ensure that your codebase remains reliable and maintainable as it evolves.

Definition and Purpose of Unit Testing

Unit testing is a software testing method where individual components of a software application, typically functions or methods, are tested in isolation from the rest of the application. The primary goal of unit testing is to validate that each unit of the software performs as expected, which ensures that the smallest, testable parts of the application are working correctly.

A "unit" in unit testing usually refers to the smallest part of the code that can be tested, such as a function, method, or class. Each unit test focuses on a specific aspect of the unit is functionality and checks if the output matches the expected result for a given input. By testing these small units individually, developers can identify and fix issues early in the development process before they evolve into more complex problems.

Unit testing is typically automated, which allows tests to be run repeatedly and consistently throughout the development lifecycle. Automated unit tests provide a quick and efficient way to ensure that code changes do not introduce new bugs or regressions.

Benefits of Unit Testing in Software Development

Unit testing offers the following benefits that contribute to the overall quality and stability of a software application:

- **Early Detection of Bugs:** By testing individual components early in the development process, unit testing helps identify and fix bugs before they can affect other parts of the application. This reduces the cost and complexity of fixing issues later in the development cycle.
- **Improved Code Quality:** Unit tests encourage developers to write cleaner, more modular code. Testable code is typically well-structured, with clear responsibilities and fewer dependencies, which improves the overall code quality.
- **Facilitates Refactoring:** With a comprehensive suite of unit tests, developers can confidently refactor code, knowing that the tests will catch any unintended changes or regressions. This allows for continuous improvement of the codebase without the fear of breaking existing functionality.
- **Supports Continuous Integration:** Unit tests are an integral part of continuous integration (CI) pipelines, where code changes are automatically tested before being integrated into the main codebase. This ensures that only code that passes all tests is merged, and the stability of the project is maintained.
- **Provides Documentation:** Unit tests can serve as documentation for the code. They demonstrate how the code is intended to be used and what results are expected, which makes it easier for new developers to understand the codebase.
- **Reduces Debugging Time:** When a unit test fails, it usually indicates an issue in a specific part of the code. This makes it easier to locate and fix the problem compared to debugging the entire application.

- **Encourages Best Practices:** Writing unit tests promotes the adoption of best practices such as writing small, focused functions, using dependency injection, and keeping code decoupled. These practices contribute to a more maintainable and scalable codebase.

Overview of Unit Testing Best Practices

To get the most out of unit testing, it is important to follow best practices that ensure your tests are effective, maintainable, and reliable:

- **Write Independent Tests:** Each unit test should be independent of others. Tests should not rely on shared state or external resources, as this can lead to unpredictable results. This ensures that tests can be run in any order without affecting the outcome.
- **Follow the AAA Pattern:** Structure your tests using the Arrange, Act, Assert (AAA) pattern.
    - **Arrange:** Set up the initial conditions and inputs for the test.
    - **Act:** Execute the code being tested.
    - **Assert:** Verify that the outcome is matching with the expected result.
- **Test One Thing at a Time:** Each unit test should focus on a single aspect of the functionality being tested. This makes it easier to identify the cause of a failure and ensures that tests are clear and concise.
- **Keep Tests Simple and Fast:** Unit tests should be fast to execute, which will cause them to be run frequently. Avoid complex logic in tests; the simpler the test, the easier it is to understand and maintain.
- **Use Descriptive Names:** Give your tests descriptive names that clearly indicate what they are testing. This makes it easier to understand what the test is verifying and aids in diagnosing test failures.
- **Mock External Dependencies:** When a unit interacts with external systems (for example, databases, web services), use mocking to simulate these dependencies. This isolates the unit from the external system and ensures that the test only focuses on the unit's functionality.
- **Ensure Tests Are Repeatable:** Tests should produce the same result every time they are run, regardless of the environment or the order in which they are executed. Avoid relying on external data sources or system states that may change between test runs.
- **Review and Refactor Tests:** Just like production code, unit tests should be reviewed and refactored as needed. Regularly revisit your test suite to remove redundant tests, improve clarity, and ensure that tests remain relevant as the code evolves.

- **Aim for High Coverage, But Don't Obsess Over It:** While it is important to have a high level of test coverage, quality is more important than quantity. Focus on testing critical paths and edge cases rather than trying to achieve 100% coverage, as the latter may lead to diminishing returns.
- **Integrate Tests into the Development Workflow:** Make unit testing a regular part of your development process. Run tests frequently, especially before committing code, and integrate them into your CI pipeline to catch issues early.

By adhering to these best practices, you can create a robust unit testing suite that not only improves the quality of your code, but also enhances your development workflow. Unit testing, when done right, is a powerful tool that contributes significantly to the success of software projects.

Importance of Unit Testing in Visual Studio

Visual Studio's deep integration with testing frameworks and its wide array of features make it an ideal environment for unit testing. Whether you are a solo developer or part of a large team, Visual Studio provides the tools you need to ensure that your code is reliable, maintainable, and ready for production. By adopting unit testing as part of your development process in Visual Studio, you can catch bugs early, facilitate code refactoring, and improve the overall quality of your software projects.

Key Features of Unit Testing in Visual Studio

Some of the key features of Unit testing in Visual Studio are as follows:

- **Test Explorer:** Visual Studio's Test Explorer provides a centralized location to manage and run your tests. It displays the status of all your tests, which makes it easy to identify and troubleshoot failing tests. You can also group and filter tests, allowing you to focus on specific areas of your code.
- **Test Project Templates:** Visual Studio offers built-in templates for creating test projects, pre-configured for the testing framework of your choice. This streamlines the process of setting up your testing environment and ensures that you can start writing tests quickly and efficiently.
- **Code Coverage:** Visual Studio includes tools for measuring code coverage, which helps you understand how much of your code is being tested. By analyzing code coverage reports, you can identify untested parts of your code and improve your test suite to cover these areas.
- **Debugging Support:** One of the powerful features of Visual Studio is its integrated debugging capabilities. You can set breakpoints within your tests, step through code, and inspect variables to diagnose issues in your code. This

makes it easier to understand why a test is failing and to fix the underlying problem.

- **Continuous Testing:** Visual Studio integrates with continuous integration (CI) tools like Azure DevOps and GitHub Actions, which allows you to run tests automatically with every code change. This ensures that your code remains stable and that any issues are caught early in the development process.

Getting Started with Unit Testing in Visual Studio

In this section, we will go through the step-by-step process of Creating and Configuring a Unit Test Project in Visual Studio 2022

System Requirements: Before you begin creating a unit test project in Visual Studio 2022, ensure that your development environment meets the following system requirements:

- **Operating System**: Windows 10 version 1909 or higher, Windows Server 2016, or higher
- **Visual Studio 2022**: The latest version of Visual Studio 2022 installed with the "**`.NET desktop development`**" and "**`ASP.NET and web development`**" workloads (if you are working on web projects).
- **.NET SDK**: Ensure the appropriate version of the .NET SDK is installed, depending on your project's requirements.
- **Disk Space**: At least 20 GB of free disk space
- **RAM**: Minimum of 8 GB of RAM (16 GB recommended for large projects)

Steps to Create a Unit Test Project in Visual Studio 2022

1. **Open Visual Studio 2022.**
   a. Launch Visual Studio 2022 from the Start menu or desktop shortcut.
2. **Create a New Project.**
   a. From the Start Window, click on "**`Create a new project`**."
   b. In the "**`Create a new project`**" dialog, search for "**`Unit Test Project`**" in the search box.
3. **Select the Unit Test Project Template.**
   a. Select the Unit Test Project (.NET) template from the list.
   b. Click on Next to proceed.

4. **Configure Your Project.**
    a. **`Project Name`**: Enter a name for your unit test project.
    b. **`Location`:** Choose the location where you want to save the project.
    c. **`Solution Name`:** If you are adding the test project to an existing solution, choose the solution name or create a new one.
    d. Click on **`Next`** to continue.
5. **Select Framework.**
    a. Choose the appropriate .NET framework version for your project. The default is usually the latest version, but you can select an earlier version if required.
        i. Click on **`Create`** to generate the project.

Additional Steps to Configure the Project

1. **Install Additional Test Frameworks (Optional).**
    a. If you want to use a testing framework other than MSTest (for example, NUnit or xUnit), you can install the corresponding NuGet package.
    b. Right-click on the project in Solution Explorer, then select Manage NuGet Packages.
    c. Search for and install the desired test framework (for example, NUnit, xUnit).
2. **Add References to the Project Under Test.**
    a. If your unit test project needs to test code from another project in the same solution, you must add a reference to that project.
    b. Right-click on the References node under your test project in **`Solution Explorer`**, then select **`Add Reference`**.
    c. In the "**`Reference Manager`**" dialog, check the box next to the project you want to test, then click **`OK`**.
3. **Organize Test Classes and Methods.**
    a. Create test classes for each class or module you are testing. Ensure that each test class and method follows naming conventions that clearly describe their purpose.

4. **Configure Test Settings (Optional).**
   a. You can customize test settings by editing the `.runsettings` file, which controls how tests are run and reported.
   b. To add a `.runsettings` file, right-click on the solution, select `Add` > `New Item`, and choose XML File. Rename it with a `.runsettings` extension.

How to Run the Unit Test Project

1. **Build the Solution.**
   a. Before running the tests, build the solution to ensure that all projects compile successfully. Go to `Build` > `Build Solution`.
2. **Run Tests.**
   a. Open the `Test Explorer` by navigating to `Test` > `Test Explorer`.
   b. The `Test Explorer` will automatically discover all the test methods in your solution.
   c. To run all tests, click on Run All at the top of the `Test Explorer`.
   d. You can also run specific tests or groups of tests by right-clicking on them in the `Test Explorer` and selecting `Run Selected Tests`.
3. **View Test Results.**
   a. Once the tests have completed, the Test Explorer will display the results, indicating which tests passed, failed, or were skipped.
   b. You can click on any test to view detailed results, including error messages and stack traces for failed tests.
4. **Debug Failing Tests:** If a test fails, you can debug it by right-clicking the test in the Test Explorer and selecting Debug. This will run the test with the debugger attached, allowing you to step through the code.

Thus, by following these steps, you can effectively create, configure, and run unit test projects in Visual Studio 2022, while ensuring that your application remains robust and reliable throughout its development lifecycle.

Overview of Available Unit Test Frameworks in Visual Studio (MSTest, NUnit, xUnit)

Visual Studio supports several popular unit testing frameworks, each with its own set of features, advantages, and use cases. The primary frameworks supported are

MSTest, NUnit, and xUnit. Here is a breakdown of these frameworks, their advantages, disadvantages, and when to use each:

MSTest

MSTest is the unit testing framework developed by Microsoft and is integrated by default into Visual Studio. It has been around for a long time and is the go-to framework for many developers who use the Microsoft ecosystem.

Advantages of using MSTest

- **Seamless Integration**: MSTest is deeply integrated into Visual Studio, which provides an out-of-the-box experience with no additional setup required.
- **Supported by Microsoft**: As a Microsoft product, MSTest is well-supported, with extensive documentation and community resources.
- **Data-Driven Testing**: MSTest provides built-in support for data-driven tests, which allows tests to be run with different sets of input data.
- **Compatibility**: MSTest works well with other Microsoft technologies such as Azure DevOps and Visual Studio Test Explorer.

Disadvantages of using MSTest

- **Feature Set**: While MSTest v2 supports most core testing features, it still lacks some of the extensibility and advanced customization options provided by frameworks like NUnit and xUnit.
- **Verbose Syntax:** Some developers find the MSTest syntax to be more verbose and less intuitive compared to other frameworks.
- **Performance**: MSTest may not perform as efficiently as xUnit in scenarios that require the execution of large test suites. For large test suites, xUnit may perform more efficiently than MSTest due to its default parallel execution and lightweight architecture.

When to Use MSTest:

- **Microsoft Ecosystem:** If you are working within a Microsoft-centric environment and need tight integration with Visual Studio and Azure DevOps, MSTest is a strong choice.
- **Legacy Projects**: For projects that have been using MSTest historically, continuing with MSTest can make maintenance and team onboarding smoother.

NUnit

NUnit is a popular open-source unit testing framework for .NET, known for its flexibility and wide range of features. It has been a long-standing choice for .NET developers and offers extensive customization options.

Advantages of using NUnit

- **Rich Feature Set**: NUnit offers a broad range of features, including advanced assertions, setup/teardown functions, and parameterized tests.
- **Maturity and Stability**: As a mature framework with a large user base, NUnit is stable and well-documented, with many resources available for learning and troubleshooting.
- **Flexibility**: NUnit provides extensive options for customizing test execution, which makes it suitable for complex test scenarios.

Disadvantages of using NUnit

- **Less Integration**: While NUnit integrates with Visual Studio, it requires additional setup (such as installing the NUnit NuGet package) and is not as seamlessly integrated as MSTest.
- **Learning Curve**: Due to its extensive feature set, NUnit might have a steeper learning curve for developers who are new to unit testing.

When to Use NUnit

- **Complex Testing Scenarios**: If your project requires advanced testing features or complex setup and teardown logic, NUnit is a great choice.
- **Cross-Platform Projects**: NUnit is well-suited for projects that need to run tests across different platforms like .NET Core and Mono.

xUnit

xUnit is a modern, open-source unit testing framework created by the original authors of NUnit. It is designed to address some of the shortcomings of older frameworks and follows modern software development practices.

Advantages of using xUnit

- **Modern Design**: xUnit embraces modern .NET development practices, with features like automatic parallel test execution and better isolation of test cases.
- **Lightweigh**t: xUnit is lightweight and has a clean, straightforward API, which makes it easy to write and maintain tests.
- **Parallelism**: xUnit supports parallel test execution out-of-the-box, which can significantly reduce test execution time for large test suites.
- **Community Support**: xUnit has a strong community and is widely adopted in open-source projects, which means there are plenty of resources and extensions available.

Disadvantages of using xUnit

- **Less Built-In Features:** Compared to NUnit, xUnit has fewer built-in features, which may require developers to write more custom code or use additional libraries for certain scenarios.
- **Different Concepts:** xUnit introduces some concepts that may be unfamiliar to developers used to MSTest or NUnit, such as the lack of setup/teardown attributes in favor of constructor-based setup.

When to Use xUnit

- **Modern Projects**: If you are starting a new project and want to follow modern .NET practices, xUnit is an excellent choice.
- **Performance**: For projects with large test suites where test execution time is a concern, xUnit is parallel test execution can offer significant performance benefits.
- **Open Source and Community Projects:** xUnit is widely used in the open-source community, which make it a good choice if you want to align with community standards.

Differences Between MSTest, NUnit, and xUnit

Feature/Aspect	MSTest	NUnit	xUnit
Integration	Best integrated with Visual Studio	Requires setup with Visual Studio	Requires setup with Visual Studio
Setup/Teardown	`[TestInitialize]`, `[TestCleanup]`	`[SetUp]`, `[TearDown]`	Constructor for setup, IDisposable for cleanup
Parallel Execution	Limited support	Supported with some configuration	Supported by default
Data-Driven Testing	Built-in attributes like `[DataTestMethod]`	Supported via `[TestCase]` and `[TestCaseSource]`	Supported via `[Theory]` and `[InlineData]`
Assertions	MSTest assertions library	Rich assertions library	Rich assertions library
Performance	Moderate, can slow down with large suites	Generally faster, but varies with complexity	Fastest, especially with large suites
Community and Support	Strong Microsoft support	Strong community and mature ecosystem	Strong community and modern practices

***Table 5.1**: Key Differences among Different Test Frameworks*

Choosing the Right Framework

- Use MSTest if you need deep integration with Visual Studio, are working on a project heavily reliant on Microsoft technologies, or are maintaining legacy codebases.
- Use NUnit if you require a mature framework with a rich feature set, need advanced testing capabilities, or are working on cross-platform projects.
- Use xUnit if you are starting a new project, want to follow modern .NET practices, or need efficient test execution for large test suites.

Each of these frameworks has its strengths, and the choice depends on your project's specific needs, your team's familiarity with the frameworks, and the testing requirements of your application.

Creating Your First Unit Test

Step-by-Step Process to Create Your First Unit Test Using xUnit in Visual Studio 2022

Step 1: Set Up Your Development Environment.

Before creating your first xUnit test, ensure that you have Visual Studio 2022 installed with the necessary workloads.

a. **Workloads**: Make sure the "`.NET desktop development`" and "`ASP.NET and web development`" workloads are installed.

b. **Framework**: Ensure that the appropriate version of the .NET SDK is installed based on your project's requirements.

Step 2: Create a New Solution and Project.

a. **Open Visual Studio 2022.**

   i. Launch Visual Studio 2022 from the Start menu or desktop shortcut.

b. **Create a New Project.**

   i. From the Start Window, click on "`Create a new project`."

   ii. In the "`Create a new project`" dialog, search for "`xUnit Test`" or choose it from the list of templates.

   iii. Select the "`xUnit Test Project`" template and click `Next`.

c. **Configure the Project.**

   i. `Project Name`: Enter a name for your project (for example, `MyFirstXUnitProject`).

ii. **`Location`**: Choose the location where you want to save the project.

iii. **`Solution Name`**: You can use the default solution name or create a custom one.

iv. Click on **`Next`**.

d. **Select Framework**.

i. Choose the appropriate .NET framework version for your project (for example, .NET 6 or .NET 7).

ii. Click on **`Create to generate the project`**.

Step 3: Add xUnit to Your Project.

a. **Manage NuGet Packages**

i. Right-click on the project in the **`Solution Explorer`** and select **`Manage NuGet`** Packages.

ii. In the NuGet Package Manager, click on the Browse tab and search for xunit.

iii. Select the xunit package from the search results and click Install.

iv. Repeat the process to install the **`xunit.runner.visualstudio`** package, which integrates xUnit with Visual Studio's Test Explorer.

b. **Confirm Installation**.

c. After installation, you should see both **`xunit`** and **`xunit.runner.visualstudio`** listed under the "**`Installed`**" tab in the NuGet Package Manager.

Step 4: Write Your First Unit Test.

a. **Add a `Test Class`**.

i. In the **`Solution Explorer`**, right-click on the project and select **`Add`** > New **`Item`**.

ii. Choose **`Class`** from the list of items, name it **`CalculatorTests.cs`** and click on **`Add`**.

b. **Write the Test Code**.

i. Open the **`CalculatorTests.cs`** file and replace the content with the following code:

```
using Xunit;

public class CalculatorTests
{
```

```
        [Fact]
        public void Adding_Two_Numbers_Should_Return_Correct_
Sum()
        {
            // Arrange
            var calculator = new Calculator();
            int a = 5;
            int b = 10;

            // Act
            int result = calculator.Add(a, b);

            // Assert
            Assert.Equal(15, result);
        }
    }

    public class Calculator
    {
        public int Add(int x, int y)
        {
            return x + y;
        }
    }
```

This code defines a simple unit test using xUnit. The [Fact] attribute indicates that the method is a test that should be run by the test runner. The Calculator class is the system under test, and the **Add** method is the function being tested.

Step 5: Run the Unit Test.

a. **Build the Solution.**

   - Before running the tests, build the solution to ensure that everything compiles correctly. Go to **`Build`** > **`Build Solution`** or press *Ctrl+Shift+B*.

Open the Test Explorer.

a. Navigate to **`Test`** > **`Test Explorer`** to open the **`Test Explorer`** window, where you can view and run your tests.

Run the Test.

a. In the Test Explorer, you should see the:

   i. **`Adding_Two_Numbers_Should_Return_Correct_Sum`** test listed.

b. Click on **`Run All`** to run the test.

c. After the test runs, the result will be displayed in the **`Test Explorer`**. If the test passes, it will be marked with a green checkmark; if it fails, it will be marked with a red cross.

View Test Results.

a. You can click on the test name to view detailed results, including any error messages and the output of assertions.

Step 6: Debugging the Test (Optional).

- Set a Breakpoint.
  - To debug a test, set a breakpoint in your test method (for example, click in the margin next to a line of code to set a breakpoint).
- Debug the Test.
  - Right-click on the test in the `Test Explorer` and select `Debug`.
  - Visual Studio will start the debugger and pause execution at the breakpoint, which will allow you to step through the code and inspect variables.

Summary

Congratulations! You have successfully created and run your first unit test using xUnit in Visual Studio 2022. This basic example shows how straightforward it is to get started with xUnit, but the framework also provides many powerful features for more complex testing scenarios. As you continue to develop your skills, you will find xUnit to be a flexible and efficient tool for ensuring the reliability of your code.

Understanding Basic Testing Concepts

In Visual Studio, developers can leverage several testing methodologies to ensure the quality, reliability, and performance of their applications. These methodologies encompass various testing levels and types to cover different aspects of the software's functionality. Here are some of the most commonly used testing methodologies in Visual Studio:

- **Unit Testing:** Unit testing focuses on testing individual units or components of a software application, typically at the method or function level. The goal is to validate that each small unit of the application performs as expected in isolation from the rest of the system.
  - **Tools**: MSTest, NUnit, xUnit
  - **Use Cases**: Ensuring that individual functions or classes behave as expected
  - **Benefits**: Early bug detection, better code quality, and support for refactoring

- **Integration Testing:** Integration testing verifies that multiple components or systems work together as intended. It focuses on the interactions between different modules and can involve testing interfaces, APIs, or third-party services.
  - **Tools**: MSTest, NUnit, xUnit, ASP.NET Core integration testing tools
  - **Use Cases**: Testing the interaction between a database and the application, or between multiple microservices
  - **Benefits**: Ensures that integrated components work together correctly, identifies issues in data flow and communication between modules
- **Functional Testing:** Functional testing validates that the application works according to specified requirements by focusing on the output produced in response to a particular input. This type of testing often involves verifying user interface behaviors and business logic.
  - **Tools**: MSTest, NUnit, xUnit, Selenium for web applications
  - **Use Cases**: Testing features and user stories; verifying that the software meets business and functional requirements
  - **Benefits**: Ensures that the software functions as intended from the user's perspective
- **UI Testing (Automated UI Testing):** UI testing focuses on testing the graphical user interface of an application to ensure that the interface behaves correctly in different scenarios. Automated UI testing tests the user interface without manual intervention, while simulating user interactions.
  - **Tools**: Selenium, WinAppDriver, Playwright, TestComplete
  - **Use Cases**: Validating button clicks, form submissions, page navigation, and ensuring UI consistency across browsers or platforms
  - **Benefits**: Detects issues with user interaction, visual elements, and layout discrepancies
- **Regression Testing:** Regression testing involves re-running previously passed tests after code changes to ensure that new changes do not introduce new defects or break existing functionality. Automated regression testing helps minimize the risk of regressions when continuously updating code.
  - **Tools**: MSTest, NUnit, xUnit, Visual Studio Test Explorer for test automation
  - **Use Cases**: After code refactoring, bug fixes, or adding new features to confirm that existing functionality remains intact
  - **Benefits**: Prevents the introduction of bugs into previously working code and ensures stability after updates
- **Load Testing (Performance Testing):** Load testing evaluates how well an application performs under heavy loads. It is used to determine the application's

ability to maintain performance, scalability, and reliability under varying levels of stress.

  - **Tools**: Apache JMeter, Azure Load Testing
  - **Use Cases**: Testing performance during high traffic or heavy computation scenarios, while evaluating server load and response time
  - **Benefits**: Identifies performance bottlenecks and ensures that the application can handle anticipated user loads

- **Stress Testing:** Stress testing pushes the system beyond its operational limits to evaluate how it performs under extreme conditions. The objective is to ensure the system fails gracefully and recovers properly after the stress is removed.
  - **Tools**: Apache JMeter, Azure Load Testing
  - **Use Cases**: Testing database connections under heavy load, while simulating high traffic conditions on web servers
  - **Benefits**: Helps identify the system's breaking point and assesses its ability to recover from failure
- **Acceptance Testing:** Acceptance testing ensures that the application meets the acceptance criteria defined by stakeholders. This is often the final stage before a release and focuses on verifying that the system satisfies business requirements and functions correctly in a production-like environment.
  - **Tools**: MSTest, NUnit, xUnit, Selenium, SpecFlow for Behavior-Driven Development (BDD)
  - **Use Cases**: Running tests based on user stories, verifying that the application meets business needs
  - **Benefits**: Ensures that the application meets stakeholder expectations and is ready for release
- **Behavior-Driven Development (BDD):** BDD is a collaborative testing methodology that encourages communication between developers, testers, and business stakeholders. BDD focuses on describing the behavior of an application in simple, understandable language, usually in the form of scenarios.
  - **Tools**: SpecFlow (Cucumber for .NET), xBehave.net
  - **Use Cases**: Writing tests in a natural language syntax (Gherkin), which helps to ensure that everyone, including non-technical stakeholders, understands the application's expected behavior
  - **Benefits**: Encourages collaboration, aligns tests with business requirements, and makes tests more readable
- **Code Coverage Testing:** Code coverage testing measures the percentage of

the codebase that is covered by automated tests. It helps ensure that all parts of the code are being tested adequately.

  - **Tools**: Visual Studio Code Coverage, dotCover (by JetBrains), Coverlet
  - **Use Cases**: Analyzing test coverage to identify areas of code that are not tested, improving test completeness
  - **Benefits**: Provides a quantitative measure of test coverage, while helping developers ensure that critical paths and edge cases are tested

- **Static Code Analysis:** Static code analysis involves inspecting the source code without executing it to identify potential issues such as code smells, security vulnerabilities, and adherence to coding standards. This can help catch issues early in the development process.
  - **Tools**: SonarQube, ReSharper, Visual Studio's built-in analyzers
  - **Use Cases**: Analyzing code quality, detecting security vulnerabilities, and enforcing coding standards
  - **Benefits**: Helps maintain high code quality, detects issues before they lead to bugs, and ensures compliance with best practices
- **Code Profiling (Performance Profiling):** Code profiling is used to measure the performance of an application, identify bottlenecks, and determine which parts of the code consume the most resources (for example, CPU, memory).
  - **Tools**: Visual Studio Profiler, dotTrace (by JetBrains), PerfView
  - **Use Cases**: Analyzing performance-critical code, identifying slow functions, memory leaks, and optimizing resource usage
  - **Benefits**: Optimizes code performance, improves application efficiency, and prevents performance degradation

Summary

In Visual Studio, developers have access to a wide variety of testing methodologies that cater to different aspects of software quality. From unit and integration testing to load and acceptance testing, each methodology plays a crucial role in ensuring that applications meet the necessary quality standards before release. By combining these testing approaches, developers can create robust, reliable, and performant applications.

Basic Concepts of xUnit

xUnit is a popular unit testing framework for .NET that promotes modern development practices and provides a flexible, lightweight approach to writing tests. Before diving into writing unit tests with xUnit, developers should familiarize themselves with the following basic concepts:

Test Attributes

xUnit uses attributes to indicate which methods are tests and how they should behave.

- **[Fact]**: The **[Fact]** attribute is used to define a single test case. This is the most basic attribute in xUnit and is used when you want to test a specific scenario with a fixed set of inputs.

```
[Fact]
public void TestMethodName()
{
    // Test code here
}
```

- **[Theory]**: The **[Theory]** attribute is used when you want to test a method with multiple sets of data. It works in conjunction with data attributes like **[InlineData]**, **[MemberData]**, and **[ClassData]** to pass different values into the test method.

```
[Theory]
[InlineData(3, 5, 8)]
[InlineData(2, 4, 6)]
public void TestMethodWithDifferentData(int a, int b, int
expected)
{
    // Test code here
}
```

Assertions

Assertions are used to verify that the output of the code under test matches the expected outcome. xUnit provides a variety of assertion methods through the Assert class.

- **Assert.Equal(expected, actual)**: Verifies that two values are equal
- **Assert.NotEqual(expected, actual)**: Verifies that two values are not equal
- **Assert.True(condition)**: Verifies that a condition is true
- **Assert.False(condition)**: Verifies that a condition is false
- **Assert.Throws<TException>(() => action)**: Verifies that a specific exception is thrown by a piece of code

Test Class Lifecycle

xUnit uses a simple and intuitive lifecycle for test classes and methods to ensure that tests are isolated and easy to manage.

- **Constructor and Dispose**: xUnit doesn't use **`[SetUp]`** and **`[TearDown]`** methods (like NUnit). Instead, it uses the class constructor for setup and the **`IDisposable`** interface for teardown. The constructor is executed before each test method, and Dispose is called after each test method.

```
public class MyTests : IDisposable
{
    public MyTests()
    {
        // Setup code here
    }

    public void Dispose()
    {
        // Teardown code here
    }

    [Fact]
    public void MyTest()
    {
        // Test code here
    }
}
```

- **Class Fixtures and Collection Fixtures**: For shared setup across multiple tests or test classes, xUnit provides **`IClassFixture<T>`** and **`ICollectionFixture<T>`**. These interfaces allow you to share context or expensive setup across tests in a class or across multiple classes.

Data-Driven Tests

xUnit supports data-driven tests through the **`[Theory]`** attribute, which enable you to run a test method multiple times with different input values.

- **`[InlineData]`**: Supplies inline values to the test method
- **`[MemberData]`**: Supplies data from a member (method or property) in the same class or another class
- **`[ClassData]`**: Supplies data from a separate class that implements the **`IEnumerable<object[]>`** interface

Parallel Test Execution

xUnit executes tests in parallel by default, which can significantly speed up test execution, especially for large test suites.

- **Control Parallelism**: You can control parallelism at the class or method level using **`[Collection]`** or by setting up parallelism options in the **`xunit.runner.json`** configuration file.

```
[Collection("MyNonParallelTests")]
public class MyTests
{
    // This class will not be run in parallel with other
classes in the same collection
}
```

Test Output

xUnit provides a mechanism for capturing and viewing test output, which is useful for debugging and analyzing test results.

- **`ITestOutputHelper`**: This interface allows you to write output from your test methods that can be viewed in the test runner's output.

```
public class MyTests
{
    private readonly ITestOutputHelper _output;

    public MyTests(ITestOutputHelper output)
    {
        _output = output;
    }

    [Fact]
    public void MyTest()
    {
        _output.WriteLine("This is a test output message.");
    }
}
```

Extensibility

xUnit is designed with extensibility in mind. You can create custom attributes, assertions, and even custom test case discoverers and runners to fit your specific testing needs.

- **Custom Traits**: You can define custom traits (categories) for tests using the [Trait] attribute, which helps in organizing and filtering tests.
- **Custom Assertions**: Developers can create their own assertions if the built-in ones are not sufficient for their needs.

Important Basics of xUnit That Developers Should Know

- **Understand Test Attributes (`[Fact]` vs. `[Theory]`):** Knowing when to use `[Fact]` for simple, single-scenario tests and `` `[Theory]` `` for data-driven tests is crucial.
- **Assertion Methods:** Familiarize yourself with the various assertion methods (`Equal`, `NotEqual`, `True`, `False`, `Throws`, and so on) to validate test outcomes effectively.
- **Constructor and Dispose for Setup/Teardown:** Learn how to use the constructor for test setup and the 'Dispose' method for teardown, as xUnit doesn't use `[SetUp]` and `[TearDown]` like other frameworks.
- **Data-Driven Testing:** Leverage xUnit is powerful data-driven testing capabilities with `[Theory]`, `[InlineData]`, `[MemberData]`, and `[ClassData]`.
- **Parallel Test Execution:** Be aware of xUnit is default parallel execution and how to manage or disable it when necessary.
- **Using `ITestOutputHelper` for Logging:** Learn how to capture test output using ITestOutputHelper to assist in debugging tests.
- **Shared Contexts with Fixtures:** Understand how to share context between tests using class and collection fixtures.
- **Extensibility:** Explore xUnit is extensibility features if you need custom behaviors or additional functionality not provided out-of-the-box.

By mastering these basic concepts, developers can effectively write, organize, and manage unit tests using xUnit, which ensures robust and maintainable test suites.

Test-Driven Development Model (TDD)

Test-Driven Development (TDD) is a software development process where tests are written before the actual code. The TDD process typically follows a cycle known as Red-Green-Refactor, which is elaborated as follows:

- **Red:** Write a test for a new feature or functionality. Initially, this test will fail because the feature has not been implemented yet.
- **Green:** Write the minimal amount of code necessary to pass the test. The goal is to make the test pass quickly without worrying about the quality or structure of the code.
- **Refactor:** Refactor the code to improve its structure and design while ensuring that the tests still pass. This step focuses on code quality, optimization, and maintainability.

The main objectives of TDD are to ensure that the code is fully tested, to guide the design of the software, and to reduce the occurrence of bugs. TDD encourages developers to think about the requirements and design before writing code, which often leads to cleaner and more maintainable codebases.

Behavior Driven Development Model (BDD)

Behavior-Driven Development (BDD) is an extension of TDD that emphasizes collaboration between developers, testers, and business stakeholders. BDD focuses on the behavior of the application and uses natural language descriptions of software behavior to define tests. These descriptions are usually written in a structured format called Gherkin, which uses Given-When-Then syntax. Its components are elaborated as follows:

- **Given:** The initial context or state before an action occurs
- **When:** The action or event that triggers the behavior
- **Then:** The expected outcome or result of the action

BDD aims to bridge the communication gap between technical and non-technical stakeholders by using plain language to describe the behavior of the system. It ensures that all stakeholders have a common understanding of how the application should behave in various scenarios.

Differences Between TDD and BDD

Aspect	TDD	BDD
Focus	TDD focuses on writing tests before code, emphasizing code correctness and design.	BDD focuses on the behavior of the system from the user's perspective, emphasizing collaboration and communication.
Participants	Primarily involves developers who write tests and code	Involves developers, testers, and business stakeholders in defining behaviors and writing tests
Test Description	Tests are written in code, usually with unit testing frameworks.	Tests are written in natural language using Gherkin syntax (Given-When-Then), which is then automated.
Language	Uses programming languages to define tests	Uses a shared language (for example, Gherkin) to describe behavior, which makes it accessible to non-technical stakeholders
Granularity	Typically focuses on low-level units of code, such as methods or functions	Focuses on higher-level scenarios and behaviors that span multiple components
Output	Tests that validate the correctness of individual units of code	Scenarios that validate the behavior of the application from an end-user perspective

Goal	To ensure that all code is tested and to guide the design of the software	To ensure that the application behaves as expected according to business requirements

Table 5.2: *Key Differences between TDD and BDD*

Scenarios That Suit TDD

- **Low-Level Component Development:** TDD is ideal for situations where the focus is on developing and testing small, isolated units of code, such as individual functions, methods, or classes.

  Example: Developing a complex algorithm where correctness is critical and each step needs to be thoroughly tested

- **Refactoring Existing Code:** TDD is useful when refactoring legacy code. By writing tests first, you can ensure that the refactoring does not introduce new bugs.

  Example: Refactoring a large codebase with minimal existing tests, where the goal is to improve code structure without changing functionality

- **Ensuring Code Quality:** TDD helps maintain high code quality by ensuring that each unit is tested as it is written, reducing the likelihood of bugs.

  Example: Developing a library or API where reliability and correctness are paramount

Scenarios That Suit BDD

- **Complex Business Logic**: BDD is ideal for projects where understanding and verifying business requirements is crucial. It ensures that the software meets business needs by focusing on user behavior and scenarios.

  Example: Developing a financial application where the correct implementation of business rules is critical, and stakeholder collaboration is needed to define expected behaviors

- **Cross-Functional Teams**: BDD is beneficial in environments where collaboration between developers, testers, and business stakeholders is essential. It fosters communication and ensures that everyone has a shared understanding of the project.

  Example: Building a customer-facing web application where the behavior and user experience need to be validated by both technical and non-technical team members

- **Agile Development**: BDD fits well with Agile methodologies, where features are delivered in small, iterative increments. It ensures that each feature behaves as expected and meets user requirements.

  Example: An e-commerce platform where new features are continuously added and need to be validated against business scenarios and user expectations.

Summary

Both TDD and BDD are valuable methodologies that help improve software quality, but they serve different purposes and are suited to different types of projects. TDD is more focused on code correctness and design, making it ideal for low-level development and refactoring. BDD, on the other hand, emphasizes behavior and collaboration, which makes it well-suited for projects where understanding and validating business requirements is key. Depending on the project's needs, developers may choose one methodology over the other or even combine elements of both.

Understanding the Visual Studio Testing Environment

In this section, we will understand the Test Explorer feature and how to utilize it to make the most out of our test cases and how to efficiently and effectively maximize the potential of handling test cases.

Test Explorer in Visual Studio 2022 for C# Projects

Purpose of Test Explorer : Test Explorer in Visual Studio 2022 is a tool window that provides a centralized interface to manage and run unit tests within your C# projects. It enables developers to write, execute, and debug tests with ease, while offering various functionalities to help ensure the quality and reliability of the code. The Test Explorer is particularly useful in maintaining the health of the codebase by allowing you to quickly verify that your code behaves as expected.

Components and Features of Test Explorer

- **Test List**
  - **Description**: Displays all the discovered tests from your solution, categorized by various criteria such as project, class, or trait (for example, category or priority)
  - **Use:** It provides an overview of all the tests, allowing you to see which ones have been run, their outcomes, and to navigate directly to the test code.

- **Search and Filter Box**
    - **Description**: A search bar at the top of the Test Explorer window.
    - **Use**: Allows you to quickly find specific tests by name. You can also apply filters to show only the tests that match certain criteria such as passed, failed, or not run tests.
- **Run Tests Button**
    - **Description**: A button to execute the selected tests or all tests within the solution.
    - **Use**: You can choose to run all tests, or a subset by selecting them in the test list. This button also includes options for running tests with different settings like running in parallel.
- **Test Results Pane**
    - **Description**: Displays the results of the tests after they have been executed, including status (for example, passed, failed, skipped) and any associated messages or stack traces
    - **Use**: Allows you to see the outcome of each test run, while providing quick access to debugging information in case of failures
- **Group by Dropdown**
    - **Description**: A dropdown menu that allows you to group tests by various criteria, such as project, class, outcome, or traits.
    - **Use**: Helps in organizing and managing tests, which makes it easier to focus on specific subsets of tests during development
- **Run History**
    - **Description**: Shows a historical view of the test runs, including the number of tests that passed, failed, or were skipped in each run
    - **Use**: Enables you to track the progress of your tests over time and identify any regressions or improvements in your codebase
- **Test Output Window**
    - **Description**: A pane that shows the detailed output of the test execution, including logs and diagnostic messages.
    - **Use**: Essential for understanding what happened during a test run, especially when dealing with complex scenarios or intermittent failures
- **Test Playlist**
    - **Description**: A feature that allows you to create and manage playlists of tests, which are essentially subsets of your entire test suite.

    - **Use**: Useful for running a specific group of tests regularly without having to manually select them each time
- **Code Coverage**
    - **Description**: An option to run tests with code coverage analysis.
    - **Use**: Helps you determine how much of your code is covered by tests, while highlighting untested parts of your application
- **Test Settings**
    - **Description**: Options to configure test execution, such as timeout settings, deployment options, and parallel execution settings.
    - **Use**: Customizes the behavior of your tests according to the specific needs of your project or environment

Managing and Navigating Through Tests in Test Explorer

Managing and navigating through tests in Test Explorer is crucial for efficiently handling your test suite, especially as it grows. Visual Studio 2022 offers several features and techniques to help you organize and move through your tests effectively.

These are the ways to effectively manage tests:

Grouping Tests

- **How to Group**: Use the "`Group By`" dropdown menu in the Test Explorer to group tests by various criteria such as:
- **Project**: Groups tests based on the project they belong to
- **Class**: Groups tests by the class in which they are defined
- **Namespace**: Groups tests according to their namespace
- **Outcome**: Groups tests by their last run outcome (for example, `Passed`, `Failed`)
- **Traits**: Groups tests based on custom attributes (like Category or Priority)

Purpose: Grouping helps in managing large test suites by making it easier to focus on specific subsets of tests, such as those belonging to a particular feature or module.

Filtering Tests

- **How to Filter**: Use the search and filter box at the top of the `Test Explorer`. You can enter specific text to search for test names or apply predefined filters to show:
    - Only passed tests

- Only failed tests
- Not run tests
- Tests with specific traits or characteristics

Purpose: Filtering is useful when you need to focus on a particular set of tests, like only those that failed in the last run, or when searching for a specific test.

Creating and Managing Playlists

- **How to Create a Playlist**: Right-click on selected tests in the `Test Explorer` and choose "`Add to Playlist`" > "`New Playlist`." You can then name and save the playlist.
- **Managing Playlists**: Once created, playlists can be managed through the "`Playlists`" tab in Test Explorer, where you can run, edit, or delete them.

Purpose: Playlists allow you to create custom test groups that you can run independently of the rest of your test suite, which is particularly useful for regression testing or focusing on specific features.

Running Tests with Different Configurations

- **How to Run Tests**: Select the tests you want to run, then use the "`Run`" button. You can choose to:

    i. Run all tests in the solution

    ii. Run selected tests

    iii. Run failed tests only

    iv. Run tests in parallel

Purpose: Running tests in different configurations helps you optimize your testing workflow and ensures that you can target specific areas of your application efficiently.

Navigating through Tests in the Project

Test List Navigation

- **How to Navigate**: Simply click on any test in the Test List to navigate directly to its definition in the code editor.

Purpose: This provides a quick way to review, edit, or debug a particular test without having to manually search for it in your codebase.

Using the Run History

- **How to Use**: The Run History at the bottom of the Test Explorer shows the results of recent test runs. You can click on any previous run to see its results and directly navigate to the code from the results pane.

Purpose: This allows you to review the history of test outcomes and investigate any test that has changed its result status, which helps in identifying flaky tests or regressions.

Navigating Failed Tests

- **How to Navigate**: After a test run, failed tests are typically highlighted. You can click on any failed test to view the error message and stack trace. Then, you can directly navigate to the point in the code where the failure occurred.

Purpose: This facilitates quick debugging and correction of issues by immediately taking you to the problematic code.

Navigating between Grouped Tests

- **How to Navigate**: When you group tests by class, project, or namespace, you can collapse and expand these groups for easier navigation. Clicking on a group header will select all tests within that group, which allows you to run or manage them as a batch.

Purpose: Grouping and navigating between groups help you manage large test suites by breaking them down into more manageable sections, making it easier to focus on one part of the suite at a time.

Navigating with Keyboard Shortcuts

- **How to Navigate**: Visual Studio supports several keyboard shortcuts for navigating within Test Explorer, such as:
  - *Ctrl* + R, A: Run all tests
  - *Ctrl* + R, T: Run selected tests
  - *Ctrl* + R, F: Run failed tests

Purpose: Keyboard shortcuts increase efficiency by allowing you to quickly navigate and execute tests without having to switch between mouse and keyboard.

Managing and navigating tests in Test Explorer is streamlined through features like grouping, filtering, playlists, and keyboard shortcuts. These tools and techniques help you efficiently organize, run, and debug your tests, which ensure that your testing process is both effective and manageable, even as your test suite grows in size.

Test Project Templates Available in Visual Studio

Visual Studio 2022 offers several test project templates to help you set up and configure unit testing projects quickly and efficiently. Each template is tailored for specific testing frameworks or scenarios, which allows you to choose the most appropriate one for your project needs.

MSTest Test Project: The MSTest template creates a project that uses the MSTest framework, which is Microsoft's default testing framework. It is fully integrated with Visual Studio and provides support for a wide range of testing scenarios.

Advantages:

- Deep integration with Visual Studio, including features like Live Unit Testing and Test Explorer
- Supports data-driven tests using data attributes
- Offers extensive documentation and community support

Use Case: Ideal for teams already familiar with MSTest or those using other Microsoft tools like Azure DevOps. It is a good choice when you need a testing framework that is well-supported and integrated into the Microsoft ecosystem.

xUnit Test Project: The xUnit template sets up a project that uses the xUnit.net framework, which is a popular open-source testing framework. xUnit is known for its simplicity and extensibility.

Advantages:

- Strong community support and regularly updated
- Designed after considering modern development practices such as parallel test execution
- Supports parameterized tests and theory-based testing

Use Case: Best suited for teams looking for a lightweight, flexible, and modern testing framework. It is commonly used in open-source projects and is well-suited for testing large-scale applications.

NUnit Test Project: The NUnit template creates a project based on the NUnit framework, another widely used open-source testing framework. NUnit is known for its robust feature set and compatibility with various platforms.

Advantages:

- Rich set of attributes for test customization, such as TestCase, SetUp, and TearDown
- Supports running tests on multiple platforms, including .NET Core and .NET Framework
- Good integration with third-party tools and services

Use Case: Ideal for projects that require extensive test customization or need to run on multiple platforms. It is also a good choice for teams with existing NUnit experience or legacy NUnit test suites.

.NET Core Test Project (Using MSTest, xUnit, or NUnit): This template is designed for creating test projects targeting .NET Core. It allows you to choose between MSTest, xUnit, or NUnit as the testing framework.

Advantages:

- Supports cross-platform testing (Windows, macOS, Linux)
- Provides flexibility in choosing the most appropriate testing framework for your project
- Integrated with .NET Core CLI tools for command-line test execution

Use Case: Best suited for cross-platform .NET Core applications, especially when you want to leverage the benefits of .NET Core's performance and scalability. Choose this template if your application targets .NET Core and you want to maintain compatibility across different environments.

ASP.NET Core Test Project: This template is specifically tailored for testing ASP.NET Core applications. It allows you to create a test project using your choice of testing framework (MSTest, xUnit, or NUnit).

Advantages:

- Designed for integration with ASP.NET Core applications, including support for dependency injection and other ASP.NET Core-specific features
- Supports testing of ASP.NET Core MVC, Web API, and Razor Pages
- Compatible with cross-platform testing environments

Use Case: Ideal for projects that involve ASP.NET Core applications. Choose this template when you need to test ASP.NET Core-specific functionalities like controllers, middleware, or Razor Pages.

Generic Test Project: This is a more general-purpose test project template that does not tie you to a specific framework. You can customize it by adding the desired testing framework and libraries manually.

Advantages:

- Maximum flexibility, which allows you to integrate any testing framework or library
- Suitable for scenarios where none of the pre-configured templates meet your needs

- Can be customized for specialized testing scenarios, such as integration tests or performance tests

Use Case: Use this template when you have specific requirements that are not covered by the other templates or when you want to experiment with non-standard or multiple testing frameworks.

Summary

Choosing the right test project template in Visual Studio depends on the specific needs of your project, the frameworks you are familiar with, and the environment in which your application will run. Each template offers unique advantages, which makes it important to select the one that aligns best with your development and testing requirements.

Configuring Test Settings

Step-by-Step Guide for Configuring Test Settings in Visual Studio Using C# and xUnit

Configuring test settings in Visual Studio is essential for customizing how your tests run, particularly when using xUnit as your testing framework. This guide walks you through the process of configuring these settings in a C# project using xUnit.

Step 1: Create an xUnit Test Project.

a. Open Visual Studio: Start by launching Visual Studio 2022.

b. Create a New Project.

   i. Click on "**`Create a new project`**".

   ii. In the search bar, type "**`xUnit Test Project`**".

   iii. Select the **`xUnit Test Project`** template and click on **`Next`**.

c. Configure Your Project.

   i. Name your project (for example, `` `MyXUnitTestProject` ``).

   ii. Choose a location for your project files.

   iii. Select the .NET framework version (for example, `` `.NET 6.0` ``).

   iv. Click **`Create`**.

Step 2: Install Additional xUnit Packages (Optional).

If you need additional features or extensions, such as parallel test execution or test case ordering, you may need to install additional xUnit packages through the following steps:

a. Open the **NuGet Package Manager**.

   i. Right-click on your test project in the **Solution Explorer**.

   ii. Select **Manage NuGet Packages**.

b. Search for xUnit Packages.

   i. Browse for packages like **xunit.runner.visualstudio** or **xunit.extensions**.

   ii. Click **Install** to add the package to your project.

Step 3: Configure Test Settings in the xunit.runner.json File.

xUnit allows you to configure test settings using a JSON configuration file named '**xunit.runner.json**'. This file needs to be placed in the root of your test project.

a. Add a New JSON File.

   i. Right-click on your test project in the **Solution Explorer**.

   ii. Select **Add** > **New Item**.

   iii. Choose JSON File and name it '**xunit.runner.json**'.

b. Edit the '**xunit.runner.json**' File:

   i. Open '**xunit.runner.json**' in the code editor.

   ii. Add the following JSON configuration to customize your test settings:

```
{
  "parallelizeAssembly": true,
  "parallelizeTestCollections": true,
  "maxParallelThreads": 4,
  "longRunningTestSeconds": 60,
  "diagnosticMessages": true,
  "methodDisplay": "method"
}
```

Here is an explanation of the mentioned settings:

a. **parallelizeAssembly**: Enables or disables parallel execution of test assemblies

b. **parallelizeTestCollections**: Enables or disables parallel execution of test collections within an assembly

c. **maxParallelThreads**: Sets the maximum number of threads to use for parallel test execution.

d. **longRunningTestSeconds**: Specifies the duration (in seconds) after which a test is considered long-running

e. **diagnosticMessages**: Enables diagnostic messages, which are useful for troubleshooting

f. **methodDisplay**: Controls how test methods are displayed (for example, '**method**' for method names, '**classandmethod**' for full method names)

Finally save the file. Save the '**xunit.runner.json**' file to apply these settings.

Step 4: Configure Test Settings in the Test Explorer.

a. Open **Test Explorer**.

   i. Navigate to **Test** > **Test Explorer** to open the **Test Explorer** window.

b. Select **Tests** to Run.

   i. In **Test Explorer**, select the tests you want to run with your configured settings.

c. Run tests.

d. Click the **Run All** button or right-click on selected tests and choose '**Run Selected Tests**'. Your tests will now execute according to the settings configured in the '**xunit.runner.json**' file.

Step 5: Customize Run Configurations (Optional).

Visual Studio allows further customization through **RunSettings** files, though xUnit primarily uses the '**xunit.runner.json**' for configuration. If you need to configure specific settings like test timeout or deployment options, you can use a '**.runsettings**' file.

a. Create a '**.runsettings**' File.

   i. Right-click on the solution in **Solution Explorer**.

   ii. Select **Add** > **New Item** and choose XML File.

   iii. Name it '**MyTestSettings.runsettings**'.

b. Edit the '**.runsettings**' File.

   i. Add your desired configurations like test timeouts or custom data collectors.

```
<?xml version="1.0" encoding="utf-8"?>
<RunSettings>
  <RunConfiguration>
    <MaxCpuCount>2</MaxCpuCount>
```

```
        <TestSessionTimeout>600000</TestSessionTimeout>
      </RunConfiguration>
    </RunSettings>
```

Here is an explanation of the mentioned settings:

- **MaxCpuCount**: Limits the number of CPUs to use for running tests
- **TestSessionTimeout**: Sets the timeout duration for the test session

c. Apply the '**.runsettings**' File.

   i. In Visual Studio, go to **Test** > **Configure Run Settings** > Select **Solution Wide runsettings** File.

   ii. Select your '**.runsettings**' file.

Step 6: Run and Monitor Tests.

- **Run Tests.** Run your tests as you normally would via the **Test Explorer**.
- **Monitor Results.** Test results will appear in **Test Explorer**, and the settings you configured will influence how tests are executed.

Summary

By following these steps, you can configure test settings in Visual Studio for a C# project using xUnit, which further allows you to customize how your tests run. This includes setting parallel execution, controlling how test results are displayed, and fine-tuning your testing process to meet the specific needs of your project.

Writing Effective Unit Tests Using C# and Visual Studio

Writing effective unit tests is essential for maintaining the quality and reliability of your code. In C# and Visual Studio, there are several best practices and techniques that can help you write unit tests that are both meaningful and maintainable. It involves following best practices such as naming conventions, using the AAA pattern, mocking dependencies, and ensuring tests are independent and maintainable. By adhering to these principles, you can create a robust suite of unit tests that help ensure the quality and reliability of your code.

Understand the Purpose of Unit Tests

- **Definition**: A unit test is a small, focused test that verifies the behavior of a single method or function in isolation from other parts of the application.
- **Goal**: The primary goal is to ensure that individual units of code (for example, methods, classes) work as expected under various conditions.

Use a Consistent Naming Convention

- **Why**: Clear and descriptive names make it easier to understand what the test is doing and what behavior it is verifying.
- **How**: Use a consistent pattern like **`MethodName_StateUnderTest_ExpectedBehavior`**. For example:
  - `CalculateDiscount_CustomerIsLoyal_ApplyDiscount`
  - `WithdrawFunds_InsufficientBalance_ThrowException`

Arrange-Act-Assert (AAA) Pattern

- **Arrange:** Set up the necessary objects and prepare the context.
- **Act:** Invoke the method under test.
- **Assert:** Verify that the outcome is as expected.

Example:

```
[Fact]
public void CalculateDiscount_CustomerIsLoyal_ApplyDiscount()
{
    // Arrange
    var customer = new Customer { IsLoyal = true };
    var order = new Order { Amount = 100 };

    // Act
    var discount = order.CalculateDiscount(customer);

    // Assert
    Assert.Equal(10, discount); // Assuming a loyal customer gets
a $10 discount
}
```

Test One Thing at a Time

- **Why**: Testing one behavior per test ensures that when a test fails, you can quickly identify the cause.
- **How**: Keep your tests focused on a single scenario or condition. Avoid testing multiple behaviors in one test.

Example:

```
[Fact]
public void WithdrawFunds_InsufficientBalance_ThrowException()
{
    // Arrange
    var account = new BankAccount { Balance = 50 };
```

```
        // Act & Assert
        Assert.Throws<InvalidOperationException>(() => account.With-
    draw(100));
    }
```

Use Test Data Generously

- **Why**: Testing with a variety of data inputs ensures that your code handles different scenarios and edge cases.
- **How**: Use techniques like data-driven tests to run the same test logic with different data sets.

Example:

```
[Theory]
[InlineData(100, 50, 50)]
[InlineData(200, 100, 100)]
[InlineData(150, 150, 0)]
public void WithdrawFunds_ValidAmount_DecreaseBalance(int
initialBalance, int withdrawalAmount, int expectedBalance)
{
    // Arrange
    var account = new BankAccount { Balance = initialBalance };

    // Act
    account.Withdraw(withdrawalAmount);

    // Assert
    Assert.Equal(expectedBalance, account.Balance);
}
```

Mock External Dependencies

- **Why**: Unit tests should test your code in isolation, without being influenced by external factors like databases, file systems, or APIs.
- **How**: Use mocking frameworks like `Moq` to create mock objects that simulate the behavior of external dependencies.

Example:

```
[Fact]
public void ProcessOrder_WhenCalled_SaveOrderToDatabase()
{
    // Arrange
    var mockRepository = new Mock<IOrderRepository>();
    var orderProcessor = new OrderProcessor(mockRepository.
Object);
    var order = new Order();
```

```
        // Act
        orderProcessor.Process(order);

        // Assert
        mockRepository.Verify(r => r.Save(order), Times.Once);
    }
```

Ensure That Tests are Independent.

- **Why**: Each test should be able to run independently of others to avoid unpredictable results.
- **How**: Avoid sharing state between tests. Each test should set up its own context and clean up afterward if necessary.

Write Readable and Maintainable Tests

- **Why**: Tests are just as important as production code and should be easy to read and maintain.
- **How**: Keep tests simple and to the point. Avoid complex logic in tests. If setup logic is repeated, consider using helper methods or SetUp methods.

Run Tests Frequently

- **Why**: Regularly running tests ensures that your code remains robust as it evolves.
- **How**: Use Visual Studio's Test Explorer to run tests frequently, especially before committing code. Integrate tests into your CI/CD pipeline.

Use Code Coverage Tools.

- **Why**: Code coverage tools help you identify untested parts of your codebase.
- **How**: Visual Studio Enterprise Edition provides built-in code coverage analysis. Use it to ensure that critical paths in your code are covered by tests.

Handle Exceptions and Edge Cases.

- **Why**: Robust tests should account for edge cases and unexpected inputs.
- **How**: Write tests that verify how your code behaves when encountering errors or unusual conditions.

Example:

```
[Fact]
public void CalculateDiscount_InvalidCustomer_ThrowArgumentNull-
Exception()
{
    // Arrange
    var order = new Order();
```

```
        // Act & Assert
        Assert.Throws<ArgumentNullException>(() => order.Calculate-
    Discount(null));
    }
```

Structuring Unit Tests: Arrange, Act, Assert (AAA) Pattern

The Arrange, Act, Assert (AAA) pattern is a widely accepted approach to structuring unit tests, providing clarity and consistency in how tests are written and understood. This guide will walk you through each step of the AAA pattern, while illustrating how to structure your unit tests effectively.

Overview of the AAA Pattern

- **Arrange**: Set up the test scenario by initializing objects, setting up dependencies, and preparing the system under test.
- **Act**: Execute the method or functionality that you are testing.
- **Assert**: Verify that the outcome is as expected to ensure that the system behaves correctly.

Step 1: Set Up Your Unit Test Project.

a. Create a Test Project.

   i. Open Visual Studio.

   ii. Create a new unit test project (for example, xUnit Test Project, MSTest, or NUnit) for your C# application.

b. Add a Reference to the Project Under Test.

   i. In **`Solution Explorer`**, right-click on your test project.

   ii. Select **`Add`** > **`Project Reference`**.

   iii. Choose the project that contains the code you want to test and click **`OK`**.

Step 2: Write a Basic Unit Test Using the AAA Pattern.

Let us write a unit test for a simple method that calculates the discount for a customer based on their loyalty status:

```
public class Order
{
    public decimal CalculateDiscount(Customer customer)
    {
        if (customer.IsLoyal)
        {
```

```
                return 10m; // Loyal customers get a $10 discount
            }
            return 0m;
        }
    }

    public class Customer
    {
        public bool IsLoyal { get; set; }
    }
```

Step 3: Arrange - Set Up the Test Scenario.

a. **Initialize the Objects**: In the Arrange step, create and configure the objects that your test will use. This often includes the system under test (SUT) and any dependencies or input data.

```
[Fact]
public void CalculateDiscount_CustomerIsLoyal_ReturnsDiscount()
{
    // Arrange
    var customer = new Customer { IsLoyal = true };
    var order = new Order();
}
```

Explanation: Here, we create an instance of '**Customer**' and set '**IsLoyal**' to 'true'. We also create an instance of '**Order**', which is the system under test (SUT).

a. **Set Up Dependencies (If Any)**: If your method relies on external dependencies, you would mock or initialize them in this step. In this case, no external dependencies are involved.

Step 4: Act - Execute the Method Under Test

Invoke the Method: Call the method that you want to test and capture the result.

```
    // Act
    var discount = order.CalculateDiscount(customer);
```

Explanation: We call the '**CalculateDiscount**' method on the '**order**' object, passing in the '**customer**' as an argument. The result is stored in the '**discount**' variable.

Step 5: Assert - Verify the Outcome

Check the Result: Use assertion methods to verify that the result matches your expectations.

```
    // Assert
    Assert.Equal(10, discount);
```

Explanation: The **Assert.Equal** method checks that the calculated discount is $10, which is the expected outcome for a loyal customer. If the assertion fails, the test will fail, indicating that the method does not behave as expected.

Step 6: Run and Verify the Test.

a. **Run the Test.**

   i. In Visual Studio, open the **`Test Explorer`** (**`Test`** > **`Test Explorer`**).

   ii. Run the test you just wrote.

b. **Check the Results**: Verify that the test passes. If it fails, review the **`Arrange`**, **`Act`**, and **`Assert`** steps to identify any mistakes or issues.

Step 7: Apply the AAA Pattern to More Complex Scenarios.

As your tests grow in complexity, the AAA pattern remains useful for keeping your tests organized and understandable. For instance:

Handling Exceptions: Use the AAA pattern to test that exceptions are thrown under certain conditions.

```
[Fact]
public void CalculateDiscount_InvalidCustomer_ThrowsArgumentNull-
Exception()
{
    // Arrange
    var order = new Order();

    // Act & Assert
    Assert.Throws<ArgumentNullException>(() => order.Calculate-
Discount(null));
}
```

Data-Driven Tests: When using data-driven tests (for example, xUnit is **`[Theory]` `attribute`**), you can still structure each test case using AAA.

```
[Theory]
[InlineData(true, 10)]
[InlineData(false, 0)]
public void CalculateDiscount_VariousCustomerLoyalty_Returns
ExpectedDiscount(bool isLoyal, decimal expectedDiscount)
{
    // Arrange
    var customer = new Customer { IsLoyal = isLoyal };
    var order = new Order();

    // Act
    var discount = order.CalculateDiscount(customer);
```

```
        // Assert
        Assert.Equal(expectedDiscount, discount);
    }
```

Step 8: Refactor Tests for Readability and Maintainability.

a. **Use Helper Methods**: If your Arrange or Assert steps are complex, consider refactoring them into helper methods to keep your test code clean.

b. **Avoid Duplication**: Reuse setup code by leveraging test setup methods like `[SetUp]` in NUnit or constructor setups in xUnit.

```
public class OrderTests
{
    private Order _order;
    private Customer _customer;

    public OrderTests()
    {
        _order = new Order();
        _customer = new Customer();
    }

    [Fact]
    public void CalculateDiscount_CustomerIsLoyal_ReturnsDis-
count()
    {
        // Arrange
        _customer.IsLoyal = true;

        // Act
        var discount = _order.CalculateDiscount(_customer);

        // Assert
        Assert.Equal(10, discount);
    }
}
```

Summary

The Arrange, Act, Assert (AAA) pattern is a simple yet powerful way to structure your unit tests. By organizing your tests into these three distinct sections, you can create tests that are clear, consistent, and easy to maintain. This approach helps ensure that your tests are focused on verifying specific behaviors and that failures are easy to diagnose and fix.

Writing Testable Code: Dependency Injection, Mocking, and Stubbing

Writing testable code is a crucial part of ensuring that your applications are maintainable and reliable. By using techniques like Dependency Injection (DI), Mocking, and Stubbing, you can decouple your code from its dependencies, which makes it easier to write unit tests. This guide will explain each concept in detail, with code samples to illustrate how they work together.

Dependency Injection (DI)

Definition: Dependency Injection is a design pattern that allows you to inject dependencies (for example, services, repositories) into a class rather than having the class create these dependencies itself. This makes the class easier to test because you can provide mock or stub implementations of these dependencies during testing.

Why It is Important:

- **Decouples Code**: By injecting dependencies, your code becomes less dependent on specific implementations.
- **Enhances Testability**: You can easily swap out real dependencies for mock or stub versions in your tests.

Example: Suppose you have a service that depends on a repository, as shown here:

```
public interface IProductRepository
{
    Product GetProductById(int id);
}

public class ProductService
{
    private readonly IProductRepository _productRepository;

    public ProductService(IProductRepository productRepository)
    {
        _productRepository = productRepository;
    }

    public decimal GetProductPrice(int productId)
    {
        var product = _productRepository.GetProductById(productId);
        return product?.Price ?? 0m;
    }
}
```

Explanation:

- The **ProductService** class depends on **IProductRepository**.
- Instead of creating the **IProductRepository** instance inside the **ProductService**, it is injected through the constructor.

Step-by-Step: Implementing Dependency Injection

a. **Define the Dependency Interface**: Create an interface for the dependency (**IProductRepository**).

b. **Inject the Dependency**: Use constructor injection to inject the dependency into your class (**ProductService**).

c. **Register and Resolve Dependencies (in an Actual Application)**: If you are using a DI container (like in ASP.NET Core), you would register the dependency and its implementation in the **Startup.cs** file, as shown here:

```
services.AddScoped<IProductRepository, ProductRepository>();
services.AddScoped<ProductService>();
```

Mocking

Definition: Mocking is a technique where you create a mock object that simulates the behavior of a real object. In unit tests, mocks are used to verify interactions with dependencies (for example, method calls) without relying on the actual implementation.

Why It is Important:

- **Isolates Tests**: Mocking allows you to isolate the unit of work you are testing from its dependencies.
- **Verifies Interactions**: You can verify that certain methods were called with expected parameters.

Example: Let us continue with the **ProductService** example and write a test that verifies the **GetProductPrice** method:

```
[Fact]
public void GetProductPrice_ValidProductId_ReturnsCorrectPrice()
{
    // Arrange
    var mockRepository = new Mock<IProductRepository>();
    mockRepository.Setup(repo => repo.GetProductById(1))
                  .Returns(new Product { Id = 1, Price = 100m });

    var productService = new ProductService(mockRepository.
Object);
```

```
        // Act
        var price = productService.GetProductPrice(1);

        // Assert
        Assert.Equal(100m, price);
        mockRepository.Verify(repo => repo.GetProductById(1), Times.
    Once);
    }
```

Explanation:

- '`Mock<IProductRepository>`' creates a mock object of the `IProductRepository`.
- '`Setup`' configures the mock to return a specific result when `GetProductById` is called with an ID of 1.
- '`Verify`' checks that the method was called exactly once.

Step-by-Step: Implementing Mocking

a. **Install a Mocking Library**: Install a mocking library like `Moq` via NuGet:

```
dotnet add package Moq
```

b. **Create a Mock Object**: Use '`Mock<T>`' to create a mock object for the dependency.

c. **Set Up Behavior**: Use the '`Setup`' method to define how the mock should behave when certain methods are called.

d. **Inject the Mock Object**. Pass the mock object into your class under test, just like you would with a real dependency.

e. **Verify Interactions**: Use the '`Verify`' method to check that the expected interactions with the mock occurred.

Stubbing

Definition: Stubbing is similar to mocking, but instead of verifying interactions, you use stubs to provide canned responses for the methods of your dependencies. Stubs are typically used to return fixed data to the system under test.

Why It is Important:

- **Simplifies Testing**: Stubs provide predictable and controlled outputs, which simplify the testing of code in isolation.
- **Focus on Logic**: Stubbing allows you to focus on testing the logic of the method under test without worrying about the behavior of dependencies.

Example: Let us write a test using a stub to simulate the **IProductRepository**:

```
public class StubProductRepository : IProductRepository
{
    public Product GetProductById(int id)
    {
        return new Product { Id = id, Price = 100m };
    }
}

[Fact]
public void GetProductPrice_StubRepository_ReturnsFixedPrice()
{
    // Arrange
    var stubRepository = new StubProductRepository();
    var productService = new ProductService(stubRepository);

    // Act
    var price = productService.GetProductPrice(1);

    // Assert
    Assert.Equal(100m, price);
}
```

Explanation:

- '**StubProductRepository**' is a stub implementation of **IProductRepository** that always returns a Product with a price of 100m.
- This allows the **ProductService** to be tested in isolation without depending on the actual **ProductRepository** implementation.

Step-by-Step: Implementing Stubbing

- **Create a Stub Class**: Implement a stub version of the dependency, where methods return fixed data.
- **Inject the Stub**: Pass the stub object into your class under test, similar to how you would inject a mock or real object.
- **Use Stubs for Testing Logic**: Use stubs when you want to test how your code handles specific inputs without worrying about the complexity or correctness of dependencies.

Putting It All Together

By combining Dependency Injection, Mocking, and Stubbing, you can write highly testable code. Here is a quick summary of when to use each technique:

- **Dependency Injection**: Use DI to inject dependencies to make your code more flexible and easier to test.

- **Mocking**: Use mocks when you need to verify that your code interacts correctly with its dependencies.
- **Stubbing**: Use stubs when you need to provide controlled, predictable outputs from your dependencies to focus on testing the logic of your code.

Summary

Writing testable code requires careful consideration of how you manage dependencies. By applying Dependency Injection, you can decouple your classes from their dependencies. Mocking allows you to verify interactions with dependencies, while stubbing provides fixed responses to focus on testing the logic. Together, these practices lead to more robust, maintainable, and testable code in your C# applications.

Using Data-Driven Tests to Cover Multiple Test Cases in xUnit with C#

Data-driven testing is a technique that allows you to run the same test logic with different sets of input data. xUnit supports data-driven tests through the use of the `[Theory]` attribute combined with data attributes like `[InlineData]`, `[MemberData]`, or `[ClassData]`. This approach enables you to efficiently test multiple scenarios with a single test method.

Step 1: Install xUnit

Before writing data-driven tests, ensure that you have xUnit installed in your test project. If you have not set up an xUnit project yet:

a. Create an xUnit Test Project.

   i. Open Visual Studio.

   ii. Create a new xUnit Test Project.

b. Add xUnit via NuGet.

   i. Right-click on your test project in Solution Explorer.

   ii. Choose Manage NuGet Packages.

   iii. Search for `xunit` and `xunit.runner.visualstudio`, and install them.

Step 2: Write a Basic Data-Driven Test Using `[InlineData]`

The simplest form of data-driven testing in xUnit is using the `[InlineData]` attribute. This allows you to pass multiple sets of parameters to a single test method.

Example: Testing a method that checks whether a number is even:

```
public class MathTests-
{
    [Theory]
    [InlineData(2, true)]
    [InlineData(3, false)]
    [InlineData(4, true)]
    [InlineData(5, false)]
    public void IsEvenTest(int number, bool expected)
    {
        // Act
        bool result = IsEven(number);

        // Assert
        Assert.Equal(expected, result);
    }

    // Method under test
    private bool IsEven(int number)
    {
        return number % 2 == 0;
    }
}
```

Explanation:

- The **`[Theory]`** attribute indicates that this test method will be run multiple times with different input values.
- Each **`[InlineData]`** attribute specifies a set of arguments for the test method. In this example, the test runs four times with different integers, while checking whether they are even.

Step 3: Use `[MemberData]` for Complex Data

When you need more complex data or want to reuse data across multiple tests, you can use the **`[MemberData]`** attribute. This attribute allows you to supply test data from a method, property, or field.

Example: Testing a method that calculates the sum of two numbers:

```
public class MathTests
{
    [Theory]
    [MemberData(nameof(GetSumTestData))]
    public void AddTest(int number1, int number2, int expected-
Sum)
    {
```

```
            // Act
            int result = Add(number1, number2);

            // Assert
            Assert.Equal(expectedSum, result);
        }

        public static IEnumerable<object[]> GetSumTestData()
        {
            yield return new object[] { 1, 2, 3 };
            yield return new object[] { 5, 7, 12 };
            yield return new object[] { 10, 20, 30 };
            yield return new object[] { -1, -1, -2 };
        }

        // Method under test
        private int Add(int x, int y)
        {
            return x + y;
        }
    }
```

Explanation:

- **[MemberData(nameof(GetSumTestData))]** tells xUnit to retrieve test data from the **GetSumTestData** method.
- **GetSumTestData** returns an **IEnumerable<object[]>**, where each **object[]** contains the parameters for a single test run.
- This approach allows for more complex and reusable test data like collections, objects, or even data fetched from external sources.

Step 4: Use [ClassData] for Even More Flexibility

For even more complex scenarios, you can use **[ClassData]**, which allows you to create a custom class to provide test data. This is particularly useful when the data needs to be generated or processed before use.

Example: Testing a method that multiplies two numbers:

```
public class MathTests
{
    [Theory]
    [ClassData(typeof(MultiplyTestData))]
    public void MultiplyTest(int number1, int number2, int
expectedProduct)
    {
        // Act
        int result = Multiply(number1, number2);
```

```
            // Assert
            Assert.Equal(expectedProduct, result);
        }

        // Method under test
        private int Multiply(int x, int y)
        {
            return x * y;
        }
    }

    // Custom class to provide test data
    public class MultiplyTestData : IEnumerable<object[]>
    {
        public IEnumerator<object[]> GetEnumerator()
        {
            yield return new object[] { 2, 3, 6 };
            yield return new object[] { 5, 5, 25 };
            yield return new object[] { 10, 10, 100 };
            yield return new object[] { 0, 10, 0 };
        }

        IEnumerator IEnumerable.GetEnumerator() => GetEnumerator();
    }
```

Explanation:

- **`[ClassData(typeof(MultiplyTestData))]`** tells xUnit to use the **`MultiplyTestData`** class to provide test data.
- **`MultiplyTestData`** implements **`IEnumerable<object[]>`**, where each **`object[]`** is a set of parameters for a single test run.
- This method offers maximum flexibility, as you can generate, process, or even retrieve data from external sources before providing it to the test.

Step 5: Running Data-Driven Tests.

a. Run Tests in Visual Studio

   i. Open the Test Explorer in Visual Studio.

   ii. Run the tests as you normally would.

   iii. Each combination of data will result in a separate test run, and you will see the results for each case.

b. **Interpret Test Results**: **`Test Explorer`** will display each data-driven test case as a separate entry, which makes it easy to identify which cases passed or failed.

Summary

Data-driven testing in xUnit allows you to cover multiple test cases with a single test method by passing different sets of input data. You can use `[InlineData]` for simple cases, `[MemberData]` for more complex or reusable data, and `[ClassData]` for highly customized scenarios. By leveraging these features, you can efficiently test a wide range of inputs and conditions, while ensuring that your code is robust and reliable.

Debugging Failing xUnit Tests in Visual Studio

Debugging failing xUnit tests in Visual Studio is an essential skill to diagnose issues within your code. Visual Studio provides powerful tools to help you identify the root cause of a failing btest, which makes the debugging process efficient and straightforward. Here is a step-by-step guide on how to debug failing xUnit tests in Visual Studio.

Step 1: Identify the Failing Test.

a. **Run All Tests.**

   i. Open `Test Explorer` in Visual Studio (Go to `Test` > `Test Explorer`).

   ii. Click on `Run All` to execute all your tests.

b. **Locate the Failing Test**: In the `Test Explorer`, find the test that has failed. Failing tests will typically be highlighted in red, and you can click on the test to see the error message and stack trace.

Step 2: Analyze the Error Message

a. **Review the Error Message**: Click on the failing test in `Test Explorer` to view the detailed error message and stack trace. This information can give you clues about what went wrong.

b. **Examine the Stack Trace**: The stack trace will show the sequence of method calls that led to the failure, which will help you trace the issue back to the source code.

Step 3: Set a Breakpoint

a. **Open the Test Method**: Double-click on the failing test in `Test Explorer` to navigate directly to the test method in the code editor.

b. **Set a Breakpoint**: Click on the left margin next to the line of code where you suspect the issue might be. This will place a breakpoint, which will pause the execution of the test when it reaches this line.

Consider setting breakpoints at:

- The beginning of the test method
- Inside any conditional statements or loops
- On the method call that is directly related to the test failure

Step 4: Start Debugging.

a. **Run Tests in Debug Mode**

i. Right-click on the failing test in **`Test Explorer`** and select **`Debug Selected Tests`**. This will start the test in debug mode.

ii. Alternatively, you can click on the Debug All Tests button if you want to debug all tests.

b. **Examine the State at Each Breakpoint**: When the test execution reaches a breakpoint, Visual Studio will pause, which will allow you to inspect variables, evaluate expressions, and step through the code.

c. **Use Debugging Tools**

i. **`Watch Window`**: Add variables or expressions to the Watch Window to monitor their values as you step through the code.

ii. **`Locals Window`**: Use the Locals Window to see the values of variables in the current scope.

iii. **`Step Into (F11)`**: Step into the code to follow the execution into methods and see how they behave.

iv. **`Step Over (F10)`**: Skip over method calls to move to the next line of code.

v. **`Step Out (Shift + F11)`**: Exit the current method and return to the calling method.

Step 5: Modify the Code and Re-Run the Test

a. **Make Code Changes**: After identifying the issue, make the necessary code changes to fix the problem.

b. **Re-run the Test**: Save your changes and re-run the test in Test Explorer to see if the issue is resolved. You can do this by clicking Run or Debug Selected Tests again.

c. **Repeat If Necessary**: If the test fails again, repeat the debugging process until you resolve the issue.

Step 6: Use Additional Debugging Techniques

a. Use `Debug.WriteLine` or `Console.WriteLine`: Insert `Debug.WriteLine` or `Console.WriteLine` statements in your code to output diagnostic messages to the Output window during test execution. This can help you understand the flow of the program and the state of variables at specific points.

```
Debug.WriteLine($"Value of x: {x}");
```

b. **Test with Different Data**: If the failing test uses data-driven testing (for example, `[Theory]` with `[InlineData]`), consider running the test with different sets of data to isolate the issue.

c. **Check for Side Effects**: Ensure that the test is independent and that no side effects from previous tests are causing the failure. If necessary, refactor your test to avoid shared state or dependencies.

Step 7: Analyze and Improve Test Coverage

1. Run Code Coverage Analysis: Use Visual Studio's built-in code coverage tools to analyze how much of your code is covered by tests. This can help you identify untested paths that might be causing issues.

2. Add More Tests: If necessary, add more unit tests to cover additional scenarios and edge cases that might reveal hidden bugs.

Summary

Debugging failing xUnit tests in Visual Studio involves identifying the failing test, setting breakpoints, running the test in debug mode, and analyzing the state of your code as it executes. By using Visual Studio's debugging tools effectively, you can quickly diagnose and fix issues in your code, ensuring that your tests pass and your application is behaving as expected.

Setting Up Unit Tests to Run as Part of a CI Pipeline in Azure DevOps

Integrating unit tests into your Continuous Integration (CI) pipeline ensures that your code is automatically tested every time you commit changes. Azure DevOps provides a robust platform to set up and run your unit tests as part of the CI process. This guide will walk you through the steps to configure unit tests in a CI pipeline using Azure DevOps.

Step 1: Create an Azure DevOps Project.

a. **Sign in to Azure DevOps**: Go to dev.azure.com (https://dev.azure.com) and sign in with your Microsoft account.

b. **Create a New Project**

   i. Click on **`New Project`**.

   ii. Enter a name for your project (for example, **`MyTestProject`**).

   iii. Choose visibility (public or private) and click Create.

Step 2: Set Up a Git Repository

a. **Create a Git Repository**

   i. Navigate to Repos in your Azure DevOps project.

   ii. If you do not have a repository yet, click on Initialize to create one.

b. **Clone the Repository**: Clone the repository to your local machine using the following command:

```
git clone https://dev.azure.com/your-organization/your-project/_
git/your-repo
```

c. **Add Your Code**

   i. Add your C# project code and unit tests to the repository.

   ii. Commit and push the changes to the Azure DevOps repository.

```
git add .
git commit -m "Initial commit with unit tests"
git push origin main
```

Step 3: Create a CI Pipeline in Azure DevOps.

a. **Navigate to Pipelines**

   i. Go to the Pipelines section in Azure DevOps.

   ii. Click on Create Pipeline.

b. **Select a Repository**: Choose your repository from the list.

c. **Configure the Pipeline**

   i. Azure DevOps provides multiple ways to configure a pipeline. Choose **`YAML`** to define the pipeline as code, which is the recommended approach.

   ii. Azure DevOps will attempt to automatically detect your project type and generate a basic pipeline configuration.

d. **Define the Pipeline with YAML**: If Azure DevOps doesn't automatically generate the correct YAML, you can customize it. Here is an example YAML file for a .NET Core project with xUnit tests:

```
trigger:
  - main

pool:
  vmImage: 'windows-latest'

steps:
- task: UseDotNet@2
  inputs:
    packageType: 'sdk'
    version: '6.x'
    installationPath: $(Agent.ToolsDirectory)/dotnet

- script: dotnet restore
  displayName: 'Restore dependencies'

- script: dotnet build --configuration Release --no-restore
  displayName: 'Build the solution'

- script: dotnet test --configuration Release --no-build
--verbosity normal --logger trx
  displayName: 'Run unit tests'

- task: PublishTestResults@2
  inputs:
    testResultsFiles: '*/*.trx'
    testRunTitle: 'Unit Test Results'
```

Explanation:

- **`trigger`**: Automatically triggers the pipeline on commits to the main branch
- **`pool`**: Specifies the virtual machine image to use (Windows in this case)

Steps:

a. **`UseDotNet@2`**: Installs the .NET SDK on the agent

b. **`dotnet restore`**: Restores NuGet packages

c. **`dotnet build`**: Builds the solution in Release mode

d. **`dotnet test`**: Runs the unit tests and outputs results in the .trx format

e. **`PublishTestResults@2`**: Publishes the test results to Azure DevOps

e. **Save and Run the Pipeline**

   i. Click **`Save`** and **`Run`** to save the pipeline configuration and start the CI process.

   ii. Azure DevOps will automatically build your project and run the unit tests.

Step 4: Monitor and Review Test Results.

a. **View the Pipeline Run**

   i. After the pipeline is completed, you can view the results in the Pipelines section.

   ii. Click on the latest pipeline run to see the detailed output, including test results.

b. **Review Test Results**

   i. Navigate to the Tests tab within the pipeline run details.

   ii. You will see a summary of all the tests that were executed, including **`pass/ fail`** status, duration, and any error messages.

c. **Set Up Alerts (Optional)**: You can configure Azure DevOps to send alerts when tests fail. Go to **`Project Settings`** > **`Notifications`** and set up a notification rule to receive emails or other notifications when a pipeline fails.

Step 5: (Optional) Advanced Configuration and Integration.

a. **Test Coverage**: You can integrate code coverage tools (like **`Coverlet`**) into your pipeline to get detailed reports on how much of your code is covered by tests.

```
    - script: dotnet test --configuration Release --no-build
--collect:"XPlat Code Coverage"
      displayName: 'Run tests with code coverage'

    - task: PublishCodeCoverageResults@1
      inputs:
        codeCoverageTool: 'Cobertura'
        summaryFileLocation: '$(System.DefaultWorkingDirectory)/
coverage.cobertura.xml'
```

b. **Branch Policies**

   i. Set up branch policies in Azure Repos to require that the pipeline passes (including all tests) before any pull request can be merged.

   ii. Navigate to **`Repos`** > **`Branches`**, select the branch, and configure branch policies to include build validation.

3. **Parallel Test Execution**: For large test suites, consider parallelizing your tests to speed up execution. This can be done by configuring the '`dotnet test`' command to specify the maximum number of concurrent tests.

Summary

By integrating unit tests into your Azure DevOps CI pipeline, you ensure that your code is automatically tested with every commit. This setup helps maintain high code quality, prevents regressions, and provides quick feedback to developers. Azure DevOps makes it straightforward to configure, run, and monitor your tests as part of your CI/CD process.

Conclusion

In this chapter, we have explored the essential concepts and best practices for unit testing in Visual Studio. We have covered the basics of writing effective unit tests, including the importance of keeping tests small and focused, using the Arrange, Act, Assert (AAA) pattern, and ensuring that tests are independent and repeatable. We discussed how to leverage tools like mocking and stubbing to isolate dependencies, which will make your tests more reliable and easier to maintain. Additionally, we explored the benefits of data-driven testing to cover multiple scenarios with minimal code and emphasized the importance of running tests frequently, whether manually or as part of a Continuous Integration (CI) pipeline in Azure DevOps. By following these practices, you can ensure that your code is well-tested, robust, and ready for deployment.

As we move beyond the realm of isolated unit tests, the next chapter delves into the complexities of integrating your application with databases. Database integration is a critical aspect of modern software development, where ensuring seamless interaction between your application code and persistent data storage can make or break your system's reliability and performance. In this upcoming chapter, you will learn how to set up, configure, and test database connections, write efficient queries, and manage database migrations. We will also explore best practices for maintaining data integrity, optimizing performance, and testing database-related code to ensure your application runs smoothly in production environments. Whether you are working with relational databases, NoSQL, or cloud-based solutions, this chapter will equip you with the knowledge and tools needed to effectively integrate databases into your application.

Chapter 6
Database Integration

Introduction

Database integration is more than just a means of storing data; it is a crucial element that empowers applications with the ability to manage, manipulate, and secure data effectively. In Visual Studio, developers are provided with a wide range of tools and frameworks to streamline this integration, from traditional ADO.NET to the more modern Entity Framework Core (EF Core), and even cloud-based solutions like Azure SQL Database.

In modern software development, databases are integral to almost every application, providing the backbone for data storage, retrieval, and manipulation. Whether you are building a small web application, an enterprise-level solution, or even mobile apps, connecting your software to a reliable and well-structured database is crucial for maintaining data consistency, scalability, and performance. In this chapter, we will explore the importance of database integration, how it can be achieved within Visual Studio, and why it is indispensable for project development.

Structure

In this chapter, we will cover the following topics:

- Importance of Database Integration
- Different ways to integrate database in Visual Studio
- ADO.Net, Entity Framework (EF), SQL Server, Azure SQL
- Alternatives to Entity Framework - Dapper, NHibernate, Micro-ORMs
- LINQ - Language Integrated Query
- Code-First Approach for EF
- Database-First Approach for EF
- Model-First Approach for EF

Why Database Integration is Important

Data is one of the most valuable assets of any application. User information, transaction details, product inventories, and all other important data must be stored, accessed, and updated frequently. As a result, database integration provides a critical link between the application's interface and its data repository. Here is why it is essential:

- **Data Management**: Applications need a structured way to store, manage, and retrieve data. Databases allow developers to query, update, and manipulate data efficiently without losing consistency.
- **Persistent Storage**: Unlike in-memory data structures, databases allow for long-term storage of data. This persistence is essential in real-world applications where data must survive system reboots, crashes, or updates.
- **Concurrency**: Modern applications handle multiple users or transactions simultaneously. Databases are designed to manage concurrent access and ensure that data integrity is maintained even under heavy loads.
- **Security**: Databases provide robust mechanisms for controlling access to data. By integrating with authentication systems, they ensure that only authorized users can access or modify sensitive information.
- **Scalability**: As applications grow, so does their need for data storage and retrieval. Databases, particularly those with cloud integration, can scale with the application, while ensuring that performance does not degrade as data volumes increase.

Why Database Integration is Needed for Project Development

- **Centralized Data Handling**: As applications scale, managing data locally (for example, in files or arrays) becomes infeasible. Databases provide a centralized, reliable system for handling large volumes of data in a structured manner.
- **Separation of Concerns**: By using databases, developers can separate the data storage and management layer from the application logic. This not only improves the maintainability of the application, but also promotes scalability and flexibility in the architecture.
- **Enabling Complex Business Logic**: Databases allow for the implementation of complex business logic, such as transactions, data validation, and rules enforcement, through stored procedures, triggers, and views.
- **Data-Driven Applications**: Modern applications, especially in the enterprise domain, are increasingly data-driven. Features like reporting, analytics, and

real-time updates are only possible with a solid database backend integrated into the application.

- **User Management and Security**: Databases are central to handling user credentials, permissions, and data privacy. Integrating a secure database ensures that sensitive data is protected, and user access is controlled.
- **Performance Optimization**: Databases come with optimization techniques like indexing, caching, and partitioning, which are essential for maintaining the performance of applications as they scale. Visual Studio's integrated tools help developers analyze and optimize queries for faster data access.

How Database Integration is Done in Visual Studio

Visual Studio simplifies database integration through a range of tools and frameworks, enabling developers to work seamlessly with databases. Here are the key approaches:

ADO.NET for Direct Database Access

ADO.NET is a powerful data access framework that allows developers to communicate directly with databases using SQL commands. Visual Studio provides full support for ADO.NET, which makes it easy to connect, query, and manage data.

- **Setup**: Developers can add a database connection from the **Server Explorer** in Visual Studio.
- **Data Retrieval**: Using data adapters and readers, developers can execute SQL queries and retrieve data directly into their applications.
- **Integration with Datasets**: ADO.NET allows the creation of strongly-typed datasets for structured data management.

Entity Framework (EF)

Entity Framework Core is an Object-Relational Mapping (ORM) framework that simplifies database interactions by allowing developers to work with data as .NET objects. It abstracts the complexities of SQL, which lets developers interact with databases through LINQ queries and model classes.

- **Code-First Approach**: Developers define their database schema using C# code, and Entity Framework generates the corresponding database structure automatically.
- **Database-First Approach**: In scenarios where a database already exists, EF can

reverse-engineer the database and generate models that correspond to the existing schema.

- **Migrations**: Entity Framework supports migrations, allowing developers to manage changes to the database schema over time, while ensuring that existing data remains intact.

SQL Server Integration

Visual Studio offers native integration with SQL Server, one of the most widely-used database management systems. With tools like SQL Server Data Tools (SSDT), developers can manage database projects, design schemas, and deploy them directly from the IDE.

- **Database Projects**: Developers can create SQL Server database projects in Visual Studio, design tables, stored procedures, and views, and manage version control for database changes.
- **Query Editor**: Visual Studio's integrated SQL query editor allows developers to write, execute, and test SQL queries within the IDE.
- **Data Comparison and Synchronization**: SSDT enables developers to compare different versions of databases and synchronize changes easily.

Azure SQL and Cloud Databases

With the increasing adoption of cloud technologies, many applications leverage cloud databases such as Azure SQL Database or Cosmos DB. Visual Studio provides robust support for cloud databases, which makes it easy to integrate with Azure services directly.

- **Azure SQL Database**: Developers can manage, deploy, and interact with Azure SQL databases from within Visual Studio, while taking advantage of scalable, high-performance cloud storage solutions. However, creating new Azure SQL databases requires the Azure Portal, CLI or PowerShell.
- **Cosmos DB**: For non-relational data models, Cosmos DB offers a globally distributed, multi-model database solution. While Visual Studio provides SDK-based integration and the Cosmos DB Emulator for development, full in-IDE tooling for direct interaction with Cosmos DB is limited.

Here is a step-by-step process to connect to a SQL Server from Visual Studio:

Step 1: Open Server Explorer

a. Open Visual Studio.

b. In the `View` menu, select `Server Explorer`. This window allows you to manage database connections, servers, and other resources.

Step 2: Add a New Connection

a. In the **`Server Explorer`** window, right-click on **`Data Connections`**.

b. Click **`Add Connection...`** from the context menu.

Step 3: Configure the Connection Settings

a. In the **`Add Connection`** window, choose **`Microsoft SQL Server`** as the data source.

   i. If you do not see **`Microsoft SQL Server`**, click on the **`Change`** button, and select it from the list.

b. In the **`Server Name`** field, enter the name of your SQL Server instance. This can be:

   i. **`localhost`** or (**`local`**) for a local SQL Server

   ii. The name of a remote SQL Server instance, if you are connecting to a server on another machine

Step 4: Select Authentication Method

a. Choose the authentication method:

   i. **Windows Authentication**: This uses your Windows credentials to log in to the SQL Server.

   ii. **SQL Server Authentication**: You need to provide a username and password for a SQL Server login.

Step 5: Choose the Database

a. After the server connection is established, in the **`Select or enter a database name`** dropdown, choose the database you want to connect to.

   i. If you are unsure, click the **`Test Connection`** button to verify the connection to the server first.

   ii. If successful, proceed to select the **`database`**.

Step 6: Test the Connection

a. Click **`Test Connection`** to ensure that Visual Studio can successfully connect to the SQL Server and database.

   i. If the test is successful, you will see a message indicating that the connection is valid.

   ii. If the test fails, verify the server name, authentication method, and credentials.

Step 7: Finalize the Connection

a. Once the test is successful, click `OK` to finish the connection.

b. The connection will now appear under `Data Connections` in the `Server Explorer` window.

Step 8: Explore and Work with the Database

a. Expand the connected database node under `Data Connections` in the `Server Explorer`.

b. From here, you can explore tables, views, stored procedures, and other database objects.

c. Right-click on tables or views to retrieve data or execute queries using the built-in query editor.

Step 9: Query the Database (Optional)

a. If you want to query the database, right-click on the database name in `Server Explorer` and choose `New Query`.

b. Write your SQL queries and execute them directly within Visual Studio.

By following these steps, you will successfully connect to a SQL Server instance from Visual Studio, which will enable you to manage and interact with your databases directly within the IDE.

Now that we know all the different ways using which we can integrate database with our application. Let us dive in deeper into each way starting with ADO.NET.

As data-driven applications have become the norm, managing the connection between your .NET application and various data sources is critical. ADO.NET is a foundational technology within the .NET Framework that provides the means to connect, retrieve, manipulate, and update data in a relational database. While the data-access landscape has evolved over time, ADO.NET remains a robust and efficient way to interact with databases at a low level.

ADO.NET

ADO.NET stands for ActiveX Data Objects for .NET. It is a set of classes within the .NET Framework designed to facilitate communication between .NET applications and data sources such as SQL Server, Oracle, MySQL, and others. ADO.NET provides:

- **Connection Objects** to establish a communication line with the database
- **Command Objects** to execute SQL queries and stored procedures

- **Data Reader Objects** to retrieve data in a fast, forward-only, read-only manner
- **Data Adapter and DataSet Objects** to manage disconnected data operations

At its core, ADO.NET serves as a bridge between your application's business logic and the underlying data store. It is part of the `System.Data` namespace and is fully integrated into the .NET environment.

Importance for .NET Application Development and Lifecycle

- **Maturity and Stability:** ADO.NET is a well-established technology that has been around since the early days of .NET. It is stable, well-documented, and widely supported.
- **Performance:** For developers who need fine-grained control over database operations and the highest possible performance, ADO.NET offers low-level APIs and efficient, while streaming reads of large datasets.
- **Control and Flexibility:** Unlike ORM (Object-Relational Mapping) tools, ADO.NET does not abstract away the SQL or the database structure. Developers retain full control over queries, transaction management, and error handling.
- **Broad Data Source Support:** ADO.NET providers are available for most major databases, while ensuring that it can be a one-stop solution for many different data access needs.

Advantages of Using ADO.NET in a Project

- **High Performance:** Directly working with SQL commands and readers can be more performant than using ORMs.
- **Low-Level Control:** Developers can hand-tune queries, manage connections explicitly, and optimize data access patterns.
- **Ease of Understanding:** For those familiar with SQL and relational databases, ADO.NET provides a straightforward mapping to database interactions.
- **Disconnected Model:** The DataSet and DataTable provide a disconnected model that simplifies working with data offline or asynchronously.

Disadvantages of Using ADO.NET in a Project

- **Verbosity:** Compared to modern ORMs, the amount of boilerplate code can be higher.
- **Manual Mapping:** You must manually handle query results and map them to objects or data structures, while increasing development time.
- **Higher Maintenance:** Changes in database schema or business logic can lead to a lot of code updates if queries are spread throughout the codebase.

Better Options Available Compared to ADO.NET

In recent years, the following higher-level data access technologies have emerged that simplify the developer experience:

- **Entity Framework Core (EF):** An ORM that reduces the need for repetitive SQL writing by allowing you to work with strongly typed objects.
- **Dapper:** A lightweight ORM or micro-ORM that simplifies data access code while still giving you full SQL control.
- **LINQ to SQL:** A built-in solution for mapping objects to SQL tables directly. LINQ to SQL is effectively deprecated for modern .NET development.
- **Third-Party ORM Tools:** Tools like NHibernate and others offer more features than raw ADO.NET.

Step-by-Step Process to Connect a C# Application to a Database Using ADO.NET

Step 1: Install or Reference the Appropriate ADO.NET Provider

If you are connecting to SQL Server, you will likely use **`System.Data.SqlClient`**, which is typically included with .NET. For other databases like MySQL or Oracle, you must install their respective .NET data providers.

Define the Connection String

The connection string is a key-value string that specifies the database server, the database name, and the necessary credentials.

Example of SQL Server Authentication:

```
string connectionString = "Server=your_server_name;Database=your_
database_name;User Id=your_username;Password=your_password;";
```

Windows Authentication (SQL Server):

```
string connectionString = "Server=your_server_name;Database=your_
database_name;Integrated Security=True;";
```

Step 2: Create and Open a Connection

```
using System.Data.SqlClient;
// Define the connection string
string connectionString = "Server=.;Database=SampleDB;Integrated
Security=True;";

// Create the connection object
using (SqlConnection conn = new SqlConnection(connectionString))
{
```

```
        // Open the connection
        conn.Open();
        // At this point, you are connected to the database
        // and can execute commands or queries
}
```

Step 3: Execute a Command and Retrieve Data

To retrieve data, you can use a **SqlCommand** and a **SqlDataReader** (for forward-only, read-only data):

```
using (SqlConnection conn = new SqlConnection(connectionString))
{
        conn.Open();
        string query = "SELECT Id, Name, Email FROM Users";
        using (SqlCommand cmd = new SqlCommand(query, conn))
        {
                using (SqlDataReader reader = cmd.ExecuteReader())
                {
                        while (reader.Read())
                        {
                                int id = reader.GetInt32(0);
                                string name = reader.GetString(1);
                                string email = reader.GetString(2);
                                // Process the retrieved data
                        }
                }
        }
}
```

Step 4: Display the Data in a C# User Interface

If you are developing a Windows Forms or WPF application, you might populate the data into a **DataGridView** (WinForms) or a **DataGrid** (WPF).

Example (WinForms with DataGridView):

```
DataTable dataTable = new DataTable();
using (SqlConnection conn = new SqlConnection(connectionString))
{
        conn.Open();
        string query = "SELECT Id, Name, Email FROM Users";
        using (SqlCommand cmd = new SqlCommand(query, conn))
                {
                        using (SqlDataReader reader = cmd.Exe-
cuteReader())
                        {
                                dataTable.Load(reader);
                        }
                }
```

```
}

// Assume you have a DataGridView control named dataGridView1
dataGridView1.DataSource = dataTable;
```

This approach loads the data directly into a **DataTable**, which is then assigned as the **DataSource** of the UI element.

Step 5: Save and Update Data Back to the Database

When updating the database, you can either execute SQL **INSERT**, **UPDATE**, or **DELETE** commands directly via **SqlCommand**, or you can use a **SqlDataAdapter** connected to a **DataSet** or **DataTable**.

Direct Insert Example:

```
using (SqlConnection conn = new SqlConnection(connectionString))
{
	conn.Open();
	string insertQuery = "INSERT INTO Users (Name, Email)
VALUES (@Name, @Email)";
	using (SqlCommand cmd = new SqlCommand(insertQuery, conn))
	{
		cmd.Parameters.AddWithValue("@Name", "New User");
		cmd.Parameters.AddWithValue("@Email",
"newuser@example.com");
		int rowsAffected = cmd.ExecuteNonQuery();
		// rowsAffected indicates how many rows were inserted
	}
}
```

Using a DataAdapter for Disconnected Updates:

```
DataTable dataTable = new DataTable();

using (SqlConnection conn = new SqlConnection(connectionString))
{
	conn.Open();
	using (SqlDataAdapter adapter = new SqlDataAdapter
("SELECT Id, Name, Email FROM Users", conn))
	{
		// Automatically generate commands for Insert/Up-
date/Delete
		SqlCommandBuilder builder = new SqlCommandBuilder
(adapter);
		// Fill the DataTable
		adapter.Fill(dataTable);
		// Modify the data locally
		DataRow row = dataTable.NewRow();
		row["Name"] = "Another User";
```

```
                row["Email"] = "another@example.com";
                dataTable.Rows.Add(row);

                // Now push changes back to the database
                adapter.Update(dataTable);
            }
        }
```

Summary

ADO.NET remains an essential part of the .NET ecosystem for developers who want to exercise fine control over database operations. While newer abstractions and ORMs can simplify data access, ADO.NET's direct approach can result in better performance and a deeper understanding of what is happening behind the scenes. By following the steps outlined above, you can establish a robust, maintainable connection between your .NET application and a relational database, retrieve and display data, and handle updates with confidence.

Before getting into the details of database integration, let us take a look at Entity Framework and see how we can leverage it.

Entity Framework Core

Entity Framework Core is Microsoft's recommended ORM solution for .NET developers. It acts as a bridge between the relational databases and the object-oriented world of .NET languages like C#. Instead of working directly with tables, columns, and SQL commands, developers can work with C# classes (known as entities) and leverage LINQ (Language-Integrated Query) to query and manipulate data. EF handles the translation of these queries into SQL and maps the returned results into objects. This improves developer productivity by significantly reducing the amount of boilerplate code and SQL required.

With EF, you can:

- Map database tables to .NET classes.
- Use LINQ (Language Integrated Query) to query data.
- Automatically handle database schema changes through migrations.
- Manage relationships between entities with ease.

Importance of EF Core for .NET Application Development and Lifecycle

- **Rapid Development:** EF Core accelerates the development process by eliminating much of the repetitive code needed for database interactions.

This allows developers to focus on business logic rather than on database plumbing.

- **Maintainability:** Because EF models are strongly typed, refactoring (such as renaming a property) is simpler and less error-prone. The application can evolve over time without breaking large swaths of data access code.
- **Portability and Flexibility:** EF supports multiple database providers (for example, SQL Server, MySQL, PostgreSQL), which makes it relatively straightforward to switch or capable of supporting multiple databases in different environments.
- **Consistent Patterns:** EF enforces patterns and best practices in data access, which encourages a clean, well-structured codebase that is easier to understand and maintain as the project grows.
- **Tight Integration with .NET:** EF is developed and maintained by Microsoft, which ensures first-class integration with the .NET ecosystem, language features, and tooling support such as Visual Studio.

Advantages of Using Entity Framework Core

- **Productivity Gains:** EF reduces the need to write raw SQL. Developers can quickly get started by generating a model from an existing database or by creating classes first and letting EF create the database schema.
- **Strong Typing and IntelliSense:** Since EF uses C# classes for entities, you get compile-time type checking, IntelliSense support in Visual Studio, and easier debugging.
- **LINQ Support:** LINQ provides a unified way to query data in a strongly typed manner. Queries become more readable, maintainable, and testable.
- **Change Tracking:** EF automatically tracks changes made to your entity objects, which simplifies the create, update, and delete operations.
- **Migrations:** EF supports schema migrations, which allows you to version and evolve your database schema over time with minimal manual effort.

Disadvantages of Using Entity Framework

- **Performance Overhead:** EF's abstraction introduces a performance cost compared to raw SQL or micro-ORMs. For very large-scale and performance-critical systems, EF might be too heavy.
- **Complexity in Certain Scenarios:** While EF makes common scenarios easier, complex queries or bulk operations might require falling back to raw SQL or stored procedures.
- **Learning Curve:** Understanding the EF lifecycle, tracking states, and query optimization strategies can be challenging for beginners.

- **Less Control Over Generated SQL:** Although EF gives some control via raw SQL or stored procedures, the generated SQL might not always be as optimized as hand-tuned queries.

Better Options Compared to EF

While EF is a solid choice for many projects, there are alternatives worth considering:

- **Dapper:** A lightweight micro-ORM developed by Stack Overflow, which is known for its excellent performance and minimal overhead. It is closer to raw SQL, providing more control, but less abstraction.
- **NHibernate:** A mature, feature-rich ORM that can match EF in capabilities and often surpasses it in configurability and support for complex domain modeling.
- **Raw ADO.NET:** For scenarios that demand maximum performance and minimal overhead, writing raw SQL and using data readers might be more appropriate.
- **Micro-ORMs (like `PetaPoco`, `ServiceStack.OrmLite`):** Similar to Dapper, these libraries provide a balance between ease-of-use and control, with less overhead than EF.

Step-By-Step: Connecting a C# Application to a Database Using EF

We have provided a walkthrough of setting up Entity Framework in a .NET application and have defined a connection string, how to query data, and display or update it in your application.

Prerequisites

- A .NET development environment (Visual Studio or VS Code with .NET SDK)
- A database installed and running (for example, SQL Server)
- The Entity Framework NuGet packages (for example, **`Microsoft.EntityFrameworkCore and Microsoft.EntityFrameworkCore.SqlServer`**, if targeting SQL Server)

Step 1: Install Entity Framework NuGet Packages

Open the Package Manager Console (in Visual Studio) or a terminal window and run the following commands:

```
Install-Package Microsoft.EntityFrameworkCore
Install-Package Microsoft.EntityFrameworkCore.SqlServer
Install-Package Microsoft.EntityFrameworkCore.Tools
```

Step 2. Define the Connection String

A connection string defines how your application connects to the database. It typically resides in the **appsettings.json** (for .NET Core/5+) or the **Web.config/ App.config** (for .NET Framework) and looks like this:

appsettings.json settings (for .Net Core/.Net 5+ versions):

```
{
      "ConnectionStrings": {
            "DefaultConnection":
            "Server=YOUR_SERVER_NAME;Database=YOUR_DATABASE_
NAME;User Id=YOUR_USERNAME;Password=YOUR_PASSWORD;"
      }
}
```

Web.config settings (for .NET Framework):

```
<configuration>
      <connectionStrings>
            <add name="DefaultConnection" connectionString
="Server=YOUR_SERVER_NAME;Database=YOUR_DATABASE_NAME;User
Id=YOUR_USERNAME;Password=YOUR_PASSWORD;" providerName="System.
Data.SqlClient" />
      </connectionStrings>
</configuration>
```

Step 3: Create Your Entity Classes

Create C# classes that represent tables in your database. For example, if you have a **Products** table, it will look like this:

```
public class Product
{
      public int ProductId { get; set; }
      public string Name { get; set; }
      public decimal Price { get; set; }
}
```

Step 4: Create the EF DbContext

A **DbContext** class defines which entities are included and how EF maps them to the database. Consider this example code:

```
using Microsoft.EntityFrameworkCore;
public class AppDbContext : DbContext
{
      private readonly string _connectionString;
      public AppDbContext(DbContextOptions<AppDbContext> options):
base(options) { }AppDbContext(string connectionString)
```

```
        public DbSet<Product> Products { get; set; }

        protected override void OnConfiguring(DbContextOptions-
Builder optionsBuilder)
        {
                optionsBuilder.UseSqlServer(_connectionString);
        }
}
```

.NET Core/5+ Approach Using Dependency Injection:

If you are using a modern .NET application, you might define your **`DbContext`** in **`Startup.cs`** or **`Program.cs`** through the following:

```
builder.Services.AddDbContext<AppDbContext>(options =>
options.UseSqlServer(builder.Configuration.GetConnection-
String("DefaultConnection")));
```

Step 5: Calling the Connection String from C# Code

If you are using a simple console or WinForms/WPF application, use the following:

```
string connectionString = "Server=YOUR_SERVER_NAME;Database=YOUR_
DATABASE_NAME;User Id=YOUR_USERNAME;Password=YOUR_PASSWORD;";
using (var context = new AppDbContext(connectionString))
{
        // context is now ready to use
}
```

For .NET Core/5+, you would read this connection string from configuration:

```
var configuration = new ConfigurationBuilder()
                        .AddJsonFile("appsettings.json")
                        .Build();

string connectionString = configuration.GetConnectionString
("DefaultConnection");
using (var context = new AppDbContext(connectionString))
{
        // …
}
```

Step 6: Retrieve Data Using EF

Once the context is set up, retrieving data is pretty much straightforward, if you use LINQ queries as follows:

```
using (var context = new AppDbContext(connectionString))
{
        var products = context.Products.ToList(); // Retrieve all
products
```

```
        var cheapProducts = context.Products.Where(p => p.Price < 
10).ToList(); // Filtered query
}
```

Step 7. Displaying Data in a C# User Interface (for example, WinForms, WPF)

If you have a WinForms application with a **DataGridView** control, you can bind data directly, as shown here:

```
using (var context = new AppDbContext(connectionString))
{
        var products = context.Products.ToList();
        dataGridView1.DataSource = products;
}
```

For WPF, you might set the **ItemsSource** of a **DataGrid** in the following manner:

```
using (var context = new AppDbContext(connectionString))
{
        var products = context.Products.ToList();
        myDataGrid.ItemsSource = products;
}
```

If you are using ASP.NET Core MVC or Razor Pages, you can pass the collection to the view and render it using HTML tables.

Step 8: Save and Update the Data Back to the Database

Inserting a New Record:

```
using (var context = new AppDbContext(connectionString))
{
        var newProduct = new Product { Name = "New Widget", Price 
= 19.99m };
        context.Products.Add(newProduct);
        context.SaveChanges(); // Execute INSERT in the database
}
```

Updating an Existing Record:

```
using (var context = new AppDbContext(connectionString))
{
        var product = context.Products.FirstOrDefault(p => p.
ProductId == 1);
        if (product != null)
        {
                product.Price = 9.99m; // Update a property
                context.SaveChanges(); // Execute UPDATE in the 
database
        }
}
```

Deleting a Record:

```
using (var context = new AppDbContext(connectionString))
{
	var product = context.Products.FirstOrDefault(p => p.
ProductId == 1);
	if (product != null)
	{
		context.Products.Remove(product);
		context.SaveChanges(); // Execute DELETE in the da-
tabase
	}
}
```

Summary

Entity Framework simplifies and accelerates data access in .NET projects by eliminating much of the boilerplate code and allowing developers to work with strongly typed objects rather than raw SQL. Its integration into the .NET ecosystem, support for migrations, and tooling make it a popular choice for many applications. However, it is not without trade-offs, particularly during performance-critical scenarios.

While EF can be an excellent starting point and often the right tool for CRUD-focused business apps, remember to consider alternatives like Dapper or NHibernate for specific performance or complexity requirements. Nonetheless, mastering Entity Framework remains a valuable skill for any .NET developer and can substantially improve productivity, maintainability, and overall development experience.

LINQ is used to query the data in Entity Framework.

What is LINQ?

LINQ (Language Integrated Query) is a feature of the .NET platform that provides a consistent, readable, and declarative way to query data from various sources such as databases, collections, XML, or data retrieved from web services directly within the C# or VB.NET language. LINQ enables developers to use a uniform syntax to access data irrespective of the data source.

Key Characteristics of LINQ

- Integrated directly into .NET languages like C#
- Strongly-typed queries with compile-time checking
- Uses query syntax (from, where, select) or method syntax (**`.Where()`**, **`.Select()`**)
- Can query data from collections, databases (via LINQ to SQL/Entity Framework), XML, and more

Some key basic concepts of LINQ are as follows:

Namespaces: To use LINQ, include the required namespace in the following way:

```
using System.Linq;
```

Data Sources: LINQ works with a variety of data sources, as explained here:

- **LINQ to Objects**: Queries collections like **List<T>** or Array
- **LINQ to Entity Framework Core**: Queries relational databases
- **LINQ to XML**: Queries XML documents

Query Syntax: This is a declarative, SQL-like syntax for writing LINQ queries.

```
var result = from item in collection
             where item.Property == value
             select item;
```

Method Syntax: This is a functional syntax that uses extension methods.

```
    var result = collection.Where(item => item.Property == value).
Select(item => item);
```

Common LINQ Methods:

- `Where`: Filters elements based on a condition
- `Select`: Projects each element into a new form
- `OrderBy/OrderByDescending`: Orders elements
- `GroupBy`: Groups elements based on a key
- `Aggregate`, `Sum`, `Count`, `Average`: Aggregation functions

Deferred Execution: Queries are not executed until you iterate over the results at runtime, such as with '`foreach`'.

Key differences between Traditional Data Access and LINQ are mentioned below:

Feature	Traditional Data Access	LINQ
Syntax	SQL strings or custom logic for collections	Unified query syntax for all data sources
Type Safety	Requires careful validation of SQL strings	Strongly-typed queries checked at compile-time
Integration	Queries written separately (for example, SQL in stored procs)	Integrated into C# or VB.NET language
Readability	Can be verbose or hard to read	Clean, concise, and declarative syntax.

Data Source	Separate logic for databases, collections, XML, and so on	Unified approach for multiple data sources
Error Detection	Errors are often caught at runtime.	Errors are caught at compile-time.

Table 6.1: *Differences between Traditional Data Access and LINQ*

Why Using LINQ is Better

- **Unified Query Language:** LINQ provides a consistent way to query various data sources, whether it is an in-memory collection, a relational database, or XML.
- **Strongly Typed and Compile-Time Checked:** LINQ queries are strongly typed, and errors are caught at compile time rather than runtime. This reduces bugs and increases reliability.
- **Improved Readability:** LINQ uses a declarative syntax that is easy to read and understand compared to traditional nested loops or string-based SQL queries.
- **Less Code, More Functionality:** With LINQ, you can achieve more with fewer lines of code. This makes code concise and easier to maintain.
- **Deferred Execution:** LINQ queries support deferred execution, meaning they are executed only when the data is needed. This can improve performance by avoiding unnecessary computations.
- **Intellisense Support:** LINQ integrates seamlessly with Visual Studio, offering features like IntelliSense for method suggestions, property access, and query construction.
- **Composability:** LINQ allows you to compose queries dynamically by chaining multiple methods or queries together.
- **Data Transformations:** LINQ makes it easy to transform data into different shapes or structures using methods like '`Select`' and '`GroupBy`'.
- **Integration with Entity Framework:** When using LINQ with Entity Framework, you can work with high-level abstractions rather than worrying about SQL queries and database interactions.
- **Eliminates Magic Strings:** Traditional approaches often require SQL strings, which can lead to runtime errors if column names change. LINQ eliminates this risk by relying on strongly-typed members.

Example: Traditional vs LINQ

Traditional SQL Query:

```
string query = "SELECT * FROM Customers WHERE Country = 'USA'";
SqlCommand command = new SqlCommand(query, connection);
```

```
SqlDataReader reader = command.ExecuteReader();
while (reader.Read())
{
        Console.WriteLine(reader["Name"]);
}
```

LINQ Query:

```
var result = from customer in db.Customers
             where customer.Country == "USA"
             select customer.Name;
foreach (var name in result)
{
        Console.WriteLine(name);
}
```

Summary

LINQ enhances data access in .NET by unifying query syntax, enhancing readability, and reducing errors through strong typing and compile-time checks. It integrates seamlessly into .NET languages, which makes it the preferred choice for modern development over traditional data access methods. Whether you are querying in-memory objects, databases, or XML, LINQ is a powerful tool that enhances productivity and simplifies code.

Different Ways to Use EF in a .NET Core Project

Entity Framework Core (EF Core) offers three primary approaches for interacting with databases in .NET Core projects:

Code-First Approach: This section explores what EF Code First is, why it matters, and how to implement it in your .NET applications. We will delve into the advantages and disadvantages, compare it with other options, and provide step-by-step guidance on connecting to a database, retrieving data, displaying it in a user interface, and saving or updating records back to the database.

Code First is an Entity Framework development approach in which you primarily focus on writing your .NET model classes first. Once you have defined your domain models, the underlying database schema (tables, columns, relationships) is derived automatically based on conventions or configuration through data annotations or the fluent API.

Key Points

- You begin by writing C# classes that represent your domain entities.
- EF generates the database schema from these classes, often without needing you to write database scripts manually.

Database changes can be handled via migrations, which keep your database schema aligned with your evolving C# models.

- **How It Works**
  a. Create classes to represent your entities (tables)
  b. Configure relationships and data annotations within your classes
  c. Use migrations to generate and apply database schema changes
- **When to Use**
  - When starting a new project without an existing database
  - When you prefer to define the database schema in your application code
- **Advantages**
  - Full control over the database schema from your codebase
  - Seamless schema evolution with migrations

The Importance of Code First for .NET Application Development and Lifecycle

- **Developer Productivity:** By starting with **POCO (Plain Old CLR Object) classes**, developers can focus on the business logic and domain modeling first. This leads to a more domain-driven approach, where the code models the real-world entities without database-centric distractions.
- **Flexibility and Agility:** As requirements change, Code First allows developers to modify the domain classes and use migrations to smoothly update the database schema. This reduces friction in iterative development cycles and shortens the time-to-market.
- **Maintainability:** Having the schema defined in code makes it easier for teams to version-control database changes, review them, and collaborate effectively. Migrations can be part of your continuous integration and deployment pipeline, ensuring that database changes are tracked and reproducible.
- **Decoupling from Database Details:** You are not tied to a specific database technology at the onset. The abstraction offered by EF Code First allows you to switch underlying database providers (SQL Server, MySQL, PostgreSQL, and so on) with minimal changes in the codebase.

Advantages of Using the Code First Approach

- **Convention Over Configuration:** EF uses sensible defaults to create database schema from your classes, which minimizes configuration overhead.
- **Migrations for Database Evolution:** As you alter your models, you can use `Add-Migration` and `Update-Database` commands to manage schema

changes. This streamlined approach simplifies synchronization between code and database.

- **Strongly-Typed Models and LINQ Support:** By having models defined in code, you gain type-safety. LINQ queries over these models are easier to write and maintain compared to working directly with SQL strings.
- **Domain-Driven Design Friendly:** Code First naturally aligns with domain-driven design principles, which encourages a focus on the domain model rather than database schema.

Disadvantages of Using the Code First Approach

- **Initial Learning Curve:** Developers unfamiliar with EF or Code First conventions may find the initial setup and configuration confusing.
- **Limited Direct Control Over Generated Schema:** Although you can customize the schema through attributes and the fluent API, it can be more complex than using a Database First approach where you start from a known schema.
- **Performance Overheads:** In some scenarios, the added abstraction can lead to slight performance hits compared to direct ADO.NET or handcrafted stored procedures.
- **Complex Legacy Integration:** If you are integrating with a legacy database that already has a complex schema, Code First might not be as straightforward as Database First.

Alternative Approaches Compared to Code First

- **Database First:** In this approach, you start with an existing database, and EF generates model classes based on that schema. This is beneficial when working with a well-established legacy database, but it is less flexible when evolving the schema frequently.
- **Model First:** You visually design an EF model using the Entity Framework Designer, and then generate both code and database schema from that conceptual model. While it provides a nice graphical approach, it often adds complexity to version control and CI/CD pipelines.
- **Micro-ORMs (for example, Dapper):** For scenarios where performance and fine-grained control are paramount, micro-ORMs like Dapper provide direct SQL mapping with fewer abstractions. However, they lack the productivity features of EF's Code First approach.

Step-by-Step Process: Connecting a C# Application to a Database Using Code-First

Prerequisites

- .NET 5+ or .NET Framework 4.x Environment

- Visual Studio or VS Code
- EF Core or EF 6 NuGet Packages

For the following demonstration, we will assume EF Core and a SQL Server database.

Step 1: Create a New C# Project

Open Visual Studio and create a new Console App (.NET Core) or ASP.NET Core Web Application.

Install the necessary EF Core packages through the following commands:

```
dotnet add package Microsoft.EntityFrameworkCore
dotnet add package Microsoft.EntityFrameworkCore.SqlServer
dotnet add package Microsoft.EntityFrameworkCore.Tools
```

Step 2: Define Your Domain Model Classes

Create a folder named **`Models`** and define your entity classes. For example, a simple **`Product`** class can look like:

```
public class Product
{
        public int Id { get; set; }
        public string Name { get; set; }
        public decimal Price { get; set; }
}
```

Step 3: Create a `DbContext` Class

The **`DbContext`** class acts as a bridge between your model classes and the database. Create a **`MyAppContext`**, as shown here:

```
using Microsoft.EntityFrameworkCore;

public class MyAppContext : DbContext
{
        public DbSet<Product> Products { get; set; }
        // Define the connection string configuration in
OnConfiguring if not using dependency injection
        protected override void OnConfiguring(DbContextOptions-
Builder optionsBuilder)
        {
                // Connection string can be placed here or in
appsettings.json for ASP.NET Core
optionsBuilder.UseSqlServer("Server=.;Database=MyAppDb;Trusted_
Connection=True;");
        }
}
```

Defining the Connection String

For a Console Application: The simplest approach is to hardcode the connection string in the **OnConfiguring** method as shown above. A more maintainable way is to store it in **app.config** or **appsettings.json**.

app.config settings:

```
<configuration>
      <connectionStrings>
      <add name="MyAppContext" connectionString="Server=.;Data-
base=MyAppDb;Trusted_Connection=True;" providerName="System.Data.
SqlClient"/>
      </connectionStrings>
</configuration>
```

In C# (DbContext constructor):

```
using System.Configuration;
using Microsoft.EntityFrameworkCore;

public class MyAppContext : DbContext
{
      public DbSet<Product> Products { get; set; }
      public MyAppContext() : base() { }
      protected override void OnConfiguring(DbContextOptions-
Builder optionsBuilder)
      {
            string connStr = ConfigurationManager.Connection-
Strings["MyAppContext"].ConnectionString;
            optionsBuilder.UseSqlServer(connStr);
      }
}
```

For ASP.NET Core Applications:

You would typically define the connection string in **appsettings.json** and inject it via **Startup.cs** or **Program.cs**:

```
{
      "ConnectionStrings": {
      "MyAppContext": "Server=.;Database=MyAppDb;Trusted_Connec-
tion=True;"
      }
}
services.AddDbContext<MyAppContext>(options =>
options.UseSqlServer(Configuration.GetConnectionString
("MyAppContext")));
```

How to Call It from C# Code to Connect to the Database

Once your **DbContext** is defined and your connection string is configured, you can use it directly in code. For example:

```
using (var context = new MyAppContext())
{
        // This triggers EF to connect to the database
        var productCount = context.Products.Count();
        Console.WriteLine($"Total Products: {productCount}");
}
```

The **using** statement ensures that the context and its underlying database connection are properly disposed of after use.

How to Retrieve Data Using the Code First Approach:

You can query the database using LINQ queries directly on the **DbSet** properties, as shown here:

```
using (var context = new MyAppContext())
{
        // Retrieve all products
        var products = context.Products.ToList();
        // Retrieve products with a filter
        var expensiveProducts = context.Products
                                       .Where(p => p.Price > 100)
                                       .ToList();
}
```

EF translates these LINQ queries into SQL, executes them against the database, and materializes the results into C# objects.

How to Display the Data in a C# User Interface

For a WPF or Windows Forms Application:

Bind to a DataGrid (WPF):

```
using (var context = new MyAppContext())
{
        var products = context.Products.ToList();
        myDataGrid.ItemsSource = products; // Assuming
'myDataGrid' is a WPF DataGrid in XAML
}
```

Bind to a DataGridView (Windows Forms):

```
using (var context = new MyAppContext())
{
        var products = context.Products.ToList();
```

```
        myDataGridView.DataSource = products; // Assuming
'myDataGridView' is a WinForms DataGridView
}
```

For ASP.NET Core MVC or Razor Pages applications, you would pass the retrieved data to your view and render it in HTML tables or other UI elements.

How to Save and Update Data Back to the Database Using Code First

Inserting New Records:

```
using (var context = new MyAppContext())
{
        var newProduct = new Product { Name = "New Product", Price
= 19.99m };
        context.Products.Add(newProduct);
        context.SaveChanges(); // Executes INSERT statement
}
```

Updating Existing Records:

```
using (var context = new MyAppContext())
{
        var existingProduct = context.Products.FirstOrDefault(p =>
p.Id == 1);
        if (existingProduct != null)
        {
                existingProduct.Price = 24.99m;
                context.SaveChanges(); // Executes UPDATE statement
        }
}
```

EF automatically tracks changes to entities by default, unless you disable tracking using **AsNoTracking** or detach entities. When you call **SaveChanges()**, EF determines which entities need **INSERT**, **UPDATE**, or **DELETE** operations and runs the appropriate SQL statements.

The Code First approach in Entity Framework offers a powerful, code-centric way to design and evolve your application's data layer. Its alignment with domain-driven design, flexibility in handling schema changes through migrations, and integration with LINQ queries make it a popular choice among .NET developers.

While it may not be the best fit in scenarios where a stable, pre-existing database schema exists, it provides substantial advantages in greenfield projects, agile development environments, and any situation where developer productivity and maintainability take precedence.

By following the steps outlined above, you can quickly get up and running with EF Code First, from defining your domain models to displaying data in the UI and persisting changes back to the database, making it a cornerstone strategy in modern .NET app**lication development.**

Database-First Approach

In the Database-First approach, EF generates the entity classes and **`DbContext`** based on an existing database.

- **How It Works:**
  a. Use the '**`Scaffold-DbContext`**' command to generate entity classes from a database schema.
  b. Perform further customizations as needed.
- **When to Use**:
  a. When working with an existing database that you cannot modify
  b. When you want to quickly integrate an existing schema into your project
- **Advantages**:
  a. Saves time by generating code for an existing schema
  b. Ensures that entity classes are in sync with the database structure

Step-By-Step Process for Connecting a C# Application to a Database Using the Database-First Approach in Visual Studio 2022

Step 1: Create a C# Project in Visual Studio

Open Visual Studio 2022.

Go to **`File`** → **`New`** → **`Project`**.

Select Console App (.NET Core) or ASP.NET Core Web Application based on your requirements.

Name your project (for example, **`DatabaseFirstApp`**) and select a location. Click on Create to generate the project.

Step 2: Install Required NuGet Packages

To enable the Entity Framework Core Database-First approach, install the following NuGet packages:

In **`Solution Explorer`**, right-click on the project → select **`Manage NuGet Packages`**.

Search for and install the following packages:

- **`Microsoft.EntityFrameworkCore`**
- **`Microsoft.EntityFrameworkCore.SqlServer`** (if using SQL Server)

- **`Microsoft.EntityFrameworkCore.Tools`**

Alternatively, use the Package Manager Console to install the following:

```
Install-Package Microsoft.EntityFrameworkCore
Install-Package Microsoft.EntityFrameworkCore.SqlServer
Install-Package Microsoft.EntityFrameworkCore.Tools
```

Step 3: Create or Connect to a Database

a. Ensure you have a database ready. Use an existing SQL Server database or create one via SQL Server Management Studio (SSMS) or Azure SQL.

b. Make a note of the Connection String.

Example Connection String:

```
"Server=YourServerName;Database=YourDatabaseName;Trusted_
Connection=True;"
```

Step 4: Scaffold the Database.

Use the EF Core Scaffold-**`DbContext`** command to generate the model classes and **`DbContext`** based on the database schema.

```
Open Tools → NuGet Package Manager → Package Manager Console
```

Run the following command:

```
Scaffold-DbContext "Server=YourServerName;Database=YourData-
baseName;Trusted_Connection=True;"

Microsoft.EntityFrameworkCore.SqlServer -OutputDir Models
```

- **`Server=YourServerName`**: Replace with your SQL Server instance.
- **`Database=YourDatabaseName`**: Replace with your database name.
- **`OutputDir` Models**: This specifies the folder where the generated classes will be stored.

After the command is executed:

- The **`DbContext`** class and entity models are generated in the **`Models`** folder.
- Each table in the database has a corresponding class.

Step 5: Register `DbContext` in the Application.

Register the generated **`DbContext`** in your project so it can be used for database operations.

Open **`Program.cs`** (for Console Apps) or **`Startup.cs`** (for Web Apps).

Add the connection string and register the context:

```
using Microsoft.EntityFrameworkCore;
using YourNamespace.Models;

var optionsBuilder = new DbContextOptionsBuilder<YourDbCon-
text>();
optionsBuilder.UseSqlServer("Server=YourServerName;Database=Your-
DatabaseName;Trusted_Connection=True;");

var dbContext = new YourDbContext(optionsBuilder.Options);
```

For Web Applications: In **Startup.cs** → **ConfigureServices** method:

```
services.AddDbContext<YourDbContext>(options =>
options.UseSqlServer(Configuration.GetConnectionString("Default
Connection")));
```

Step 6: Use the Generated DbContext.

You can now use the generated **DbContext** and entity classes to perform CRUD operations.

Example: Fetching Data from a Table

```
using System;
using System.Linq;
using YourNamespace.Models;
class Program
{
        static void Main(string[] args)
        {
                using (var context = new YourDbContext())
                {
                        // Fetch all records from a table
                        var users = context.Users.ToList();
                        foreach (var user in users)
                        {
                                Console.WriteLine($"ID: {user.Id},
Name: {user.Name}");
                        }
                }
        }
}
```

Step 7: Build and Test the Application.

a. Build the application: **Build → Build Solution**.

b. Run the application to ensure it connects to the database and retrieves data.

Troubleshooting Tips

- If the **`Scaffold-DbContext`** command fails, ensure:
    - Your database server is accessible.
    - The correct NuGet packages are installed.
    - Proper permissions are granted for the database.
- If you encounter "**`No provider found`**" errors, verify that **`Microsoft.EntityFrameworkCore.SqlServer`** is installed.

By following these steps, your C# application will be connected to a database using the Database-First approach. You can now extend the application to include advanced database operations such as inserts, updates, and deletes.

Here are the examples of CRUD operations (Create, Read, Update, and Delete) using Entity Framework Core with the Database-First approach in a C# application:

Prerequisites

Ensure that you have the following:

- The **`DbContext`** and model classes generated using **`Scaffold-DbContext`**
- The correctly configured database connection

The following examples assume we have a table named `Users` with the following schema:

- **`Id (int, Primary Key)`**
- **`Name (nvarchar)`**
- **`Email (nvarchar)`**

Create Operation (Insert Data): Insert a New Record.

Here is how you can add a new user to the Users table:

```
using System;
using YourNamespace.Models;
class Program
{
   static void Main(string[] args)
   {
          using (var context = new YourDbContext())
          {
                 var newUser = new User
                 {
                        Name = "John Doe",
                        Email = "john.doe@example.com"
                 };
```

```
                context.Users.Add(newUser); // Add the new user to
the DbSet
                context.SaveChanges();      // Save changes to the
database
                Console.WriteLine("New user added
successfully.");
        }
    }
}
```

Read Operation (Retrieve Data): Fetch All Records.

Retrieve all records from the Users table, as shown here:

```
using System;
using System.Linq;
using YourNamespace.Models;

class Program
{
    static void Main(string[] args)
    {
        using (var context = new YourDbContext())
        {
            var users = context.Users.ToList();
            foreach (var user in users)
            {
                Console.WriteLine($"ID: {user.Id}, Name:
{user.Name}, Email: {user.Email}");
            }
        }
    }
}
```

Fetch a Single Record by ID: Retrieve a specific user based on their ID, as shown here:

```
var userId = 1; // Example ID to search for
using (var context = new YourDbContext())
{
    var user = context.Users.FirstOrDefault(u => u.Id == userId);
    if (user != null)
    {
        Console.WriteLine($"User Found: {user.Name}, Email: {user.
Email}");
    }
    else
    {
        Console.WriteLine("User not found.");
    }
}
```

Update Operation (Modify Data): Update an Existing Record.

Update the **Name** and **Email** of an existing user, as is shown:

```
using System;
using System.Linq;
using YourNamespace.Models;
class Program
{
	static void Main(string[] args)
	{
		var userId = 1; // ID of the user to update
		using (var context = new YourDbContext())
		{
			var user = context.Users.FirstOrDefault(u =>
u.Id == userId);
			if (user != null)
			{
				user.Name = "Jane Doe";
				user.Email = "jane.doe@example.com";
				context.SaveChanges(); // Save changes
to the database
				Console.WriteLine("User updated
successfully.");
			}
			else
			{
				Console.WriteLine("User not found.");
			}
		}
	}
}
```

Delete Operation (Remove Data): Delete a Record by ID.

Remove a user based on their ID in the following way:

```
using System;
using System.Linq;
using YourNamespace.Models;
class Program
{
	static void Main(string[] args)
	{
		var userId = 1; // ID of the user to delete
		using (var context = new YourDbContext())
		{
			var user = context.Users.FirstOrDefault(u =>
u.Id == userId);
```

```
                    if (user != null)
                    {
                          context.Users.Remove(user); // Remove
      the user from DbSet
                          context.SaveChanges();      // Save
      changes to the database
                          Console.WriteLine("User deleted suc-
      cessfully.");
                    }
                    else
                    {
                          Console.WriteLine("User not found.");
                    }
              }
        }
      }
```

Summary of CRUD Operations:

a. **Create:** Add a new record using **`DbContext.Add()`** and **`SaveChanges()`**.

b. **Read:** Fetch data using LINQ queries like **`ToList()`**, **`FirstOrDefault()`**, and so on.

c. **Update:** Modify existing records, update properties, and call **`SaveChanges()`**.

d. **Delete:** Remove records using **`DbContext.Remove()`** and save changes.

Model-First Approach

In the Model-First approach, developers use a graphical designer to create an entity model, and EF generates the database schema and code.

- **How It Works:**
  a. Design the data model using a visual tool.
  b. Generate the database and classes from the designed model.
- **When to Use:**
  - When you prefer to work visually and design the database using diagrams
  - When collaborating with a team that uses visual database modeling
- **Advantages:**
  - Provides a visual representation of the database and relationships
  - Easy for non-developers to understand

Note: *Model-First is not natively supported in EF Core, but it can be used with third-party tools.*

Here is a **Step-by-Step Process** for connecting a **C# application** to a database using the **Model-First** approach in Visual Studio 2022. Model-First is feature of **Entity Framework (EF6)** and allows you to create your database schema visually from a model.

Step 1: Create a New Project in Visual Studio.

a. Open `Visual Studio 2022`.

b. Select '`Create a new project`'.

c. Choose the `Console App (.NET)` or `ASP.NET Core Web Application` template based on your requirement.

d. Name the project (for example, `ModelFirstDemoApp`) and choose a suitable location.

e. Click on `Create`.

Step 2: Add Entity Framework.

In the Solution Explorer, right-click on the project and select **Manage NuGet Packages.**

Search for `EntityFramework` and install the package.

- For .NET Framework, install `EntityFramework` (v6.x)
- For .NET Core or .NET 5/6+, use `Microsoft.EntityFrameworkCore`

Note: *Ensure the correct version of EF is installed based on your .NET version.*

Step 3: Add the ADO.NET Entity Data Model (Valid for EF 6.x Only).

In Solution Explorer,

a. right-click on the project and choose `Add > New Item`.

b. Select `Data` from the left-hand panel.

c. Choose `ADO.NET Entity Data Model`.

d. Name the file (for example, `ModelFirst.edmx`) and click on `Add`.

Step 4: Choose the Model-First Workflow.

a. In the `Entity Data Model Wizard`, select `Empty EF Designer Model` and click on `Finish`.

b. A blank `Entity Framework Designer` surface will open.

Step 5: Define the Model Using the Designer.

In the `EF Designer`, right-click on the design surface and select `Add New > Entity`.

Create entities by naming them and defining properties:

a. Name the entity (for example, **`Student`**)

b. Add properties such as:

   i. **`Id`** (Primary Key, **`int`**)

   ii. **`Name`** (**`string`**)

   iii. **`Age`** (**`int`**)

Repeat the above step to create additional entities, if needed.

Define **relationships in the following manner**:

a. Right-click on the designer surface and select **`Add Association`**.

b. Set relationships (for example, one-to-many, many-to-many).

Step 6: Generate the Database from the Model.

a. In the **`EF Designer`**, right-click on the design surface and choose **`Generate Database from Model`**.

b. The **`Generate Database Wizard`** opens.

c. Click on **`New Connection`** to set up your database:

   i. Choose **SQL Server**.

   ii. Enter the **`Server Name`** and **`Database Name`**.

   iii. Choose **`Windows Authentication`** or **`SQL Server Authentication`**.

d. Click on **`OK`** to create the connection.

e. Review the generated **`SQL script`**.

f. Click on **`Finish`** to execute the script and create the database.

Step 7: Verify the Database.

a. Open **SQL Server Management Studio (SSMS)** or use the **SQL Server Object Explorer** in Visual Studio.

b. Connect to your database server and verify the newly created database and tables.

Step 8: Generate the Context and Entity Classes.

After generating the database, Entity Framework will automatically create:

- A **`DbContext`** class

- Entity classes that correspond to your model

For example:

```
public class Student
{
    public int Id { get; set; }
    public string Name { get; set; }
    public int Age { get; set; }
}

public class ModelFirstDemoContext : DbContext
{
    public DbSet<Student> Students { get; set; }
}
```

Step 9: Perform CRUD Operations in Code.

Use the generated **`DbContext`** to interact with the database. For example:

```
using (var context = new ModelFirstDemoContext())
{
    // Add a new Student
    var student = new Student { Name = "John Doe", Age = 22 };
    context.Students.Add(student);
    context.SaveChanges();

    // Retrieve and display students
    var students = context.Students.ToList();
    foreach (var s in students)
    {
        Console.WriteLine($"{s.Id}: {s.Name} ({s.Age} years
old)");
    }
}
```

Step 10: Build and Run the Application.

a. Build the project (*Ctrl+Shift+B*) to ensure that there are no errors.

b. Run the application (F5) and verify that data is added to the database.

In this process, you:

a. Created a C# project

b. Used the Model-First approach to design your database schema visually

c. Generated the database and entity classes

d. Performed CRUD operations using Entity Framework

The **Model-First** approach is useful when you need to design the database schema before implementing the actual database, while providing a clean and maintainable workflow.

Conclusion

This chapter highlights the importance of database integration in developing data-driven applications. Tools like **ADO.NET** and **Entity Framework** cater to both low-level database control and high-level abstractions, which enables developers to choose the approach that best suits their project needs. Visual Studio's powerful tools streamline the integration process and make database management efficient, secure, and scalable.

Foreword for the Next Chapter: Developing Web Applications

As we move beyond the database integration, the next chapter will explore the world of web application development in Visual Studio. Whether you are creating a lightweight single-page application (SPA), a robust ASP.NET Core MVC web app, or integrating advanced front-end frameworks like React, Angular, or Blazor, Visual Studio provides the ideal platform to bring your ideas to life.

CHAPTER 7

Developing Web Applications

Introduction

Microsoft .NET is a powerful, modern development framework designed to build secure and high-performance web applications. At its core is the Common Language Runtime (CLR), which executes code and manages important features such as memory, security, and exception handling. The .NET ecosystem also includes a broad set of tools and libraries that streamline everything from database connectivity and caching, to deployment and scaling.

One of the main web-focused technologies in .NET is **ASP.NET Core**, a cross-platform, open-source framework for building cloud-ready web apps and services. ASP.NET Core delivers high performance, easy integration with databases (via Entity Framework Core), and support for modern coding patterns like Model-View-Controller (MVC). Additionally, you can create real-time, bidirectional communication with your web clients using SignalR for chat apps, IoT dashboards, and more.

A relatively new option for building rich, interactive client-side experiences in .NET is **Blazor**. Blazor allows you to write client-side web applications in C# instead of JavaScript and enables code sharing across both the server and client. This results in faster development, a smaller set of technologies to master, and the powerful debugging experience you would usually expect from .NET.

Whether you're building a content management system, e-commerce platform, or enterprise dashboard, Microsoft .NET offers the flexibility, performance, and security demanded by modern web applications. Backed by robust support, extensive libraries, and seamless cloud integration, it is a comprehensive solution for creating fast, maintainable, and scalable web-based applications.

Structure

In this chapter, we will cover the following topics:

- Web Application Model-Architecture
- Tier-based Web Application and how to implement it
- Authentication and Authorization for security
- Caching for performance improvement
- Types of Caching : In-Memory, Distributed, Response
- .Net MAUI for Multi Platform App development
- React for developing web based applications
- .Net Core Web API

Few Reasons Microsoft .NET Is a Top Choice for Enterprise-Level Web Applications:

Proven Enterprise-Grade Performance

.NET has been a staple in enterprise development for decades and has powered countless mission-critical business applications. Over several years, Microsoft has continuously improved .NET by releasing updates that enhance performance, reduce memory usage, and support modern development practices. The framework's Common Language Runtime (CLR) is engineered for speed, which makes it highly optimized for large, complex workloads.

Comprehensive Ecosystem and Tooling

A significant advantage of .NET is its comprehensive ecosystem and integration with the broader Microsoft suite of products, which are explained as follows:

- **Visual Studio Family**: Visual Studio and Visual Studio Code are powerful tools that support a wide range of development needs. Visual Studio is a full-featured IDE ideal for complex applications, while Visual Studio Code is a lightweight, extensible editor suited for a broad set of programming languages and workflows. Together, they help streamline coding, debugging, and deployment through extensions and integrations.
- **Azure Integration**: For organizations migrating to or expanding in the cloud, .NET's native integration with Microsoft Azure offers easy scaling, containerization, and streamlined deployment options.
- **Extensive Libraries and Frameworks**: From ASP.NET Core for web applications to Entity Framework Core for data access and ML.NET for machine learning, .NET offers a one-stop shop of frameworks that integrate seamlessly.

Cross-Platform Flexibility

With the advent of .NET Core (now merged into .NET 5+), Microsoft has moved away from Windows-only development. .NET now runs on Windows, Linux, and macOS, which grants teams the freedom to choose hosting platforms based on performance, compliance, or cost considerations without losing language features or ecosystem benefits.

Security-First Approach

Enterprises handle sensitive data, including financial transactions and personal information. .NET helps mitigate security risks:

- **In-Built Security Measures**: .NET enforces code access security and includes out-of-the-box protections like input validation and encryption libraries. Code Access Security (CAS) was part of .NET Framework but has been removed from .NET Core and later (.NET 5+ including .NET 6/7/8).
- **Regular Updates**: Microsoft releases frequent security patches and enhancements, which ensures that applications remain protected against new threats.
- **Secure Coding Guidance**: Extensive documentation and best-practice patterns from Microsoft and the community help developers follow secure coding principles.

Consistency and Stability

Enterprise organizations often need platforms that promise stability and long-term support. Microsoft follows a defined product roadmap for .NET and offers the following features:

- **Long-Term Support (LTS)**: Certain .NET versions come with multi-year support, which gives businesses time to plan and execute upgrades strategically.
- **Clear Versioning and Release Cycles**: Predictable release schedules empower enterprises to align internal development schedules with .NET updates.

Below is an overview of the typical components and layers you would find in a modern, enterprise-ready web application built on Microsoft .NET technologies. The goal is to help you understand *what* each layer does, *why* it is there, and *how* to distinguish all the parts that are required to build a robust enterprise solution.

Web Application Model/Architecture

Building an enterprise web-based application in .NET involves carefully structuring your code into layers—*Presentation*, *Business (Domain/Service)*, *Data Access*, and

Database–and incorporating cross-cutting concerns such as security, logging, and configuration. By understanding and distinguishing each layer's responsibility and leveraging the right .NET frameworks (ASP.NET Core, EF Core, and so on), you will be able to create scalable, maintainable, and robust solutions that meet enterprise requirements.

Ultimately, your choice of architecture and technology within the .NET ecosystem should reflect your project's scale, complexity, and performance needs, which ensures that each layer and service is well-organized and easy to maintain over the long term.

Typical Layers in a .NET Web Application

Most enterprise .NET applications follow a layered architecture (sometimes called n-tier). The exact naming of layers can vary, but a common convention is:

- Presentation Layer (UI)
- Business Logic Layer (Domain/Service Layer)
- Data Access Layer (Repository Layer)
- Database Layer

Example of a Project Structure in Visual Studio:

```
MySolution
    ├── MySolution.Web          (Presentation Layer: ASP.NET Core MVC/Blazor)
    ├── MySolution.Business     (Business Layer: Services, Models, Validators)
    ├── MySolution.Data         (Data Access Layer: Repositories, EF Core)
    └── MySolution.Tests        (Unit Tests)
```

Additionally, enterprise applications often include *cross-cutting* layers or services such as security, logging, configuration, caching, and so on.

Presentation Layer (UI)

It interacts directly with the end user (or client). It is responsible for displaying data and capturing user input.

Some common technologies used for creating User Interface (UI) are:

- **ASP.NET Core MVC** or **Razor Pages** for server-side rendering
- **Blazor** (server-side or WebAssembly) for interactive client-side applications in C#
- **ASP.NET Web Forms** (legacy) in older applications
- **JavaScript frameworks** (Angular, React, Vue) + ASP.NET Core Web APIs for SPA (Single Page Applications)

Purpose of Creating Presentation Layer:

- Holds controllers (in MVC) or pages (in Razor Pages) that handle requests
- Returns views (HTML/CSS/JS) or JSON data (when building REST APIs)
- Often integrates with client-side libraries (Bootstrap, jQuery, and so on)
- Should contain minimal business logic (for example, validations, formatting) and primarily coordinate with the service/business layer

Business Logic Layer (Domain/Service Layer)

It encapsulates the core rules, workflows, and behaviors unique to the business domain.

- **Common Approaches**
  - Plain C# classes (services, domain models)
  - Domain-Driven Design (DDD) patterns with Aggregates, Entities, Value Objects, Domain Events
  - Dependency Injection (DI) is commonly used to inject required services
- **Key Points**
  - Should be technology-agnostic regarding the UI and data storage details
  - Contains the application services (for example, **`CustomerService`**, **`OrderService`**) or domain logic
  - Enforces validation rules, coordinates data from multiple repositories, implements business workflows

Data Access Layer (Repository Layer)

It abstracts the operations of reading and writing data to the underlying database or data sources.

- **Common Ways to Create a Data Layer**
  - **Entity Framework Core** (EF Core) for ORM-based data access
  - **Dapper** for lightweight, micro-ORM-based querying
  - **ADO.NET** for direct SQL data access (lower-level)
- **Key Points**
  - Typically defines *Repository* classes (for example, **`CustomerRepository`**, **`OrderRepository`**) or EF **`DbContext`** classes
  - Isolates the rest of the application from database details (schema, SQL queries)

- Supports unit testing by allowing repositories to be mocked or stubbed

Database Layer

- **Purpose**: The physical or logical data store where your data resides
- **Common Technologies**
    - **SQL Server**, **Azure SQL Database,** or other databases if needed
- **Key Points**
    - Stores tables, stored procedures, views, functions (in a relational scenario)
    - For EF Core, you might use migrations to manage schema changes (in a relational scenario)
    - Security, performance tuning, indexing, and backups are critical at this layer

In an enterprise web application, you often have additional components or layers that cut across the entire architecture. These layers are:

- **Security/Identity**
    - ASP.NET Core Identity, OAuth/OpenID Connect (with Azure AD, for example), JWT-based auth
    - Role-based or claims-based authorization
- **Logging and Monitoring**
    - .NET built-in logging (ILogger), Serilog, NLog, or similar frameworks
    - Azure Monitor, Application Insights for cloud-based telemetry
- **Caching:** In-memory cache, Redis distributed cache, or other caching strategies
- **Configuration Management:** `appsettings.json`, environment variables, Azure Key Vault, and so on
- **Exception Handling:** Centralized handling via ASP.NET Core middleware, global filters, or custom frameworks
- **CI/CD Pipeline**
    - Automated builds/tests (Azure DevOps, GitHub Actions)
    - Deployment pipelines to on-prem or cloud platforms (Azure Web Apps, Azure Kubernetes, and so on)
- **APIs / Integrations**
    - ASP.NET Core Web API for RESTful services
    - gRPC for high-performance, contract-based communication

- Integration with third-party APIs or microservices via **`HttpClient`**, **`Refit`**, and so on

Key Distinctions and Considerations

- **Layer Responsibility**: Each layer should only do one thing; UI handles user interaction, business layer enforces rules, while the data layer deals with persistence.
- **Dependency Rules**: Upper layers can depend on lower layers (for example, UI depends on business layer), but not vice versa.
- **Loose Coupling and High Cohesion**: Use interfaces and DI to decouple implementations and keep related functionalities tightly grouped.
- **Scaling Up or Out**: If requirements grow, the layered architecture or a microservice approach can help you scale specific parts of the system independently.

In this chapter, you will learn how to build a N-tier ASP.NET 8.0 web application using Visual Studio 2022. The application will include a presentation layer, a business logic layer, and a data access layer, with functionality to manage countries, states, and cities.

Step 1: Create the ASP.NET 8.0 Solution and Projects

Add Presentation Layer Project

a. Open Visual Studio 2022 and select Create a new project.

b. Choose ASP.NET Core Web App (Model-View-Controller) as the template.

c. Name the project **`CountryApp.Web`** (presentation layer) and the solution as '**`CountryApp`**'.

d. Ensure that .NET 8.0 is selected as the framework.

Add Business Layer Project.

a. Right-click on the solution → **`Add`** → **`New Project`**.

b. Select Class Library and name it **`CountryApp.Business`**.

c. Delete the default '**`Class1.cs`**' file.

Add Data Access Layer Project.

a. Right-click on the solution → **`Add`** → **`New Project`**.

b. Select Class Library and name it **`CountryApp.Data`**.

c. Delete the default '**Class1.cs**' file.

Add Project References.

a. Right-click on '**CountryApp.Web**' → **Add** → **Project Reference** → Select **CountryApp.Business**.

b. Right-click '**CountryApp.Business**' → **Add** → **Project Reference** → Select **CountryApp.Data**.

Step 2: Configure the Data Access Layer

Install Entity Framework Packages

In the '**CountryApp.Data**' project, install these NuGet packages:

- **Microsoft.EntityFrameworkCore**
- **Microsoft.EntityFrameworkCore.SqlServer**
- **Microsoft.EntityFrameworkCore.Tools**

Create Database Models

In '**CountryApp.Business**', create a '**Models**' folder.

Add classes for **Country**, **State**, and **City**, as shown in the example here:

```
//Country.cs
public class Country
{
    public int Id { get; set; }
    public string Name { get; set; }
    public List<State> States { get; set; } = new();
}

// State.cs
public class State
{
    public int Id { get; set; }
    public string Name { get; set; }
    public int CountryId { get; set; }
    public List<City> Cities { get; set; } = new();
}

// City.cs
public class City
{
    public int Id { get; set; }
    public string Name { get; set; }
```

```
        public int StateId { get; set; }
    }
```

Create DbContext

In '**CountryApp.Data**', create '**AppDbContext.cs**', as shown in the following example:

```
using Microsoft.EntityFrameworkCore;
using CountryApp.Business.Models;
public class AppDbContext : DbContext
{
        public AppDbContext(DbContextOptions<AppDbContext>
options) : base(options) { }
        public DbSet<Country> Countries { get; set; }
        public DbSet<State> States { get; set; }
        public DbSet<City> Cities { get; set; }
}
```

Configure SQL Server Connection

In '**CountryApp.Web/appsettings.json**', add the connection string, as indicated here:

```
"ConnectionStrings": {
        "DefaultConnection":
"Server=(localdb)\\mssqllocaldb;Database=CountryDb;Trusted_
Connection=True;"
}
```

In 'Program.cs', register the 'AppDbContext ', as shown here:

```
using CountryApp.Data;
using Microsoft.EntityFrameworkCore;

var builder = WebApplication.CreateBuilder(args);
builder.Services.AddDbContext<AppDbContext>(options =>
options.UseSqlServer(builder.Configuration.GetConnection-
String("DefaultConnection")));
```

Step 3: Implement the Business Layer

Create Services

In '**CountryApp.Business**', add a '**Services**' folder and create '**CountryService.cs**', as shown here:

```
using CountryApp.Data;
using CountryApp.Business.Models;

public class CountryService
{
        private readonly AppDbContext _context;
```

```
        public CountryService(AppDbContext context) => _context =
context;
        public List<Country> GetCountries() => _context.Countries.
Include(c =>
c.States).ThenInclude(s => s.Cities).ToList();

        public void AddCountry(Country country)
        {
                _context.Countries.Add(country);
                _context.SaveChanges();
        }
//Add similar methods for states and cities
}
```

Step 4: Build the Presentation Layer

Home Page (Display Countries and States)

In '**CountryApp.Web/Controllers/HomeController.cs**', implement the following code:

```
using Microsoft.AspNetCore.Mvc;
using CountryApp.Business.Services;

public class HomeController : Controller
{
        private readonly CountryService _countryService;
        public HomeController(CountryService countryService) =>
_countryService = countryService;

        public IActionResult Index()
        {
                var countries = _countryService.GetCountries();
                return View(countries);
        }
}
```

Create 'Views/Home/Index.cshtml'

```
@model List<CountryApp.Business.Models.Country>
<h1>Countries</h1>
<select id="countryDropdown" asp-items="@(new SelectList(Model,
"Id", "Name"))">
<option value="">Select Country</option></select>
<div id="statesGrid">
<!-- States and cities will load here via JavaScript →
</div>
```

```
@section Scripts
{
	<script>
		$("#countryDropdown").change(function ()
		{
		var countryId = $(this).val();
		$.get(`/Home/GetStatesByCountry?countryId=${country-
Id}`, function (data)
			{
				$("#statesGrid").html(data);
			});
		});
	</script>
}
```

Add a Partial View for States and Cities (`Views/Home/GetStatesByCountry.cshtml`)

```
@model List<State>
<table class="table">
	<thead>
		<tr>
			<th>State</th>
			<th>Cities</th>
		</tr>
	</thead>
	<tbody>
		@foreach (var state in Model)
		{
			<tr>
			<td>@state.Name</td>
			<td>@string.Join(", ", state.Cities.Select(c
=> c.Name))</td>
			</tr>
		}
	</tbody>
</table>
```

Step 5: CRUD Page for Managing Countries, States, and Cities

Create '**`ManageController`**' and add '**`ManageController.cs`**', as shown here:

```
public class ManageController : Controller
{
	private readonly ICountryService _countryService;
	public ManageController(CountryService countryService) =>
_countryService = countryService;
	public IActionResult Index() => View();
```

```
        [HttpPost]
        public IActionResult AddCountry(Country country)
        {
              _countryService.AddCountry(country);
              return RedirectToAction("Index");
        }// Add similar actions for states and cities
  }
```

Create the Manage View: In 'Views/Manage/Index.cshtml', add forms and controls for CRUD operations. Use modals or nested forms to handle states and cities.

Step 6: Add Styling and Enhance the UI with Bootstrap, CSS, and JavaScript

Add Bootstrap and Custom CSS and install Bootstrap

In '**CountryApp.Web**', add Bootstrap 5 via CDN in '**Views/Shared/_Layout.cshtml**' inside the '**<head>**' tag, implement the following code:

```
      <link href="https://cdn.jsdelivr.net/npm/bootstrap@5.3.0/
dist/css/bootstrap.min.css" rel="stylesheet">
      <script src="https://cdn.jsdelivr.net/npm/bootstrap@5.3.0/
dist/js/bootstrap.bundle.min.js"></script>
```

Add Custom CSS

Create a '**wwwroot/css**' folder in the '**CountryApp.Web**' project.

Add a file '**custom.css**' with styles for the grid, forms, and dropdown, as shown here:

```
/* Custom CSS */
.dropdown-container {
    margin: 20px 0;
    padding: 15px;
    background-color: #f8f9fa;
    border-radius: 5px;
}

#statesGrid {
    margin-top: 20px;
}

.table-hover tbody tr:hover {
    background-color: rgba(0, 123, 255, 0.1);
}

.btn-custom {
    margin: 5px;
```

```
            min-width: 100px;
        }
```

Include CSS in Layout and update '**_Layout.cshtml**' to include 'custom.css', as shown here:

```
<link rel="stylesheet" href="~/css/custom.css" />
```

Style the **Home Page** (**Index.cshtml**) and update the dropdown and grid with Bootstrap classes, as shown here:

```
@model List<CountryApp.Business.Models.Country>

<div class="container mt-4">
    <div class="dropdown-container shadow-sm">
        <h3 class="mb-3">Select a Country</h3>
        <select id="countryDropdown" class="form-select"
asp-items="@(new SelectList(Model, "Id", "Name"))">
            <option value="">-- Select Country --</option>
        </select>
    </div>

    <div id="statesGrid" class="table-responsive">
        <!-- States/Cities load here -->
    </div>
</div>

@section Scripts {
    <script>
        // Add loading spinner during AJAX call
        $("#countryDropdown").change(function () {
            var countryId = $(this).val();
            $("#statesGrid").html('<div class="text-center"><div
class="spinner-border text-primary"></div></div>');

            $.get(`/Home/GetStatesByCountry?countryId=${country-
Id}`, function (data) {
                $("#statesGrid").html(data);
            });
        });
    </script>
}
```

Style the Partial View (**GetStatesByCountry.cshtml**) and use Bootstrap table styling, as shown here:

```
@model List<State>

<table class="table table-hover table-striped">
    <thead class="table-dark">
        <tr>
```

```
                <th>State</th>
                <th>Cities</th>
            </tr>
        </thead>
        <tbody>
            @foreach (var state in Model)
            {
                <tr>
                    <td class="fw-bold">@state.Name</td>
                    <td>
                        @foreach (var city in state.Cities)
                        {
                            <span class="badge bg-primary me-1">@
city.Name</span>
                        }
                    </td>
                </tr>
            }
        </tbody>
</table>
```

Style the CRUD Page (**Manage/Index.cshtml**) and add a responsive form with Bootstrap, as indicated here:

```
<div class="container mt-4">
    <div class="card shadow">
        <div class="card-header bg-primary text-white">
            <h3 class="mb-0">Manage Countries, States, and
Cities</h3>
        </div>
        <div class="card-body">
            <!-- Add Country -->
            <div class="mb-4">
                <h4>Add Country</h4>
                <form asp-action="AddCountry" class="row g-3">
                    <div class="col-md-6">
                        <input type="text" name="Name"
class="form-control" placeholder="Country Name" required>
                    </div>
                    <div class="col-md-2">
                        <button type="submit" class="btn
btn-success btn-custom">Add Country</button>
                    </div>
                </form>
            </div>

            <!-- Add State to Country -->
            <div class="mb-4">
```

```
                <h4>Add State</h4>
                <form id="addStateForm" class="row g-3">
                    <div class="col-md-4">
                        <select id="countryList" class="form-se-
lect" asp-items="ViewBag.Countries">
                            <option value="">Select
Country</option>
                        </select>
                    </div>
                    <div class="col-md-4">
                        <input type="text" id="stateName"
class="form-control" placeholder="State Name" required>
                    </div>
                    <div class="col-md-2">
                        <button type="button" class="btn btn-info
btn-custom" onclick="addState()">Add State</button>
                    </div>
                </form>
            </div>

            <!-- Dynamic City Inputs (JavaScript-Powered) -->
            <div id="citySection" style="display: none;">
                <h4>Add Cities</h4>
                <div id="cityInputs" class="row g-3"></div>
                <button type="button" class="btn btn-secondary
mt-3" onclick="addCityField()">+ Add City</button>
                <button type="button" class="btn btn-success
mt-3" onclick="saveCities()">Save Cities</button>
            </div>
        </div>
    </div>
</div>

@section Scripts {
    <script>
        // Dynamically add city input fields
        function addCityField() {
            const inputGroup = document.createElement("div");
            inputGroup.className = "col-md-4";
            inputGroup.innerHTML = `
                <div class="input-group mb-3">
                    <input type="text" class="form-control"
placeholder="City Name">
                    <button class="btn btn-danger" type="button"
onclick="this.parentElement.parentElement.remove()">×</button>
                </div>
            `;
```

```
            document.getElementById("cityInputs").appendChild
(inputGroup);
        }

        // Example AJAX call to save cities
        function saveCities() {
            const cityNames = Array.from(document.querySelector-
All('#cityInputs input'))
                .map(input => input.value);

            // Call API to save cities here
        }
    </script>
}
```

Add Responsive Design and update '**_Layout.cshtml**'. Add a responsive navbar and Bootstrap grid, as shown here:

```
<nav class="navbar navbar-expand-lg navbar-dark bg-dark">
    <div class="container">
        <a class="navbar-brand" href="/">Country App</a>
        <div class="collapse navbar-collapse">
            <ul class="navbar-nav me-auto">
                <li class="nav-item">
                    <a class="nav-link" href="/Home">Home</a>
                </li>
                <li class="nav-item">
                    <a class="nav-link" href="/Manage">
Manage Data</a>
                </li>
            </ul>
        </div>
    </div>
</nav>
```

Add Mobile-Friendly Media Queries: In '**custom.css**', add:

```
@media (max-width: 768px) {
    .dropdown-container {
        margin: 10px;
        padding: 10px;
    }
    .btn-custom {
        width: 100%;
        margin: 5px 0;
    }
}
```

Add JavaScript Enhancements:

Form Validation: Add client-side validation to the CRUD forms using javascript, as demonstrated here:

```
document.getElementById("addStateForm").addEventListener
("submit", function (e) {
        if (!document.getElementById("countryList").value ||
!document.getElementById("stateName").value) {
            e.preventDefault();
            alert("Please select a country and enter a state
name!");
        }
    });
```

Confirmation for Deletes: Add a delete confirmation dialog using javascript via:

```
function confirmDelete(itemType) {
      return confirm(`Are you sure you want to delete this ${item-
Type}?`);
}
```

Final UI Preview will display the following:

- **Home Page**: A clean dropdown with a responsive grid showing states and cities as badges
- **Manage Page**: Card-based layout with independent form sections, dynamic city inputs, and Bootstrap modals for edits

You have enhanced the UI using Bootstrap for responsive layouts, CSS for custom styling, and JavaScript for dynamic interactions. The application now has a modern, mobile-friendly design and also has interactive forms with client-side validation.

Run the application and navigate to '`/Home`' to test the dropdown and grid.

Visit '`/Manage`' to add countries, states, and cities.

In this chapter, you have built a layered ASP.NET 8.0 web application using Visual Studio 2022. The presentation layer handles user interactions, the business layer manages models and services, and the data access layer connects to SQL Server via Entity Framework. The application allows users to view hierarchical data and perform CRUD operations, which demonstrates clean separation of concerns.

Now, here is a step-by-step guide to creating a **Blazor application** in Visual Studio.

Blazor allows you to build interactive web UIs using C# instead of JavaScript and supports two hosting models: Blazor WebAssembly (client-side) and Blazor Server (server-side).

Step 1: Create a New Blazor Project

a. Open Visual Studio.

b. Click on '`Create a new project`' on the start screen.

c. Search for Blazor in the template search bar.

d. Select either:

   - Blazor WebAssembly App (runs client-side in the browser via WebAssembly)
   - Blazor Server App (runs server-side with real-time updates via SignalR)

e. Click on `Next`.

Step 2: Configure the Project

a. Enter a Project Name (for example, MyBlazorApp).

b. Choose a Location for the project.

c. Set the Solution Name (if needed).

d. Ensure that Configure for HTTPS is checked (recommended for security).

e. Under Authentication, select:

   - None (default) or Individual Accounts (for user authentication)

f. Click on Create.

Step 3: Explore the Project Structure

After creation, the solution will include:

a. Pages: Contains Razor components (for example, `Index.razor`, `Counter.razor`)

b. Shared: Shared components (for example, `MainLayout.razor`\`, \``NavMenu.razor`)

c. `wwwroot`: Static files (CSS, images, JS)

d. `Program.cs`: Entry point for the app

e. `App.razor`: Root component for routing

Step 4: Build and Run the Application

a. Press F5 or click the Run button to build and launch the app.

b. A browser will open to 'https://localhost:PORT' (HTTPS enabled by default).

c. Explore the default template.

d. Navigate to the Counter or Fetch Data pages to see dynamic components.

Step 5: Modify a Component (Example: Counter)

a. Open '**Pages/Counter.razor**'.

b. Modify the increment logic. For example:

```
@page "/counter"
<h1>Counter</h1>
<p>Current count: @currentCount</p>
<button class="btn btn-primary" @onclick="IncrementCount">Click
me</button>
@code {
        private int currentCount = 0;
        private void IncrementCount()
        {
            currentCount += 2; // Changed from 1 to 2
        }
    }
```

Save the file. The app will auto-reload in the browser.

Step 6: Add a New Component

Right-click the Pages folder and select **Add** > **Razor Component**.

Name it '**Todo.razor**'.

Add a simple **todo** list like the one shown here:

```
@page "/todo"
<h1>Todo List</h1>
<input @bind="newTodo" placeholder="Add a task..." />
<button @onclick="AddTodo">Add</button>
<ul>
    @foreach (var todo in todos)
    {
        <li>@todo</li>
    }
</ul>

@code {
    private List<string> todos = new();
    private string newTodo = "";

    private void AddTodo()
    {
```

```
            if (!string.IsNullOrWhiteSpace(newTodo))
            {
                todos.Add(newTodo);
                newTodo = "";
            }
        }
    }
```

Navigate to '**/todo**' in the browser to test.

Step 7: Add Authentication (Optional)

If you have selected Individual Accounts during setup, run the app and click Register to create a test user.

Apply database migrations, as indicated here:

a. Open **Package Manager Console** (**Tools** > **NuGet Package Manager**).

b. Run '**Update-Database**' to create the Identity database.

Step 8: Add a Service (Dependency Injection)

Create a folder named Services.

Add a class '**WeatherService.cs**', as indicated here:

```
public class WeatherService
   {
       public Task<WeatherForecast[]> GetForecastAsync()
       {
           // Simulate fetching data
           return Task.FromResult(new[]
           {
               new WeatherForecast { Date = DateTime.Now, Tem-
peratureC = 20, Summary = "Sunny" }
           });
       }
   }

   public class WeatherForecast
   {
       public DateTime Date { get; set; }
       public int TemperatureC { get; set; }
       public string Summary { get; set; }
   }
```

Register the service in '**Program.cs**':

```
builder.Services.AddScoped<WeatherService>();
```

Inject the service into a component (for example, **FetchData.razor**) via:

```
@inject WeatherService
```

Step 9: Debugging

a. Set breakpoints in C# code (for example, in `Counter.razor`).

b. Use Browser Developer Tools (F12) for client-side debugging.

c. Check the Output Window in Visual Studio for runtime logs.

Step 10: Publish the Application

a. Right-click on the project and select Publish.

b. Choose from the given targets:

   - `Folder` (for manual deployment)
   - `Azure` (for cloud hosting)
   - `Docker` Container (for containerization)

c. Follow the wizard to configure settings and deploy.

By following these steps, you can create, customize, and deploy a Blazor application using Visual Studio. The framework's integration with C# and .NET simplifies full-stack development with a single language.

Implementing Authentication and Authorization in .Net Core Web API

Authentication: Verifies the identity of a user or system (for example, checking credentials like username/password, tokens, or certificates)

Authorization: Determines what an authenticated user is allowed to do (for example, granting access to specific endpoints based on roles or policies)

Different Ways to Implement Authentication/Authorization in .NET Core Web API

JWT (JSON Web Tokens):

- Stateless tokens containing user claims, signed for security
- Ideal for APIs and SPAs (Single-Page Applications)

Identity Framework

- Built-in ASP.NET Core Identity system with user management, roles, and claims
- Integrates with Entity Framework Core for user storage

OAuth 2.0 / OpenID Connect: Delegated authentication using providers like Google, Microsoft, or Auth0

API Key Authentication: Validate clients via a secret key passed in headers or query strings

Azure Active Directory (AAD): Enterprise-grade authentication using Microsoft's cloud identity service

Custom Middleware: Build your own authentication logic (for example, HMAC signatures)

Here is the step-by-step process to Implement JWT Authentication in .NET Core Web API: Let us use JWT for this example:

Create a New .NET Core Web API Project

a. Open Visual Studio.

b. Create a new project: ASP.NET Core Web API

c. Name the project (for example, `` `JwtAuthDemo` ``).

Add Required NuGet Packages: Install these packages via NuGet Package Manager:

```
Microsoft.AspNetCore.Authentication.JwtBearer
Microsoft.AspNetCore.Identity.EntityFrameworkCore (optional for
user management)
System.IdentityModel.Tokens.Jwt
```

Configure JWT Settings in '`appsettings.json`': Add a JWT configuration section, as indicated here:

```
{
"Jwt": {
       "Key": "your_256-bit_secret_key_here",
       "Issuer": "https://localhost:5001",
       "Audience": "https://localhost:5001",
       "ExpiryInMinutes": 60
       }
}
```

Create a User Model (Optional): For simplicity, use a basic login DTO, as shown here:

```
public class LoginModel
{
       public string Username { get; set; }
       public string Password { get; set; }
}
```

Configure Authentication in '`Program.cs`': Add JWT authentication to the services, as demonstrated here:

```
using Microsoft.AspNetCore.Authentication.JwtBearer;
using Microsoft.IdentityModel.Tokens;
using System.Text;

var builder = WebApplication.CreateBuilder(args);
// Add JWT Authentication
builder.Services.AddAuthentication(options =>
{
        options.DefaultAuthenticateScheme = JwtBearerDefaults.
AuthenticationScheme;
        options.DefaultChallengeScheme = JwtBearerDefaults.
AuthenticationScheme;
        options.DefaultScheme = JwtBearerDefaults.Authentication-
Scheme;
}).AddJwtBearer(options =>
{
        options.TokenValidationParameters = new TokenValidationPa-
rameters
    {
        ValidateIssuer = true,
        ValidateAudience = true,
        ValidateLifetime = true,
        ValidateIssuerSigningKey = true,
        ValidIssuer = builder.Configuration["Jwt:Issuer"],
        ValidAudience = builder.Configuration["Jwt:Audience"],
        IssuerSigningKey = new SymmetricSecurityKey(Encoding.UTF8.
GetBytes(builder.Configuration["Jwt:Key"]))
  };
});

builder.Services.AddAuthorization();
```

Create a Token Generation Service: Add a service to generate JWT tokens through:

```
public class TokenService
{
        private readonly IConfiguration _config;
        public TokenService(IConfiguration config) => _config = config;
        public string GenerateToken(string username)
        {
        var securityKey = new SymmetricSecurityKey(Encoding.UTF8.
GetBytes(_config["Jwt:Key"]));
        var credentials = new SigningCredentials(securityKey,
SecurityAlgorithms.HmacSha256);
```

```
        var token = new JwtSecurityToken(issuer: _config
["Jwt:Issuer"],
        audience: _config["Jwt:Audience"],
        claims: new[] { new Claim(ClaimTypes.Name, username)
},

            expires: DateTime.UtcNow.AddMinutes(Convert.To
Double(_config["Jwt:ExpiryInMinutes"])),
        signingCredentials: credentials
        );
        return new JwtSecurityTokenHandler().WriteToken(token);
        }
}
```

Create an Auth Controller: Add an endpoint to authenticate users and issue tokens via:

```
[ApiController]
[Route("api/[controller]")]
public class AuthController : ControllerBase
{
        private readonly TokenService _tokenService;
        public AuthController(TokenService tokenService)
        {
                _tokenService = tokenService;
        }

        [HttpPost("login")]
        public async Task<IActionResult> Login([FromBody]
LoginModel login)
        {
                if (login == null || string.IsNullOrEmpty
(login.Username) || string.IsNullOrEmpty(login.Password))
                return BadRequest("Username and password are
required.");
                var user = await _userManager.FindByNameAsync(login.
Username);
                if (user == null)
                return Unauthorized("Invalid username or password.");
                var passwordValid = await _userManager.CheckPass-
wordAsync(user, login.Password);
                if (!passwordValid)
                return Unauthorized("Invalid username or pass-
word.");
                var token = _tokenService.GenerateToken(user.User-
Name);
```

```
                return Ok(new { Token = token });
        }
}
```

Secure Endpoints with Authorization: Use the [Authorize] attribute to protect endpoints, as indicated here:

```
[ApiController]
[Route("api/[controller]")]
[Authorize] // Requires authentication
public class SecureController : ControllerBase
{
        [HttpGet]
        public IActionResult Get() => Ok("This is a secure
endpoint!");
}
```

Test with Postman

Login Request:

```
POST `https://localhost:PORT/api/auth/login`
{
        "username": "admin",
        "password": "admin"
}
```

Response: JWT token.

Access Secure Endpoint

GET https://localhost:PORT/api/secure
Add the token to the Authorization header as 'Bearer {token}'.

Implement Role-Based Authorization: Add roles to the token, as indicated:

```
// In TokenService.GenerateToken()
var claims = new[]
{
new Claim(ClaimTypes.Name, username),
new Claim(ClaimTypes.Role, "Admin") // Assign role
};

Protect endpoints by role:
[Authorize(Roles = "Admin")]
[HttpGet("admin-only")]
public IActionResult AdminOnly() => Ok("Admins only!");
```

Additionally, follow these key security best practices:

- Always use HTTPS.

- Store secrets (for example, JWT keys) in Azure Key Vault or environment variables.
- Set short token expiration times.
- Use refresh tokens for long sessions.

By following these steps, you can implement secure authentication and authorization in your .NET Core Web API using JWT. For production, integrate with a database (for example, Entity Framework Core) and enhance validation logic.

Caching in Web Applications

Caching is a technique used to temporarily store copies of frequently accessed data or resources in a fast-access storage layer, reducing the need to repeatedly fetch or compute the same data from its original source (for example, a database, API, or file system). It acts as a "*short-term memory*" for applications, which enables faster responses to repetitive requests.

Importance of Caching

- **Dramatically Improves Performance**
    - Reduces latency by serving data from memory (nanoseconds access) instead of slower sources like databases (milliseconds) or disk storage (seconds)
    - **Example**: A product catalog fetched once from a database and cached can serve thousands of subsequent requests instantly.
- **Reduces Server/Resource Load**
    - Minimizes repetitive compute-heavy operations (for example, database queries, API calls, or complex calculations).
    - **Example**: Caching the results of a CPU-intensive report generation avoids recalculating it for every user.
- **Enhances Scalability**
    - Allows applications to handle more concurrent users with the same hardware by reducing backend load
    - **Example**: An e-commerce site can manage Black Friday traffic spikes by caching product listings.
- **Cost Efficiency**
    - Reduces costs associated with:
        - Database operations (fewer queries = lower cloud database costs)
        - Network bandwidth (fewer data transfers)

    - Compute resources (less CPU/memory usage)

- **Improves User Experience**
    - Faster page loads and smoother interactions (critical for retaining users)
    - **Example**: A social media app caches profile pictures to load them instantly.
- **Supports Offline/Fault Tolerance**
    - Cached data can be served during:
        - Network outages
        - Backend system failures
        - High-latency scenarios (for example, mobile apps in poor connectivity)
- **Reduces Redundant Work**
    - Avoids reprocessing identical requests
    - **Example**: Caching weather data for 10 minutes prevents repeated API calls for the same location.

Types of Caching (explained in tabular format)

Type	Use Case	Example
In-Memory Cache	Single-server, temporary data	Session data, configuration
Distributed Cache	Multi-server environments	Redis, Azure Cache for Redis
Client-Side Cache	Browser/app-level caching	Static assets (CSS, images)
CDN Cache	Global content delivery	Cached videos/images on edge servers
Database Cache	Query result caching	Redis cache

Table 7.1: *Types of Caching*

Common Use Cases of Using Caching

- **Web Applications**: Caching rendered HTML pages or API responses
- **Database Queries**: Storing results of frequent read-heavy queries (for example, product listings)
- **Authentication/Authorization**: Caching user roles or permissions to avoid repeated database checks
- **Content Delivery**: Caching static assets (images, CSS, JS) on CDNs
- **Machine Learning**: Storing preprocessed datasets or model predictions

Challenges to Consider

- **Cache Invalidation**: Ensuring cached data stays fresh and synchronized with the source (for example, updating product prices)

- **Memory Management**: Preventing cache bloat (for example, using LRU or TTL expiration policies)
- **Consistency**: Handling distributed systems where multiple caches might hold different versions of data
- **Cache Stampede**: Avoiding thundering herds of requests when cached data expires

Example: Caching in Action

Imagine a news website with 10 million daily users.

- **Without Caching**: Each article page triggers database queries for content, ads, and user preferences → database overload.
- **With Caching**:
    - Articles cached for 1 hour → 90% of requests served from memory.
    - User preferences cached for 15 minutes → 50% fewer database calls.
    - Ads cached regionally → 70% faster load times.

Result will be reduced server costs by 60% and improved page load speed by 3x.

Caching is Essential for

- Building high-performance applications
- Reducing operational costs
- Scaling to handle massive traffic
- Delivering a seamless user experience

By strategically caching data at the right layer (client, server, or network), developers optimize resource usage while maintaining data accuracy and freshness.

Here is a step-by-step guide to implementing caching in .NET 8 web applications using Visual Studio:

Choose Caching Strategy: Decide which type of caching to implement:

- In-Memory Caching (local to the server)
- Distributed Caching (shared across servers)
- Response Caching (HTTP-level caching)

In-Memory Caching Implementation

Step 1: Add Required Services

In '`Program.cs`':

```
builder.Services.AddMemoryCache();
```

Step 2: Inject `IMemoryCache`

In your service/controller:

```
public class CountryService
{
    private readonly IMemoryCache _cache;

    public CountryService(IMemoryCache cache)
    {
        _cache = cache;
    }
}
```

Step 3: Store and Retrieve Data

```
public List<Country> GetCountries()
{
    const string cacheKey = "CountriesCache";

    if (!_cache.TryGetValue(cacheKey, out List<Country> countries))
    {
        // Get from database
        countries = _context.Countries.ToList();

        var cacheOptions = new MemoryCacheEntryOptions()
            .SetSlidingExpiration(TimeSpan.FromMinutes(15))
            .SetAbsoluteExpiration(TimeSpan.FromHours(1));

        _cache.Set(cacheKey, countries, cacheOptions);
    }

    return countries;
}
```

Distributed Caching (Using Redis)

Step 1: Install NuGet Packages

```
Microsoft.Extensions.Caching.StackExchangeRedis
```

Step 2: Configure Redis in `Program.cs`

```
builder.Services.AddStackExchangeRedisCache(options =>
{
    options.Configuration = builder.Configuration.GetConnection-
String("Redis");
    options.InstanceName = "CountryApp_";
});
```

Step 3: Inject `IDistributedCache`

```
public class CountryService
{
    private readonly IDistributedCache _cache;

    public CountryService(IDistributedCache cache)
    {
        _cache = cache;
    }
}
```

Step 4: Store/Retrieve Data

```
public async Task<List<Country>> GetCountriesAsync()
{
    const string cacheKey = "CountriesCache";
    var cachedData = await _cache.GetStringAsync(cacheKey);

    if (string.IsNullOrEmpty(cachedData))
    {
        var countries = _context.Countries.ToList();
        var json = JsonSerializer.Serialize(countries);

        await _cache.SetStringAsync(cacheKey, json, new
DistributedCacheEntryOptions
        {
            AbsoluteExpirationRelativeToNow = TimeSpan.From-
Hours(1)
        });

        return countries;
    }

    return JsonSerializer.Deserialize<List<Country>>(cachedData);
}
```

Response Caching

Step 1: Enable in `Program.cs`

```
builder.Services.AddResponseCaching();
var app = builder.Build();
app.UseRouting();
app.UseResponseCaching();
```

Step 2: Add Cache Profile (Program.cs)

```
builder.Services.AddControllers(options =>
{
    options.CacheProfiles.Add("Default30",
        new CacheProfile()
        {
            Duration = 30,
            Location = ResponseCacheLocation.Any
        });
});
```

Step 3: Apply to Controller Actions

```
[HttpGet]
[ResponseCache(Duration = 60, Location = ResponseCacheLocation.
Any)]
public IActionResult GetCountries()
{
    // ...
}
// Or use named profile
[ResponseCache(CacheProfileName = "Default30")]
```

Cache Invalidation: Manual Cache Removal

```
// For MemoryCache
_cache.Remove(cacheKey);

// For DistributedCache
await _cache.RemoveAsync(cacheKey);
```

Cache Dependencies

```
var cancellationTokenSource = new CancellationTokenSource();
var cacheEntryOptions = new MemoryCacheEntryOptions()
    .AddExpirationToken(new CancellationChangeToken(cancellation-
TokenSource.Token));

// Trigger expiration later
cancellationTokenSource.Cancel();
```

Cache Configuration Best Practices

- Use appropriate expiration policies.
- Implement cache-busting strategies.
- Monitor cache hit/miss ratios.
- Use semantic cache keys (for example, "**`countries_v1`**").
- Consider cache size limits.

Testing Caching

- Use '**`dotnet-counters`**' for monitoring, it helps with general performance metrics, but does not provide detailed cache-specific monitoring like hit/miss rates.
- Verify cache behavior with Fiddler/Postman.
- Test cache expiration scenarios.
- Check distributed cache synchronization.

Caching Comparison Table

Feature	In-Memory	Distributed (Redis)	Response
Persistence	Volatile	Persistent	HTTP
Server Scope	Single	Multiple	Client
Data Type	Objects	Serialized	Responses
Complexity	Low	Medium	Low
Best For	Temp data	Shared data	Static content

***Table 7.2**: Caching Comparison*

Common Use Cases

- **In-Memory**: Session data, configuration
- **Distributed**: Shopping carts, user preferences
- **Response**: Static API responses, images

By following these steps, you can significantly improve your application's performance while maintaining data consistency. Remember to choose the right caching strategy based on your specific requirements.

.Net MAUI

.NET MAUI (Multi-platform App UI) is an open-source framework by Microsoft for building cross-platform native applications using C# and XAML. It enables developers to create apps for:

- **Mobile**: iOS, Android
- **Desktop**: Windows, macOS

from a single codebase. It is the evolution of **`Xamarin.Forms`**, which is integrated into the modern .NET ecosystem (.NET 6+).

What is .NET MAUI Used For?

- **Cross-Platform Development**: Build apps for multiple platforms with one project. **Example**: A fitness app running natively on phones, tablets, and desktops
- **Native Performance**: Access platform-specific APIs (camera, GPS, sensors) using C#. **Example**: Using Bluetooth on iOS/Android with shared code
- **Enterprise Apps**: Line-of-business apps (for example, inventory management, CRM)
- **Consumer Apps**: Social media, e-commerce, or productivity tools
- **Hybrid Web+Native Apps**: Integrate Blazor for web UI components in native apps.

Differences shown in below table between .Net MAUI, Xamarin Forms, Flutter or React Native

Feature	.NET MAUI	Xamarin.Forms	Flutter/React Native
Language	C#	C#	Dart (Flutter), JS (RN)
Project Structure	Single project	Multiple platform projects	Single project
Platform Integration	Deep .NET integration	Xamarin SDK	Platform channels
UI Framework	XAML or C# (declarative)	XAML	Widgets (Flutter), JSX (RN)
Hot Reload	Yes	Limited	Yes

***Table 7.3**: Differences between .Net MAUI, Xamarin Forms, Flutter/React Native*

Key Advantages of .NET MAUI

- **Single Codebase, Multiple Platforms**
  - Write once, deploy everywhere.
  - Shared UI, business logic, and platform-specific code
- **Native Performance**
  - Compiles to native binaries (not interpreted)
  - Direct access to platform APIs via platform-specific code or helpers like `CommunityToolkit.Maui`
- **Modern Development Experience**
  - **Hot Reload**: Instantly see UI changes without rebuilding.

   - **Single Project**: Simplified file structure (no platform-specific projects)
- **Rich Ecosystem**
   - Leverage .NET libraries (EF Core, ASP.NET Core).
   - NuGet packages and .NET tooling (Visual Studio, VS Code).
- **Flexible UI**
   - Use XAML for declarative UI or C# for code-driven layouts.
   - Customize UI per platform with `OnPlatform` or `Handler` customization.
- **Cost-Effective**: Free, open-source, and reduces development time/costs.
- **Blazor Hybrid Support**: Mix web (Blazor) and native UI components in the same app.

Example Workflow of a .Net MAUI Project:

a. Create a .NET MAUI project in Visual Studio.

b. Design UI in XAML/C# (shared across platforms).

c. Add platform-specific code using '#if' directives or dependency injection.

d. Test on emulators/devices with hot reload.

e. Deploy to app stores or package installers.

When to Use .NET MAUI

- You want native performance with shared code.
- Your team already uses C#/.NET.
- Targeting mobile + desktop platforms.
- Building enterprise/internal tools.

When Not to Use

- Apps requiring heavy platform-specific customization.
- Teams preferring JavaScript/React (choose React Native) or Dart (Flutter).

.NET MAUI is Microsoft's answer to modern cross-platform app development, as it combines the power of .NET with the flexibility of native UI. It is ideal for developers seeking a unified workflow to target mobile and desktop platforms while leveraging existing C# skills.

Here is a step-by-step guide to creating a .NET MAUI application in Visual Studio 2022, complete with a simple "Hello MAUI" sample app:

Step 1: Install Prerequisites

a. Install Visual Studio 2022 (17.3 or later).

b. During installation, select:

   i. .NET Multi-platform App UI development workload

   ii. Platform SDKs (Android, iOS, macOS, Windows)

Step 2: Create New Project

a. Open Visual Studio → Create a new project.

b. Search for "**MAUI**" → Select **.NET MAUI** App → Click **Next**.

c. Configure:

   - **Project name**: MauiDemo
   - **Location**: Choose folder
   - **Framework**: .NET 8.0

Step 3: Understand Project Structure

Your solution will contain:

- **App.xaml**: Application resources/entry point
- **App.xaml.cs**: Application lifecycle code
- **MainPage.xaml**: Default UI page
- **Platforms**: Platform-specific code (Android, iOS, and so on)
- **Resources**: Images, fonts, styles

Step 4: Build the UI

Replace **MainPage.xaml** content with:

```
<?xml version="1.0" encoding="utf-8" ?>
<ContentPage xmlns="http://schemas.microsoft.com/dotnet/2021/maui"
             xmlns:x="http://schemas.microsoft.com/winfx/2009/xaml"
             x:Class="MauiDemo.MainPage"
             Title="MAUI Demo">

    <VerticalStackLayout Spacing="25" Padding="30">

        <!-- Header -->
        <Label Text="Welcome to .NET MAUI!"
               FontSize="32"
               HorizontalOptions="Center"/>

        <!-- Counter Button -->
        <Button Text="Click Me"
                Clicked="OnCounterClicked"
                HorizontalOptions="Center"/>
```

```
        <!-- Counter Display -->
        <Label x:Name="CounterLabel"
               Text="Count: 0"
               FontSize="18"
               HorizontalOptions="Center"/>

    </VerticalStackLayout>

</ContentPage>
```

Step 5: Add Functionality

```
using System;
using Microsoft.Maui.Controls;
using Microsoft.Maui.Devices;
using Microsoft.Maui.Devices.Sensors;
```

Update `**MainPage.xaml.cs**`:

```
namespace MauiDemo;
public partial class MainPage : ContentPage
{
    int _count = 0;

    public MainPage()
    {
        InitializeComponent();
    }

    private void OnCounterClicked(object sender, EventArgs e)
    {
        _count++;
        CounterLabel.Text = $"Count: {_count}";

        // Vibrate on click (mobile-only)
        if (DeviceInfo.Platform == DevicePlatform.Android ||
            DeviceInfo.Platform == DevicePlatform.iOS)
        {
            Vibration.Default.Vibrate(100);
        }
    }
}
```

Step 6: Add Platform-Specific Features

Add `NuGet package: CommunityToolkit.Maui`

In `'MauiProgram.cs'`:

```
builder.UseMauiApp<App>().UseMauiCommunityToolkit();
```

Add Android vibration permission:

- Right-click Android project → **`Add`** → **`New Item`**
- Select **`Android Manifest`** → Add:

```
<uses-permission android:name="android.permission.VIBRATE" />
```

Step 7: Run the App

Select target platform from the following:

a. Windows Machine (for Windows desktop)

b. Android Emulator (for mobile)

c. iOS (requires Mac)

Click on Start Debugging (F5).

Step 8: Deploy to Different Platforms.

For Android:

a. Connect physical device via USB.

b. Enable Developer Mode and USB Debugging.

c. Select device from debug dropdown.

For Windows: Built-in support - just select Windows Machine.

For iOS:

- Pair with Mac via Xcode.
- Select iOS Simulator.

Key features demonstrated in this sample project are:

- Cross-platform UI with XAML
- Event handling in C#
- Platform-specific capabilities (vibration)
- Community Toolkit integration
- Responsive layout system

These are the next steps **you can perform to further enhance the application:**

1. Add navigation:

```
await Navigation.PushAsync(new DetailsPage());
```

2. Implement MVVM pattern.

3. Add data persistence (SQLite).

4. Integrate web APIs.

This sample shows .NET MAUI's core capabilities while maintaining simplicity. The same codebase runs natively on all supported platforms.

Developing a React Application in .Net

"**React in .NET**" refers to integrating React (a JavaScript library for building user interfaces) with .NET technologies (typically ASP.NET Core) to create modern web applications. This combination allows developers to use React for the frontend UI and .NET for backend logic (APIs, services, or server-side rendering). Common implementations include:

- **ReactJS.NET**: A library that simplifies using React with ASP.NET MVC/Razor
- **ASP.NET Core + React SPA Templates**: Official Microsoft templates for building React single-page applications (SPAs) with .NET backends
- **Decoupled Architecture**: React frontend app consuming .NET Web APIs.

What is React in .NET Used For?

- Modern Web Apps: Build interactive, component-driven UIs with React while leveraging .NET for backend logic.
- Enterprise Applications: Create line-of-business apps (for example, dashboards, CRUD apps) with React frontends and .NET APIs.
- Server-Side Rendering (SSR): Use React with .NET for SEO-friendly server-rendered pages (via Next.js or ReactJS.NET).
- Full-Stack Development: Combine C#/.NET backend expertise with React's UI capabilities.

Comparison between React, Blazor and MVC/Blazor :

Aspect	**React + .NET**	**Blazor**	**ASP.NET MVC/Razor**
Frontend Language	JavaScript/TypeScript	C#	C#/Razor Syntax
UI Framework	React (Component-based)	Blazor Components	Razor Pages
Rendering	Client-side or SSR	WebAssembly (client) or Server	Server-side
Ecosystem	React's npm packages	.NET NuGet Packages	.NET Libraries
Use Case	Modern SPAs with rich interactivity	C#-centric full-stack apps	Traditional server-rendered apps

Table 7.4: *Comparison between React, Blazor and MVC/Blazor*

Advantages of Using React with .NET

- **Best of Both Worlds:**
  - **React**: Rich UI ecosystem, virtual DOM for performance, reusable components
  - **.NET**: Robust backend (APIs, security, scalability) with C#
- **Decoupled Architecture:**
  - Frontend (React) and backend (.NET) can evolve independently.
  - **Example**: A React app can consume multiple .NET microservices.
- **Large Ecosystem**: Access to React's npm packages (for example, Material-UI, Redux) and .NET NuGet packages (for example, Entity Framework Core)
- **Performance**: React's efficient DOM updates + .NET's high-performance APIs
- **Developer Flexibility**: Teams can work on frontend (JavaScript/TypeScript) and backend (C#) separately.
- **SSR Capabilities**: Use ReactJS.NET or Next.js for SEO-friendly server-side rendering.
- **Enterprise-Ready**: .NET's security, dependency injection, and logging pair well with React's scalability.

Example application showing combination of React + .NET Workflow:

Backend (ASP.NET Core Web API):

```
// WeatherForecastController.cs
[ApiController]
[Route("[controller]")]
public class WeatherController : ControllerBase
{
    [HttpGet]
    public IEnumerable<WeatherForecast> Get()
    {
        // Return data from a .NET service
    }
}
```

Frontend (React):

```
// Weather.js
import React, { useEffect, useState } from 'react';

function Weather() {
  const [forecasts, setForecasts] = useState([]);

  useEffect(() => {
```

```
        fetch('/weather')
          .then(response => response.json())
          .then(data => setForecasts(data));
      }, []);

      return (
        <ul>
          {forecasts.map(f => <li key={f.date}>{f.temperatu-
reC}°C</li>)}
        </ul>
      );
    }
```

When to Use React with .NET?

- You want a modern SPA frontend with a scalable .NET backend.
- Your team has expertise in both JavaScript/React and C#.
- You need to integrate with React's ecosystem (for example, third-party UI libraries).
- Building enterprise apps where .NET's backend strengths are critical

When Not to Use

- Small projects where a full-stack framework like Blazor simplifies development
- Teams unfamiliar with JavaScript/React

Key tools for React + .Net:

Create a ASP.NET Core React Template with following command in Terminal:

```
dotnet new react -o MyApp
```

- ReactJS.NET (for SSR with MVC/Razor)
- Swagger/OpenAPI (for API documentation)
- Azure DevOps (CI/CD for full-stack apps)

React in .NET combines the flexibility of React's UI ecosystem with the power of .NET's backend capabilities. It is ideal for teams building modern web apps that require:

- Rich interactivity
- Scalable APIs
- Enterprise-grade security
- Cross-team collaboration (frontend/backend separation)

By leveraging both technologies, developers can create high-performance applications while maximizing existing .NET investments.

Here is a step-by-step guide to creating a React application integrated with a .NET backend using ASP.NET Core and the React project template:

Step 1: Install Prerequisites.

a. Install .NET SDK 8.0 (or 6.0)

b. Install Node.js (v18+)

c. Install IDE: Visual Studio 2022+ or VS Code

Step 2: Create New Project.

Open command prompt and run:

```
dotnet new react -o ReactNetDemo
cd ReactNetDemo
```

This creates a project with:

- ASP.NET Core Web API backend
- React frontend (in '**`ClientApp`**' folder)

Step 3: Project Structure

```
ReactNetDemo/
├── Controllers/          # .NET API controllers
├── ClientApp/            # React application
│   ├── src/                    # React components
│   ├── public/           # Static assets
│   └── package.json      # React dependencies
├── Program.cs            # .NET startup
└── appsettings.json      # Configuration
```

Step 4: Restore Dependencies

.NET dependencies

```
dotnet restore
```

React dependencies (from **`ClientApp`** folder)

```
cd ClientApp
npm install
cd ..
```

Step 5: Run the Application

```
dotnet run
```

The app will:

- Start .NET backend on https://localhost:7119.

- Start React dev server on https://localhost:44470.
- Auto-open browser to the React app

Step 6: Explore Key Files

Backend API (`WeatherForecastController.cs`):

```
[ApiController]
[Route("[controller]")]
public class WeatherForecastController : ControllerBase
{
    [HttpGet]
    public IEnumerable<WeatherForecast> Get()
    {
        // Returns sample data
    }
}
```

Frontend Fetch (`ClientApp/src/FetchData.js`):

```
async populateWeatherData() {
  const response = await fetch('weatherforecast');
  const data = await response.json();
  this.setState({ forecasts: data, loading: false });
}
```

Step 7: Modify the React Frontend

Edit `ClientApp/src/App.js`:

```
import React from 'react';

export default class App extends React.Component {
  render() {
    return (
      <div className="container mt-5">
        <h1>React + .NET Demo</h1>
        <p>Count: {this.state?.count ?? 0}</p>
        <button
          className="btn btn-primary"
          onClick={async () => {
            const res = await fetch('/api/counter');
            const data = await res.json();
            this.setState({ count: data.count });
          }}
        >
          Increment Counter
        </button>
      </div>
    );
```

```
    }
}
```

Step 8: Add .NET API Endpoint.

Create `**CounterController.cs**`:

```
[ApiController]
[Route("api/[controller]")]
public class CounterController : ControllerBase
{
    private static int _count = 0;

    [HttpGet]
    public IActionResult Get()
    {
        _count++;
        return Ok(new { count = _count });
    }
}
```

Step 9: Build and Run.

```
dotnet build
dotnet run
```

Step 10: Test the Application

a. Visit https://localhost:44470.

b. Click the button to see the counter increment.

c. Observe network calls to .NET API endpoints.

This setup combines React's dynamic frontend capabilities with .NET's robust backend services, which is ideal for enterprise-grade applications. The integrated template provides a seamless development experience with hot reloading for both C# and React code.

.Net Core Web API

A .NET Core Web API project (built with ASP.NET Core) is a framework for creating HTTP-based services that serve data to clients (for example, web apps, mobile apps, IoT devices) over RESTful APIs. It is designed to build lightweight, scalable, and platform-agnostic backend services that communicate via standard HTTP methods (GET, POST, PUT, DELETE) and return data in formats like JSON or XML.

Key Features of a .NET Core Web API Project

- **RESTful Design:**
  - Follows REST principles for resource-based interactions (for example, `/api/products`)
  - Uses HTTP verbs (`GET`, `POST`, and so on) to define actions
- **Cross-Platform**: Runs on Windows, Linux, and macOS
- **Minimalist and Fast**: Optimized for performance with minimal overhead
- **Integration with Modern Tools**:
  - Built-in support for OpenAPI (Swagger) for API documentation
  - Works seamlessly with Entity Framework Core (for databases) and Dependency Injection
- **Security**: Supports authentication/authorization via JWT, OAuth2, or Azure AD
- **Flexibility**: Can be hosted in IIS, Docker, Kubernetes, or cloud platforms (Azure, AWS)

Structure of a .NET Core Web API Project

A typical project includes:

- `Controllers`: Define API endpoints (for example, `ProductsController.cs`).
- `Models`: Represent data objects (for example, `Product.cs`).
- `Program.cs`: Configures services and middleware (dependency injection, routing)
- `appsettings.json`: Stores configuration (database strings, API keys)
- `Dependencies`: NuGet packages (for example, `Swashbuckle.AspNetCore` for Swagger)

Example Workflow:

- **Client Request**: A mobile app sends an HTTP '`GET`' request to https://api.example.com/products/1.
- **Routing**: The request is routed to the `ProductsController`'s '`GetProduct(int id)`' method.
- **Processing**: The controller fetches data (from a database, cache, or service) and returns a JSON response.
- **Response**: The client receives a JSON object like:
  ```
  { "id": 1, "name": "Laptop", "price": 999.99 }
  ```

When to Use a .NET Core Web API

- Building a backend for SPA frameworks (React, Angular, Vue)
- Creating microservices architectures
- Serving data to mobile apps or IoT devices
- Integrating with third-party APIs or legacy systems

Key features and comparison between .Net Core Web API, ASP.NET MVC, Node.js/ Express :

Feature	.NET Core Web API	ASP.NET MVC	Node.js/Express
Purpose	HTTP APIs	Server-rendered web apps	JavaScript APIs
Performance	High (compiled)	Moderate	Moderate (interpreted)
Cross-Platform	Yes	Yes	Yes
Type Safety	Strong (C#)	Strong (C#)	Weak, dynamic (JavaScript)
Tooling	Visual Studio, CLI	Visual Studio	VS Code, npm

***Table 7.5**: Key Features and Comparison between .Net Core Web API, ASP.NET MVC, Node.js/Express*

Sample Code Snippets:

Controller (`ProductsController.cs`):

```
[ApiController]
   [Route("api/[controller]")]
   public class ProductsController : ControllerBase
   {
       [HttpGet]
       public IActionResult GetAllProducts()
       {
           return Ok(new List<Product> { /* ... */ });
       }
   }
```

Model (`Product.cs`):

```
public class Product
   {
       public int Id { get; set; }
       public string Name { get; set; }
       public decimal Price { get; set; }
   }
```

Swagger Configuration (`Program.cs`):

```
builder.Services.AddSwaggerGen();
   app.UseSwagger();
   app.UseSwaggerUI();
```

Why Choose .NET Core Web API

- **Speed**: Optimized for high-throughput scenarios
- **Scalability**: Built for cloud-native and microservices architectures
- **Ecosystem**: Integrates with Azure, Docker, and DevOps tools
- **Community**: Backed by Microsoft and a large developer community

Thus, by leveraging a .NET Core Web API, developers can build robust, secure, and maintainable services that power modern applications across platforms.

Here is a step-by-step guide to creating and managing a .NET Core Web API in Visual Studio:

Step 1: Prerequisites

a. Install Visual Studio 2022+ (Community/Professional).

b. Install .NET SDK 8.0 (or 6/7).

c. Optional: Postman/Swagger for API testing

Step 2: Create a New Project.

a. Open Visual Studio → Create a new project.

b. Search for "**`ASP.NET Core Web API`**" → Select the template.

c. Configure:

   - **Project name**: ProductApi
   - **Framework**: .NET 8.0
   - **Authentication**: None
   - Enable OpenAPI (Swagger).

Step 3: Explore Project Structure.

Key files/folders:

- **Program.cs**: Startup/configuration
- **Controllers/**: API endpoints
- **`appsettings.json`**: Configuration
- **Properties/`launchSettings.json`**: Runtime profiles

Step 4: Create a Model Class.

Add a '**Models**' folder and create '**Product.cs**', as shown:

```
namespace ProductApi.Models;
public class Product
{
    public int Id { get; set; }
    public string? Name { get; set; }
    public decimal Price { get; set; }
}
```

Step 5: Add a Controller

a. Right-click on '**Controllers**' → **Add** → **Controller**.

b. Select API Controller with read/write actions → Name: '**ProductsController**'.

```
using Microsoft.AspNetCore.Mvc;
using ProductApi.Models;

namespace ProductApi.Controllers;

[Route("api/[controller]")]
[ApiController]
public class ProductsController : ControllerBase
{
    private static List<Product> _products = new()
    {
        new Product { Id = 1, Name = "Laptop", Price = 999.99m },
        new Product { Id = 2, Name = "Mouse", Price = 25.50m }
    };

    // GET: api/products
    [HttpGet]
    public ActionResult<IEnumerable<Product>> GetProducts()
    {
        return _products;
    }

    // GET: api/products/5
    [HttpGet("{id}")]
    public ActionResult<Product> GetProduct(int id)
    {
        var product = _products.FirstOrDefault(p => p.Id == id);
        if (product == null) return NotFound();
        return product;
    }
```

```
        // POST: api/products
        [HttpPost]
        public ActionResult<Product> PostProduct(Product product)
        {
            product.Id = _products.Max(p => p.Id) + 1;
            _products.Add(product);
            return CreatedAtAction(nameof(GetProduct), new { id = 
    product.Id }, product);
        }

        // PUT: api/products/5
        [HttpPut("{id}")]
        public IActionResult PutProduct(int id, Product product)
        {
            var existing = _products.FirstOrDefault(p => p.Id == id);
            if (existing == null) return NotFound();

            existing.Name = product.Name;
            existing.Price = product.Price;
            return NoContent();
        }

        // DELETE: api/products/5
        [HttpDelete("{id}")]
        public IActionResult DeleteProduct(int id)
        {
            var product = _products.FirstOrDefault(p => p.Id == id);
            if (product == null) return NotFound();

            _products.Remove(product);
            return NoContent();
        }
    }
```

Step 6: Test with Swagger

Press F5 to run the app.

Swagger UI opens at https://localhost:PORT/swagger.

Test endpoints:

- **`GET /api/products`**: Retrieve all products.
- **`POST /api/products`**: Add new product (JSON body).
- **`PUT/DELETE`**: Modify/remove products.

Step 7: Add Validation

Enhance the '**PostProduct**' method, as shown here:

```
[HttpPost]
public ActionResult<Product> PostProduct(Product product)
{
    if (!ModelState.IsValid) // Validate input
    {
        return BadRequest(ModelState);
    }

    product.Id = _products.Max(p => p.Id) + 1;
    _products.Add(product);
    return CreatedAtAction(nameof(GetProduct), new
{ id = product.Id }, product);
}
```

Step 8: Manage Configuration

Add database connection string in '**appsettings.json**':

```
{
  "ConnectionStrings": {
    "DefaultConnection": "Server=(localdb)\\mssqllocaldb;Data-
base=ProductDb;Trusted_Connection=True;"
  }
}
```

Now, you can access the following in '**Program.cs**':

```
var connectionString = builder.Configuration.GetConnection-
String("DefaultConnection");
```

Step 9: Deploy the API.

a. Right-click on project → **Publish**.

b. Choose target:

- **Azure**: App Service
- **Docker**: Container Registry
- **Folder**: Self-contained executable

Key Features of the Sample API

- RESTful endpoints
- In-memory data store (replace with EF Core for production)
- Swagger/OpenAPI documentation
- Model validation

- HTTP status codes

Troubleshooting Tips

- **`Swagger Not Loading`**:
  - Check '**`launchSettings.json`**' for correct launch URL.
  - Ensure that '**`Swashbuckle.AspNetCore NuGet`**' package is installed.
- **`404 Errors`**:
  - Verify route attributes (**`[Route("api/[controller]")]`**).
  - Check HTTP verb annotations (**`[HttpGet]`**`, `**`[HttpPost]`**).

Next steps for you to complete as a practice test:

1. Add Entity Framework Core for database integration.
2. Implement JWT authentication.
3. Add logging (**`ILogger<ProductController>`**).
4. Write unit tests with xUnit.

This Web API demonstrates core concepts like routing, CRUD operations, and REST principles. You have now built a foundation for scalable .NET Core APIs.

Conclusion

This chapter showcased how to create web based applications using different technologies. Visual Studio's integrated environment empowers developers to navigate these frameworks efficiently, as it offers tools for development, debugging, testing, and deployment. While each technology has trade-offs such as React's JavaScript ecosystem complexity or MAUI's platform-specific nuances, the choice ultimately depends on project goals, team expertise, and long-term maintainability.

As web development evolves, embracing trends like cloud-native architectures, AI integration, and progressive web apps (PWAs) will further enhance these frameworks' capabilities. By mastering these tools within Visual Studio, developers are well-equipped to build adaptable, high-performance applications that meet the demands of today's digital landscape.

As we move beyond the web development basics, the next chapter invites you to unlock the full potential of this powerful IDE by exploring the vibrant ecosystem of extensions that can transform how you code, debug, and innovate. They empower developers to transcend the IDE's default features by injecting specialized tools, automation, and integrations that align with specific workflows, languages, or project demands.

CHAPTER 8
Using Extensions in Visual Studio

Introduction

In the dynamic landscape of software development, adaptability is the key to formulating smart solutions. Visual Studio, Microsoft's flagship integrated development environment (IDE), embraces this philosophy through its robust support for **extensions**. Extensions are modular add-ons that empower developers to tailor and enhance their coding experience, while transforming the IDE into a personalized powerhouse. Whether streamlining workflows, integrating cutting-edge tools, or supporting new programming languages, these extensions can unlock endless possibilities for customization.

From productivity-boosting utilities like code snippet managers and real-time linters to advanced integrations with cloud platforms such as Azure and GitHub, extensions cater to diverse needs across the development lifecycle. Available via the Visual Studio Marketplace, they range from Microsoft-authored tools to innovative contributions by the global developer community. With seamless installation through the IDE's Extensions Manager, even novice users can effortlessly expand Visual Studio's capabilities. By bridging gaps between functionality and creativity, extensions not only optimize efficiency but also foster innovation, while allowing developers to focus on building exceptional software.

Structure

In this chapter, we will cover the following topics:

- Understanding VS Extensions
- Searching and Installing Extensions
- Popular Extension Categories and Must-Have Tools
- Customizing Extensions in Visual S

- Assigning Keyboard shortcuts to Extension Features
- Building Custom Extensions & Publishing to VS Marketplace
- Automated Builds with Extensions in CI/CD

Understanding Extensions

Extensions in Visual Studio are modular components or plugins that augment the IDE's core functionality. They also allow developers to customize and optimize their development environment for specific tasks, workflows, or technologies. Think of them as "*power-ups*" that integrate seamlessly into Visual Studio, while expanding its capabilities without altering its foundational architecture. These add-ons can range from simple utilities like code formatters or shortcut enhancers, to complex tools that integrate with external services, debuggers, or frameworks.

Key Characteristics of Extensions

- **Modularity:** Extensions are designed to be lightweight and focused. Developers can install only what they need, while avoiding unnecessary bloat.
- **Integration:** They interact with Visual Studio's APIs to access and modify features such as the code editor, debugger, project system, or user interface.
- **Customization:** Extensions let users tailor the IDE to their preferences by adding new language support, themes, or keyboard shortcuts.
- **Community-Driven:** While Microsoft offers official extensions, the Visual Studio Marketplace thrives on contributions from third-party developers, while fostering a rich ecosystem of tools.

How Do Extensions Work?

Extensions leverage Visual Studio's extensibility model, which provides APIs (Application Programming Interfaces) for interacting with the IDE's components. These often include:

- **Editor Extensions:** Modify code highlighting, autocompletion, or linting using the .NET Compiler Platform (Roslyn).
- **Project Templates:** Add scaffolding for frameworks like React, Angular, or .NET MAUI.
- **Debugging Tools:** Integrate with specialized debuggers for databases, containers, or IoT devices.
- **UI Enhancements:** Customize toolbars, panels, or themes to improve usability.

Developers can build extensions using the Visual Studio SDK (Software Development Kit) and distribute them via the Visual Studio Marketplace. Once installed, extensions are managed through the Extensions Manager, where users can enable, disable, or update them with minimal disruption.

Why Use Extensions in Visual Studio?

Extensions are a cornerstone of the Visual Studio experience and offer unparalleled flexibility to adapt the IDE to their unique needs. Here is why they are indispensable:

They boost productivity.

Extensions automate repetitive tasks, reduce context-switching, and streamline workflows. The following tools eliminate manual effort, while allowing developers to focus on solving complex problems:

- ReSharper (code analysis/refactoring)
- GitHub Copilot (AI-driven code suggestions)
- CodeMaid (code cleanup/organization)

They help you customize your workflow.

Not every team or project has the same requirements. Extensions let you tailor Visual Studio to match your preferences via the following tools and features:

- Themes (for example, Dark Theme Enhancers) for visual comfort
- Key Bindings (for example, Vim Emulation) for familiar keyboard shortcuts
- Project Templates for scaffolding frameworks like React or Blazor

They help you expand built-in capabilities.

Visual Studio's core features are powerful, but extensions fill gaps for niche or emerging needs like the ones mentioned here:

- **Language Support:** Add compilers, debuggers, or syntax highlighting for languages like Python, Rust, or Go.
- **Cloud Integration:** Tools like Azure DevOps or AWS Toolkit streamline cloud development.
- **Advanced Debugging:** Extensions for Docker, IoT, or game engines (for example, Unity/Unreal).

They help you access cutting-edge tools.

The developer ecosystem evolves rapidly, and extensions let you adopt innovations without waiting for official updates. These tools are:

- AI-Assisted Coding (for example, IntelliCode)
- Real-Time Collaboration (for example, Live Share)
- Performance Optimizers (for example, OzCode for debugging)

They help you leverage community expertise.

The Visual Studio Marketplace hosts thousands of extensions built by developers worldwide, while offering solutions for almost every use case. Whether it is a niche tool for legacy systems or a trending framework, the community has likely already created an extension for it.

They help you achieve cost-effective scalability.

Many extensions are free or low-cost, which allow teams to enhance their toolchain without significant investment. Even premium tools (for example, ReSharper) often save time and resources in the long run.

They help you stay agile in modern development.

Extensions ensure that Visual Studio stays relevant as technology trends shift. These extensions can perform functions like:

- Integrating DevOps pipelines (for example, Azure Pipelines)
- Supporting containerization (for example, Docker Tools)
- Enabling cross-platform development (for example, .NET MAUI).

Extensions can transform Visual Studio from a generic IDE into a personalized, future-ready development hub. They empower developers to work faster, smarter, and more creatively while adapting to the ever-changing demands of software engineering. By leveraging extensions, you can ensure that your toolkit grows alongside your skills and projects, which will keep you ahead in a competitive tech landscape.

By bridging gaps in the IDE's native features, extensions empower developers to work smarter, faster, and more creatively. They transform Visual Studio from a general-purpose tool into a finely tuned environment that aligns with individual or team needs. This ensures that the IDE evolves alongside the ever-changing demands of modern software development.

Finding and Installing Extensions in Visual Studio

Visual Studio's true power lies in its ability to adapt to your needs through extensions, which are third-party or Microsoft-built tools that enhance the IDE's functionality. Whether you are optimizing code quality, integrating with Git, or leveraging AI-driven assistance, extensions can transform Visual Studio into a tailored development environment.

Here is a step-by-step guide to discovering, installing, and managing extensions effectively.

Visual Studio Marketplace: The Visual Studio Marketplace is the official repository for extensions, while offering thousands of free and premium tools. Here is how to navigate it:

Step-by-Step Guide to Finding Extensions in Visual Studio

Follow these simple steps to discover and explore extensions in Visual Studio:

Step 1: Open Visual Studio.

Launch Visual Studio and open an existing project or start a new one.

Step 2: Access the Extensions Manager.

a. Go to the top menu bar.

b. Click on `Extensions` > `Manage Extensions`.

   - This opens the `Extensions Manager` window.

Step 3: Browse or Search for Extensions.

In the `Extensions Manager`, you will see two main tabs:

- `Installed`: Lists extensions already added to your IDE
- `Online`: Lets you search for new extensions

To find new extensions:

a. Click on the `Online` tab.

b. Use the search bar in the top-right corner to type keywords (for example, "`Git`," "`Theme`," or "`Debugging`").

   - **Example**: Search for `SonarLint` to find code quality tools.

Step 4: Filter and Sort Results.

- **Filter by Category**: Click on the dropdown under the search bar to narrow results by categories like "`Coding Tools`," "`Cloud`," or "`Languages`".
- **Sort by Relevance or Popularity**: Use the "`Sort by`" dropdown to prioritize highly rated or trending extensions.

Step 5: Review Extension Details.

Click any extension from the list to view the following details:

- **Description**: Features and use cases
- **Ratings and Reviews**: User feedback and ratings (for example, ★★★★☆)

- **Compatibility**: Supported Visual Studio versions (for example, VS 2022, 2019)
- **Publisher**: Verify if it's Microsoft or a trusted third party

Step 6: Install the Extension.

a. Click on the Download or Install button next to the extension.

b. Wait for the download to complete.

c. Restart Visual Studio to activate the extension.

Alternative: Use the Visual Studio Marketplace Website.

a. Visit https://marketplace.visualstudio.com/.

b. Search for extensions using keywords or categories.

c. Click **`Download`** to get a **`.vsix`** file for manual installation (see Step 7).

Tips for Success

Use Specific Keywords: Narrow results by searching for precise terms like "**`Azure DevOps`**" or "**`Python support`**."

- **Check Compatibility:** Ensure that the extensions are working with your Visual Studio version to avoid crashes.
- **Prioritize Ratings:** Highly rated extensions are often more reliable and well-maintained.

Step 7 : Installation Methods

a. **Method 1: Install Directly via Visual Studio.**

  i. Open **`Extensions`** > **`Manage Extensions`**.

  ii. Search for an extension (for example, "**`SonarLint`**").

  iii. Click on **`Download`** or **`Install`**.

  iv. Restart Visual Studio to activate the extension.

Note: *Extensions are managed under the Installed tab, where you can enable, disable, or update them.*

b. **Method 2: Manual Installation with `.vsix` Files.**

  i. Some extensions are distributed as **`.vsix`** files, useful for offline setups or custom tools.

  ii. Download the **`.vsix`** file from the Marketplace or a trusted source.

  iii. In Visual Studio, navigate to **`Extensions`** > **`Manage Extensions`**.

iv. Click on the `More Options` menu and select `Install` from VSIX.

v. Browse to the `.vsix` file and confirm installation.

Pro Tip: Use manual installation for testing beta versions or internal company tools.

Step 8: Verify Installation.

a. After restarting Visual Studio, check the Installed tab in the Extensions Manager.

b. Ensure the extension is listed and enabled.

Popular Extension Categories and Must-Have Tools

- **Code Quality and Analysis**
  - **SonarLint:** A real-time code linter that detects bugs, vulnerabilities, and code smells in C#, VB.NET, and C++
  - **ReSharper:** Enhances code refactoring, navigation, and static analysis (paid tool)
- **Git and Version Control**
  - **GitHub for Visual Studio:** Seamlessly commit, push, and pull code without leaving the IDE.
  - **GitLens:** Supercharge Git with blame annotations, history tracking, and branch comparisons.
- **AI-Powered Coding Assistants**
  - **IntelliCode:** Uses machine learning to prioritize context-aware code completions
  - **GitHub Copilot:** Generates code snippets and entire functions based on natural language prompts
- **Database Tools**
  - **SQL Server Data Tools (SSDT):** Design, debug, and deploy SQL Server databases
  - **Entity Framework Core Tools:** Simplify database scaffolding and migrations for .NET projects
- **Other Notable Categories**
  - **Themes & UI Tweaks:** Customize the IDE with dark themes (for example, Dark Theme 2022) or icon packs.
  - **Cloud and DevOps:** Integrate with Azure, AWS, or Docker via official toolkits.

- **Testing and Debugging:** Tools like OzCode (debugging assistant) or NCrunch (automated test runner)

Best Practices for Managing Extensions

- **Avoid Overloading**: Install only what you need to keep Visual Studio fast and responsive.
- **Update Regularly**: Check for updates in `Manage Extensions` > `Updates`.
- **Security First**: Stick to trusted publishers to avoid malicious add-ons.

Extensions are the secret sauce to unlocking Visual Studio's full potential. By mastering the Marketplace, leveraging installation methods, and choosing the right tools for your workflow, you can supercharge productivity, improve code quality, and stay ahead in modern software development. Whether you are a solo developer or part of a team, extensions ensure your IDE evolves with your ambitions.

Must-Have Visual Studio Extensions for Developers

Visual Studio's extensibility makes it a powerhouse for developers across domains. Whether you are refining code quality, debugging complex issues, or polishing your IDE's aesthetics, these extensions are game-changers. Here is a curated list of essential tools to supercharge your workflow:

Productivity Boosters:

- **ReSharper:** Enhances code analysis, refactoring, and navigation for C# and VB.NET
- **ReSharper C++**: Provides similar features for C++ development

  Key Features:

  - Smart code completion and error detection
  - Automated code cleanup and pattern matching
  - Seamless integration with unit testing frameworks
  - Saves hours by streamlining repetitive tasks and enforcing best practices (Remember, it is a paid tool.)

- **Visual Studio Live Share:** Enables real-time collaborative coding with shared editing, debugging, and terminals

  Key Features:

  - Multi-user pair programming with audio chat
  - No need to clone repos or sync environments
  - Perfect for remote teams, code reviews, or mentoring sessions

- **CodeMaid:** Automates code cleanup, formatting, and organization

  Key Features:

  - Sorts and groups code elements (methods, properties)
  - Removes unused code and simplifies navigation
  - Keeps your codebase pristine with minimal effort

Debugging and Error Handling:

- **OzCode:** Supercharges debugging with advanced visualization tools

  Key Features:

  - **Time Travel Debugging**: Enables stepping backward during debugging sessions to inspect previous states
  - **LINQ Query Insights**: Visualize and debug complex LINQ expressions
  - Reduces debugging time by making complex data flows transparent
- **Exception Assistant:** Simplifies error resolution with actionable insights

  Key Features:

  - Detailed exception explanations and troubleshooting steps
  - Quick access to relevant documentation
  - Turns cryptic errors into solvable problems

Frontend Development

- **Web Essentials:** Adds modern tooling for CSS, JavaScript, and HTML development

  Key Features:

  - **CSS Autoprefixer**: Automatically adds vendor prefixes
  - **Browser Compatibility Warnings**: Flags unsupported features
  - Streamlines frontend workflows for frameworks like React or Angular
- **Browser Link:** Syncs Visual Studio with browsers for real-time updates

  Key Features:

  - Live reloading for CSS/HTML changes
  - Inspect DOM elements directly from the IDE
  - Eliminates manual refreshes during UI tweaks

Themes and UI Customization

- **Material Theme:** Modernizes Visual Studio with Material Design-inspired styling

Key Features:

- Sleek icons, syntax highlighting, and dark/light themes
- Customizable color schemes for reduced eye strain
- Makes coding visually appealing and ergonomic

- **Productivity Power Tools:** Enhances IDE usability with layout and navigation tweaks

Key Features:

- Custom Document Well: Organizes open tabs by project or type
- Solution Explorer Filtering: Quickly finds files in large projects
- Tailors the IDE to your workflow preferences

Pro Tips for Extension Mastery

- **Avoid Overloading**: Install only what you need to keep Visual Studio snappy.
- **Check Compatibility**: Ensure extensions support your VS version (for example, 2022).
- **Explore the Marketplace**: Discover niche tools for your stack (for example, Docker, IoT).
- Pair these with Git integrations (for example, GitHub for Visual Studio) and AI tools (for example, IntelliCode) for an unstoppable workflow.

Customizing Extensions in Visual Studio: Tailoring Tools to Your Workflow

Visual Studio's extensions are powerful out of the box, but their true potential is unlocked when you customize them to align with your workflow. From tweaking settings to syncing preferences across devices, personalizing extensions ensures they work for you and not against you. Here is a detailed guide to mastering extension customization in Visual Studio.

Configuring Extension Settings

Most extensions offer configurable options to adapt their behavior to your needs. Here is how to fine-tune them:

Accessing Extension Settings

a. Open **`Visual Studio`**.

b. Navigate to **`Tools`** > **`Options`** (Windows) or **`Visual Studio`** > **`Preferences`** (macOS).

c. In the **`Options`** dialog, expand the tree view to find your extension's settings.
   - Extensions often group their settings under their name or a related category (for example, Web Essentials or ReSharper).

Example: Customizing Code Snippets with Snippet Designer

a. Install the Snippet Designer extension (via the Marketplace).

b. Go to **`Tools`** > **`Options`** > **`Snippet Designer`**.

c. Adjust settings like:
   - **Default Language**: Set to C#, TypeScript, or other supported languages.
   - **Snippet Shortcuts**: Define prefixes for quick insertion (for example, '**`tryf`**' for a try-finally block).
   - **Placeholder Styles**: Customize how variables appear in snippets.

d. Save changes and test snippets in the code editor.

Tailoring snippet shortcuts or language defaults saves keystrokes and ensures consistency across projects.

Assigning Keyboard Shortcuts to Extension Features

Many extensions add commands that are not bound to keys by default. Assigning hotkeys lets you trigger these features instantly.

How to Set Custom Shortcuts:

1. Go to **`Tools`** > **`Options`** > **`Environment`** > **`Keyboard`**.
2. In the **`Show`** commands containing search bar, type the extension's command name.
   - **Example**: Search for `` `CodeMaid.CleanupCode` `` to find CodeMaid's cleanup command.
3. Select the command from the list.
4. In the Press shortcut keys field, type your desired key combination (for example, `Ctrl+K, Ctrl+M`).
5. Click **`Assign`** and confirm.

Pro Tip: *Use the Global scope for shortcuts that work everywhere or Text Editor for context-specific actions.*

Example: Shortcut for Snippet Designer

a. Assign 'Ctrl+K, Ctrl+X' to insert a snippet.

b. Press the keys, type the snippet shortcut (for example, '`tryf`'), and hit Tab to insert the code block.

c. Hotkeys eliminate mouse dependency, which speeds up repetitive tasks like code cleanup or snippet insertion.

Syncing Extensions Across Devices with Visual Studio Settings Sync

If you work across multiple machines, Visual Studio's Settings Sync ensures your extensions and configurations follow you everywhere.

How to Enable Settings Sync:

1. Sign in to Visual Studio with your Microsoft or work/school account.
2. Go to **`Tools`** > **`Options`** > **`Environment`** > **`Accounts`**.
3. Check **`Synchronize`** settings across devices and choose what to **`sync`**:
   - **Extensions**: Installed extensions and their versions
   - **Keyboard Shortcuts**: Custom key bindings
   - **`Tools`** > **`Options`** **`Settings`**: Extension configurations (for example, ReSharper rules).
4. Click on **`OK`** to save.

How It Works:

- When you install Visual Studio on a new device, sign in to automatically download synced extensions and settings.
- Updates to extensions or settings on one machine propagate to others.

Example: If you customize OzCode's debugging filters on your office PC, those preferences will sync to your home laptop.

Best Practices for Customization:

- **Avoid Conflicts**
  - Test new shortcuts to ensure they don't clash with built-in commands (for example, *Ctrl*+S for save).
  - Reset conflicting shortcuts via **`Tools`** > **`Options`** > **`Keyboard`** > **`Reset`**.
- **Backup Custom Configurations**: Export settings manually via **`Tools`** > **`Import and Export Settings`** for extra redundancy.
- **Stay Updated**: Check extension changelogs after updates—new features might require reconfiguring settings.

Customizing extensions transforms Visual Studio from a generic IDE into a finely tuned instrument for your coding symphony. These tweaks compound into significant productivity gains when you are streamlining snippets, blazing through tasks with hotkeys, and syncing setups across devices.

Building Custom Extensions for Visual Studio: A Developer's Guide

Visual Studio's extensibility model empowers developers to create custom tools that enhance the IDE's functionality. Whether automating workflows, integrating new languages, or adding niche debugging features, building your own extensions unlocks endless possibilities. This guide walks you through the process—from crafting a "`Hello World`" extension to publishing it on the Visual Studio Marketplace.

What Is the Extension SDK

The Visual Studio Software Development Kit (SDK) provides the tools, templates, and APIs needed to build, debug, and deploy extensions. Some of its key components are:

- **VSIX Project Template:** Scaffolds extension projects with boilerplate code
- **Visual Studio IDE Services:** APIs to interact with editors, tool windows, debuggers, and more
- **Debugging Tools:** Test extensions in an isolated "Experimental Instance" of Visual Studio

Prerequisites

- Visual Studio 2022 (Community, Professional, or Enterprise)
- Visual Studio Extension Development Workload
    - Install via the **`Visual Studio Installer`** > **`Workloads`** > **`Other Toolsets`**.

Getting Started: Building a "`Hello World`" Extension

Step 1: Create a VSIX Project.

a. Open Visual Studio.

b. Go to **`File`** > **`New`** > **`Project`**.

c. Search for VSIX Project (under Extensibility).

d. Name the project (for example, `` `HelloWorldExtension` ``) and click on Create.

Step 2: Add a Custom Command.

Let us create a button that displays a "**Hello World**" message.

a. Right-click on the project in **Solution Explorer**.

b. Select **Add** > **New Item** > **Extensibility** > **Command**.

c. Name the file '**HelloWorldCommand.cs**' and click on Add.

Step 3: Modify the Command Code.

In '**HelloWorldCommand.cs**', locate the **Execute** method and modify it to show the message, as indicated here:

```
private void Execute(object sender, EventArgs e)
{
    string message = "Hello from your first extension!";
    VsShellUtilities.ShowMessageBox(
        this.package,
        message,
        "Hello World",
        OLEMSGICON.OLEMSGICON_INFO,
        OLEMSGBUTTON.OLEMSGBUTTON_OK,
        OLEMSGDEFBUTTON.OLEMSGDEFBUTTON_FIRST);
}
```

Step 4: Update the Manifest.

Open '**source.extension.vsixmanifest**' to configure metadata, as shown here:

- **General Tab**: Set display name, author, and description.
- **Assets Tab**: Ensure that the **HelloWorldCommand** is included.

Debugging and Packaging Extensions

a. Press F5 to launch the Experimental Instance of Visual Studio.
    - This sandboxed environment isolates your extension for testing.

b. In the experimental instance:

    i. Go to **Tools** > **Extensions** to confirm your extension is installed.

    ii. Trigger your command via **View** > **Other Windows** > **HelloWorldCommand** (or your assigned menu path).

Packaging

a. In **Solution Explorer**, right-click on the project and select **Build**.

b. Navigate to the **bin\Debug** or **bin\Release** folder.

c. Locate the `.vsix` file; this is your distributable extension package.

Pro Tip: Test the `.vsix` file in a clean Visual Studio installation to catch compatibility issues.

Publishing to the Visual Studio Marketplace

Step 1: Prepare for Publishing.

a. **Finalize Metadata**:

   i. Ensure that `source.extension.vsixmanifest` has a clear description, version number, and license.

   ii. Add screenshots or GIFs to showcase functionality.

b. **Test Thoroughly**: Verify compatibility with target Visual Studio versions (for example, 2022 and 2019).

Step 2: Create a Publisher Account:

a. Go to the `Visual Studio Marketplace Publisher Portal` (https://marketplace.visualstudio.com/manage).

b. Sign in with your Microsoft account.

c. Click on Create Publisher and fill in your profile (for example, name, logo, website).

Step 3: Upload Your Extension:

a. In the `Publisher Portal`, click `Create New Extension` > `Visual Studio`.

b. Upload your `.vsix` file.

c. Complete the following listing details:

   - `Title`: A clear, search-friendly name (for example, "`Hello World Extension`")
   - `Categories`: Relevant tags (for example, Coding Tools, Debugging)
   - `Pricing`: Free, Paid, or Trial

d. Click `Upload` to publish.

Step 4: Manage Your Listing:

- **Updates**: Upload new `.vsix` files to release patches or features.
- **Analytics**: Track downloads, ratings, and user reviews.
- **Respond to Feedback**: Engage with users to improve your extension.

Best Practices for Building Extensions

- **Follow Naming Conventions:**
  - Prefix commands with your extension's name (for example, **`HelloWorld.ShowMessage`**).
  - Use **`PascalCase`** for classes and **`camelCase`** for variables.
- **Prioritize Performance:**
  - Avoid blocking the UI thread with long-running tasks.
  - Use asynchronous methods for operations like file I/O or web requests.
- **Handle Errors Gracefully:**
  - Wrap risky operations in try-catch blocks.
  - Log errors to the Output Window or a dedicated log file.
- **Versioning:**
  - Use semantic versioning (for example, 1.0.0 for initial release, 1.0.1 for bug fixes).
  - Update the **`vsixmanifest`** file with each release.
- **Community Engagement:**
  - Open-source your extension on GitHub to encourage contributions.
  - Write documentation with usage examples and troubleshooting tips.

Building custom extensions for Visual Studio is a rewarding way to contribute to the developer ecosystem while solving your own workflow challenges. From a simple "Hello World" experiment to complex tools like linters or cloud integrations, the VSIX framework provides the flexibility to create almost anything.

Integrating Extensions into Development Workflows: Streamlining Collaboration, Automation, and Standardization

Visual Studio extensions are not just individual tools; they are building blocks for creating cohesive, efficient, and scalable development workflows. By integrating extensions into team collaboration, CI/CD pipelines, and curated tool bundles, teams can eliminate friction, reduce setup time, and ensure consistency. Here is how to leverage extensions to supercharge your workflows:

Team Collaboration: Sharing Extensions with `.vsconfig` and `.vsextensions`

Why Standardize Extensions: Teams often face inconsistencies when developers use different tools, leading to "**`works on my machine`**" issues. Sharing recommended extensions ensures everyone uses the same tools like:

- Code Analyzers (for example, SonarLint)

- Version Control Tools (for example, GitHub for Visual Studio)
- Debugging Utilities (for example, OzCode)

Method 1: Using `.vsconfig` Files

A **`.vsconfig`** file lists required components and extensions for a project. Visual Studio uses this to auto-install missing tools.

Here is the step-by-step process for it:

Step 1. Export Your Configuration:

a. In Visual Studio, go to **`Tools`** > **`Get Tools and Features`**.

b. Click on **`Export configuration`** and save the **`.vsconfig`** file.

Step 2. Add Extensions to `.vsconfig`: Open the file and include extension IDs (from the Marketplace URL): [json code provided here]

```
{
  "version": "1.0",
  "components": [
    "Microsoft.VisualStudio.Component.CoreEditor",
    "MyCompany.MyExtension,version=1.0.0"
  ]
}
```

Step 3. Share with the Team:

a. Commit the **`.vsconfig`** to your repository.

b. New developers open the file via **`File`** > **`Open`** > **`File to install dependencies`**.

Method 2: `.vsextensions` Manifests

For granular control, create a .vsextensions manifest to specify exact extension versions:

a. Create a **`extensions.json`** file as shown here:

```
{
    "recommendations": [
      "SonarSource.sonarlint-visualstudio",
      "GitHub.GitHubExtension",
      "ms-dotnettools.dotnet-core-extensions"
    ]
  }
```

b. **Place it in the `` `.vs` `` folder:** Save to `` `.vs/vsextensions/extensions.json` `` in your project root.

c. **Visual Studio Prompts Users to install:** When the project loads, developers will see a notification to install missing extensions.

Best Practices to Follow

a. Use **`.vsconfig`** for broad environment standardization (components + extensions).

b. Use **`.vsextensions`** for project-specific tooling.

c. Update files regularly as dependencies evolve.

CI/CD Pipelines: Automating Builds with Extensions

Extensions are not limited to the IDE; they can supercharge CI/CD pipelines too.

Example: Azure DevOps Tasks

Many extensions in the Azure DevOps Marketplace (https://marketplace.visualstudio.com/azuredevops) add custom tasks to pipelines such as:

- **SonarQube**: Integrates code quality gates
- **Azure Pipelines**: Deploys to cloud services
- **`ReportGenerator`**: Generates test coverage reports

Here is a quick walkthrough for how to integrate them step-by-step:

a. Install the Extension in Azure DevOps:

    i. Navigate to your organization's Marketplace.

    ii. Add the extension (for example, SonarQube Scanner for Azure DevOps).

b. Add Tasks to **`azure-pipelines.yml`**, as indicated here:

```
steps:
  - task: SonarQubePrepare@5
    inputs:
      SonarQube: "SonarCloud"
      scannerMode: "MSBuild"
      projectKey: "my-project"
  - task: DotNetCoreCLI@2
    inputs:
      command: "build"
  - task: SonarQubeAnalyze@5
  - task: SonarQubePublish@5
```

Using Visual Studio Extensions in Build Agents

For extensions that impact builds (for example, SQL Server Data Tools), you must follow these steps:

Install Extensions on Build Agents: Use PowerShell to install `.vsix` files.

[PowerShell code mentioned here.]

```
Install-Vsix -Path "C:\path\to\extension.vsix"
```

Validate in Pipeline Scripts:

```
- script: |
    if (-not (Test-Path "C:\VS\Extensions\MyExtension")) {
      exit 1
    }
  displayName: "Check Extension Installation"
```

Extension Packs: Curated Tool Bundles for Specific Scenarios

Extension packs group related tools into a single installable unit, which reduces setup time for specialized workflows.

Example: ASP.NET Core Developer Pack

A hypothetical pack could include:

- **Razor Syntax Highlighting**: For **`.cshtml`** files
- **Swagger UI Integration**: API documentation tools
- **Entity Framework Core Tools**: Database scaffolding

Here is the complete process to create an Extension Pack:

a. **Create a VSIX Project:** Use the VSIX Project template in Visual Studio.

b. **Add Dependencies:** In **`source.extension.vsixmanifest`**, list extension IDs under **`<Dependencies>`**:

c. xml, as indicated here:

```
    <Dependency Id="Microsoft.AspNetCore.Razor.VSCode"
Version="1.0.0" />
    <Dependency Id="Swashbuckle.AspNetCore.SwaggerUI"
Version="6.0.0" />
```

d. **Build and Share:** Distribute the **`.vsix`** file internally or publish to the Marketplace.

Popular Packs to Inspire You:

- **Web Development Pack**: Bundles CSS/JS tools, browser sync, and REST client utilities
- **Game Dev Pack**: Integrates Unity, Unreal, and debugging tools

Best Practices:

- Target specific roles (for example, frontend vs. backend developers).

- Include documentation for pack components.

Real-World Workflow Integration Examples:

Scenario 1: Onboarding a New Team Member

a. Clone the repo with `.vsconfig` and `.vsextensions`.

b. Open the solution; Visual Studio auto-installs required extensions.

c. Start coding immediately with standardized tools.

Scenario 2: Enforcing Code Quality in CI/CD

a. PR triggers pipeline with SonarQube analysis.

b. Build fails if code quality thresholds are not met.

c. Developers fix issues using SonarLint in Visual Studio.

Scenario 3: Rapid Prototyping with Extension Packs

a. Install ASP.NET Core Pack for API development.

b. Use built-in tools to scaffold endpoints, debug, and generate Swagger docs.

Integrating extensions into workflows transforms disjointed tools into a unified engine for productivity. By standardizing team environments, automating CI/CD tasks, and curating extension packs, developers can focus on solving problems instead of configuring tools.

With the right extensions in the right places, your team can ship faster, collaborate smarter, and innovate boldly.

Conclusion

Extensions in Visual Studio are more than just add-ons; they are the linchpin of a modern, adaptable, and efficient development experience. By transforming the IDE into a personalized toolkit tailored to your unique needs, extensions bridge the gap between out-of-the-box functionality and the ever-evolving demands of software development.

Throughout this chapter, we explored how extensions empower developers to:

- **Boost Productivity:** Automate repetitive tasks, enhance code quality with tools like SonarLint, and leverage AI-driven aids such as IntelliCode.
- **Customize Workflows:** Tailor shortcuts, themes, and tooling via **`Tools`** > **`Options`** or **`sync`** preferences across devices with Settings Sync.

- **Collaborate Effectively:** Standardize team environments using `.vsconfig` files and streamline CI/CD pipelines with Azure DevOps extensions.
- **Innovate Freely:** Build and publish custom extensions to solve niche challenges or share solutions with the global developer community.

The Visual Studio Marketplace stands as a testament to the vibrant ecosystem of tools created by developers, for developers. Whether you are adopting extensions for frontend frameworks, cloud integrations, or debugging complex systems, they ensure that your IDE evolves alongside technology trends.

Next Steps:

1. **Explore the Marketplace**: Discover tools that align with your current projects.
2. **Experiment Boldly**: Customize existing extensions or build your own to address unmet needs.
3. **Share Knowledge**: Contribute to the community by publishing extensions or curating packs for your team.

In a world where agility and efficiency define success, extensions are essential. By embracing them, you future-proof your workflows, unlock creativity, and turn Visual Studio into a dynamic engine for innovation. The possibilities are limitless; dive in and redefine what your IDE can do.

Your toolkit is only as powerful as the extensions you choose. Choose wisely, build boldly, and code joyfully.

Foreword for the Next Chapter: Performance Optimization and Memory Management

As we transition from the dynamic world of extensions to the meticulous art of performance optimization and memory management, we will shift our focus from enhancing tools to refining code itself. While extensions empower your workflow, the true measure of exceptional software lies in its efficiency, scalability, and reliability.

In the next chapter, we delve into the critical discipline of crafting code that not only works, but thrives under pressure. Performance optimization is more than just speed; it is about resource stewardship, minimizing latency, and eliminating bottlenecks that plague user experiences. Memory management, meanwhile, is the unsung hero of stability, as it ensures that your applications run smoothly without leaks, bloat, or unexpected crashes.

Chapter 9
Performance Optimization and Memory Management

Introduction

Visual Studio provides a robust suite of tools and features to help developers optimize application performance and manage memory efficiently. Performance optimization focuses on identifying and resolving bottlenecks like slow algorithms, excessive CPU usage, or inefficient I/O operations. Tools like the **Performance Profiler** and **Diagnostic Tools** enable real-time analysis of CPU, memory, and GPU usage, while code optimization techniques like asynchronous programming and multithreading support enhance responsiveness.

Memory management is critical to preventing leaks, reducing overhead, and ensuring resource efficiency. Visual Studio's **Memory Usage Profiler** and **Debugging Tools** (for example, heap analysis and garbage collection tracking) pinpoint issues like unmanaged resource leaks or excessive allocations in .NET applications. By leveraging features such as **memory snapshots** and **static code analysis**, and best practices like object pooling or `` `IDisposable` `` patterns, developers can build applications that balance speed, scalability, and resource sustainability.

Together, these tools empower developers to create high-performance, reliable software while minimizing runtime inefficiencies and memory-related errors.

Structure

In this chapter, we will cover the following topics:

- Performance Profiler
- Memory & CPU Usage Tools

- Diagnostic Tools in Action
- Intellitrace for advanced debugging
- Static Code Analysis (SCA)
- Performance Anti-Patterns
- Async/Await Patterns
- Thread-Pool Optimization
- Best Practices

Performance Profiler is a powerful diagnostic tool designed to help developers identify and resolve these issues efficiently. This section explores how the Performance Profiler works, its key features, and a step-by-step guide to leveraging it effectively.

- Here are the most widely used tools:
    - Performance Profiler
    - CPU Usage Tool
    - Memory Usage Tool
    - Application Timeline (UI Responsiveness)
    - GPU Usage Tool
    - Diagnostic Tools (Real-time CPU/Memory during debugging)
    - Static Code Analysis (Performance warnings)
    - IntelliTrace (Historical debugging)
    - PerfView (Advanced ETW analysis). PerfView is not part of Visual Studio. It is a separate, standalone performance analysis tool developed by Microsoft.
    - JetBrains dotMemory/ANTS Profiler (Third-party integrations)

Commonly Used Tools and their use-cases:

Tool	**Primary Use Case**
CPU Usage Tool	Identifying slow methods, loops, or algorithms
Memory Usage Tool	Detecting leaks, fragmentation, or excessive allocations
Application Timeline	Diagnosing UI freezes in WPF/UWP/MAUI apps
Diagnostic Tools	Real-time monitoring during debugging
Static Code Analysis	Flagging inefficient code patterns (for example, `string concat`)

***Table 9.1**: Commonly Used Tools and Their Use-cases*

Here is the step-by-step guide to use each of these tools:

CPU Usage Tool

- Open **`project`** > **`Debug`** > **`Performance Profiler`** > Select **`CPU Usage`**
- Start the profiler, execute the slow operation, and stop profiling.
- Check "**`Hot Paths`**" in the call tree to find CPU-intensive methods.

Example: CPU Bottleneck (Identified via CPU Usage Tool)

Inefficient Code:

```
public void ProcessOrders(List<Order> orders) {
    foreach (var order in orders) {
        // Nested loop causing O(n²) complexity
        foreach (var item in order.Items) {
            item.Price = CalculateTax(item.Price);
        }
    }
}
```

Fix: Cache tax rates or parallelize using the following code:

```
Parallel.ForEach(orders, order => {
    foreach (var item in order.Items) {
        item.Price = CalculateTax(item.Price);
    }
});
```

Memory Usage Tool

- **`Debug`** > **`Performance Profiler`** > Select **`Memory Usage`**.
- **Take Snapshots**: Take a snapshot before and after a suspected leak operation.
- **Compare**: Identify growing object counts or retained memory in the comparison view.

Example: Memory Leak (Detected via Memory Usage Tool)

Leaky Code:

```
public class EventManager {
    public static event Action OnDataLoaded;

    public void LoadData() {
        // Leak: Subscriber never unregisters
        OnDataLoaded += HandleData;
    }

    private void HandleData() { /* ... */ }
}
```

Fix: Deregister the event using:

```
OnDataLoaded -= HandleData;
```

Application Timeline Tool

- **Debug** > **Performance Profiler** > Select **Application Timeline**.
- Reproduce the UI freeze scenario.
- **Analyze**: Check "**UI Thread**" for long-running tasks blocking responsiveness.

Example 3: UI Freeze (Diagnosed via Application Timeline)

Blocking UI Thread:

```
private void LoadData_Click(object sender, EventArgs e) {
    // Synchronous call freezes UI
    var data = File.ReadAllText("large.json");
    UpdateUI(data);
}
```

Fix: Use '**async/await**' to make the call asynchronous, as shown here:

```
private async void LoadData_Click(object sender, EventArgs e) {
    var data = await File.ReadAllTextAsync("large.json");
    UpdateUI(data);
}
```

Diagnostic Tools in Action

Real-Time Memory Monitoring:

1. Start debugging (F5).
2. Open Diagnostic Tools (**Debug** > **Windows** > **Diagnostic Tools**).
3. Observe Memory Usage graph while interacting with the app.

Static Code Analysis Warning

Inefficient Code:

```
string result = "";
for (int i = 0; i < 1000; i++) {
    result += i; // Warning: "Implicit string concatenation in
loop"
}
```

Fix: Use StringBuilder instead of string concatenation, as shown here:

```
var builder = new StringBuilder();
for (int i = 0; i < 1000; i++) {
    builder.Append(i);
```

```
    }
    string result = builder.ToString();
```

These tools empower developers to resolve performance issues systematically, while ensuring that applications are fast, responsive, and resource-efficient.

In software development, performance issues like slow response times, memory leaks, or excessive CPU usage can degrade user experience and scalability. Visual Studio's diagnostic tools can help in identifying such issues at both compile time and run time and improve application stability and performance.

Step-by-Step Guide to Use the Performance Profiler:

Consider that a project (for example, .NET, C++, ASP.NET) is open in Visual Studio.

1. **Launch the Performance Profiler**.
    a. **Method 1**: Navigate to `Debug` > `Performance Profiler` (or press 'Alt+F2').
    b. **Method 2**: Use the Analyze menu: `Analyze` > `Performance Profiler`.
2. **Configure Profiling Session**.
    a. Select your target project or executable.
    b. Choose from among the following profiling tools based on your goals:
        - **CPU Usage**: For CPU-intensive code analysis
        - **Memory Usage**: To track heap allocations and garbage collection
        - **GPU Usage**: For GPU-bound applications
        - **File I/O**: Diagnose slow read/write operations
        - **.NET Async**: Analyze asynchronous operations
        - **Application Timeline**: Profile WPF/UWP UI performance
3. **Start Profiling**.
    a. Click on `Start` to launch the application with profiling enabled.
    b. Interact with your app to reproduce the performance issue (for example, load a heavy feature).
4. **Stop the Session**.
    a. Return to `Visual Studio` and click `Stop Collection`.
    b. The profiler generates a detailed report.
5. **Analyze Results**. CPU Usage Report:
    - It shows a flame graph or call tree highlights methods with high exclusive (self-time) or inclusive (total time) CPU consumption.

- Look for "**`hot paths`**" to optimize.

6. **Memory Report:**
    a. Inspect the Heap Snapshot to see object counts and sizes.
    b. Compare snapshots before/after an operation to spot leaks.
7. **Diagnose and Fix Issues.**
    a. **Example 1**: A method taking 80% CPU time may need algorithmic optimization.
    b. **Example 2**: Unreleased '**`Idisposable`**' objects in the memory report indicate leaks.
    c. **Example 3**: Frequent disk I/O calls might require caching.

Pro Tips:

- **Profile in Release Mode**: Debug mode skews results if optimizations are disabled.
- **Compare Snapshots**: For memory issues, take snapshots before/after a suspect operation.
- **Filter Data**: Exclude system or framework code to focus on your application logic.
- **Iterate**: Profile after each optimization to measure impact.

Visual Studio's Performance Profiler is an indispensable tool for maintaining high-performing applications. By systematically analyzing CPU, memory, I/O, and UI behavior, developers can preemptively resolve bottlenecks and deliver smoother user experiences. Incorporate profiling into your regular testing cycle to catch issues early and iterate with confidence. Remember, a well-optimized application is scalable, reliable, and resource-efficient.

Unlocking Advanced Debugging with IntelliTrace in Visual Studio

IntelliTrace is a powerful diagnostic tool in Visual Studio that has revolutionized debugging by recording application execution events and method calls. Unlike traditional debugging which requires you to reproduce issues step-by-step, IntelliTrace enables historical debugging, which allows developers to "*travel back in time*" and analyze events leading to crashes, exceptions, or unexpected behavior. This is especially useful for intermittent or hard-to-reproduce bugs.

Advantages of IntelliTrace:

- **Historical Debugging**: Inspect past application states, variable values, and method calls without restarting the debugging session.
- **Production Debugging**: Collect logs from deployed environments (for example, Azure, IIS) and analyze them locally in Visual Studio.
- **Reduced Reproducibility Hassles**: Debug issues reported by users without needing to replicate their exact environment or steps.
- **Event and Call Tracking**: Track specific events (for example, exceptions, file operations) and method calls with parameters and return values.
- **Time Travel Debugging**: Travel back and forth through recorded execution to pinpoint root causes. TTD is a separate feature available in Visual Studio Enterprise for C++ on Windows using the Windows Debugger (WinDbg) or Azure-hosted environments with Snapshot Debugging for .NET Core.

Step-by-Step Guide for Using IntelliTrace

Prerequisites:

- Visual Studio 2019/2022 Enterprise Edition (IntelliTrace is not available in Community/Pro)
- A .NET Framework project (IntelliTrace supports .NET, ASP.NET, WPF, and so on)
- Enable IntelliTrace.
    a. Open your project in Visual Studio.
    b. Go to **`Debug`** > **`Windows`** > **`IntelliTrace Events`** to open the IntelliTrace panel.
- Configure IntelliTrace Settings.
    a. Navigate to **`Tools`** > **`Options`** > **`IntelliTrace`**.
    b. Choose from the following recording modes:
        - **`Events Only`**: Records exceptions, file I/O, and other system events.
        - **`Events and Call Information`**: Logs method calls and parameters (more detailed but resource-intensive).
- Start Debugging with IntelliTrace.
    a. Press F5 to start debugging.
    b. IntelliTrace automatically begins recording events and method calls.
    c. Reproduce the issue (for example, click a button that triggers an exception).

- Analyze Recorded Events.
  a. When an exception occurs, the IntelliTrace Events window lists all logged events (for example, exceptions, HTTP requests).
  b. Double-click on an event to jump to the exact code location and inspect variables, call stacks, and threads.
- Step Backward in Time.
  a. Use the **Step Backward** button in the **Debug** toolbar to navigate to previous application states.
  b. Inspect variable values and method parameters at each step to trace the root cause.
- Export and Analyze Logs in Production.
  a. **Collect Logs in Production**:
     i. Deploy the IntelliTrace collector to your server.
     ii. Run: powershell
     ```
     IntelliTraceCollector.exe /Launch /Configuration:collection_plan.ASP.NET.xml
     ```
  b. Reproduce the issue, then stop the collector to generate an '**.iTrace**' file.
- Open Logs in Visual Studio:
  a. Go to **File** > **Open** > **File** and load the '**.iTrace**' file.
  b. Analyze events, exceptions, and threads as if debugging locally.

Best Scenarios for IntelliTrace (with Examples):

- **Debugging Intermittent Exceptions**:
  - **Scenario**: A user reports sporadic '**NullReferenceException**' in a payment processing module. This is further illustrated in the following code:
  ```
  public void ProcessPayment(PaymentRequest request)
  {
     var user = _userService.GetUser(request.UserId); // user
  could be null
  user.DeductBalance(request.Amount); // Throws if user is null
  }
  ```
- **Here is the sequence of steps to follow:**
  - Use IntelliTrace to record method calls and events.
  - When the exception occurs, step backward to see why '**_userService.GetUser()**' returned '**null**'.

   - Discover if '**request.UserId**' was invalid due to a race condition in a prior method.
- **Diagnosing Production Crashes:**
   - **Scenario**: A deployed ASP.NET app crashes randomly.
   - Here is the sequence of steps to follow:
      a. Collect an '**.iTrace**' log from the production server.
      b. Open it in Visual Studio to find an '**OutOfMemoryException**' caused by a memory leak in a background service.
      c. Use the **Memory Usage** tab to analyze object allocations and memory retention. For detecting undisposed resources like **SqlConnection**, consider using static analysis or dedicated memory profilers.
- **Tracing Concurrency Issues:**
   - **Scenario**: A WPF app freezes due to UI thread blocking.

```
private void LoadData_Click(object sender, EventArgs e) {
    var data = _service.GetDataSync(); // Blocks UI thread
    dataGrid.ItemsSource = data;
}
```

   - Record events with IntelliTrace and notice long-running synchronous calls on the UI thread.
   - Refactor the method to use '**async/await**' and verify via historical debugging.
- **Validating Event Sequences:**
   - **Scenario**: An e-commerce cart fails to apply discounts correctly.
   - **Steps**: Use IntelliTrace to track the order of method calls, as shown here:
     `AddToCart() → ApplyCoupon() → CalculateTotal()`
   - Discover that '**ApplyCoupon()**' is called after '**CalculateTotal()**', leading to incorrect totals.

Best Practices

- Use Events Only mode for minimal performance overhead.
- Limit call tracking to critical modules to reduce log size.
- Combine IntelliTrace with other tools (for example, Performance Profiler) for comprehensive diagnostics.
- Avoid using it in performance-critical production environments due to resource usage.

IntelliTrace is a game-changer for debugging complex issues as it provides a time-travel audit trail of your application's execution. Whether diagnosing elusive production bugs, concurrency problems, or unexpected exceptions, it empowers developers to resolve issues faster and with greater precision. By integrating IntelliTrace into your debugging workflow, you can reduce guesswork, improve code quality, and deliver more robust applications.

Static Code Analysis in Visual Studio: Enhancing Code Quality and Security

Static Code Analysis (SCA) is a technique used to analyze source code **without executing it** to identify potential bugs, security vulnerabilities, and deviations from coding standards. In Visual Studio, tools like Roslyn Analyzers (for C#/VB.NET) and legacy Code Analysis (FxCop) automatically review code against predefined or custom rulesets. This proactive approach helps developers catch issues early, enforce best practices, and maintain clean, efficient code.

Advantages of Static Code Analysis

- **Early Bug Detection**: Identify logic errors, null reference risks, and resource leaks during development.
- **Security Compliance**: Detect vulnerabilities like SQL injection, hard-coded passwords, or insecure deserialization.
- **Code Consistency**: Enforce naming conventions, architecture guidelines, and design patterns.
- **Performance Insights**: Flag common inefficient code patterns, such as potential boxing or costly string concatenations, especially when supplemented with additional analyzers or extensions.
- **Maintainability**: Simplify code reviews by automating checks for complexity, duplication, and readability.

Step-by-Step Process to Run Static Code Analysis

1. **Enabling Code Analysis:** For Legacy Projects (FxCop), follow these steps:
    a. Right-click on the project > `Properties` > `Code Analysis` > Check `Enable Code Analysis` on Build.
    b. Select a ruleset (for example, "*Microsoft All Rules*").
2. **For .NET Core/5+ (Roslyn Analyzers)**:
    a. Analyzers are enabled by default. Configure rules via '`.editorconfig`' or `Solution Explorer` > `Dependencies` > `Analyzers`.

3. **Running Analysis:**

    a. **Manual Run**: Go to **`Build`** > **`Run Code Analysis`** > **`On Solution`**.

    b. **Automatic Run**: Warnings appear in the Error List as you code or build.

4. **Analyzing Results:**

    a. Open the Error List ('*Ctrl*+\, *Ctrl*+E') to view warnings.

    b. Click on a warning to navigate to the problematic code.

    c. Hover over the issue for a description and suggested fixes.

5. **Fixing or Suppressing Issues:**

    a. **Quick Fixes**: Use the lightbulb icon ('*Ctrl*+.') to apply auto-fixes (for example, null-checking, disposing resources).

    b. **Suppress Warnings**: Right-click on a warning > **`Suppress`** > In **`Source/Suppression`** File (if justified).

6. **Customizing Rulesets:**

    a. Create a custom ruleset:

        i. Right-click on **`Project`** > **`Add`** > **`New Item`** > **`Code Analysis Rule Set`**.

        ii. Toggle rules to Error, Warning, or None based on team standards.

        iii. Apply the ruleset via project properties.

Best Scenarios for Static Code Analysis (with Examples)

- **Security Vulnerability Detection**
    - **Issue**: Unsanitized input leading to SQL injection

```
public void ExecuteQuery(string userInput) {
    var query = $"SELECT * FROM Users WHERE Name
= '{userInput}'";
    SqlCommand cmd = new SqlCommand(query, connection);
// Warning: CA2100
}
```

You need to explicitly add **`Microsoft.CodeAnalysis.NetAnalyzers`** with security rules enabled as this rule will not trigger by default.

Fix: Use parameterized queries, as shown here:

```
var query = "SELECT * FROM Users WHERE Name = @name";
cmd.Parameters.AddWithValue("@name", userInput);
```

- **Null Reference Prevention**
  - **Issue**: Potential '**NullReferenceException**' when dereferencing unvalidated objects

```
public void PrintName(Person person) {
    Console.WriteLine(person.Name.ToUpper()); // Warning:
CA1062
}
```

Fix: Validate input with null checks, as shown here:

```
Console.WriteLine(person?.Name?.ToUpper() ?? "Unknown");
```

- **Resource Leak Detection**
  - **Issue**: Undisposed '**Idisposable**' objects (for example, file streams)

```
public void ReadFile() {
    var stream = new FileStream("file.txt", FileMode.Open);
// Warning: CA2000
}

Fix: Use 'using' blocks, as shown here:
using (var stream = new FileStream("file.txt", FileMode.Open)) {
... }
```

Identifying and Resolving Performance Anti-Patterns

Performance anti-patterns are coding practices that degrade application efficiency. Common examples include:

- String Concatenation in Loops (Excessive Allocations)
- Boxing/Unboxing in Collections.
- Synchronous I/O in Async Methods
- Redundant Database Queries

Step-by-Step Process to Identify and Fix Anti-Patterns

1. **Use the Performance Profiler.**

   a. **Launch Profiler**: **Debug** > **Performance Profiler** > Select **CPU Usage/ Memory Usage**.

   b. **Reproduce the Issue**: Execute the slow operation (for example, loading a large dataset).

   c. **Analyze Hot Paths**:

      - **CPU Report**: Identify methods with high exclusive time.

- o **Memory Report**: Check for excessive allocations or retained objects.

2. **Identify Anti-Patterns in Code.**

   a. **Example 1**: String Concatenation in Loops

```
string result = "";
for (int i = 0; i < 10000; i++) {
        result += i.ToString(); // Allocates 10,000 strings
}
```

Fix: Use `StringBuilder`.

```
var sb = new StringBuilder();
  for (int i = 0; i < 10000; i++) {
        sb.Append(i);
  }
```

   b. **Example 2**: Redundant Queries

```
  public void RenderPage(int userId) {
      var user = _db.GetUser(userId); // Called on every
render
  }
```

Fix: Cache results, as shown here:

```
  private User _cachedUser;
  public void RenderPage(int userId) {
      _cachedUser ??= _db.GetUser(userId);
  }
```

3. **Leverage Static Analysis for Performance.** Enable rules like CA1822 (Mark members as static) or CA1831 (Use '**AsSpan**' instead of '**Substring**').

   Example:

```
 public string GetSubstring(string s) => s.Substring(0, 10); //
CA1831
```

   Fix:

```
  public ReadOnlySpan<char> GetSubstring(string s) => s.AsSpan().
Slice(0, 10);
```

4. **Optimize Async Code**

   Anti-Pattern: Blocking async calls with '**.Result**' or '**.Wait()**'

```
public string LoadData() {
    return _httpClient.GetStringAsync(url).Result; // Blocks the
thread
}
```

Fix: Use 'async/await' correctly.

```
public async Task<string> LoadDataAsync() {
    return await _httpClient.GetStringAsync(url);
}
```

Best Practices for Performance

- Profile in Release Mode for accurate results.
- Use ETW Events or Application Insights for production monitoring.
- Regularly review Code Analysis warnings for performance hints.

Static Code Analysis and **Performance Profiling** in Visual Studio are essential tools for building robust, high-performance applications. By integrating SCA into your workflow, you can preemptively eliminate bugs and security risks, while the Performance Profiler roots out inefficiencies. Together, they empower developers to deliver code which is not only functional, but also scalable and maintainable.

Here is a step-by-step guide to implementing these optimization techniques in Visual Studio:

Code-Level Optimization

1. **Ensuring Algorithmic Efficiency (Big-O Analysis):**
    a. **Identify Critical Paths.**
        i. Use Visual Studio's `*Performance Profiler*` (Alt+F2 → Check "`CPU Usage`").
        ii. Run profiling during typical usage scenarios.
2. **Analyze Complexity.**
    a. Manually review code for nested loops.
    b. Look for $O(n^2)$ patterns in sorting/searching algorithms.
3. **Optimize Algorithms.**
    a. Replace inefficient algorithms (for example, switch from bubble sort to quicksort).
    b. Implement caching/memoization patterns.
4. **Validate Improvements.**
    a. Re-run profiler and compare execution times.
    b. Use `BenchmarkDotNet` for micro-measurements.

Reducing Boxing/Unboxing Overheads:

- Detect Boxing Operations.
  - Use ***Debug → Windows → Disassembly*** to inspect IL code.
  - Look for box instructions in critical paths.
- Eliminate Object Casting.
  - Replace '**ArrayList**' with '**List<T>**'.
  - Convert '**Hashtable**' to '**Dictionary<TKey,TValue>**'.
- Using Generic Methods:

```
// Before
void Process(object data) { ... }
// After
void Process<T>(T data) where T : struct { ... }
```

- Optimizing Value Type Usage:
  - Implement interfaces on structs to avoid boxing.
  - Use '**Enum.HasFlag**' optimization in C# 7.3+.

Stringing Manipulation Best Practices:

- Identify Problematic Code.
  - Search for '+=' string operations in loops.
  - Check for multiple '**String.Split**'/'**Substring**' calls.
- Implement StringBuilder.

```
// Before
string result = "";
foreach(var item in collection) result += item;

// After
var sb = new StringBuilder(estimatedCapacity);
foreach(var item in collection) sb.Append(item);
```

- Use Efficient Methods.
  - Prefer '**StringComparison.Ordinal**' for culture-agnostic compares
  - Use '**Span<char>**' for parsing operations.
- Optimize Memory Allocation.
  - Pool **StringBuilders** using '**ObjectPool<StringBuilder>**'.
  - Pre-calculate sizes for arrays/buffers.

Concurrency and Parallelism

- Task Parallel Library (TPL). Identify Parallelizable Work.

   - Locate CPU-intensive, independent operations.
   - Check for '**for/foreach**' loops with >1000 iterations.
- Implement Parallel Execution.

```
// Before
foreach(var item in items) Process(item);

// After
Parallel.ForEach(items, item => Process(item));
```

- Configure Parallel Options.

```
      var options = new ParallelOptions {
      MaxDegreeOfParallelism = Environment.ProcessorCount - 1
  };
  Parallel.ForEach(items, options, Process);
```

- Handle Exceptions.
   - Wrap in try/catch with '**AggregateException**'.
   - Use '**CancellationToken**' for cooperative cancellation.

Async/Await Patterns

- **Identify I/O-Bound Operations**. Locate database calls, file I/O, or network requests.
- **Convert Synchronous Methods.**

```
// Before
  public int GetData() { return _client.Get(); }

// After
   public async Task<int> GetDataAsync() {
       return await _client.GetAsync();
   }
```

- **Configure Context**. Add '**ConfigureAwait(false)**' for library code

```
var data = await GetDataAsync().ConfigureAwait(false);
```

- **Avoid Deadlocks.**
   - Never use **.Result** or **.Wait()** on **async** methods.
   - Use **async** void only for event handlers.

Thread Pool Optimization

- **Monitor Thread Usage.**
   - Use **Diagnostic Tools** window (**Debug** → **Windows** → **Diagnostic Tools**).
   - Check "**Threads**" view during load.

- **Adjust Pool Settings.**

```
ThreadPool.SetMinThreads(100, 100); // For burst workloads
ThreadPool.SetMaxThreads(32767, 32767); // maximum limit
```

- **Optimize Task Scheduling.**
  - Use **`TaskCreationOptions.LongRunning`** for >1s operations.
  - Implement custom **`TaskScheduler`** for specialized scenarios.
- **Avoid Thread Starvation.**
  - Use **`ValueTask`** for high-throughput scenarios.
  - Limit concurrent async I/O operations with **`SemaphoreSlim`**.

General Optimization Process

- **Baseline Measurement**
  - Record current performance metrics.
- **Implement Changes**
  - Apply one optimization at a time.
- **Verify Results**
  - Use Visual Studio's **`*CPU Usage*`** tool.
  - Check allocation rates in **`Memory Usage`** tool.
- **Regression Testing**
  - Ensure functional correctness after optimizations.
  - Use unit tests with performance constraints.

Visual Studio Tools Checklist

- Performance Profiler (*Alt*+F2)
- Diagnostic Tools (**`Debug`** → **`Windows`**)
- Parallel Stacks Window (**`Debug`** → **`Windows`** → **`Parallel Stacks`**)
- Memory Usage Analyzer
- Code Metrics (**`Analyze`** → **`Calculate Code Metrics`**)

Remember to always measure before and after optimizations, and prioritize changes based on actual performance bottlenecks rather than focusing on premature optimization.

Conclusion

This chapter underscores the critical balance between computational efficiency and resource utilization in software development. By exploring strategies such as algorithmic optimization, memory allocation techniques, and tools for profiling and leak detection, the chapter highlights the necessity of proactive management to avoid bottlenecks and ensure application stability. Mastering these principles empowers developers to craft scalable, responsive, and resource-efficient systems. As software complexity grows, these foundational skills remain indispensable for delivering robust solutions that meet evolving performance demands and user expectations.

Foreword for the Next Chapter:

As software systems increasingly migrate to distributed, cloud-native architectures, mastering modern development paradigms becomes essential for building resilient and scalable applications. This chapter transitions from localized performance optimization to the expansive world of cloud development and containerization, where Visual Studio's robust toolset empowers developers to streamline deployment, orchestration, and resource management. By delving into Docker integration, Kubernetes orchestration, and Azure services, we will explore how containerization bridges the gap between development and production environments, while ensuring consistency and agility. Whether deploying microservices or managing hybrid cloud workflows, the next chapter will equip you with the practices and tools to thrive in an era defined by cloud-first innovation and DevOps collaboration. Prepare to elevate your development workflow, harnessing the cloud's potential to deliver seamless and scalable solutions.

CHAPTER 10
Cloud Development and Containerization

Introduction

The rapid evolution of software development has been reshaped by two transformative paradigms: **cloud development** and **containerization**. Cloud development empowers developers to build, deploy, and scale applications using remote, on-demand infrastructure and services to eliminate the constraints of physical hardware. By leveraging platforms like Microsoft Azure, AWS, or Google Cloud, teams can focus on innovation rather than on infrastructure management, while adopting scalable architectures, serverless computing, and DevOps workflows to deliver solutions faster and more efficiently.

Containerization, when spearheaded by tools like Docker and Kubernetes, revolutionizes how applications are packaged and run. Containers encapsulate code, dependencies, and configurations into portable, isolated environments, while ensuring consistency across development, testing, and production. Unlike traditional virtualization, containers are lightweight, start instantly, and simplify microservices-based architectures. When combined with cloud platforms, they enable seamless deployment, scaling, and orchestration of applications at a global scale.

Together, cloud development and containerization form the backbone of modern cloud-native ecosystems. Visual Studio 2022 bridges these worlds and offers integrated tools to streamline containerized app development, debug in cloud environments, and deploy to Kubernetes clusters, while adhering to security and scalability best practices. This synergy not only accelerates time-to-market but also makes applications more resilient to upcoming challenges in an era defined by agility, resilience, and distributed innovation.

Structure

In this chapter, the following topics will be covered:

- Cloud Service Models : IaaS, PaaS, SaaS
- Creating Cloud-Optimized Asp.Net Core Web Application
- Best Practices for scalable and secure cloud applications
- Security Best Practices
- DevOps and Monitoring
- Containerization for deployment and hosting

Understanding Cloud Service Models: IaaS, PaaS, and SaaS

Cloud computing offers three primary service models–**Infrastructure as a Service (IaaS), Platform as a Service (PaaS), and Software as a Service (SaaS)**. Each of them caters to different business and technical needs. We have also broken down their definitions, use cases, differences, pros/cons, and have mentioned how to implement them using Visual Studio 2022.

Infrastructure as a Service (IaaS): This consists of virtualized computing resources (servers, storage, networking) that are hosted in the cloud. Users can manage the OS, runtime, and applications.

Here are its use cases:

- Hosting custom applications
- Disaster recovery setups
- Running legacy systems in the cloud

Examples: Azure VMs and AWS EC2

Platform as a Service (PaaS): This is a cloud platform that provides tools and frameworks for building, testing, and deploying applications. Users can focus on code, while the provider manages the infrastructure.

Here are its use cases:

- Web/mobile app development
- API development and deployment
- DevOps pipelines

Examples: Azure App Service and Google App Engine

Software as a Service (SaaS): This refers to fully managed software applications delivered over the internet. Users can access them via web browsers, desktop apps, or mobile apps.

Here are its use cases:

- Email/collaboration tools (for example, Microsoft 365)
- CRM systems (for example, Salesforce)
- Cloud storage (for example, Dropbox)

Key differences between these models:

Factor	IaaS	PaaS	SaaS
Control	Full infrastructure control	Code and app control only	No control over software
Management Overhead	High (manage OS, patches)	Medium (manage code)	None (vendor-managed)
Scalability	Manual scaling	Auto-scaling	Built-in scaling
Time to Market	Slow (setup required)	Fast (focus on code)	Instant (plug-and-play)
Cost	Pay for infrastructure	Pay for platform tools	Pay per user/feature

***Table 10.1**: Key Differences between These Models*

Pros and Cons of each model are mentioned as follows :

Model	Pros	Cons
IaaS	Full control, flexible, cost-efficient	High management overhead, security risks
PaaS	Faster development, auto-scaling, no infra	Vendor lock-in, limited runtime control
SaaS	Zero maintenance, easy access	Limited customization, data privacy concerns

***Table 10.2:** Pros and Cons of Each Model*

Using IaaS in Visual Studio with an example: Deploying a VM on Azure

1. **Creating an Azure VM**:
   a. Open Cloud Explorer (`View` > `Cloud Explorer`).
   b. Sign in to Azure, right-click `Virtual Machines` > `Create VM`.

c. Configure OS, size, and network settings.

2. **Connecting via Visual Studio**:

    a. Use Server Explorer to connect to the VM's IP.

    b. Deploy the code using SSH or Remote Debugging.

Using PaaS in Visual Studio with an example: Deploying a Web App to Azure App Service

- Creating a Project: In VS, choose ASP.NET Core **`Web App`** > **`Create`**.
- Publishing to Azure:

    a. Right-click on the project > **`Publish`** > **`Azure`** > **`Azure App Service`**.

    b. Create a new App Service instance or select an existing one.

    c. Click on **`Publish`** to deploy.

Using SaaS in Visual Studio with an example: Integrating Microsoft Graph API (Office 365)

- Adding Authentication:
    - Create an Azure AD app registration via Azure Portal.
    - Note the Client ID and Tenant ID.
- Integrating the Code:
    - Install the **`Microsoft.Graph`** NuGet package in Visual Studio.
    - Use the following SDK to access Office 365 data:

```
var graphClient = new GraphServiceClient(new AuthProvider());
var user = await graphClient.Me.Request().GetAsync();
```

When to Use Each Model

Choose IaaS If:

- You need full infrastructure control (for example, custom network configurations).
- You have to migrate legacy systems to the cloud.
- You have to run highly specialized workloads (for example, GPU-intensive machine learning).
- **Example Use Cases**:
    - Hosting a custom Linux/Windows VM on Azure Virtual Machines or AWS EC2
    - Disaster recovery setups with on-premises + cloud hybrid environments

Choose PaaS If:

- You want to focus on code without managing servers.
- You have to build modern web/mobile apps or APIs.
- You have to use serverless functions (for example, Azure Functions, AWS Lambda).
- **Example Use Cases:**
  - Deploying a .NET Core app to Azure App Service
  - Running a CI/CD pipeline with AWS Elastic Beanstalk or Google App Engine

Choose SaaS If:

- You need off-the-shelf software with minimal IT involvement.
- You want to prioritize quick adoption (for example, collaboration tools).
- You wish to avoid maintenance practices (updates, security patches).
- **Example Use Cases**:
  - Using Microsoft 365 for email and Office tools
  - Managing customer relationships with Salesforce

Understanding these models helps in optimizing metrics like costs, scalability, and development efficiency. Visual Studio 2022 streamlines cloud integration for all three objectives, whether you are connecting to and deploying VMs (IaaS), building apps (PaaS), or consuming APIs (SaaS). You may begin with Azure Free Tier to experiment and find the best fit for your projects.

Step-by-Step Guide: Creating a Cloud-Optimized ASP.NET Core Application in Visual Studio

Prerequisites:

- Visual Studio 2022 (with ASP.NET and web development workload installed)
- Azure Account (for cloud deployment; sign up for a [free trial](https://azure.microsoft.com/free/))
- .NET 6/7 SDK

Create a New ASP.NET Core Web App.

a. Open **`Visual Studio`** > **`Create a new project`**.

b. Select ASP.NET Core Web App (Model-View-Controller).

c. Name the project (for example, `` `CloudReadyApp` ``) and choose .NET 6/7 as the framework.

d. Ensure Configure for HTTPS and Enable Docker are checked (optional but recommended).

e. Click on **Create**.

Configure Cloud-Ready Settings.

Use Environment-Specific Configuration: Modify **`appsettings.json`** and **`appsettings.Development.json`** to include cloud settings, as shown in the following code:

```
// appsettings.json
{
  "Logging": {
    "LogLevel": {
      "Default": "Information",
      "Microsoft.AspNetCore": "Warning"
    }
  },
  "AllowedHosts": "*",
  "Azure": {
    "StorageConnectionString": "<AZURE_STORAGE_CONNECTION_
STRING>",
    "DatabaseConnectionString": "<SQL_CONNECTION_STRING>"
  }
}
```

Use **`appsettings.Development.json`** for local overrides.

Access Configuration in Code.

```
// In Program.cs
var builder = WebApplication.CreateBuilder(args);
var connectionString = builder.Configuration.GetConnection-
String("Azure:DatabaseConnectionString");
```

Integrate with Azure SQL Database.

Install the following Nuget Packages:

- **Microsoft.EntityFrameworkCore.SqlServer**
- **Microsoft.EntityFrameworkCore.Tools**

Create a Model and DbContext.

```
public class Product
   {
       public int Id { get; set; }
       public string Name { get; set; }
   }
```

```
    public class AppDbContext : DbContext
    {
        public AppDbContext(DbContextOptions<AppDbContext>
options) : base(options) { }
        public DbSet<Product> Products { get; set; }
    }
```

Register DbContext in 'Program.cs'.

```
    builder.Services.AddDbContext<AppDbContext>(options =>
options.UseSqlServer(builder.Configuration["Azure:Database
ConnectionString"]));
```

Add Azure Blob Storage Integration.

1. **Install Package**: '**`Azure.Storage.Blobs`**'
2. Create a Service to Handle Blobs:

```
public class BlobStorageService
    {
        private readonly BlobServiceClient _blobServiceClient;
        private readonly string _containerName = "mycontainer";

        public BlobStorageService(IConfiguration config)
        {
            var connectionString = config["Azure:Storage
ConnectionString"];
            _blobServiceClient = new BlobServiceClient
(connectionString);
        }

        public async Task UploadFileAsync(Stream fileStream, string
fileName)
        {
            var containerClient = _blobServiceClient.GetBlob
ContainerClient(_containerName);
            await containerClient.CreateIfNotExistsAsync();
            var blobClient = containerClient.GetBlobClient
(fileName);
            await blobClient.UploadAsync(fileStream, true);
        }
    }
```

- Register the Service in '**`Program.cs`**'.

```
builder.Services.AddScoped<BlobStorageService>();
```

Enable Logging with Application Insights:

a. Install **`Microsoft.ApplicationInsights.AspNetCore`**.

b. Add Application Insights in '**Program.cs**' using the following command:

```
builder.Services.AddApplicationInsightsTelemetry(options =>
   {
       options.ConnectionString = builder.Configuration
["APPLICATIONINSIGHTS_CONNECTION_STRING"];
   });
```

Set the connection string in 'appsettings.json' or Azure environment variables.

Containerize with Docker.

- Add Docker Support via the following steps:
    - Right-click the project > **Add** > **Docker Support**.
    - Choose Linux as the OS.
- **Dockerfile Example**: The following code goes in the dockerfile:

```
FROM mcr.microsoft.com/dotnet/aspnet:7.0 AS base
   WORKDIR /app
   EXPOSE 80
   EXPOSE 443
   FROM mcr.microsoft.com/dotnet/sdk:7.0 AS build
   WORKDIR /src
   COPY ["CloudReadyApp.csproj", "."]
   RUN dotnet restore "CloudReadyApp.csproj"
   COPY . .
   RUN dotnet build "CloudReadyApp.csproj" -c Release -o /app/
build

   FROM build AS publish
   RUN dotnet publish "CloudReadyApp.csproj" -c Release -o /app/
publish

   FROM base AS final
   WORKDIR /app
   COPY --from=publish /app/publish .
   ENTRYPOINT ["dotnet", "CloudReadyApp.dll"]
```

Deploy to Azure App Service.

a. Right-click on the **project** > **Publish**.

b. Select **Azure** > Azure App Service (Windows/Linux).

c. Create a new App Service or select an existing one.

d. Configure deployment settings and click on Publish.

Cloud Optimization Best Practices:

- Use Environment Variables for secrets (for example, Azure Key Vault).
- Enable Auto-Scaling in Azure App Service for traffic spikes.
- Use Azure CDN for static files.
- Leverage Caching (for example, Redis Cache).

Sample Controller Using Cloud Services:

```
public class HomeController : Controller
{
    private readonly AppDbContext _dbContext;
    private readonly BlobStorageService _blobService;

    public HomeController(AppDbContext dbContext, BlobStorage
Service blobService)
    {
        _dbContext = dbContext;
        _blobService = blobService;
    }

    public IActionResult Index()
    {
        var products = _dbContext.Products.ToList();
        return View(products);
    }

    [HttpPost]
    public async Task<IActionResult> Upload(IFormFile file)
    {
        using var stream = file.OpenReadStream();
        await _blobService.UploadFileAsync(stream, file.FileName);
        return RedirectToAction("Index");
    }
}
```

Your ASP.NET Core app is now cloud-optimized with:

- Database Integration (Azure SQL)
- Blob Storage (Azure Storage)
- Monitoring (Application Insights)
- Containerization (Docker)
- Scalability (Azure App Service)

Test locally and then deploy to Azure for a fully-managed cloud experience.

Best Practices for Scalable and Secure Cloud Applications Using Visual Studio

Building scalable and secure cloud applications requires a mix of architectural design, tooling, and adherence to modern DevOps practices. We have mentioned the key best practices tailored for Visual Studio and Azure ecosystems as follows:

Scalability Best Practices: Follow these best practices to make your projects scalable:

Design Stateless Applications : Stateless apps scale horizontally without session affinity issues.

- Use Azure App Service or Azure Functions (serverless).
- Store session data in Azure Redis Cache or Cosmos DB through the following command:

```
  // Store session data in Redis
  services.AddStackExchangeRedisCache(options => {
      options.Configuration = Configuration.GetConnectionString
("Redis");
  });
```

Use Asynchronous Programming: You can do this to avoid blocking threads to handle high traffic.

- Use '**async/await**' in C# for I/O-bound operations, as shown here:

```
public async Task<IActionResult> GetData()
  {
      var data = await _httpClient.GetAsync("https://api.example.
com");
      return View(data);
  }
```

Leverage Auto-Scaling: Automatically adjust resources based on demand.

- Configure Azure App Service Auto-Scale Rules via the Azure Portal.
- Use Azure Kubernetes Service (AKS) for containerized apps.

Optimize Database Access: It prevent bottlenecks in high-traffic scenarios.

- Use Entity Framework Core with '**AsNoTracking()**' for read-only queries.
- Implement caching with Azure Cache for Redis through the following command:

```
var products = await _context.Products.AsNoTracking().
ToListAsync();
```

Containerize with Docker: Ensure consistency across environments and simplify scaling through this step.

a. Right-click on your project in Visual Studio > **`Add`** > **`Docker Support`**.

b. Deploy containers to Azure Container Instances (ACI) or AKS.

Security Best Practices

Follow these best practices to make your projects scalable:

Secure Configuration Management: To avoid exposing secrets (for example, connection strings, API keys)

- Use Azure Key Vault to store secrets.
- Integrate Key Vault in Visual Studio through the following command:

```
// In Program.cs
builder.Configuration.AddAzureKeyVault(
    new Uri("https://your-keyvault-name.vault.azure.net/"),
    new DefaultAzureCredential()
);
```

[Never hardcode secrets in '**`appsettings.json`**']

Enable Managed Identities: To eliminate the need for credentials in code

- Assign a Managed Identity to your Azure App Service.
- Access Azure resources without secrets through the following command:

```
 var blobClient = new BlobServiceClient(new Uri("https://
your-storage.blob.core.windows.net"),
        new DefaultAzureCredential());
```

Implement Authentication/Authorization: To protect APIs and endpoints from unauthorized access,

- Use Azure Active Directory (AAD) or Microsoft Identity Platform.
- Right-click on **`project`** > **`Add`** > **`New Scaffolded Item`** > **`Identity`**.
- Integrate AAD via '**`Microsoft.Identity.Web`**' as shown here:

```
services.AddMicrosoftIdentityWebAppAuthentication(Configuration);
```

Encrypt Data at Rest and in Transit: To prevent data breaches

- Enable HTTPS in ASP.NET Core through the following command:

```
// In Program.cs
builder.Services.AddHttpsRedirection(options => {
    options.HttpsPort = 443;
});
```

Use Azure Disk Encryption for VMs and Transparent Data Encryption (TDE) for Azure SQL.

Regular Dependency Updates: To avoid vulnerabilities in third-party libraries

- Use Visual Studio's NuGet Package Manager to update packages.
- Enable `Dependabot` in GitHub for automated updates.

DevOps and Monitoring

CI/CD Pipelines: To streamline deployments and reduce human error

- Use Azure DevOps or GitHub Actions with Visual Studio's built-in Git tools.
- Configure pipelines to auto-deploy to Azure App Service or AKS.

Centralized Logging and Monitoring: To detect issues early and optimize performance

- Use Azure Monitor to set alerts for abnormal traffic or errors.
- Integrate Application Insights into your project through the following command:

```
// In Program.cs
    builder.Services.AddApplicationInsightsTelemetry();
```

Load Testing: To validate scalability under stress

- Use Azure Load Testing or third-party tools (for example, JMeter, k6) for load/stress testing.

Cost Optimization: To avoid overspending on unused resources

- Use Azure Cost Management to analyze spending.
- Scale down non-production environments during off-hours.
- Choose Azure Spot Instances for batch workloads.

Through these practices, you can build cloud applications that are resilient to traffic spikes and hardened against threats, while leveraging Visual Studio's powerful toolset.

Containerization is a lightweight, portable way to package and deploy applications along with their dependencies, which ensures consistency across environments. **Docker**, the leading containerization platform, simplifies building, shipping, and running applications. Visual Studio integrates seamlessly with Docker, which enables developers to create, debug, and deploy containerized apps directly from the IDE.

Docker Images: A read-only template with instructions to create a container. Think of it as a "*snapshot*" of your app, including the OS, runtime, code, and dependencies.

- **Base Image**: '**mcr.microsoft.com/dotnet/aspnet:7.0**' (contains the .NET runtime)
- **Custom Image**: Built from a '**Dockerfile**' (see the following examples)

Containers: This refers to a runnable instance of an image. Containers are isolated, lightweight, and share the host OS kernel.

```
docker run <image>    # Start a container from an image
docker ps             # List running containers
docker stop <container-id>  # Stop a container
```

Registries: These are repositories for storing and sharing Docker images (for example, Docker Hub, Azure Container Registry).

- Push an image to Azure Container Registry (ACR) through the following command:

```
docker tag my-app:latest myacr.azurecr.io/my-app:latest
    docker push myacr.azurecr.io/my-app:latest
```

Dockerfile: This is a text file with instructions to build a Docker image, as is shown here:

```
# Use the .NET SDK to build the app
FROM mcr.microsoft.com/dotnet/sdk:7.0 AS build
WORKDIR /src
COPY . .
RUN dotnet restore
RUN dotnet publish -c Release -o /app/publish

# Use the ASP.NET runtime to run the app
FROM mcr.microsoft.com/dotnet/aspnet:7.0 AS final
WORKDIR /app
COPY --from=build /app/publish .
ENTRYPOINT ["dotnet", "MyApp.dll"]
```

Using Docker with Visual Studio: Add Docker Support to a Project through the following steps:

Create an ASP.NET Core Web App.

- In Visual Studio, select **File** > **New** > **Project** > **ASP.NET Core Web App**.

Enable Docker.

- Check Enable Docker during project creation.
- Choose Linux or Windows as the container OS.

(Alternatively, you can right-click on an existing project > **Add** > **Docker Support**.)

Understand the Generated Dockerfile.

Visual Studio auto-generates a Dockerfile optimized for your project, as shown here:

```
# Build stage
FROM mcr.microsoft.com/dotnet/sdk:7.0 AS build
WORKDIR /src
COPY ["MyApp.csproj", "."]
RUN dotnet restore "MyApp.csproj"
COPY . .
RUN dotnet build "MyApp.csproj" -c Release -o /app/build

# Publish stage
FROM build AS publish
RUN dotnet publish "MyApp.csproj" -c Release -o /app/publish

# Runtime stage
FROM mcr.microsoft.com/dotnet/aspnet:7.0 AS final
WORKDIR /app
COPY --from=publish /app/publish .
ENTRYPOINT ["dotnet", "MyApp.dll"]
```

Debug in a Container: Run: Press F5 to start debugging. Visual Studio will:

a. Build the Docker image

b. Start a container from the image

c. Attach the debugger to the container

View Containers: Use the Docker Tools window (Tools > Docker) to manage running containers.

Publish to a Registry.

a. Right-click on the **`project`** > **`Publish`**.

b. Select Azure Container Registry or Docker Hub.

c. Configure credentials and push the image.

Key Benefits of Docker in Visual Studio:

- **Consistency**: Eliminate "**`works on my machine`**" issues.
- **Isolation**: Avoid dependency conflicts (for example, different .NET versions).
- **Scalability**: Deploy containers to Kubernetes (for example, Azure Kubernetes Service).
- **DevOps Integration**: Streamline CI/CD pipelines with containerized builds.

How to run a Containerized App

a. **Build the image through:**

```
docker build -t my-app .
```

b. **Run the container** via:

```
docker run -p 5000:80 --name my-app-container my-app
```

c. **Access the app at 'http://localhost:5000'**

You can follow these steps after completing the preceding sequence:

i. **Docker Compose**: Define multi-container apps (for example, app + database).

ii. **Azure Integration**: Deploy containers to Azure App Service or AKS.

iii. **Security**: Scan images for vulnerabilities with tools like Trivy and Azure Security Center.

With Visual Studio and Docker, you can focus on coding while ensuring that your app runs reliably everywhere.

Conclusion

The integration of cloud development and containerization in Visual Studio marks a transformative leap in modern software engineering, which empowers developers to build, deploy, and scale applications with unprecedented efficiency. By leveraging the robust toolset of Visual Studio alongside cloud platforms like Azure and containerization technologies like Docker, teams can bridge the gap between local development and production environments, while ensuring consistency, portability, and resilience.

Visual Studio's seamless integration with Azure simplifies cloud-native app creation, which allows developers to deploy directly to services like Azure App Service, Azure Functions, and Azure Kubernetes Service (AKS). Adopting IaaS, PaaS, or SaaS models depends on balancing control, scalability, and maintenance needs, with PaaS emerging as the go-to choice for streamlined, code-focused workflows.

Docker containers eliminate the "*it works on my machine*" problem by packaging apps and dependencies into isolated, reproducible environments.

Visual Studio's built-in Docker support automates image creation, debugging, and deployment, which reduces the learning curve for containerization.

Combining Azure cloud services with Docker containers unlocks auto-scaling, cost optimization, and hybrid-cloud flexibility. Tools like Azure Container Registry (ACR) and Kubernetes orchestration streamline container management at scale.

As cloud-native architectures and microservices dominate the tech landscape, mastering Visual Studio's cloud and container tools is no longer optional, but is an essential practice. Whether deploying a serverless API, migrating legacy systems to the cloud, or orchestrating containers in Kubernetes, Visual Studio provides the agility to innovate while maintaining enterprise-grade security and scalability.

By embracing these practices, developers and organizations can future-proof their workflows, deliver solutions faster, and stay competitive in an increasingly cloud-driven world. The journey from code to cloud has never been more intuitive or powerful.

Foreword for Next Chapter:

In the ever-evolving landscape of software development, mastery of tools is not merely a convenience–it is a necessity. Visual Studio, Microsoft's flagship integrated development environment (IDE), is a testament to the power of technology when wielded with precision. Yet, like any sophisticated instrument, its true potential can be unlocked by using it effectively.

Visual Studio has a vast array of features like debugging prowess, extensibility, project management capabilities, and seamless cloud integration. These features can overwhelm the uninitiated and the seasoned developers alike. Without a roadmap, it is easy to miss shortcuts that save hours, overlook extensions that automate drudgery, or misuse features that could otherwise prevent costly errors.

As you move forward, remember: tools shape outcomes, but technique defines excellence. Let this guide transform how you interact with Visual Studio and turn complexity into clarity. Your journey toward mastery begins here.

CHAPTER 11
Best Practices and Tips

Introduction

Modern software development is a high-stakes balancing act. As applications grow in complexity while spanning cloud services, distributed architectures, and ever-evolving user demands, the margin for error shrinks. **Therefore, following best practices** are no longer optional; they are the guardrails that keep projects on track and ensure that codebases remain scalable, secure, and maintainable. In this context, Visual Studio 2022 emerges as more than just an IDE; it is a catalyst for disciplined, future-ready development.

Adhering to best practices in Visual Studio 2022 streamlines collaboration, reduces technical debt, and mitigates risks. For instance, leveraging **IntelliCode's AI-driven suggestions** enforces consistent coding standards, while using **integrated Git tools** promotes seamless version control. Automated testing frameworks and **CI/CD pipelines** embedded in the IDE prevent fragile deployments, and robust debugging tools like **Performance Profilers** and **Live Share** help teams resolve issues before they escalate.

Ignoring best practices, on the other hand, often leads to brittle code, security vulnerabilities, and costly rework. Visual Studio 2022's built-in analyzers and containerization support act as proactive safeguards, which help developers follow secure coding practices and align with general principles found in industry standards like OWASP and GDPR.

Ultimately, best practices in Visual Studio 2022 empower developers to focus on innovation rather than firefighting. By embedding efficiency, security, and collaboration into every phase of the development lifecycle, they transform the IDE from a coding tool into a strategic asset, which future-proofs applications in an era where agility and resilience define success.

In the fast-paced world of software development, an optimized environment is the unsung hero of productivity. A finely tuned setup reduces friction, accelerates workflows, and empowers developers to focus on solving problems instead of fidgeting with tools. Whether you are a seasoned coder or just starting, investing time to configure your development environment pays dividends in speed, clarity, and satisfaction. This guide dives into practical steps to transform Visual Studio into a lean, efficient engine for innovation, while ensuring that your tools work for you and not against you.

Structure

In this chapter, the following topics will be covered:

- Visual Studio Configuration for Efficiency
- Essential Extensions
- Customizing Themes, Layouts, and Keyboard Shortcuts
- Best Practices for Managing Workspaces and Solutions
- Resharper for code refactoring and code analysis
- Best Practices for Managing Workspaces and Solutions in Visual Studio
- Productivity Tips
- Keyboard Shortcuts
- Logging and Exception Handling
- Best Practices for Working with Large Codebases

Configuring Visual Studio for Maximum Efficiency

Step 1: Optimizing Performance Settings

a. Go to `Tools > Options > Environment > Startup` and disable "`Download content every update`" and "`Show startup page`."

b. Under `Projects and Solutions > General`, uncheck "`Reopen documents on solution load`" to reduce load times.

Step 2: Streamlining Code Editing

- Enable IntelliSense and CodeLens (`Tools` > `Options` > `Text Editor` > `All Languages`).
- Adjust scrollbar settings (`Tools` > `Options` > `Text Editor` > `All Languages` > `Scroll Bars`) to map mode for better code navigation.

Step 3: Tweaking Debugging and Builds

- Under **`Debugging > General`**, disable "**`Enable Diagnostic Tools`**" unless it is required.
- In **`Projects and Solutions > Build and Run`**, set "**`MSBuild project build output verbosity`**" to **`Minimal`** to declutter logs.

Step 4: Integrating Version Control

- Use **`Git`** via **`View > Team Explorer`**. Configure global Git settings (**`Tools > Options > Source Control`**).

Essential Extensions and Plugins

Step 1: Installing Productivity Extensions

a. Open **`Extensions > Manage Extensions`** and install:
    - ReSharper (code analysis, refactoring)
    - CodeMaid (automatic code cleanup)
    - GitHub Copilot (AI-driven code suggestions)

Step 2: Configuring Extensions

- **For ReSharper**: Set up code inspection severity and keyboard shortcuts (**`ReSharper`** > **`Options`**).
- **For CodeMaid**: Customize cleanup rules (**`Tools`** > **`Options`** > **`CodeMaid`**).

Step 3: Adding Auxiliary Tools

- **`VSColorOutput`** (color-coded build logs)
- Markdown Editor (preview **`.md`** files)

Customizing Themes, Layouts, and Keyboard Shortcuts

Step 1: Personalizing Themes

- Navigate to **`Tools > Options > Environment > General`** and select a dark/light theme.
- Install custom themes via **`Extensions > Marketplace`** (for example, Solarized).

Step 2: Arrange Window Layouts

- Dock panels like **`Solution Explorer`** and **`Error List`** for quick access.
- Save layouts via **`Window`** > **`Save Window Layout`**.

Step 3: Master Keyboard Shortcuts

- Reset to "**`Visual Studio Default`**" under **`Tools`** > **`Options`** > **`Environment`** > **`Keyboard`**.
- Customize shortcuts (for example, map "*Ctrl+E, Ctrl+D*" to CodeMaid cleanup).

Best Practices for Managing Workspaces and Solutions

Step 1: Structuring Solutions Logically

- Split large solutions into smaller projects (for example, Core, API, Tests).
- Use Solution Folders to group related projects.

Step 2: Optimizing Workspace Layout

- Use Virtual Desktops (Windows) or Spaces (macOS) to separate coding, debugging, and research tasks.
- Pin frequently used files via **`Window`** > **`Auto Hide`** to keep panels tidy.

Step 3: Maintaining Consistency

- Adopt naming conventions (for example, **`Company.Product.Module`**).
- Use **`.editorconfig`** files to enforce coding standards across projects.

Step 4: Leveraging Linked Files

- Share common code between projects via Add > Existing Item > Add as Link.

Resharper

ReSharper is a powerful **developer productivity extension** for Microsoft Visual Studio, created by JetBrains. It enhances the IDE with advanced code analysis, refactoring tools, navigation aids, and coding assistance for C, VB.NET, JavaScript, TypeScript, CSS, and other languages. Below is a breakdown of its use cases, benefits, and key features:

ReSharper acts as a "*smart assistant*" for developers by:

- Analyzing code in real time
- Detecting errors, redundancies, and code smells
- Automating repetitive tasks
- Providing instant fixes and refactoring tools
- Enforcing coding standards and best practices

Key Use Cases for using ReSharper:

Code Quality Improvement

- Detects issues like unused variables, potential `null` exceptions, and incorrect syntax.
- Suggests optimizations (for example, converting loops to LINQ expressions).

Refactoring Legacy Code

- Safely rename symbols (classes, methods, variables) across the entire solution.
- Extract methods, interfaces, or variables to simplify complex code.
- Restructure code (for example, convert a `switch` statement to a dictionary).

Navigation in Large Codebases

a. Go to Everything (*Ctrl*+T) to instantly find files, types, or members.

b. Find Usages (*Alt*+F7) to track where a method or property is referenced.

c. Navigate to Declaration (*Ctrl*+B) to jump to a symbol's definition.

Code Generation

- Auto-generate boilerplate code like constructors, properties, equality checks, or '**`InotifyPropertyChanged`**' implementations.
- **Example**: Press '*Alt*+*Insert*' to generate a constructor for a class.

Unit Testing

a. Run and debug tests directly from the code editor.

b. Analyze code coverage to identify untested paths.

Enforce Coding Standards

a. Define custom naming conventions (for example, '**`_camelCase`**' for private fields).

b. Apply consistent code formatting with Code Cleanup (*Ctrl*+E, C).

Cross-Language Support offers full support for C#, VB.NET, ASP.NET, and XAML, with additional assistance for JavaScript, TypeScript, HTML, and CSS

Top Benefits of ReSharper:

Increased Productivity

a. Reduces manual work with quick-fixes (*Alt*+*Enter*) and code generation

b. Accelerates navigation in large projects

Higher Code Quality

- Catches errors early with 1,900+ code inspections
- Ensures adherence to best practices (for example,, SOLID principles)

Consistency

- Automatically applies code style rules across the team
- Integrates with **`EditorConfig`** and team-shared settings

Reduced Technical Debt

- Simplifies refactoring legacy code with safe, automated tools
- Eliminates dead code and redundancies

Learning Tool

- Teaches better coding practices through real-time suggestions

Seamless Integration

- Works within Visual Studio's native UI
- Compatible with Rider (JetBrains' standalone .NET IDE)

Example Workflow with ReSharper

Write Code: ReSharper highlights issues (for example, a possible **`NullReferenceException`**).

```
var result = GetUser()?.Name; // Suggests adding a null check
```

Fix Issues: Press *Alt+Enter* to apply a quick-fix (for example, add a null conditional operator).

Refactor: Right-click → **`Refactor`** → **`Extract Method`** to break down a complex function.

Navigate: Use *Ctrl+T* to jump to a class definition in another project.

Clean Up: Run Code Cleanup to format code and remove redundancies.

ReSharper vs. Built-in Visual Studio Features

While Visual Studio has basic refactoring and analysis tools, ReSharper offers:

- Deeper code inspections (for example, detecting **`async/await`** misuse)
- Advanced refactorings (for example, "*Introduce Variable*" for complex expressions)
- Cross-language support (for example, CSS/HTML/JavaScript analysis)
- Customizable code styles and team-shared settings

When to Use ReSharper?

- While working on large, complex projects with legacy code
- When your team needs enforced coding standards
- When you want to reduce code review time by catching issues early
- When you frequently refactor or write boilerplate code

Limitations

- Performance Impact: Can slow down older machines or very large solutions
- Learning Curve: Requires time to master shortcuts and features
- Cost: Licensed tool (free trial available)

ReSharper is indispensable for developers who aim to write clean, maintainable code faster. Its real-time feedback, refactoring tools, and navigation features make it a staple for .NET teams. However, its benefits extend to frontend and multi-language projects.

Try the 30-day free trial for ReSharper via https://www.jetbrains.com/resharper/ to evaluate its fit for your workflow.

Here is a step-by-step guide to using ReSharper in Visual Studio to improve productivity, code quality, and refactoring:

Step 1: Installing ReSharper

Download:

a. Go to JetBrains ReSharper (https://www.jetbrains.com/resharper/) and download the installer.

b. Ensure that your Visual Studio version is supported (for example, VS 2019/2022).

Install:

a. Run the installer and follow the prompts.

b. Restart Visual Studio after installation.

Step 2: Familiarizing Yourself with the ReSharper UI

Using the ReSharper Menu:

- A new ReSharper menu will appear in Visual Studio's top toolbar.
- Use it to access settings, run inspections, or disable/enable ReSharper.

Accessing the Context Menu: Right-click anywhere in the code editor to see ReSharper's context menu (for example, Refactor, Navigate, Code Cleanup).

Using Shortcuts: ReSharper uses *Alt+Enter* for quick-fix suggestions (for example, code fixes, refactorings).

Step 3: Using Code Analysis and Quick-Fixes

Code Inspections:

- ReSharper highlights code issues (for example, warnings, errors) with colored squiggles.
- **Example**: Unused variables, potential `` `null` `` exceptions, or style violations

Applying Quick-Fixes:

- Hover over a highlighted issue and press `*Alt+Enter*` to see suggested fixes.
- **Example**:

```
var unusedVariable = 5; // ReSharper will suggest removing this
```

Step 4: Navigating Code Efficiently

a. **Go to Everything (Ctrl+T):** Search for files, types, or members across the entire solution.

b. **Find Usages (*Alt*+F7):** Right-click on a symbol (for example,, method, class) and select '**`Find Usages`**' to see where it is referenced.

c. **Navigate to Declaration (*Ctrl*+B):** Jump to the definition of a symbol.

d. **File Structure Window (*Ctrl*+*Alt*+F):** View the structure of the current file (methods, classes, regions).

Step 5: Refactoring Code

Common Refactorings:

a. **Rename (*Ctrl*+R, R):** Rename a symbol (for example, class, method) and update all references.

b. **Extract Method (Ctrl+R, M):**

Select a code block → Right-click → **`Refactor`** → **`Extract`** → **`Method`**.

```
// Before:
Console.WriteLine("Hello");
Console.WriteLine("World");

// After extraction:
PrintMessages();
```

c. **Introduce Variable (*Ctrl*+R, V):** Extract an expression into a variable.

Code Cleanup (Ctrl+E, C): Reformat code, remove redundancies, and apply coding styles.

Step 6: Use Code Generation

Generate Code (Alt+Insert):

- In the editor, press `Alt+Insert` to generate:
- Constructors
- Properties
- Overrides
- Equality checks

Example:

```
// Generate a constructor for a class:
     public class Person
     {
         public Person(string name) // Auto-generated
         {
             Name = name;
         }
         public string Name { get; }
     }
```

Step 7: Unit Testing with ReSharper

Run Tests:

a. Use the Unit Test Sessions window (*Ctrl*+T, *Ctrl*+L).

b. Run individual tests or entire suites with the gutter icons in the editor.

Coverage:

- Right-click on a test → Run with Coverage to see code coverage.

Step 8: Customizing ReSharper Settings

Options ('`ReSharper` → Options'):

- Adjust code inspections, formatting rules, and keyboard shortcuts.
- **Example**: Disable specific warnings or enforce naming conventions.

Templates:

- Create live templates for code snippets (for example, **`ctor`** → generates a constructor).

Step 9: Troubleshoot Common Issues

Performance:

- Disable ReSharper temporarily with '**`ReSharper → Suspend`**'.
- Exclude large folders from analysis in **`Options → Tools → File Masks`**.

Shortcut Conflicts:

- Reset shortcuts via **`Options → Environment → Keyboard and Menus`**.

Step 10: Learn Advanced Features

Value Tracking: Track how a value propagates through the code (*Ctrl+Alt+Shift+A*).

Stacked Edits (*Alt+Shift+Click*): Edit multiple occurrences of a variable simultaneously.

Code Annotations: Use attributes like [**`NotNull`**] or [**`CanBeNull`**] to improve inspections.

Resources to learn ReSharper

- **Documentation**: The **`ReSharper Guide`** can be accessed via (https://www.jetbrains.com/help/resharper/)
- **Keyboard Shortcuts**: **`ReSharper → Help → Default Keymap Reference`**
- **Blog**: The JetBrains.NET blog can be accessed via (https://blog.jetbrains.com/dotnet/)

By following these steps, you will be able to leverage ReSharper's full potential to write cleaner, more efficient code in Visual Studio.

Best Practices for Managing Workspaces and Solutions in Visual Studio

Effectively managing workspaces and solutions in Visual Studio ensures maintainability, scalability, and collaboration. Here are some key practices to optimize your workflow:

1. **Organize Solutions and Projects.**
   - **Split solutions by responsibility as indicated here**: Use separate solutions for independent components (for example, **`WebApp.sln`**, **`Microservices.sln`**, **`SharedLibraries.sln`**).
   - Avoid monolithic solutions with unrelated projects.

Structure Projects Logically.

Group related projects into solution folders (for example, **`src`**, **`tests`**, **`docs`**, **`tools`**).

Example:

```
Solution
    ├── src/
    │    ├── WebApp (ASP.NET Core)
    │    ├── API (REST Service)
    │    └── Core (Shared Library)
    ├── tests/
    │    ├── WebApp.Tests
    │    └── Core.Tests
    └── tools/
         └── DatabaseMigrationTool
```

Use a Consistent Naming Convention.

- Prefix test projects with the target project name (for example, **`Core.Tests`** for Core).
- Name solutions after their purpose (for example, **`ECommerce.Backend.sln`**).

2. **Manage Dependencies**

Prefer Project References Over DLLs.

- Reference projects directly instead of compiled assemblies to ensure consistency.
- Use NuGet for third-party libraries.

Centralize NuGet Package Versions.

- Use a '**`Directory.Packages.props`**' file (Central Package Management) to enforce consistent versions across projects, as indicated here:

```
//xml
    <Project>
      <ItemGroup>
        <PackageVersion Include="Newtonsoft.Json" Version
="13.0.3" />
      </ItemGroup>
    </Project>
```

Avoid Circular Dependencies:

- Use dependency graphs (**`Architecture`** > **`Generate Dependency Graph`**) to visualize relationships.

3. **Optimize Build Performance**

Exclude Non-Essential Projects from Build.

- Right-click on a project → **`Build`** > **`Exclude from Build`**, to skip unused projects during development.

Use Solution Filters (`.slnf`) for Large Solutions:

- Work on subsets of projects without loading the entire solution.
- These filters are ideal for monorepos or microservices architectures.

Enable Lightweight Solution Load (Legacy):

- Load projects on-demand (right-click on solution → **`Enable Lightweight Solution Load`**).

4. **Version Control and Collaboration**

Exclude Temporary Files.

- Use **`.gitignore`** to exclude bin/, obj/, .vs/, and user-specific files.

Use Relative Paths: Ensure that project references and file paths are relative to avoid machine-specific issues.

Commit `.sln` and `.csproj` Files: These files define the solution structure and must be tracked in source control.

5. **Configuration Management**

Leverage Build Configurations.

a. Create custom configurations (for example, **`Debug`**, **`Release`**, **`Staging`**) via Configuration Manager.

b. Use '**`if DEBUG`**' pragmas sparingly.

Centralize Shared Settings.

Use **`Directory.Build.props`** to define common properties (for example, '**`<LangVersion>latest</LangVersion>`**').

6. **Testing and Quality**

Isolate Test Projects.

- Place unit, integration, and E2E tests in separate folders/projects.
- Use frameworks like xUnit, NUnit, or MSTest.

Integrate Static Analysis. Use Roslyn Analyzers or ReSharper to enforce code quality rules.

7. **IDE Performance Tips**

Disable Unused Extensions. Navigate to '**`Extensions`** > **`Manage Extensions`**' and disable tools you do not need.

Use .NET SDK-Style Projects. Migrate **`legacy.csproj`** files to SDK-style for faster loading and simpler configurations.

Avoid Overloading with Open Files: Close unused tabs and use *Ctrl+Tab* to navigate efficiently.

8. **Documentation**

Add a '`README.md`' to the Solution Root. Document setup steps, architecture, and project roles.

Use XML Comments. Generate API documentation with **`<summary>`** tags and tools like DocFX or Swagger.

Example Workflow

Create a Solution.

```
MyApp.sln
    ├── src/
    │   ├── MyApp.Web (ASP.NET Core)
    │   └── MyApp.Core (Class Library)
    ├── tests/
    │   └── MyApp.Core.Tests
    └── .gitignore
```

Configure Central Package Management. Add **`Directory.Packages.props`** to enforce **`Newtonsoft.Json`** version 13.0.3.

Exclude Test Projects from Default Build. In **`Configuration Manager`**, uncheck "**`Build`**" for test projects in Debug mode.

Tools to Enhance Workspace Management

- **ReSharper/Rider**: Advanced refactoring and code analysis.
- **Visual Studio Solution Filters (`.slnf`)**: These filters focus on subsets of large solutions.
- **NuGet Package Explorer**: Audits and manages NuGet dependencies

By following these practices, you will be able to maintain a clean, efficient workspace that scales with your team and project complexity.

Productivity Tips

Master Navigation and Search

Quick Access (*Ctrl*+Q): Quick Access lets you search for commands, settings, files, or documentation without digging through menus. It also displays keyboard shortcuts for commands in search results, which will help you learn them faster.

Example

- Press *Ctrl*+Q and type '*New Project*'.
- Results show "*Create a new project*" with the shortcut '*Ctrl+Shift+N*'.
- Select the command or use the shortcut to create a project.

Task List for Mock Code

Track incomplete code sections via '**`// TODO`**' comments. The Task List aggregates these comments and acts as a checklist for pending work.

Code Example:

```
public class UserService
{
    // TODO: Implement validation logic
    public void CreateUser(User user)
    {
        // HACK: Temporary workaround for null email
        user.Email ??= "default@example.com";
    }
}
```

1. Add '**`// TODO`**' or '**`// HACK`**' comments.
2. Open **`View`** > **`Task List`** to see all tracked items.
3. Double-click on a task to jump to the code location.

Solution Explorer Shortcuts

Use the following keyboard shortcuts to navigate projects quickly:

- ***Ctrl*+Alt+L** : Opens Toggle Solution Explorer
- ***Ctrl*+;** : Searches files/folders within the currently loaded projects in the solution

Use Case

In a large solution:

1. Press *Ctrl*+*Alt*+L to open **`Solution Explorer`**.

2. Press *Ctrl+;* and type '**UserService.cs**' to find the file instantly.

Sync with Active Document: The Sync button in Solution Explorer highlights the current file in the project hierarchy, which is useful in large projects.

1. Open a file like UserService.cs.
2. Click the Sync icon (◻) in Solution Explorer.
3. The Solution Explorer automatically expands to show the file's location.

Optimize Code Writing

IntelliSense and AI Assistance: IntelliSense provides context-aware code completions. GitHub Copilot (if installed) suggests entire code blocks based on comments.

1. Type '**DateTime.**' to see prioritized completions (for example, '**Now**').
2. For AI-generated code, consider the following example:

```
// Calculate factorial
public static int Factorial(int n)
{
    return n <= 1 ? 1 : n  Factorial(n 1);
}
```

Copilot generates this after you type the comment.

Code Snippets: Snippets insert boilerplate code. For example, '**prop**' generates a property.

- Type '**prop**' and press '**Tab**' twice.
- The snippet will expand to the following command:
  `public int MyProperty { get; set; }`

Quick Actions (Ctrl+.): Quick Actions refactor code, fix warnings, or generate methods, which is shown here:

```
var users = new List<User>();
// Place cursor on "List<User>" and press Ctrl+.
// Select "Use 'var' instead of explicit type" to simplify.
```

Paste Special

Convert JSON/XML to C classes instantly through the following steps:

a. **Copy this JSON**:

```
{ "Name": "John", "Age": 30 }
```

b. In a C file, go to **Edit** > **Paste Special** > Paste JSON as Classes.

```
public class Root
{
    public string Name { get; set; }
    public int Age { get; set; }
}
```

Debug Like a Pro

Breakpoints & DataTips

- F9 toggles breakpoints.
- *Ctrl*+F10 runs code to the cursor's position.
- DataTips let you pin variable values during debugging.

Steps:

1. Set a breakpoint on a line with `` `F9` ``.
2. Debug with `F5`.
3. Hover over a variable and click the □ icon to pin its value.

Live Share

You can collaborate in real time by sharing your debugging session.

Steps:

1. Go to **File** > **Start Collaborative Session**.
2. Share the link with a teammate.
3. Both can **edit/debug** the same code simultaneously.

Customize Your Workflow

Keyboard Shortcuts: Switch to shortcuts from other editors (for example, VS Code) through the following steps:

Steps

1. Go to **Tools** > **Options** > **Environment** > **Keyboard**.
2. Select Visual Studio Code from the scheme dropdown.

EditorConfig: Enforce coding styles with an **.editorconfig** file, as shown in the following example:

Example

```
 .editorconfig
root = true

[]
indent_style = space
indent_size = 4
charset = utf-8
```

Step 1. Right-click on the project > **Add** > **New Item** > **EditorConfig** File.

Version Control with Git

Commit, branch, and review pull requests directly in VS.

Steps:

1. Open **Git** > **Manage Branches**.
2. Right-click on a **branch** > **Merge** to combine changes.

Advanced Tools

CodeLens: CodeLens shows references, tests, and history inline, as is indicated in the following example:

Example:

```
public class Calculator // CodeLens shows "3 references" below
the class name
{
    public int Add(int a, int b) => a + b;
}
```

Pro Tips

Duplicate Lines

Steps:

1. Place the cursor on a line.
2. Press *Ctrl*+D or *Ctrl*+E, then *Ctrl*+V to duplicate it instantly.

Before:

```
Console.WriteLine("Hello");
```

After:

```
Console.WriteLine("Hello");
Console.WriteLine("Hello");
```

Format Code

Shortcut:

- Use *Ctrl*+K, *Ctrl*+D to format the entire document.
- Using Code Cleanup (*Ctrl*+K, *Ctrl*+E) applies style rules.

By combining these techniques, you can reduce boilerplate work, maintain consistency, and debug efficiently. Experiment with these tools to find your optimal workflow.

Keyboard Shortcuts

Search

Solution Explorer Search (*Ctrl* + ;)

Example: Find "**`UserService.cs`**" in a large project through the following steps:

1. Ctrl + ; opens **`Solution Explorer`** search.
2. Type "**`UserService`**".

Quick Find (*Ctrl* + F)

Code navigation: Find all "**`CalculateTotal`**" references, as is indicated here:

```
public decimal CalculateTotal() { ... }
public void ProcessOrder() {
    var total = CalculateTotal();
}
```

Ctrl + F → "**`CalculateTotal`**" → 2 matches

Code Editor

Go To All (*Ctrl* + T)

Navigation Example:

1. Type *Ctrl* + T.
2. Search "**`User`**" → jump to **`User.cs`** class

Multi-Caret Editing (*Ctrl* + *Alt* + *Click*)

Code Transformation:

```
// Original:
int item1;
int item2;
```

```
int item3;

// Add "public" modifier to all:
public int item1;
public int item2;
public int item3;
```

1. Perform the *Ctrl* + Alt + *Click* action at the beginning of each line.
2. Type "**`public `**".

Format Document (*Ctrl* + K, D)

Before Formatting:

```
public class Order{private int _id;public Order(int id){_id=id;}}
```

After pressing Ctrl + K, D:

```
public class Order
{
    private int _id;
    public Order(int id)
    {
        _id = id;
    }
}
```

Quick Actions (*Ctrl* + .)

Refactoring Example:

```
List<string> names = new List<string>();
```

1. Place cursor on **`List<string>`**.
2. *Ctrl* + . → "**`Simplify collection initialization`**"

```
var names = new List<string>();
```

Debugging

Run to Cursor (Ctrl + F10)

Debugging Loop Example:

```
for (int i = 0; i < 100; i++)
{
    ProcessItem(i); // Set cursor here
}
```

Press *Ctrl* + F10 to skip to iteration 50.

Immediate Window (*Ctrl* + Alt + I)

Debugging Session:

```
> ?i // View current value
42
> i = 50 // Modify value
> ?i
50
```

Code Navigation

Peek Definition (*Alt* + F12)

Code Inspection:

```
var service = new UserService();
```

1. Hover over **`UserService`** → Press *Alt* + F12.
2. View class definition inline without leaving the current file.

Navigate References (*Ctrl* + *Shift* + *Up/Down*)

Code Flow:

```
public void Validate(User user)
{
    user.CheckAge(); // Place cursor here
}

// In User.cs
public void CheckAge() { ... }
```

The *Ctrl* + *Shift* + *Down* action will cycle through all call sites.

Snippets and Templates

Surround With (*Ctrl* + K, S)

Code Wrapping Example:

```
try
{
    ProcessOrder();
}
```

1. Select code block,
2. Press *Ctrl* + K, S → "**`tryf`**" (try-finally)

Pro Tips

1. **Duplicate Line (*Ctrl*+D or *Ctrl* + E, then *Ctrl* +V)**

```
Console.WriteLine("Hello");  // Place cursor here
Console.WriteLine("Hello");  // After duplication
```

Block Selection (Alt + Drag)

```
FirstName = "John";      // Select vertically
LastName  = "Doe";       // to edit multiple
Age       = 30;          // lines simultaneously
```

Toggle Breakpoint (F9)

```
for (int i = 0; i < 100; i++)
{
    Process(i);  // Press F9 here
}
```

Window Management

Maximize/Minimize Windows

(Win + Up/Down Arrow)

When working with a floating code editor and **`Solution Explorer`** side-by-side, follow these steps:

1. Press *Win* + *Up* to maximize the active window.
2. Press *Win* + *Down* to restore/minimize.

Move/Dock Windows

Win + Left/Right Arrow: Arrange two code files side-by-side through the following command:

```
[FileA.cs][FileB.cs]
```

1. Open both files.
2. Press *Win* + *Left* on first file, *Win* + *Right* on second.

This structured approach helps developers quickly associate shortcuts with real-world coding scenarios. For maximum efficiency, print this as a reference sheet and gradually incorporate a few more new shortcuts into your daily workflow.

Logging and Exception Handling

Here is a structured guide to logging and exception handling best practices in Visual Studio, along with code examples and actionable insights tailored for .NET applications:

Logging Best Practices

Use Structured Logging.

Why: Enable querying and filtering logs by properties (for example, **`UserId`**, **`RequestId`**).

Tools: **ILogger** with **Serilog/NLog** or **Microsoft.Extensions.Logging**

```
// Using ILogger with structured logging
_logger.LogError(
    "Payment failed for {OrderId} with error: {ErrorMessage}",
    orderId, ex.Message
);
```

Log Levels

You can follow these guidelines:

Trace: Debugging minutiae (for example, loop iterations)

Debug: Development diagnostics

Info: Business workflows (for example, "*Order 1234 created*")

Warn: Recoverable issues (for example, retries)

Error: Unhandled exceptions

Critical: System failures (for example, database down)

```
// Configure logging levels in appsettings.json
"Logging": {
  "LogLevel": {
    "Default": "Information",
    "Microsoft": "Warning",
    "System.Net.Http": "Error"
  }
}
```

Centralize Log Configuration.

Use: Dependency Injection to inject **ILogger<T>**, as shown here:

```
public class PaymentService
{
    private readonly ILogger<PaymentService> _logger;
    public PaymentService(ILogger<PaymentService> logger)
    {
        _logger = logger;
    }
}
```

Avoid Sensitive Data.

Sanitize:

```
// logging sensitive data is wrong
_logger.LogInfo($"User logged in: {user.SSN}");
```

```
// always log generic or non sensitive data
_logger.LogInfo($"User logged in: {user.Id}");
```

Use Log Scopes.

Track Context:

```
using (_logger.BeginScope("Transaction {TransactionId}",
transactionId))
{
    _logger.LogInformation("Processing payment...");
}
```

Exception Handling Best Practices

Catch Specific Exceptions.

Why: To avoid masking issues by catching '**`Exception`**'

```
try
{
    await _paymentProcessor.ChargeAsync(order);
}
catch (PaymentGatewayException ex) // Specific exception
{
    _logger.LogError(ex, "Payment gateway error");
    throw; // Re-throw to preserve stack trace
}
```

Global Exception Handling

ASP.NET Core Middleware

```
app.UseExceptionHandler(errorApp =>
{
    errorApp.Run(async context =>
    {
        var exceptionHandler = context.Features.Get<IException-
HandlerFeature>();
        _logger.LogError(exceptionHandler.Error, "Unhandled
exception");
        await context.Response.WriteAsync("An error occurred.");
    });
});
```

Include Context.

Add Metadata

```
catch (DbUpdateException ex)
{
    var error = new
```

```
        {
            UserId = user.Id,
            Action = "UpdateProfile",
            Error = ex.InnerException?.Message
        };
        _logger.LogError("Database update failed: {@Error}", error);
    }
```

Custom Exceptions

For Business Rules:

```
public class InsufficientFundsException : Exception
{
    public decimal CurrentBalance { get; }
    public InsufficientFundsException(decimal balance)
        : base($"Insufficient funds. Current balance: {balance}")
    {
        CurrentBalance = balance;
    }
}
```

// Usage

```
throw new InsufficientFundsException(user.Balance);
```

Cleanup with 'finally'/ 'using'

Release Resources:

```
FileStream file = null;
try
{
    file = File.Open("data.txt", FileMode.Open);
}
finally
{
    file?.Dispose();
}

// Better: Use 'using'
using var file = File.Open("data.txt", FileMode.Open);
```

Visual Studio-Specific Tools

Debugging Exceptions

- **Exception Settings (*Ctrl+Alt+E*):** Configure which exceptions break the debugger.
- **Diagnostic Tools:** Monitor exceptions and logs in real-time (**Debug** > **Windows** > **Diagnostic Tools**).

Application Insights Integration

Track Telemetry:

```
services.AddApplicationInsightsTelemetry();
// Log custom events
_telemetryClient.TrackEvent("PaymentProcessed", new Dictionary
<string, string>
{
    { "OrderId", order.Id },
    { "Status", "Success" }
});
```

Code Analysis

Enable Warnings:

```
nullable enable // Enable nullable reference types
public string? GetUserName() => null; // Warns if null is
returned
```

Testing and Validation

Unit Test Exceptions

```
[Fact]
public void Charge_ThrowsInsufficientFundsException()
{
    var service = new PaymentService();
    Assert.Throws<InsufficientFundsException>(() => service.
Charge(1000));
}
```

Mock Loggers

```
var mockLogger = new Mock<ILogger<PaymentService>>();
var service = new PaymentService(mockLogger.Object);

// Verify logging
mockLogger.Verify(log => log.LogError(It.IsAny<Exception>(),
"Payment failed"), Times.Once);
```

Security and Performance

Log **`ex.Message`** and **`ex.StackTrace`** instead of the full exception. **`Exception.ToString()`** is often recommended because it includes the stack trace, inner exceptions, and full context.

Rate Limiting: Use log aggregation tools (for example, Azure Log Analytics) to avoid log flooding.

Key Takeaways

- Log with Purpose: Include enough context to debug, while avoiding noise.
- Handle Exceptions Gracefully: Never accept exceptions as they are.
- Leverage Visual Studio Tools: Use debuggers, Application Insights, and code analysis.
- Test Your Logs/Exceptions: Ensure that errors are logged and handled correctly.

By following these practices, you will be able to build robust, maintainable applications with traceable errors and actionable logs.

Best Practices for Working with Large Codebases

- **Modularization and Organization**
  - **Break into Modules**: Split the codebase into logical modules or components (for example, `UserManagement`, `PaymentService`). Use clear folder structures and namespaces.
  - **Naming Conventions**: Adopt consistent naming for files, classes, and methods (for example, `UserService.cs` in '`Services/`').
  - **Separation of Concerns**: Follow SOLID principles to decouple components (for example, separate data access, business logic, and UI layers).
- **Version Control Strategies**
  - **Branching Workflow**: Use Git Flow or GitHub Flow for feature branches, releases, and hotfixes.
  - **Atomic Commits**: Make small, focused commits with descriptive messages (for example, "*Fix null reference in UserService when user is not found*").
  - **Regular Syncing**: Frequently pull from '`main`' to avoid merge conflicts and stay updated.
- **Documentation**
  - **Onboarding Guides**: Provide a README.md with setup instructions, architecture diagrams, and key workflows.
  - **Code Comments**: Use XML comments for public APIs and complex logic. Avoid redundant comments (for example, // Increments counter).
  - **API Documentation**: Generate Swagger/OpenAPI docs for REST endpoints.

- **Testing**
  - **Automated Tests**: Implement unit, integration, and end-to-end tests (for example, xUnit, NUnit, Selenium).
  - **Test Coverage**: Aim for 70-80% coverage; focus on critical paths.
  - **CI/CD Integration**: Run tests in pipelines (for example, GitHub Actions, Azure DevOps).
- **Code Reviews and Static Analysis**
  - **Pull Requests**: Enforce reviews for knowledge sharing and quality checks.
  - **Static Analysis Tools**: Use SonarQube, ReSharper, or Roslyn Analyzers to enforce code standards and detect issues early.
- **Dependency Management**
  - **Centralized Versioning**: Use `Directory.Packages.props` (NuGet) or `package.json (npm)` to unify package versions.
  - **Audit Dependencies**: Regularly check for security vulnerabilities (for example, dotnet list package `--vulnerable`).
- **Refactoring and Technical Debt**
  - **Incremental Refactoring**: Tackle debt in small chunks during feature work.
  - **Safe Refactoring**: Use IDE tools (for example, ReSharper's "`Safe Delete`") and ensure that tests pass after changes.
- **Performance Optimization**
  - **Profiling**: Identify bottlenecks with tools like Visual Studio Profiler or JetBrains dotTrace.
  - **Caching**: Implement caching layers (for example, Redis) for frequently accessed data.
  - **Asynchronous Code**: Use `async/await` to avoid blocking calls.
- **Logging and Monitoring**
  - **Structured Logging**: Use `Serilog` or `NLog` with context (for example, `UserId`, `RequestId`).
  - **Centralized Logs**: Aggregate logs using tools like Elasticsearch or Application Insights.
  - **Alerting**: Set up alerts for critical errors (for example, via Grafana or PagerDuty).
- **Security Practices**
  - **Code Scans**: Use OWASP ZAP or GitHub CodeQL to detect vulnerabilities.
  - **Input Validation**: Sanitize user inputs to prevent SQLi, XSS, and so on.

  - **Secrets Management**: Store API keys and credentials in vaults (for example, Azure Key Vault).
- **Scalability and Architecture**
  - **Microservices**: Split monolithic apps into bounded contexts (for example, `AuthService`, `OrderService`).
  - **Event-Driven Design**: Use message brokers (for example, Kafka, RabbitMQ) for decoupled communication.
- **Team Collaboration**
  - **Coding Standards**: Enforce style with `.editorconfig` and linters (for example, ESLint, StyleCop).
  - **Knowledge Sharing**: Hold regular tech talks and maintain a wiki (for example, Confluence).
  - **Code Ownership**: Assign modules to teams with clear accountability.
- **Tooling**
  - **IDE Features**: Leverage Visual Studio's Go To Definition (F12), Find All References (*Shift*+F12), and Peek Definition (*Alt*+F12).
  - **Code Search**: Use tools like `ripgrep` or JetBrains Rider's global search.
- **Disaster Recovery**
  - **Backups**: Regularly back up repositories and databases.
  - **Rollback Plans**: Ensure that CI/CD pipelines support rolling back deployments.

Example Workflow for Adding a Feature

- `Branch`: Create a feature branch from main.
- `Develop`: Write code with unit tests.
- `Commit`: Push small, incremental changes.
- `Review`: Submit a PR with a description of changes and test results.
- `Merge`: After approval, squash and merge into `` `main` ``.
- `Deploy`: Trigger CI/CD to staging, then production.

By adhering to these practices, teams can maintain scalability, reduce friction, and ensure long-term maintainability in large codebases.

Conclusion

This chapter has equipped you with actionable strategies to maximize productivity, streamline workflows, and elevate the quality of your development projects. By adopting practices such as leveraging keyboard shortcuts, mastering debugging tools, integrating extensions, and organizing projects effectively, you can transform Visual Studio 2022 from a mere IDE into a powerful ally. Customizing the environment to suit your workflow, utilizing version control systems like Git, and prioritizing performance optimizations further ensure a seamless coding experience.

Remember, proficiency in Visual Studio is not achieved overnight; it thrives on continuous learning and adaptation. Stay curious about updates, engage with the developer community, and experiment with new features to keep your skills sharp. By embedding these best practices into your daily routine, you will be able to write more efficient code, collaborate more effectively, and make your projects resilient. Start implementing these tips today, and unlock the full potential of Visual Studio 2022 as you build innovative, robust solutions.

Appendices

Visual Studio Version History and Future Outlook

Visual Studio (VS) has evolved from a basic Windows IDE into a comprehensive development ecosystem. It supports a vast range of platforms and languages. The history of Visual Studio can be classified into distinct eras, all of which are explained as follows:

The Early Years (Pre-2010): Establishing the Foundation

- **Visual Studio 97 (v5.0):** The first release to bundle multiple development languages (Visual Basic 5.0, Visual FoxPro 5.0, and Visual SourceSafe, Visual C++, Visual J++, Visual InterDev, and MSDN) into a single package. It was a suite of tools rather than a single IDE.
- **Visual Studio 6.0 (1998):** A legendary release that was incredibly stable and long-lived. It was the last version to primarily focus on native Win32 and COM development (C++, VB6). Many legacy enterprise systems still rely on VB6 from this era.
- **Visual Studio .NET 2002 (v7.0):** A monumental shift. This release introduced the .NET Framework, C#, and ASP.NET. It rebranded the product line and focused on managed code.
- **Visual Studio .NET 2003 (v7.1):** Refined the .NET 1.0 release and included support for .NET Framework 1.1 and mobile development with the .NET Compact Framework
- **Visual Studio 2005 (v8.0):** A major overhaul with a new IDE look and feel. Key introductions included .NET Framework 2.0, generics in C# 2.0, and the `Nullable<T>` type. It also launched Visual Studio Team System for ALM (Application Lifecycle Management).
- **Visual Studio 2008 (v9.0):** Focused on multi-targeting (choosing which .NET Framework version to build against), LINQ (Language Integrated Query), and improved support for Windows Vista, WPF, and WCF

The Modern Era (2010-2019): Embracing Openness and the Cloud

This period marked a significant change in Microsoft's philosophy, as it moved towards open source and cloud-first development. The innovations characterizing this era are as follows:

- **Visual Studio 2010 (v10.0):** Introduced the WPF-based IDE for a more visually appealing experience. It brought the F# language into the box and featured improved debugging and parallel programming tools.
- **Visual Studio 2012 (v11.0):** Focused on Windows 8 and the new "Windows Store app" model. It introduced a controversial flat, all-caps interface that was later toned down. It began integrating cloud services with Azure.
- **Visual Studio 2013 (v12.0):** A refinement release with improved debugging tools, better ASP.NET support, and tighter integration with Azure. It introduced the **Community Edition**, which was a full-featured and free IDE for individual developers and small teams, as well as a game-changer for accessibility.
- **Visual Studio 2015 (v14.0):** A massive release centered on cross-platform development. It introduced the open-source .NET Core platform, Roslyn (the open-source .NET compiler platform), and extensive tools for building Android, iOS, and Windows apps with Xamarin and Apache Cordova.
- **Visual Studio 2017 (v15.0):** Focused on productivity and performance. It featured a new, modular installer, which resulted in significantly faster load times, and live code analysis with "lightbulb" suggestions. It deepened its DevOps integration with Azure.
- **Visual Studio 2019 (v16.0):** Continued the focus on productivity and modern development. Key features included AI-assisted IntelliCode, real-time collaboration with Live Share, improved search (*Ctrl*+Q), and better debugging for microservices and containers.

The Current Generation: 64-bit and Beyond

- **Visual Studio 2022 (v17.0) - Current Version:** This is the biggest leap in recent years, as it is the first 64-bit version of Visual Studio. This allows it to access more memory, which enables it to handle massive solutions and complex workloads without crashing. Other key features include:
- **Enhanced UI:** Better accessibility, themes, and updated icons
- **.NET 6+ & MAUI:** Full support for the latest .NET versions and the .NET Multi-platform App UI (MAUI) framework for building cross-platform native apps from a single codebase
- **Hot Reload:** Apply code changes to a running app without restarting it, for both .NET and C++.
- **Azure Integration:** Deep tools for developing and deploying on Azure

- **AI & ML:** Deeper integration of GitHub Copilot for AI-powered code completion

Future Outlook for Visual Studio: The future of Visual Studio is not just about the monolithic IDE; it is about an expanding ecosystem of tools.

Deepening AI Integration (The #1 Trend)

- **GitHub Copilot and IntelliCode** will become more deeply embedded, as they will evolve from code completion to AI-assisted debugging, test generation, architecture suggestions, and natural language-to-code transformation.
- **The Cloud-Based Future: Visual Studio and Codespaces**: The traditional, locally-installed IDE will remain crucial for years, but the future will be increasingly located in the cloud.

  GitHub Codespaces and Visual Studio Codespaces offer a fully configured, cloud-hosted development environment accessible from any browser. This simplifies onboarding, enables powerful hardware for complex builds, and allows developers to code from any device.
- **Visual Studio Code Synergy:** VS Code's immense popularity will continue to influence the full Visual Studio. Features often debut in the lighter, faster VS Code before they are integrated into the full IDE.
- **DevOps and GitHub:** Integration with GitHub for source control, Actions for CI/CD, and Codespaces will be seamless. This will make Visual Studio the central hub for a GitHub-centric workflow.
- **Enhanced Performance and Scalability**: The move to 64-bit is just the beginning. You may expect continued investment in making the IDE faster, more responsive, and capable of handling more complex projects, especially in areas like game development (Unreal Engine, Unity) and massive enterprise codebases.
- **Support for Emerging Technologies**: Visual Studio will continue to be the premier tool for developing applications for:
- **AI/ML Models:** With Azure Machine Learning and ONNX
- **Quantum Computing:** Through the Azure Quantum development kit (QDK)
- **Metaverse & AR/VR:** Enhanced tools for developing 3D experiences and games
- **Evolution of .NET and C++:** Visual Studio's future is tied to the platforms it supports. It will be the go-to IDE for the latest innovations in .NET (like .NET 9, 10, etc.) and will continue to receive powerful updates for modern C++ development, game development, and high-performance computing.

Glossary of Terms

The following glossary defines key terms you will encounter while using Visual Studio.

Core IDE and Project Structure

- **IDE (Integrated Development Environment):** The main application (**`devenv.exe`**) that provides a comprehensive set of tools for software development. These tools include a code editor, debugger, compilers, and designers, all wrapped up in a single interface.
- **Solution ("`.sln`" file):** A container that organizes one or more related projects. It allows you to work on multiple projects together, manage dependencies between them, and set startup configurations.
- **Project ("`.csproj`", "`.vbproj`", "`.vcxproj`", and so on):** A container for all the source code files, resources, configurations, and references that are required to build a single executable, library, or component. Each project produces a single output.
- **Workspace (Visual Studio Code Term):** In VS Code, this is the folder or the collection of folders that you have opened. In Visual Studio, the closest analog to a Workspace is the Solution.
- **Build:** The process of compiling source code files and transforming them into an executable (**`.exe`**), library (**`.dll`**), or any other output
- **Compile:** The specific act of translating source code written in a high-level language (like C# or C++) into machine code or intermediate language (IL)
- **Debug:** The process of running an application with the debugger attached to find and fix errors (bugs) in the code
- **Release:** A configuration for building a project that is optimized for performance and deployment. It typically has no symbolic debug information.
- **Platform Target (for example, x86, x64, Any CPU):** Specifies the processor architecture for which the output file is compiled
    - **x86:** 32-bit Intel/AMD architecture
    - **x64:** 64-bit Intel/AMD architecture
    - **Any CPU:** (Default for .NET) The application can run on any CPU architecture. On a 64-bit OS, it runs as 64-bit by default, unless the '**`Prefer 32-bit`**' option is enabled. In the latter case, it runs as 32-bit, as well as on a 32-bit OS.

Coding and Editing

- **IntelliSense**: The name of Microsoft's its code-completion and assistance technology. It includes:
    - **Code Completion:** Suggests and automatically completes keywords, types, methods, and variables as you type
    - **Parameter Info:** Shows information about the parameters a method requires
    - **Quick Info:** Displays the complete declaration for any identifier (like a variable or method) when you hover over it
- **CodeLens**: Displays actionable, contextual information in line with your code, such as references, authors, tests, and commit history (when connected to Git)
- **Refactoring:** The process of restructuring existing code without changing its external behavior. Common refactoring operations include Rename, Extract Method, Reorder Parameters, and Encapsulate Field.
- **Peek Definition (*Alt+F12*):** Allows you to view a method or class definition in a pop-up window without navigating away from your current file
- **Go To Definition (F12):** Navigates directly to the source code where a method or class is defined
- **Go To Implementation (*Ctrl+F12*):** Navigates to the implementation of an interface member or abstract class member
- **Snippet:** A template for commonly used code blocks (for example, a '`for`' loop, 'prop' for a property, and '`trycatch`'). Typing the shortcut and pressing 'Tab' once inserts the code.
- **Lightbulb:** The icon that appears in the left margin when Visual Studio detects an opportunity to refactor, fix an error, or improve your code. Clicking on it shows suggested actions.
- **`EditorConfig` ('`.editorconfig`' file):** A file used to define and maintain consistent coding styles (indentation, spacing, naming) across different editors and IDEs for a project

Debugging

- **Breakpoint:** A marker set on a line of code that pauses (breaks) program execution when the debugger is running, which allows you to inspect the program's state
- **Watch Window:** A debugging window where you can specify variables or expressions to monitor as you step through code

- **Locals Window:** A debugging window that automatically displays all variables local to the current scope (method)
- **Autos Window:** A debugging window that automatically shows variables used around the current line of code where execution is paused
- **Call Stack:** A window that shows the chain of method calls that led to the current execution point
- **Immediate Window:** A console-like window used during debugging to execute commands, evaluate expressions, or print variable values
- **Data Tip:** The pop-up box that appears when you hover over a variable in the editor during a debug session and shows its current value
- **Step Into (F11):** Executes the next line of code. If the line contains a method call, the debugger steps *into* that method.
- **Step Over (F10):** Executes the next line of code. If the line is a method call, it executes the entire method and pauses at the next line in the current method.
- **Step Out (Shift+F11):** Executes the remainder of the current method and pauses at the calling statement

UI and Designers

- **Designer:** A visual tool for creating application UI. Common ones include:
    - **Windows Forms Designer:** For building classic WinForms apps
    - **WPF Designer:** For building Windows Presentation Foundation (WPF) apps
    - **XAML Designer:** For building UIs for WPF, UWP, and `Xamarin.Forms` using XAML
    - **Web Forms Designer:** For building legacy ASP.NET Web Forms
- **XAML (eXtensible Application Markup Language):** A declarative XML-based language used in WPF, UWP, and `Xamarin.Forms` to define user interfaces
- **Toolbox:** A window that contains controls (buttons, textboxes, and so on) that can be dragged onto a designer surface
- **Properties Window (F4):** A window that displays the properties, events, and other configuration settings for the currently selected item in the designer or editor.
- **Event:** A message sent by a control (for example, a "`Button`") to signal that an action has occurred (for example, "`Click`"). You can write code in event handlers to respond to these events.
- **Solution Explorer:** The primary window for navigating and managing your solution's files, projects, and dependencies

- **Server Explorer/Database Explorer:** A window that provides access to server resources, such as databases, services, and Azure services. It allows you to manage data connections

Build, Deploy, and Manage

- **MSBuild:** The Microsoft Build Engine, which is the underlying platform that processes project files (`.csproj`) and builds them according to the instructions provided within
- **NuGet:** The package manager for .NET. It provides a way to create, share, and consume useful code packages (libraries, tools) in your projects.
- **Package:** A compressed file (`.nupkg`) which contains compiled code (DLLs), other files, and a descriptive manifest that includes information like the package's version number
- **Dependency:** An external library or project that your project requires to build and run. Dependencies are often managed via NuGet.
- **SDK (Software Development Kit):** A collection of tools, libraries, documentation, and samples for developing applications for a specific platform or framework (for example, .NET SDK, Windows SDK)
- **Publish:** The process of preparing and packaging an application for deployment to a specific target (for example, a folder, a web server, Azure, Docker container)
- **Docker Container:** A lightweight, standalone, and executable package of software that includes everything required to run an application. Visual Studio has built-in tools for Dockerfile generation and containerization.

Version Control

- **Git:** The distributed version control system integrated directly into Visual Studio
- **Repository (Repo):** A database that stores all the files and the complete history of changes for a project
- **Commit:** An operation that sends the latest changes you have made to the code to the local repository. It creates a new snapshot (version) of the project.
- **Push:** An operation that sends your committed changes from your local repository to a remote repository (for example, on GitHub or Azure DevOps)
- **Fetch**: An operation that retrieves changes from a remote repository but does not merge them into your local branch
- **Pull**: An operation that retrieves changes from a remote repository and merges them into your current local branch

- **Branch:** A parallel version of the repository. It allows you to work on new features or fixes without affecting the main codebase (which is often the "`main`" or the "`master`" branch).
- **Merge:** The process of integrating changes from one branch into another
- **GitHub/Azure DevOps/GitLab:** Popular cloud-based hosting services for Git repositories, which is often integrated with Visual Studio

Closing Thoughts

Beginning Your Journey

As you have reached the final pages of **Ultimate Visual Studio for Developers**, take a moment to reflect on the ground we have covered. We have journeyed from the foundational elements of the IDE–solutions, projects, and the unparalleled power of IntelliSense–through the intricate art of debugging, the efficiency of refactoring tools, and the collaborative potential of Live Share and Git integration. We have also explored how to bend the environment to your will with extensions, custom configurations, and powerful publishing tools.

You now possess a deep, working knowledge of one of the most powerful IDEs ever created. However, this is not the end. In fact, it is a profound beginning. Mastering the tools of your craft is not a destination, but a continuous path of growth. With this solid foundation, your journey has evolved from learning about Visual Studio to mastering what you can do with it.

The Playground of Possibility: Explore and Experiment

It is one thing to understand a feature conceptually and another to weave it into the muscle memory of your daily workflow. The true power of Visual Studio is not unlocked by passive reading, but by active practice.

We encourage you to treat your development environment as a playground for experimentation. Did the chapter on debugging with Data Tips and the Immediate Window spark an idea? Create a simple, throwaway project and introduce a bug on purpose. Read through it, not with the goal of finishing quickly, but with the intent of clicking every button and trying every window. Observe what happens next.

- **Challenge Yourself:** Have you always used the mouse to navigate? Force yourself to use keyboard shortcuts for a week ('Ctrl+[, S' for Solution Explorer, '*Ctrl+Q*' for Quick Launch, '*Ctrl+ -*' and '*Ctrl+Shift+ -*' for navigation). You might be surprised at the speed you will gain at using shortcuts.

- **Revisit an Old Project:** Open a personal or older codebase and look at it with a new perspective. Consider the instances where you can apply a quick refactoring? Can a new extension like CodeMaid or OzCode clean it up or can it help you understand it better?
- **Break Things:** The best way to learn the limits of a tool is to push them further. Visual Studio is a robust and resilient application. Do not be afraid to try a complex Live Share session, experiment with a custom project type, or tweak your theme and layout until it resembles what you had envisioned.

The spirit of curiosity is what transforms a competent developer into a master craftsman. Your IDE is your workshop; knowing the precise function of every tool empowers you to build masterpieces with confidence and creativity.

The Unending Ascent: The Importance of Continuous Learning

In the world of technology, stagnation can make your skills obsolete. The Visual Studio you use today is not the same application it was five years ago. Similarly, it will be vastly different five years from now. Microsoft's commitment to innovation is driven largely by the vibrant .NET and developer community. This will manifest into new features, performance enhancements, and constantly emerging paradigms.

Embrace the mindset of continuous learning. The concepts in this book are your bedrock, but the landscape will shift constantly. Subscribe to developer blogs like the Visual Studio Blog and .NET Blog. Follow the Visual Studio team on social media. Skim the release notes for every update–even a small point release might contain a feature that can save you hours of work.

This commitment to learning extends beyond the IDE itself. Visual Studio does not natively integrate new programming languages or frameworks automatically. You can install extensions, SDKs, or workloads to support new languages (like Python and Rust using extensions) or frameworks (Blazor, MAUI, and so on), but they are not automatically integrated. Your ability to leverage the IDE's full potential for Blazor, MAUI, Azure Functions, or the next groundbreaking technology depends on your willingness to learn and integrate new knowledge. You must view Visual Studio not as a static tool, but as the central hub of your entire development universe. Your curiosity will act as the fuel that keeps it spinning.

Giving Back: Contributing to the Visual Studio Community

No developer is an island. The very ecosystem you benefit from today was built by millions of developers who shared their knowledge, code, and feedback with each other. Now that you are armed with deep knowledge, you have a wonderful opportunity to give back to this community and help it grow stronger.

Your participation can take many forms. It may look like:

- **Sharing Your Knowledge:** Write a blog post or create a short video about a time-saving trick you discovered. Answer a question on Stack Overflow or the Microsoft Developer Community forums. The moment you solve a frustrating problem, you will be uniquely qualified to help the next person facing it.
- **Providing Actionable Feedback:** When you encounter a bug or have an idea for a feature that would improve your workflow, do not just grumble to your colleagues. File a detailed report through the Visual Studio Feedback mechanism. The development teams will actively monitor these channels and your input will directly shape the product's future.
- **Engaging with Extensions:** Found an amazing extension? Review it and thank the developer. Found a bug in one? Report it respectfully. Better yet, if you have an idea for a tool that does not exist, consider exploring the Visual Studio SDK and creating it yourself. The most beloved extensions begin from a single developer, who has taken the initiative to solve their own problem.
- **Mentoring Others:** As you grow more comfortable, guide those who are just beginning their journey. A simple piece of advice on using a breakpoint condition or a recommended extension can be a revelation for a junior developer.

By contributing significantly, you stop being just a user and become a stakeholder in a community dedicated to building better tools and by extension, better software.

Final Words

Ultimate Visual Studio for Developers is written to demystify the complexity and unlock the profound potential within your IDE. We hope that it has been a comprehensive guide and a trusted companion for you. However, you must remember that the ultimate Visual Studio is the one you craft. It should be perfectly configured, expertly wielded, and constantly evolving to meet the challenges of your unique projects.

Now, it is time to close this book, open your IDE, and start building. Experiment fearlessly, learn relentlessly, and contribute generously. The future of development is bright and you are now exceptionally well-equipped to shape it.

Happy coding!

Index

Symbols

A

D

E

N

O

P

R

S

T